From Class to Race

New Critical Theory
General Editors:
Patricia Huntington and Martin J. Beck Matuštík

The aim of *New Critical Theory* is to broaden the scope of critical theory beyond its two predominant strains, one generated by the research program of Jürgen Habermas and his students, the other by postmodern cultural studies. The series reinvigorates early critical theory—as developed by Theodor Adorno, Herbert Marcuse, Walter Benjamin, and others—but from more decisive postcolonial and postpatriarchal vantage points. *New Critical Theory* represents theoretical and activist concerns about class, gender, and race, seeking to learn from as well as nourish social liberation movements.

Phenomenology of Chicana Experience and Identity: Communication and Transformation in Praxis
by Jacqueline M. Martinez
The Radical Project: Sartrean Investigations
by Bill Martin
From Yugoslav Praxis to Global Pathos: Anti-Hegemonic Post-Post-Marxist Essays
by William L. McBride
Unjust Legality: A Critique of Habermas's Philosophy of Law
by James L. Marsh
New Critical Theory: Essays on Liberation
edited by William S. Wilkerson and Jeffrey Paris
The Quest for Community and Identity: Critical Essays in Africana Social Philosophy
edited by Robert E. Birt
After Capitalism
by David Schweickart
The Adventures of Transcendental Philosophy: Karl-Otto Apel's Semiotics and Discourse Ethics
by Eduardo Mendieta
Love and Revolution: A Political Memoir: People's History of the Greensboro Massacre, Its Setting and Aftermath
by Signe Waller
Beyond Philosophy: Ethics, History, Marxism, and Liberation Theology
by Enrique D. Dussel, edited by Eduardo Mendieta
From Class to Race: Essays in White Marxism and Black Radicalism
by Charles W. Mills

From Class to Race

Essays in White Marxism and Black Radicalism

Charles W. Mills

ROWMAN & LITTLEFIELD PUBLISHERS, INC.
Lanham • Boulder • New York • Oxford

ROWMAN & LITTLEFIELD PUBLISHERS, INC.

Published in the United States of America
by Rowman & Littlefield Publishers, Inc.
A wholly owned subsidiary of the Rowman & Littlefield Publishing Group, Inc.
4501 Forbes Boulevard, Suite 200, Lanham, Maryland 20706
www.rowmanlittlefield.com

PO Box 317
Oxford
OX2 9RU, UK

British Library Cataloguing in Publication Information Available

Library of Congress Cataloging-in-Publication Data

Mills, Charles W. (Charles Wade)
   From class to race : essays in white Marxism and Black radicalism / Charles W.
Mills.
      p. cm.
   Includes bibliographical references and index.
   ISBN 0-7425-1301-7 (alk. paper)—ISBN 0-7425-1302-5 (pbk. : alk. paper)
   1. Socialism. 2. Historical materialism. 3. Race relations—Philosophy. 4.
Critical theory. 5. United States—Race relations. I. Title.
   HX73.M533 2003
   335.4—dc21   2003008796

Printed in the United States of America

For the Left, black and white.

Even after a revolution, the country will still be full of crackers.

—saying in the black American community during the highpoint of white socialist activism in the 1930s

Contents

Figures/Abbreviations

FIGURES

ABBREVIATIONS

CW: References to Karl Marx and Frederick Engels, *Collected Works* (50 vols., New York: International Publishers, 1975–). Citations will be made as follows: (CW volume number)—for example, (CW 1).

MESC: References to Karl Marx and Frederick Engels, *Selected Correspondence, 1846–1895* (Westport, Conn.: Greenwood Press, 1975).

Introduction

These nine chapters mark a trajectory both personal and theoretical. For readers who know me only as the author of *The Racial Contract* (1997), it may come as a revelation that I started out as a Marxist and a fairly orthodox one at that. (This revelation will be particularly surprising for those left-wing readers and reviewers who were critical of the book for its failure to engage with, let alone utilize, a historical materialist framework.) So if one's later books usually explore one's later thoughts, here, so to speak, I have gone backward in time to reconstruct the trajectory that brought me to the present. Accordingly, my title, *From Class to Race*, indicates an evolution both of focus and approach, and the nine chapters track how I ended up here, where I am today. Not without a certain irony in my choice and arrangement of material, I begin with an analysis of the classic Marxist concept of ideology and end up with a defense, albeit qualified, of what many on the Left would see as a classic piece of bourgeois ideology—to wit, social contract theory. But read on before you judge me too harshly. . . .

This book is divided into three parts: "Marxism in Theory and Practice," "Race and Class," "Critical Race Theory." Given this disparate subject matter, the book is ineluctably hybrid in a number of ways, posing if nothing else classificatory and taxonomical problems for the library cataloger. (Should it be put with the *HX*s, under "Marxism," or with the *E*s, under "United States, race relations"?) Moreover, though the book is in Rowman & Littlefield's series in new "critical theory," a term classically associated with the Continental tradition in philosophy, the chapters are analytic rather than Continental in style. And finally, as noted, while I begin with a sympathetic exegesis of crucial terms in the apparatus of historical materialism, I wind up endorsing a framework famously foundational for liberalism. So in various ways the text resists disciplinary confinement in the standard academic boxes and labels—a reflection perhaps not merely of the author's personal evolution, but of the always somewhat awkward, always somewhat askew, always somewhat problematic relationship the black experience has traditionally had with the categories of the mainstream white academy.

But the overarching umbrella category is nonetheless critical theory, and my original (somewhat cumbersome) title was *From Critical Class Theory to Critical Race Theory*. Now, in a broad sense and by its very nature, philosophy—at least as conceived of in the Western tradition—is supposed to be "critical theory" insofar as its supposed mission is to seek wisdom and speak truth to power, rather than uncritically affirm the conventional wisdom and propitiate power. Of how many subjects in the academy, after all, can it be said that their initiator, the person standing at the head of the tradition, should have been tried, convicted, and executed for upsetting respectability? But in some ways, philosophy has been trying to live down this promising start ever since. Far too often in the subsequent two thousand years, philosophers have been complicit with power and hierarchy, rather than challenging them. Accordingly, Karl Marx famously called on philosophers to develop an understanding of the world oriented toward changing it; and critical theory, in the narrow sense of the term as linked with the 1922 founding of the Frankfurt Institute, took its inspiration from Marx's exhortation and set out to create a descriptive and normative social theory of an explicitly emancipatory kind (Rasmussen 1996). As such, critical theory indicted both capitalism and (later) Stalinism by trying to articulate a class-based analysis that was capable of explaining the deformations of reason and the nonrealization of moral universalism in both West and East.

The first part of the book, "Marxism in Theory and Practice" (chapters 1–4), is located in this tradition, at least to the extent that in these four chapters I explore some of the classic themes and problems in historical materialism: ideology, the precise significance of "materialism," the status of morality, Stalinism. But my approach to these matters is analytical, though this reflects my training as a philosopher rather than any principled hostility to Continental approaches as such. So in that sense, these four opening chapters are essays in "Analytical Marxism."

Analytical Marxism as an intellectual movement is now about a quarter-century old. Although the term itself would not be coined until the mid-eighties, its founding text is G. A. Cohen's classic 1978 *Karl Marx's Theory of History: A Defence*, reprinted in an expanded edition in 2001. (Contrasting perspectives on the movement, respectively sympathetic and hostile, can be found in Mayer [1994] and Roberts [1996].) For some, above all its practitioners, it rapidly became the only respectable form of Marxism left on the planet, a distinction unabashedly proclaimed in the self-selected title of a group of its core members: the Non-Bullshit Marxism Group. (Inevitably, in a field never shy of—indeed historically reveling in—internecine polemic and denunciation, this designation was quickly transposed by critics into the "Non-Marxist Bullshit Group.") In a "thin," or weak, sense, the defining features of Analytical Marxism are obvious enough: the application of the methods typical of analytical philosophy to Marxist theory, concepts, and claims. But "thicker," or more theoretically committed, senses were also put forward—for example, rational-choice Marxism or game-theoretic Marxism (Carver and Thomas 1995). However, these candidates have proven more controversial, in part because not all the figures prominent in the field share such methodological sympathies; thus, it is best to think of them as forming a subcategory of Analytical Marxism rather than as being coextensive with it. Certainly I have no commitment to such approaches myself. So what I see myself as carrying out here is simply the traditional analytic task of establishing—by clear initial statement of terms, textual citation, and argument—what Marx actually meant by specific concepts and what the theoretical implications would be: in short, the familiar role of philosophy as underlaborer.

As such, the first three chapters in this section are heavily textual, and I make no apologies for that. Of course, some critics might sneer that if the owl of Minerva generally spreads its wings at dusk, here it is flying at midnight. Who cares about these issues anymore? Why should anyone today be concerned about the dead ideas of a philosopher whose degree of deadness (imagine we had a thanatic metric, able to register degrees of deadness . . .) seems by conventional measures to be off the scale, underlined by the utterly post-Marxist nature of the new century? But as Bill McBride has pointed out in another volume in this series (2001, 113), the scarcity of Platonic city-states has never had any noticeably chilling effect on the Plato industry, nor have exegetes of the *Republic* ever been required to justify themselves at the philosophical bar. Systematic textual investigation to find out what a philosopher actually meant is not, one would think, an unheard-of and unprecedented exercise in the academy; but scholars who would take for granted the value of going through the corpus to clarify Plato's Theory of Forms, or Hobbes' exact position on natural law, often seem to find it strange that it should still be deemed academically worthwhile to find out what Marx actually meant by such terms as "ideology" or "materialism." Yet Marx remains one of the major thinkers of the past few hundred years; so, if only for academic reasons, it remains important to get straight on what he actually said about specific subjects. And if (as I will argue) it turns out that many commentators have in fact gotten Marx wrong, then the implications extend far beyond the academy, given Marx's influence on sociopolitical theory and movements. Finally, I am writing this in the United States in the summer of 2002, in the wake of the dot-com collapse, the wiping out of trillions of dollars by the market free fall since early 2000, the revelations of widespread corporate malfeasance, and the vertiginously growing chasm between rich and poor both nationally and globally. As I observe it all, I find it difficult to believe that a supposedly dead Marxism could have nothing of value to say to the brave new world order of a dawning twenty-first century turning out, in certain respects, to be not that different from Marx's own.[1]

The second part, "Race and Class" (chapters 5 and 6), explores what has traditionally been a problem area for Marxist theory: a major human division whose significance is awkwardly accommodated within orthodox Marxist categories. Throughout the twentieth century, many people of color were attracted to Marxism because of its far-ranging historical perspective, its theoretical centering of oppression, and its promise of liberation. But many of these recruits would later become disillusioned, both with Marxist theory and the practice of actual (white) Marxist parties. The historical vision turned out to be Eurocentric; the specificities of their racial oppression were often not recognized but were dissolved into supposedly all-encompassing class categories; and the liberation envisaged did not include as a necessary goal the dismantling of white supremacy in all its aspects. Cedric Robinson's pioneering *Black Marxism* (2000), first published in 1983, recounts the long-troubled history of left-wing black diasporic intellectuals (W. E. B. Du Bois, C. L. R. James, George Padmore, Richard Wright, Aimé Césaire) with "white Marxism," and it argues for the existence of a distinct "black radical political tradition" whose historic foci and concerns cannot be simply assimilated to mainstream white Marxist theory. So even if the origin of white supremacy is most plausibly explained within a historical materialist framework that locates it in imperialist European expansionism—as the product, ultimately, of class forces and bourgeois class interests—race as an international global structure then achieves an intersubjective reality whose dialectic cannot simply be reduced to a class dynamic. In the two chapters in this section, I try to grapple with race in a class (Marxist) framework, looking first at the so-called underclass and then going on to raise deeper questions about the foundational assumptions of historical materialism, and what should properly be counted as "material."

So we make the transition of my title to part three, "Critical Race Theory" (chapters 7–9). The titular *From . . . to . . .* should not be taken in the spirit of a complete repudiation of Marxism, since I do think that a *modified* historical materialism might be able to carry out an adequate conceptualization of the significance of race. But the rethinking necessary would have to be more thorough than most white Marxists have so far been willing to undertake. In this final part, then, I bracket the question of the possibility of a theoretical synthesis, and I simply focus on racial oppression as a system in its own right. As such, these final three chapters bring me to where I am today: using *white supremacy* as a theoretical framework, recognition of which should force liberals to concede the centrality of race to, and corresponding injustice of, the present social order.

Critical race theory, at least under that explicit designation, is a recent intellectual development, usually being traced to work in American legal theory beginning in the 1980s. The Critical Legal Studies (CLS) movement challenged mainstream conceptions of law: It demonstrated the many ways in which the law, far from being a neutral set of rules and norms standing above the political, was itself political and nonneutral (Hutchinson 1989). But minority scholars, while fully endorsing this demystificatory enterprise, argued that the largely white male leaders of the movement had failed to recognize and theorize the crucial role of *race* in social domination. They became known as critical race theorists (and their writings as critical race theory), and the term has now spread far beyond its legal origins to refer to theorizing on race much more broadly.

But it would be a major mistake to limit critical race theory to the work of the last fifteen years or so carried out under that explicit banner, or to think of it as a mere spin-off from critical theory in general. Particularly in the black diasporic tradition—not just the United States, but also the Caribbean and Latin America—there is a long tradition of oppositional intellectual engagement with the structures of white racial domination, which could reasonably be dubbed critical race theory *avant la lettre*. From this perspective, critical race theory is far from being an adjunct to, or outgrowth of, critical class theory; in fact, it long predates it, at least in its modern Marxist form. Long before Marx was born, Africans forcibly transported as slaves to the New World were struggling desperately to understand their situation; they were raising the issues of social critique and transformation as radically as—indeed even more radically than—the white European working class, who were after all beneficiaries of and accessories to the same system oppressing blacks. We associate critical theory with the Enlightenment and modernity. But modernity is usually thought of in Eurocentric terms: the modern *inside* Europe. Yet once one rethinks the conventional time and space (i.e., the periodization and the cartography) of the modern—as black and Third World theorists have long urged us to do—we should begin to appreciate, first, that the cutting edges of modernity, the outposts of the future, were to be found in the provinces rather than the metropolis (i.e., the frontiers of what would become the European world-system) and, second, that the problems of the

modern were posed in their sharpest and most unequivocal form here. As
C. L. R. James pointed out long ago (James 1989), the slave plantations of
the New World were industrially far advanced beyond the European
workshops of the time.

All the issues we now think of as defining of critical theory's concerns
were brought home to the racially subordinated, the colonized and enslaved, in the most intimate and brutal way: the human alienation, the in-
strumentalization and deformation of reason in the service of power, the
critique of abstract individualism, the paradox of reconciling proclama-
tions of humanism with mass murder, the need to harness normative theory to the practical task of human liberation. So if Marx's proletariat too
often had to have proletarian consciousness "imputed" (in Georg Lukács'
infamous phrase) to them, and if the relation between Marxism and the
actual working-class outlook was often more a matter of faith and hope-
ful counterfactuals than actuality (what the workers *would* think if only . . .),
then oppositional ideas on race have shaped the consciousness of the
racially subordinated for centuries. If white workers have been alienated
from their product, then people of color, especially black slaves, have been
alienated from their personhood; if Enlightenment reason has been complicit with bourgeois projects, then it has been even more thoroughly corrupted by its accommodation to white supremacy; if liberal individualism
has not always taken white workers fully into account, then it has often
excluded nonwhites altogether; if it was a post–World War II challenge to
explain how the "civilized" Germany of Goethe and Beethoven could
have carried out the Jewish and Romani Holocausts, then it is a far older
challenge to explain how "civilized" Europe as a whole could have carried out the savage genocide of indigenous populations and the barbaric
enslavement of millions; and, finally, if Marx's proletarians have been
called upon to see and lose their chains (and have often seemed quite
well-adjusted to them), then people of color (i.e., Native American populations, enslaved and later Jim-Crowed Africans in the New World, the
colonized) have historically had little difficulty in recognizing their oppression—after all, the chains were often literal!—and in seeking to throw
it off. So if the ideal of fusing intellectual theory with political practice has
been the long-term goal of critical class theory, it has been far more frequently realized in the nascent critical race theory of the racially subordinated, whose oppression has been more blatant and unmediated and for
whom the urgency of their situation has necessitated a direct connection
between the normative and practical emancipation.

Moreover, there are parallels between the macro-sociohistorical concerns of critical race theory and Marxism. Within the Native American,
black, and anticolonial traditions, a strong emphasis has always been
placed on studying history and revising conventional historiography.

Blacks in particular, after all, are famously the race *without* a history—see Hegel's notorious consignment of Africa to the realm of night in his *Philosophy of History* (1956). So finding a usable past (and present) has been critical to the black intellectual tradition, and debates about the role of Africa and Africans in the world long predate the controversy about Martin Bernal's recent work on the connections between ancient Greece and ancient Egypt (1987). In this respect, black radicalism's metanarrative makes pivotal the role of European expansionism in the modern period as shaping not merely a global history and geography, but, at the discursive level, a mystificatory "history" and "geography," which need to be exposed. So while some critical race theorists have been attracted to postmodernism for its iconoclasm, many have shied away from its ahistoricism and its refusal to concede the existence of macropatterns that have shaped the world and set the stage for the concerns of the present.

In Marxism/critical class theory, of course, this role is played by the analysis of capitalism or, more generally, class society; and historical materialism is supposed to be the theory of its evolution. I have argued elsewhere (Mills 1997; 1998) that white supremacy in both a local and global sense should be the overarching sociopolitical concept with which critical race theorists work. In chapters 7 and 8, accordingly, I try to map out how the idea of white supremacy could fruitfully inform descriptive and normative critical race theory. Finally, in chapter 9, the concluding chapter in the book, I draw on an apparatus historically linked with liberalism, and I show how it can be turned to radical and "critical" ends. Defending and clarifying my use of social contract theory in *The Racial Contract*, I argue against one of my critics that the "Racial Contract" (or, more generally, the "domination contract") provides an intellectual framework superior to mainstream contractarianism for tackling issues of race and racism. The resources of contract theory (the holistic descriptive picture, the normative menu of liberal rights) can then be applied to the description and condemnation of white supremacy. As such, it is an appropriate synthesizing note on which to end a book seeking to show how Marxism needs to change, how liberalism can become more "critical," and how both have been theoretically inadequate on race.

As a philosopher, some people have found me hard to classify, even before my switch some years ago from Marxism to race. Politically, as someone of color from the Third World, I have always been drawn to what is categorized as "radical" philosophy; in fact, I am a longtime member of the Radical Philosophy Association. This political orientation is usually associated with Continental philosophy's greater interest in history and social process. But my training is actually in the analytic tradition, and theoretically and methodologically it is here that I am at home. So my work is something of a hybrid: "Continental" in content, "analytic" in approach.

As a result, I hang out with two different crowds at American Philosophical Association meetings, and I have to put up with two sets of eye-rollings and surreptitious headings-for-the-exit when interlopers from the other crowd appear: one, analytic colleagues dismissive of fuzzy-minded bloviating Continentals who are unclear about everything; two, Continental colleagues dismissive of ignorant and anal analytics who are clear about nothing worthwhile. Many negative things can be said about analytic philosophy—I have said some of them myself—but I am not one of those who think that its approach is intrinsically hostile to tackling these larger sociohistorical questions. What some see as its innate conservatism, I take to be more a contingent artifact of the interests and concerns of a particular population. In other words, if you're socialized by your orthodox philosophical education into a prissily narrow picture of the proper and respectable subjects of philosophy, you will reproduce them yourself in your own writing, teaching, and mentoring of graduate students. But they are not inherent in the approach itself. The pretensions of the analytic tradition are to the making of clear statements of the issue at hand, backed up by arguments; and one would not think that this is intrinsically conservative or threatening to a radical political agenda. (If it is, then there is something wrong with that agenda.) In G. A. Cohen's dryly understated line, for the Anglophone philosophical tradition, "it is not generally supposed that a theoretical statement, to be one, must be hard to comprehend" (2001, x). In this tradition, then, I have tried to elucidate crucial concepts in Marxism and critical race theory, and I have worked out what the implications are. The inclusion of my book in a series like this is itself testimony to the open-mindedness of the series editors, Martin Matuštík and Patricia Huntington, and their recognition that "critical theory" can come in many guises. By the end, I hope to have persuaded the reader that "analytic critical theory" is not oxymoronic.

I have benefited from criticisms of and suggestions on various of the original drafts of these chapters from Sandra Bartky, G. A. Cohen, Frank Cunningham, John Deigh, Gerald A. Dworkin, Danny Goldstick, Paul Gomberg, Holly Graff, Alastair Hannay, Patricia Huntington, David Ingram, Shelly Kagan, Richard Kraut, Mark Notturno, Lois Pineau, Justin Schwartz, David Schweickart, James Sterba, Robert Stone, Olufemi Taiwo, David Waldman. Cunningham and Goldstick taught me the Marxism I know; and even if I no longer work in this area, I will always be deeply grateful to them for the education they gave me in the theory of a major global thinker. I would also like to single out and thank Martin Matuštík in particular for his very thorough, detailed, and helpful comments on the rethinking, rewriting, and reorganization of the original manuscript. The suggestions of the two anonymous Rowman and Littlefield reviewers were also very useful. Bill Hart, Department Chair at the University of

Illinois at Chicago, has been unfailingly supportive of my research, and the technical assistance and daily encouragement of Charlotte Jackson and Valerie Brown have been invaluable. As always, my father, Gladstone Mills, has been my most loyal and unwavering backer.

"The Moral Epistemology of Stalinism" was presented to the philosophy departments of the University of Illinois at Chicago and the University of Toronto in February 1992, and I have benefited from the audience discussions at both places. "Race as the Primary Contradiction," which would become a paper-within-a-paper, was presented on a panel on "Envisioning the Next Left," at the second national conference of the Radical Philosophy Association in November 1996. My thanks to Ron Aronson, the chair, for his invitation to participate, and to the audience, especially Ann Ferguson, for their vigorous criticisms. "White Supremacy and Racial Justice" was originally done at the invitation of James Sterba for a conference on "Alternative Conceptions of Justice" at the University of Notre Dame in April 2000, which was centered on his book *Justice for Here and Now* (1998); my appreciation to Jim for the invitation and for his principled receptivity to my critique. "The 'Racial Contract' as Methodology (Not Hypothesis): A Reply to Jorge Garcia" was presented as a response to Garcia on a panel on "Subversive Contractarianism" sponsored by the Society for Philosophy and Public Affairs at the Central Division meetings of the American Philosophical Association in May 2001. I would like to thank Carol Gould for organizing the panel, and Anita Superson for chairing it at short notice. Some of these chapters were originally written or revised during my 1993–1994 year as a Fellow of the Institute for the Humanities at the University of Illinois at Chicago, and I would like to express my appreciation to the institute for its support. I have also benefited, more recently, from a 1999–2002 UIC University Scholarship.

Finally, I gratefully acknowledge permission to reprint the following chapters:

"'"Ideology" in Marx and Engels' Revisited and Revised" first appeared in *The Philosophical Forum* 23, no. 4 (Summer 1992).

"Is It Immaterial That There's a 'Material' in 'Historical Materialism'?" first appeared in *Inquiry* 32, no. 3 (September 1989).

"Marxism, 'Ideology,' and Moral Objectivism" first appeared in a shorter version in the *Canadian Journal of Philosophy* 24, no. 3 (September 1994).

"The Moral Epistemology of Stalinism" first appeared in *Politics & Society* 22, no. 1 (March 1994).

"Under Class Under Standings" first appeared as a review essay in *Ethics* 104, no. 4 (July 1994). © 1994 by the University of Chicago. All rights reserved.

"European Spectres" first appeared in *The Journal of Ethics* 3, no. 2 (1999), in a special issue on Marx and Marxism. With kind permission from Kluwer Academic Publishers.

"White Supremacy as Socio-Political System" is scheduled to appear as a chapter in the forthcoming *White Out: The Continuing Significance of Racism* (Routledge), edited by Ashley Doane and Eduardo Bonilla-Silva; it is a revised and expanded version of "White Supremacy," an entry in *A Companion to African-American Philosophy*, ed. Tommy L. Lott and John P. Pittman (Malden, Mass.: Blackwell, 2003).

"White Supremacy and Racial Justice" first appeared in a shorter version in *Social and Political Philosophy: Contemporary Perspectives*, ed. James P. Sterba (New York: Routledge, 2001).

"The 'Racial Contract' as Methodology (Not Hypothesis)" first appeared as a reply to Jorge Garcia in *Philosophia Africana* 5, no. 1 (March 2002).

NOTE

1. See, for example, the startling statistics on present-day global and national capitalist inequality cited by David Schweickart in his *After Capitalism* (2002, 2): "The top 225 individuals now possess wealth equal to the combined incomes of the bottom 47 percent of the world's population. (Roughly, the average wealth of each one of these individuals is equal to the combined incomes of *ten million* people earning the average income of the bottom half of humanity.) . . . In the United States, the upper 1 percent of the population owns more wealth than the bottom 95 percent." Watch also his remarkable "parade of dwarves (and a few giants)" (88–93).

I

MARXISM IN THEORY AND PRACTICE

Ideology" was for a decade or more one of the most intensively analyzed concepts in the Marxist lexicon, though this interest would come more from "Western" Marxism than later Analytical Marxism. My first chapter, a sequel to a survey article originally published in the 1980s, offers a revisionist interpretation that argues that this huge secondary literature has produced more confusion than illumination. "Ideology" in the ideational sense, I claim, was never meant by Marx and Engels to have the all-encompassing scope it has assumed, but it is a term located in a specific polemic—with the Young Hegelians and their "idealistic" way of analyzing society—whose historical context has long been forgotten. A term of art devised for a specific localized reference has since assumed a vast significance it was never intended to have.

Insofar as Marx and Engels' usage was taken to authorize a sweeping dismissal of entire fields of thought as mere "bourgeois ideology," this misinterpretation has had a pernicious effect on left-wing theorizing and has arguably contributed to left-wing sectarianism. ("Their views are ideology; ours are science.") Not merely in the late socialist world, but in the intellectual practice of Marxist groups in the capitalist world, this simplistic equation provided a crude epistemic sorting device, intoxicating in its power. Detailed engagement with the ideas of others—the onerous task of grappling with claims, evidence, inferences—was too often short-circuited by their preemptive categorization as "ideology" and therefore as aprioristically wrong. Moreover, it was not merely the class enemy who got this treatment, but those misguided and unenlightened nonclass victims of capitalism who put forward analyses at variance with orthodoxy.

After all, if the only alternatives were bourgeois ideology and Marxist (class) science, then the nonclass ideas of other subordinated groups, clearly not being Marxist science, had to be bourgeois ideology. The tensions between the more orthodox Left, on the one hand, and the women and oppressed ethnic/racial minorities in these movements, on the other—with the struggles of the latter to get their distinctive insights and perspectives taken seriously by the white male vanguard—may be judged to have their roots in part in this straitjacketed one-dimensional analysis of the ideational. Thus we see that an apparently simple textual analysis may have much broader repercussions. Religious fundamentalisms and schisms have classically turned on rival interpretations of the sacred texts (in the beginning was the Word, after all); and if many Marxist movements of the twentieth century have, embarrassingly, had the character of millennial organizations, it might be less surprising that getting the Word wrong from the start could have disastrous consequences.

G. A. Cohen's *Karl Marx's Theory of History: A Defence* (2001) showed, first, that the fine distinction making and emphasis on lucidity typical of analytic philosophy could clarify Marx's claims and, second, that Marx's claims were neither confused nor egregiously wrong (though they might have been just plain wrong). But though anybody working in the field owes him a debt, his position then had the unhappy effect of reviving a technologically determinist Marxism that many, including myself, found implausible. (In later work, he has somewhat qualified his original position.) In my critique of Cohen in chapter 2, I show—a tribute, again, to the analytic emphasis on getting things clear—that, just by looking at how Marx used the word "material" in his writings, we can raise questions about the defensibility of this analysis. I endorse what was then known as the mode-of-production interpretation, which located primary (materialist) determination not simply in technological advance but in the complicated interaction between the forces and relations of production. So the material is in part social. The theoretical virtue of such an approach, apart from being truer to the texts, is that it provides a conceptual entry point for admitting the *negative* "material" factors that complicate—in a way that is (more importantly) truer to the world we know—the simplified technological–determinist picture of an asocial rationality driving productivist advance. In addition, I would claim as a virtue its opening-up of a space for the nonclass groups whose interactions—and whose divergent, embedded, and (socially) embodied rationalities of gender and race—would have to be incorporated into a transformed Marxism adequate to conceptualizing the *multiple* materialities of our complex social reality.

With the revival of Anglo-American political philosophy in the wake of John Rawls' *A Theory of Justice* (1971), it became important for the academic Left to determine what, if anything, Marx had to say about issues of morality and justice. The dominant interpretation of Marxism had long been an amoralist one, which seemed to be backed up by his writings; and a large industry developed in philosophy around the question of the correct adjudication of this interpretation. One important source (albeit not the only one) of this negative attitude was Marx's apparent dismissal of morality as mere "ideology." In chapter 3, I survey some of this literature, and argue that my revisionist conception of "ideology" has implications here also, since Marx's dismissal (I claim) is not really about content but about causal efficaciousness. The well-known paradox of Marx and morality (highlighted for example by Steven Lukes [1985])—that Marx seems to use moral terms and moral appeals while being negative about morality—can then be reconciled with the texts in a manner less strained than that to be found in other commentators. On the other hand, where left-wing practice has been guided by a vulgar realpolitik and indifference to moral considerations invoking Marxist inspiration ("morality is just 'ideology'"), this revision would indicate that (at least on this score) it can claim no Marxist authority.

Finally, the last chapter in this section examines one aspect of what for tens of millions of people was the nightmare of self-described Marxism in practice: Stalinism. My focus here, however, is not on Stalinism as a politico-economic system, a well-explored subject by now, especially with the post-1989 opening-up of the archives of communist parties in the former East Bloc. My interest is more in the moral psychology of the period: Stalinism as state of mind and orientation to the world. The classic philosophical analyses here have been in the Continental tradition: the Frankfurt School's diagnoses, Maurice Merleau-Ponty's work *Humanism and Terror* (1969), the postwar debates between Jean-Paul Sartre and Albert Camus. Chapter 4 tries the experiment of approaching these issues with the radically different apparatus of mainstream analytic ethics; and, by drawing on its discussion of such subjects as moral dilemmas, self-deception, and self-transformation, it attempts to track the origins and development of a Stalinist moral psychology. To the extent that the experiment is successful, it vindicates my contention that these tools are not intrinsically limited to the exploration of the humdrum, but can also be applied to more historically challenging kinds of topics.

1

"Ideology" in Marx and Engels: Revisited and Revised

In the Analytical Marxist project of clarifying Marx's concepts and claims for an Anglo-American philosophical audience, the notion of "ideology" has received comparatively little attention. Thus if we take five representative anthologies—Terence Ball and James Farr's *After Marx* (1984), John Roemer's *Analytical Marxism* (1986), Alex Callinicos' *Marxist Theory* (1989), Robert Ware and Kai Nielsen's *Analyzing Marxism* (1989), and Terrell Carver and Paul Thomas' *Rational Choice Marxism* (1995)—we will find, astonishingly, that out of sixty-three collected essays only *one* deals centrally with ideology.[1] For those who remember the classic Marxist debates of the 1960s and 1970s—with their focus on such themes as Lukács' "reification," Marcuse's "one-dimensionality," Gramsci's "hegemony," and Althusser's "ideological state apparatuses"—the shift is a truly dramatic one, which testifies to the extent to which G. A. Cohen's work (2001) has transformed the framework of debate.[2]

Yet some concept of ideology must remain pivotal in the necessary rethinking of Marxism. For those skeptical about the long-term political utility of postmodernism's epistemological relativism, for those unconvinced that the very concept of a "metanarrative" is intrinsically oppressive, and for those defiantly attached to such old-fashioned Enlightenment notions as truth and falsity—in short, for those still committed to some kind of realist program—the question of the determination and normative assessment of consciousness continues to be unavoidable. And there is a whole range of issues involved here, for which it is crucial that some adequate conception of ideology be worked out: the claim that the differential social standpoints of groups generate alternative epistemologies, the possibility of a materialist grounding of discourses, the necessary revision of the pedagogy of the intellectual resistance to oppression in the light of the failure of vanguardism, and the metaethical questions of the status of morality and the prescriptive. The concept ascribed to Marx has admittedly been traditionally problematic: it is arguably inconsistent or self-refuting to begin with; it is genealogically confused or opaque; it is class-reductively insensitive to gender and race; it is caught in an unresolved tension between epistemic and social-functional characterizations; and it too readily lends itself to moral nihilism and amoralism. Then, certainly any responsible rethinking of Marxism must seek to remedy this.

This first chapter attempts just such an elucidation through revisiting an earlier essay of mine. Some years ago, I did a survey article (Mills 1985) that reviewed twenty books and articles on "ideology," provided a rough taxonomy of different commentators' views on how Marx and Engels used the term, and then argued in support of one of those positions. A few years after its original journal appearance, it was subjected to criticism by the author whose work I spent the most time discussing, Joseph McCarney, and by two other writers, Dan Costello and Mary Ann Sushinsky (McCarney 1990; Costello 1990; Sushinsky 1990).[3] However, in the intervening years, I had already drastically modified my position as a result of discussions with a colleague at the University of Toronto, Danny Goldstick (Mills and Goldstick 1989). In this opening chapter, then, I am taking the opportunity to give a partial defense of my original article and, more important, an exposition of my new view that, paradoxically, refutes McCarney in one sense while vindicating him in another. The main virtue of this radical new interpretation lies not in its intrinsic interest (which is largely antiquarian) but in its *clearing of the conceptual ground* so that a fresh start can be made. It implies that the conventional spectrum of opinion on what Marx and Engels meant by "ideology" is quite wrong, that their own notion of "ideology" is in fact of little use to a modern audience, and that a theoretical space is therefore opened up for the construction of a new Marxist conception of ideology that can largely ignore what Marx and Engels themselves said about "ideology." To a certain extent, then, the consequence is a welcome emancipation from what in many ways (if truth be told) has always been a somewhat unhelpful text.

THE ORIGINAL ARGUMENT: THREE MAIN POSITIONS

Let me begin with a recapitulation of my original argument. It has long been taken as something of an embarrassment for Marxist theory that an apparently central concept, "ideology," seems to involve historical materialism either in self-refutation or an implausible and self-serving exceptionalism. For as critics have pointed out: if "ideology's" reference is to ideas in general or even class ideas in particular, and if it is a pejorative term, then how does Marxism escape the *tu quoque* of being itself characterized as "ideological"?

In Mills (1985), I distinguished three main positions on this question (hereafter referred to as positions *a*, *b*, and *c*): *(a)* those authors (the vast majority) who saw "ideology" as a univocal and epistemologically negative term; *(b)* those authors, most notably Joseph McCarney, who saw "ideology" as an univocal but epistemologically neutral term; *(c)* those authors who claim that Marx and Engels use "ideology" in *two* senses, a neutral sense referring generally to class ideas and a pejorative sense referring specifically to ideas of an *idealist* sort.

Since the term seems to have many appearances and derivatives that are negative—thus creating the foundation for position *a*—defenders of the existence of a single neutral sense (position *b*) must obviously find some way to account for them. The main representative of this position, Joseph McCarney, has for years waged a valiant but largely vain struggle to revise the standard understanding of Marx's concept of "ideology." McCarney's strategy, both in his book (1980) and in his critical response to me (1990), is to argue that the appearance of an epistemically negative conception, at least in Marx's own work and his coauthored writings, has simply been projected onto the texts by a generation of careless scholars who have mistaken conjunctural "concrete" attacks on *particular* ideologies for global pronouncements about "ideology" *itself*. Although he concedes that some of Engels' later remarks cannot be accommodated by this reading, he argues that these should be seen as "aberrations" (a subordinate theme in Engels' writings) that call for further research.

In my original paper, I defended position *c*, which claims that the many negative appearances of the term are no illusion; that their reference has been misunderstood, denoting idealism in particular, rather than class ideas in general; and that this restricted pejorative meaning coexists with a neutral general meaning. As will readily be appreciated, the advantage of this position is that it enables one to have it both ways: to account for what seem, *pace* McCarney, to be genuinely pejorative usages of the term, while simultaneously saving Marxism from self-refutation (since Marxism would then be an ideology in the second but not the first sense).

Before I go on to explain my new position, however, I want to address some of the criticisms of "ideology" made by McCarney and Costello. In other words, these are criticisms I still see as incorrect despite my change of views.[4]

REPLIES TO MCCARNEY'S AND COSTELLO'S POINTS

In my original paper, I placed John McMurtry, author of *The Structure of Marx's World-View* (1978), alongside McCarney in group *b*. In his "Reply," McCarney challenges this categorization, so let me give the evidence. McMurtry offers five criteria for ideology:

1. "It is constituted of *formulated ideas. . . .*"
2. "It refers to *human matters or affairs. . . .*"
3. "Its content is *materially unproductive. . . .*"
4. "It obtains in a *public mode. . . .*"
5. "It is *subject to state control. . . .*" (1978, 127–28)

McMurtry goes on to say that ideology "includes within its ambit of reference mass-media, school, church, academic, legal, political, aesthetic, and all other forms of public communication," though excluding "merely personal ideation" (130–31). He discusses the claim of some theorists that "another mark of ideology must be that it is 'unscientific,'" and he explicitly repudiates this view, saying "we are going to interpret Marx as regarding scientific and unscientific conceptions of human affairs as distinct subclasses of ideology." This interpretation, he argues, is consistent with "Marx's persistent talk of 'ideological struggle,'"[5] which implies "that he counted 'scientific socialism' as part of this struggle," so that "Marx's theory is properly conceived as both ideology *and* knowledge" (McMurtry 1978, 131–32). Overall, then, for McMurtry: "Ideology, like law and politics, is always part of the 'class struggle'—its public consciousness side" (141).

Now it should be obvious to the reader that this position is far from being *sui generis* (i.e., deserving of a separate category of its own). In its essentials, it is completely congruent with McCarney's view: "ideology" is epistemologically neutral, *not* unscientific by definition, and it consists of publicly formulated ideas about human affairs, including Marxism itself, that are part of the class struggle. Doubtless there are divergences between McMurtry's and McCarney's precise interpretations, but McMurtry is indeed, *pace* McCarney, a legitimate representative of position *b*.[6]

Another issue is more quickly disposed of. McCarney (1990) repeats a point he made in his book: that an argument against the pejorative interpretation of "ideology" is that such phrases as "ideological deception," "ideological illusion," and so forth, would then have a pleonastic character. For Marx and Engels would then be saying something like "deceptive deceptions," "illusory illusions," and so on (453).

However, if the pejorative meaning of "ideology" does not refer to "illusions" in general, but to "idealism" in particular, then "ideological distortion/illusion/deception" would *not* be pleonastic, because it would signify distortions, illusions, and deceptions of a *specific* kind: *idealistic* ones. The implicit contrast would not, then, be a "lifeless" one (McCarney 1990, 453), because Marx and Engels would be singling out a particular kind of illusion (one they regarded as peculiarly characteristic of a certain social stratum) and demarcating it from other (nonidealistic) kinds of illusion. I will elaborate on this later.

As was the case in his book, a significant portion of McCarney's reply (section 2) focuses on a rereading of one crucial passage, the *camera obscura* passage, from *The German Ideology*: "If in all ideology men and their relations appear upside-down as in a *camera obscura*. . . ." (CW 5, 36). In my original article (Mills 1985), I had suggested that one should be "a bit wary of an interpretation which rests so heavily on a single, allegedly mistranslated phrase" (335). In his reply, McCarney comments that my remark itself involves a "kind of inversion," since it is not he who has attributed such significance to this passage, but those commentators in group *a* who argue for the univocal pejorative meaning.

What we have here is an unfortunate complete misunderstanding of my original point, for which my wording might be responsible. My point was not that this is the single passage that lends support to the *second* position (position *b*). To say so would make no sense at all, since obviously (as I said in Mills [1985]) this passage is, on the contrary, a *problem* for that interpretation. My point rather was twofold: first, that it was implausible to think that position *a* had such an exiguous textual foundation (in fact, there are many passages that support it, *of which this is only one*); second, that a defender of position *b*, such as McCarney, would consequently have to do much more work to show that position *a* is *wrong* than just to offer an alternative reading of *one* of them—admittedly a central one (that most frequently cited by commentators). I will list some of these other passages later.

That brings us to Dan Costello's article. Costello defends McCarney and the epistemically neutral interpretation by claiming that all apparently pejorative usages of "ideology" can be simply accounted for by reading them specifically—by "qualify[ing] the unqualified substantive" (Costello 1990, 467). As such, his argument seems to me to be fatally marred by an elementary logical confusion: the failure to distinguish between the negative employment of a neutral term in a specific context and the employment of a generically pejorative term.

If *X* is an epistemologically neutral term, such as "belief," then obviously one can apply it equally to beliefs one thinks true and beliefs one thinks false. The burden of McCarney's book is that, for Marx, "ideology" is a term of this epistemic type (though denoting beliefs of a particular kind), rather than a term of the loaded epistemic type of "illusion," which cannot properly be used about beliefs one endorses. But clearly, whether "ideology" is epistemically neutral or negative, Marx could use it to describe specific class ideas he opposes and regards as false. In order to prove McCarney wrong, then—in order to prove that "ideology" is a term of the pejorative epistemic type of "illusion" and not a term of the neutral epistemic type of "belief"—what one would have to do is to find negative passages that make it clear that it is "ideology" *in general*, "ideology" qua "ideology," "ideology" *simpliciter*, that Marx views negatively and not just a *particular* ideology.

McCarney's recognition that some of Engels' statements fit this description is what motivates him to draw a dividing line between Marx and Engels' views. This is no "puzzling aberration," as Costello characterizes it (468), but something forced upon McCarney by the fact that, in the passages cited, it is clear that Engels is making a *general* pronouncement about the *necessarily* illusory features of "ideology" itself (and not, trivially, because "ideology" has been *defined* to mean "illusory ideas," but because of a substantive factual thesis about what it is). Thus McCarney cannot, as Costello seems to think, explain away these passages as Engels' *contextually* negative view of a particular ideology. My aim will be to show that such passages can be found in Marx's writings also.

THE NEW POSITION: "IDEOLOGY" AS "SUPERSTRUCTURE" AND "IDEALISM"

I will now outline my new position on the question of what Marx and Engels meant by "ideology."[7] Previously, as indicated, I had endorsed position *c*. However, as I would later concede in Mills and Goldstick (1989), there is something ad hoc about this view: it has no intrinsic theoretical justification, being merely an empiricist construct that seems to "save the appearances." Thus McCarney (1990) characterizes the position as "an untenable half-way house" (451). I must now agree with this judgment: position *c* is indeed a halfway house with a fatal strain in the foundations. But the solution does not lie in a move to McCarney's neighborhood, but in a more radical reconstruction and relocation altogether. Whereas previously I had thought it was necessary to accommodate a neutral ideational sense of "ideology," I would now deny this. My suggestion—let us call it position *d*—is that "ideology" has two meanings—but that *neither* of them is McCarney's. Rather, what "ideology" *really* means is: superstructure, idealism. *Thus neither of the two senses has the denotation conventionally attributed to the concept in most of the secondary literature throughout the twentieth century*—that is, partisan class ideas in general, whether bourgeois or proletarian, whether neutrally or negatively conceived.

Here is my argument. Marx's theoretical development, to recite a familiar tale, involved an influence by, and later rejection of, the thought of

Hegel and the Young Hegelians. The fatal flaw of Hegelianism for Marx was its idealism, the fact that, for Hegel, history and social evolution were determined by "the Idea." Feuerbach's "transformative method" attracted Marx because of its materialism, its righting of what had been turned "upside-down." But Marx eventually came to see Feuerbach as an inconsistent materialist, one who had not carried out the desired rectificatory program completely.

What was the nature of this inconsistency? An answer to this question requires the introduction of terminology Marx and Engels themselves did not use. "Materialism," for Marx and Engels, has both an *ontological* and a *sociological* sense.[8] Ontological materialism is, of course, the view that the universe is composed solely of material entities. Sociological materialism, on the other hand, is the view that the overall course of history is determined by economic causes. Thus, in this sense, the "material" refers to the economic realm of society, the "base" of the famous base-and-superstructure.[9] Correspondingly, "idealism" and the "ideal" each have two senses, which also need to be distinguished. "Idealism" as an ontological thesis claims that the universe is constituted by minds and ideas (e.g., some variant of a Berkeleyan view). "Idealism" in the sociological sense, however—what, by homology with "historical materialism," we could call "historical idealism"—is the view that society and history are on the whole determined by the "ideal." And the "ideal" for Marx and Engels includes not just *ideas*, but also the political and juridical regions—what Marx later termed the "superstructure." So "idealism" in the sociological sense is "superstructuralism." This set of categories and concerns was central to Marx and Engels' polemical universe, but it is so little understood and appreciated today that the tendency is to conflate the different senses of "idealism."[10] But it is crucial to keep them separate.

Now Marx and Engels believed that there was a connection between the two varieties of materialism so that the consistent carrying out of a materialist program of reconceptualizing reality required that one also be a "materialist" in the human social world—that is, that one endorse the thesis of economic determination. For a modern philosophical audience, one more sensitive to the niceties of implication, this view may seem puzzling; certainly no *logical* connection exists between the two theses. One could without contradiction, for example, simultaneously affirm the materiality of the universe so that ideas would be brain events and endorse the view that ideas determine the course of history—that is, one could be an ontological materialist and a sociological idealist.[11] But, wrongly or rightly, Marx and Engels thought some connection existed between the two—if not by logical implication, then by some weaker relationship.

In articulating their own theory of historical materialism, they were naturally led, given the claims of that theory's ability to explain other theories, to offer a materialist metatheoretical account of the causes of the failures of their contemporaries (and of previous theorists) to arrive at a sociologically materialist position. They attributed these failures to the division of material and mental labor, arguing that those who work in the nonmaterial/noneconomic/ideal sphere will be prone to exaggerate the causal role of the "products" with which they are professionally engaged. Since this complex of views initially constituted their main theoretical opponent, it was natural to identify it with a special name. My revisionary thesis is that "ideology" is simply another member of a family of terms, probably deriving from Hegel's "Idea," which came to be used by Marx and Engels to refer *both* to the ideal/noneconomic/superstructural region of society and to these theories of superstructural determination. To quote Goldstick's and my paper:

> Marx and Engels' basic claim was that if you were an *ideologist* (a member of the superstructural/ideological professions, specializing in superstructural labor), your view of society was likely to be *ideological/idealist* (superstructuralist), in that you would be inclined to see *ideology* (the ideal superstructure) as having a greater causal power and corresponding explanatory significance than it actually possessed. (Mills and Goldstick 1989, 423)

McCarney's sense of the term simply does not exist.[12]

Position *c* was a conceptual hybrid that sought, at the cost of internal unity, to retain the neutral ideational sense of "ideology." By contrast, position *d* is organically unified, since the pejorative ideational sense ("ideology" as "idealism") is derivative from the neutral sociological sense ("ideology" as "superstructure"). Nevertheless it is obvious that to a readership who has taken for granted for decades the conventional spectrum of interpretation, this view will seem quite bizarre. So let me now try to demonstrate the support for this view, drawing on some of the more obscure appearances of the terms listed earlier (see note 7). This will necessarily be a somewhat dry and wearying textual affair, but the effort will be worth it if an interpretation so radically divergent from present-day opinion can be convincingly established, thereby liberating us from the domination of a misunderstood concept.

To summarize the following, I will attempt to demonstrate that

1. the ontological and sociological senses of "materialism" and "idealism" need to be distinguished;
2. "ideology" (in the primitive sense) means "superstructure," and correspondingly "ideologists" are superstructural workers in general;
3. "ideologists," as an occupational hazard, will tend to be "idealistic";
4. for Marx, "ideology" (in the derivative ideational sense) is a pejorative term meaning just "idealism"—not ideas, or false ideas, or class ideas, in general;

5. Engels' later use of "ideology" is completely continuous with Marx's;
6. the posited neutral ideational sense of "ideology" does not exist;
7. the posited generically pejorative ideational sense of "ideology" does not exist either.

TEXTUAL EVIDENCE FOR THE NEW POSITION

The Ontological and Sociological Senses of "Materialism" and "Idealism" Need to Be Distinguished

The logical reasons adduced for this claim should be sufficiently compelling on their own, but here are some quotations to back it up. Marx began by praising Feuerbach (CW 3, 328); but by the time of the "Theses on Feuerbach" (CW 5, 3–8), he was so disenchanted with Feuerbach's failure to carry out the materialist program consistently that, in *The German Ideology*, he and Engels would conclude: "As far as Feuerbach is a materialist he does not deal with history, and as far as he considers history he is not a materialist. With him materialism and history diverge completely" (CW 5, 41; see also CW 5, 38–41, 57–59). In the terminology introduced, Feuerbach was an ontological materialist, but he remained a sociological idealist. As Engels would later put it: "he stopped halfway, was a materialist below and an idealist above" (CW 26, 382; see also CW 25, 479–80). I suggest that *ontological* materialism is what Engels means when he talks about "the materialist outlook on nature" (CW 25, 478–79), "exclusively natural-scientific materialism" (CW 26, 372), and it is what Marx means when he indicts "the abstract materialism of natural science, a materialism that excludes history and its process" (CW 35, 375–76, n. 2). Only with Marx's work, argues Engels, was "the materialistic world outlook . . . taken really seriously for the first time and . . . carried through consistently" (CW 26, 383). This marked the advent of *historical* materialism, *sociological* materialism, so that "now idealism was driven from its last refuge, the philosophy of history; now a materialistic treatment of history was propounded" (CW 25, 26–27; see also CW 25, 597 on the "tainting" of [ontological] materialism by "ideology" [sociological idealism] and cf. CW 35, 375–76, n. 2).

Throughout Marx and Engels' social thought, then, the fundamental structuring opposition is therefore: that between the "material" and the "ideal," and in the sociological sense, these antonyms correspond to the "economic base" and the "noneconomic superstructure." Since the latter identification may be less familiar, here are some illustrations. The crucial point for my case is that the "ideal" denotes not just *ideas*, but everything else in the superstructure, including the state and the juridical system.

In the 1843 *Contribution to the Critique of Hegel's Philosophy of Law*, Marx observes that, for Hegel, "[t]he idea is made the subject," though the "genuinely active elements" are the family and civil society, so that "things are inverted" and "the state issues" as "the idea's deed" (CW 3, 8–9). In the Kreuznach notebooks, he says that "Hegel makes the elements of the state idea the subject, and the old forms of existence of the state the predicate, whereas in historical reality the reverse is the case," so for Hegel "the idea of the state is made the determining factor" (CW 3, 130). I suggest that the "ideal" for Marx and Engels therefore encompasses the state. Thus, in *The German Ideology*, they assert that the "social power" of the ruling class "has its practical-*idealistic* expression in each case in the form of the state" (CW 5, 52; original emphasis removed, my emphasis added). They write that the world of "material intercourse . . . forms the basis of the state and of the rest of the *idealistic* superstructure" (CW 5, 89; my emphasis). They describe how "the conditions of existence of the ruling class . . . [are] *ideally* expressed in law, morality, etc." (CW 5, 419–20; my emphasis). In *A Contribution to the Critique of Political Economy*, Marx refers to "political, religious and other *ideal* trimmings" (CW 30, 132; my emphasis). In an 1870 letter to Paul Lafargue, Marx describes as "superannuated *idealism*" the approach "which considers the actual jurisprudence as the basis of our economical state, instead of seeing that our economical state is the basis and source of our jurisprudence" (CW 43, 490; my emphasis). Similarly, in the preparatory materials for *Anti-Dühring*, Engels remarks with respect to Dühring's conception of the "*politico-juridical foundation* of the whole of society" that: "Thus at once the *idealist* measuring stick is applied. Not production itself, but *law*" (CW 25, 616; my emphasis on "idealist").

"Ideology" (in the Primitive Sense) Means "Superstructure," and "Ideologists" Are Superstructural Workers in General

The base–superstructure distinction is, as we all know, central to Marx's sociology. But what is far less recognized is that Marx and Engels also developed a categorization of people based on this distinction: people occupationally performed either base/economic labor or superstructural/noneconomic labor. Marx saw the former as "productive" and the latter as "unproductive." Thus, in *A Contribution to the Critique of Political Economy*, Marx observes that: "Once there exists a society in which some people live without working (without participating directly in the production of use values), it is clear that the surplus labor of the workers is the condition of existence of the whole superstructure of the society," its "material basis" (CW 30, 190–91). For Marx, these people live off the surplus labor of the workers and (following Adam Smith and Jean Baptiste Say) produce "immaterial commodities" (CW 31, 30), "immaterial products" (CW 31, 164–66). Given the extensiveness and internal complexity of the super-structure, a listing of such superstructural workers will be a long and eclectic one. Thus in *Theories of Surplus Value*, Marx cites as "unproductive laborers" "parsons, government officials, soldiers, musicians" (CW 31, 20). Later, in a listing of both superstructural workers and superstructural products, he says that "alongside wheat and meat" (i.e., the "material"), there are "also prostitutes, lawyers, sermons, concerts, theatres, soldiers, politicians" (CW 31, 24). He speaks of "so-called 'higher grade' workers" who produce "'immaterial' commodities . . . such as state officials, mili-tary people, artists, doctors, priests, judges, lawyers" (CW 31, 30; see also CW 31, 166, 182–86).

My claim now is that for Marx and Engels all of these can be described as "ide-ologists," since they work in the "ideal" superstructure and produce "ideal" products. The "ideational" sense of the term (a specialist in *ideas*), which has been unquestioningly taken for granted by contemporary debate, was *not* Marx's own (though it is, of course, subsumed by it).

In an analysis of the economist Andrei Storch, Marx writes that "the contradictions in material production make necessary a superstructure of ideological strata" (CW 31, 184). Discussing Adam Smith, he refers to "un-productive laborers" as "the ideological, etc., classes" (CW 31, 30). In vol-ume one of *Capital*, in an analysis of productive and unproductive labor, he talks about "all who are too old or too young for work, all unproduc-tive women, young persons and children, *the 'ideological' classes*, such as government officials, priests, lawyers, soldiers, etc." (CW 35, 449; my em-phasis). The inclusion of "soldiers" on this listing, and the association with the criterion of "unproductivity," should make it clear that the con-ventional reading is seriously awry.[13] Likewise, when Marx and Engels re-fer to "the parasitic plants, the ideologists of the vegetable world" in *The German Ideology* (CW 5, 471), this is, I suggest, a reference to their super-structural, "parasitic," "living-off" the workers. Thus in an 1856 letter to Marx about a trip to Ireland, Engels comments: "Gendarmes, priests, lawyers, bureaucrats, lords of the manor in cheerful profusion and a total absence of any and every industry, so that one could barely conceive what all these parasitic plants live on, were there no counterpart in the wretchedness of the peasants" (CW 40, 49).

The "superstructural" reference of the term also explains the apparent heterogeneity of the lists of "ideologists" Marx and Engels give else-where: "priests, jurists, politicians (including the practical statesmen), clerics, statesmen in general, moralists, lawyers" (CW 5, 45, 62, 92, 230, 355); "lawyers, doctors" (CW 6, 526); "journalists" (CW 8, 167); "savants, lawyers, doctors" (CW 10, 49); the "spokesmen and scribes of the bour-geoisie, its platform and its press" (CW 11, 170).

"Ideologists," as an Occupational
Hazard, Will Tend to Be Idealistic

We come now to Marx and Engels' crucial materialist, metatheoretical claim, which, if my analysis is correct, has been so widely misunderstood and thus responsible for so much confusion about their position on the socioeconomic determination of belief *in general*. It is presented first in *The German Ideology* and subsequently reappears, in greater detail, in some of Engels' later writings and letters. The basic ideas are as follows:

1. because of the division of labor, some people specialize in superstructural labor;
2. these people are ideologists—they work with "ideology" (alternative name for the superstructure);
3. their jobs foster a characteristic illusion—that their immaterial/ideal products (ideas, politics, law, etc.) are causally *independent* of the material/economic base—that is, they have a largely internal logic of development, and/or they may themselves determine the development of the base and society;
4. as such, this complex of views "inverts" things, turns them "upside-down";
5. this illusion is "idealism"—or, since it implies determination by the "ideological" superstructure, it could itself be termed "ideology." (See the following two sections.)

In *The German Ideology*, in the famous passage that McCarney mistakenly thinks to be the only evidence for Marx and Engels' negative conception of "ideology," Marx and Engels write: "If in all ideology men and their relations appear upside-down as in a *camera obscura*, this phenomenon arises just as much from their historical life-process as the inversion of objects on the retina does from their physical life-process" (CW 5, 36). I suggest this should not be read counterfactually, as McCarney proposes ("If [as is not the case] in all ideology . . ."); rather, it should be read *factually*, as a characterization of (sociological) "idealism" and of its sources.[14] The point is that idealistic views themselves have a materialist genealogy and can be explained in terms of people's "historical life-process." Amplification of this claim is soon forthcoming. In a marginal note, Marx refers to "the delusion of the ideologists and the division of labor" (CW 5, 61). On the next page, Marx and Engels write that "the illusion of ideologists in general" is "explained perfectly easily from their practical position in life, their job, and the division of labor" (CW 5, 62). This is expanded in the notes at the end of part I:

Why the ideologists turn everything upside-down. Clerics, jurists, politicians. Jurists, politicians (statesmen in general), moralists, clerics. For this ideological [read: superstructural] subdivision within a class: 1) *The occupation assumes an independent existence owing to division of labor.* . . . Illusions regarding the connection between their craft and reality are the more likely to be cherished by them because of the very nature of the craft. . . . The judge, for example, applies the code, he therefore regards legislation as the real, active driving force. (CW 5, 92)

This passage is noteworthy in a number of ways. To begin with, it is hardly ever cited by anybody, since the analysis it is offering seems completely obscure and *non*illuminating about the nature of "ideology," *understood as class ideas in general.* But once it is realized that "ideology" actually means "idealism," the passage becomes transparent. The idea is that people who work in the superstructure ("ideologists": note the extended list) develop the "illusion," because of the division of labor, that the superstructural products with which they are occupationally engaged are "independent" causally, rather than determined by the material base. So the judge, for example, begins to suffer from the illusion that the legal code is the "real, active driving force," rather than the *economic* causes that Marx and Engels saw as causally primary (and note, incidentally, the matter-of-fact way in which a judge is introduced as an example of an "ideologist," with no reference to his role as a disseminator of *ideas*). This counts as "idealism" because, as earlier noted, the juridical system is "ideal" within their categorial scheme. Similarly, they later observe: "it only shows that [the writer] considers politics to be an independent sphere of activity, which develops in its own independent way, a belief he shares with all ideologists" (CW 5, 468). Both politics and the legal system are part of the superstructure, and so they do *not* "develop in their own independent way," but are determined by the economic base; the contrary belief is idealism/ideology. (See also CW 5, 446–47.)

On this basis, we can now understand why Marx and Engels were hostile to "ideologists" and "ideology" as such. But since this fact has been challenged by McCarney (for Marx) and by Costello (for both Marx and Engels), let me now put it beyond any reasonable doubt.[15]

For Marx, "Ideology" (in the Derivative Ideational Sense) Is a Pejorative Term Meaning Just "Idealism"

A hermeneutical problem: how does one differentiate a definitionally pejorative usage from a contingently pejorative usage? In reconstructing the meaning of "ideology," the mere fact that a certain usage is negative will not be sufficient to establish a pejorative conception, for one can always argue, as McCarney and Costello do, that the target makes it so—in other words, that the negative attitude evident is evoked by a *particular* ideology. Such a claim would be made more plausible by the presence of qualifiers ("the *German* ideology") or indexical terms ("this ideology," "these ideologists"), where the implicit reference is specific. Correspondingly, this interpretation will become less plausible in the absence of such qualifiers, when it seems that hostile and negative analyses of "ideology" and "ideologists" *in general* are being proffered.

Describing their own methodology in *The German Ideology*, which draws on "abstractions which are derived from the observation of the historical development of men," Marx and Engels announce that: "We shall select here some of these abstractions, which we use in contradistinction to ideology, and shall illustrate them by historical examples" (CW 5, 37). They do not say "the German ideology," or "the ideology of our opponents," or some cognate phrase—what they say is "ideology." Obviously, "ideology" *in general* is to be contraposed to their approach. They characterize Bruno Bauer's polemic against Feuerbach's "sensuousness" as motivated by Bauer's hostility to Feuerbach's "attempt to escape ideology" (CW 5, 103). Not "their ideology," note, but "ideology" *simpliciter*. They say that the True Socialists "detach the communist systems, critical and polemical writings from the real movement, of which they are but the expression," that they "detach the consciousness of certain historically conditioned spheres of life from these spheres," and that in so doing, "they have abandoned the real historical basis and returned to that of ideology" (CW 5, 456). "Ideology" without qualification, note. Later they write of the "True Socialists'" theory of property: "This theory of true property conceives *real* private property . . . merely as a semblance, whereas it views the concept abstracted from this real property as the *truth* and *reality* of the semblance; it is therefore ideological all through" (CW 5, 469). Again, "ideological" qua "ideological" is obviously functioning as a pejorative term. In all these cases, the reference is to the specific illusion of *idealism*.

In his critique of Proudhon, *The Poverty of Philosophy*, Marx says disparagingly of his theory that: "In constructing the edifice of an ideological system by means of the categories of political economy, the limbs of the social system are dislocated" (CW 6, 166–67). If "ideological" is neutral, as McCarney claims, why should these consequences follow? Similarly, in a brief 1880 journalistic note, Marx writes: "to prepare the way for the critical and materialist socialism which alone can render the real, historical development of social production intelligible, it was necessary to break abruptly with the ideological [read: idealistic] economics of which Proudhon was unwittingly the last incarnation" (CW 24, 326–27; see also CW 6, 169–70). And in an 1861 letter, there is a dismissive paragraph about a work by Ferdinand Lassalle, in which Marx comments that "Ideologism permeates everything" (CW 41, 333).[16]

Let us now consider some generically negative characterizations of "ideologists" and their characteristic errors. In an 1843 newspaper article, Marx writes: "But let us not be too hasty, let us take the world as it is, let us not be ideologists" (CW 1, 317). Can there be any doubt that being an "ideologist" implies *not* "taking the world as it is"? In *The German Ideology*, Marx and Engels refer to "the illusion of ideologists in general . . . the dogmatic dreamings and distortions of these fellows" (CW 5, 62). This statement is *explicitly* about ideologists in general. In the passage cited earlier, there is another general characterization: *"Why the ideologists turn everything upside-down"* (CW 5, 92). A few pages later they state that Bruno Bauer, "along with all philosophers and ideologists, erroneously regards thoughts and ideas . . . as the basis of this existing world" (CW 5, 99). Again, there is an explicit characterization of what *all* ideologists do. Opposing Max Stirner's idealistic concept of freedom, Marx and Engels refer to "the definition of freedom as *self-determination*, which occurs among all, and particularly German, ideologists" (CW 5, 311). (Marx and Engels' own materialistic view has been given earlier: "'Liberation' is a historical and not a mental act, and it is brought about by historical conditions" [CW 5, 38].) Since "German" ideologists are explicitly demarcated as a subgroup within a larger category, even McCarney can hardly deny that we are being given a *general* description of a characteristic illusion held by *all* ideologists. (See also CW 5, 446–47.) Later they say that "as in general with ideologists . . . they inevitably put the thing upside-down" (CW 5, 420). They state that "it only shows that [the writer] considers politics to be an independent sphere of activity, which develops in its own independent way, a belief he shares with all ideologists" (CW 5, 468). In all these references—which are prima facie generic pejorative statements about ideologists *as such*, using such terms as "the," "all," and "in general," and devoid of qualifications—McCarney has to claim, quite implausibly, that the reference is really just to certain *kinds* of ideologists.

Engels' Later Use of "Ideology" Is Completely Continuous with Marx's

As we have seen, McCarney's interpretation requires the drawing of a dividing line between Marx's and Engels' positions. My own suggestion is that we need to see Engels' genetic accounts of "ideology" simply as extrapolations from his and Marx's position in *The German Ideology*: attempts to advance, without any great philosophical sophistication (but defensibly nonetheless), a normative thesis about the causation of belief.

If one is offering a causal analysis of belief, then epistemological questions are raised about the epistemic respectability of one's own beliefs. For some philosophers, determinism rules out any chance of such respectability (we can never know whether our beliefs are well-founded or not); but for others, the criterion is simply whether or not one's adherence to a belief can (normative "can") survive exposure of its particular causal history. Thus, if one has come to believe p as a result of a causal chain without any evidential links—or because of apparently evidential links that are actually epistemically deficient—then a rational cognizer should abandon the belief.

Now if historical materialism is correct about the overall causal patterns in society, then the idealistic belief in the absolute (as against relative) autonomy of superstructural regions is *(a)* false and *(b)* preeminently caused (via a nonevidential, or deficiently evidential, causal chain) by the division of material and mental labor. Superstructural workers will therefore be inclined to propose sociologically inverted theories of society ("turning things upside-down," in the earlier language of *The German Ideology*); idealistic internalist accounts of the development of their own field; and, reflexively, false genealogies for these theories—since they will not recognize the actual, in this case epistemically subversive (because nonevidential), material determination of their own views.[17] Correspondingly, the realization of the epistemically disreputable character of the causation involved should, if one is a rational cognizer, lead one to abandon the idealistic belief. But "idealism" is "ideology." *So the result would be the end of ideology.*

First let me prove quickly (against Costello rather than McCarney) Engels' employment of the definitionally pejorative, "idealistic" sense of "ideology." In *Anti-Dühring*, Engels says: "The philosophy of reality, therefore, proves here again to be pure ideology, the deduction of reality not from itself but from a concept" (CW 25, 89). Similarly, in the preparatory writings, Engels observes: "To construct [results] in one's head, take them as the basis from which to start, and then reconstruct the world from them in one's head is *ideology*" (CW 25, 597). In *Ludwig Feuerbach*, Engels says that an ideology is "occupation with thoughts as with independent entities, developing independently and subject only to their own laws" (CW 26, 394). It should be evident that in all these cases, "ideology" is being *conceptually*, not contingently, linked to a particular kind of error (see also CW 10, 556).[18] Correspondingly, Engels derives the verb "ideologise" as itself a pejorative term, which appears, contra McCarney, in both his early and his late writings (see CW 6, 267; CW 23, 381; CW 25, 597).

Let us now move on to Engels' causal accounts, which McCarney finds so baffling and which are actually so transparent once they are seen as continuous with *The German Ideology*. A quote from the latter provides a good starting point. Marx and Engels argue that the True Socialists "detach the consciousness of certain historically conditioned spheres of life from these spheres," and in so doing "they have abandoned the real historical basis and returned to that of ideology [idealism], and *since they are ignorant of the real connection*, they can without difficulty construct some fantastic relationship with the help of . . . some . . . ideological method" (CW 5, 456; my emphasis). Ignorance of the "real connection," the "real historical basis" (i.e., material determination), makes ideological/idealistic constructions possible. Now consider what Engels says forty years later in *Ludwig Feuerbach and the End of Classical German Philosophy*. He points out there that "everything which motivates men must pass through their brains," thereby becoming "ideal powers," so that obviously idealism cannot be defined in these terms (CW 26, 373). The real distinction must be drawn elsewhere: "the question also arises. . . . What are the historical causes which transform themselves into these motives in the minds of the actors?" The deficiency of the "old materialism" (ontological, but unhistorical) is that it "never asked itself this question." Rather "it takes the ideal driving forces which operate there [in history] as ultimate causes, instead of investigating what is behind them, what are the driving forces of these driving forces." Were this investigation to be carried out, it would reveal, of course, that the "real ultimate driving forces in history" are economic (CW 26, 388–89). But those who fail to do this will remain historical idealists in their view of social causation.

As an example, Engels cites the case of juridico-political idealism. The state as well as the public and private law are all "determined by economic relations." But with the acquisition of the semblance of independence, "the connection with economic facts gets well and truly lost," so that they are "treated as separate spheres, each having its own independent historical development" (CW 26, 392–93). Engels goes on to discuss "[s]till higher ideologies" such as "philosophy and religion," where the material "connection" is more complicated, but likewise here, as for all "ideologies," a materialist genealogy and externalist dynamic can be provided (CW 26, 393). In the next paragraph, he delineates the crucial causal thesis: An ideology is

occupation with thoughts as with independent entities, developing independently and subject only to their own laws. That the material conditions of life of the persons inside whose heads this thought process goes on in the last resort determine the course of this process remains of necessity unknown to these persons, for otherwise all ideology would be finished. (CW 26, 394)

What is being articulated is a general thesis about the material determination of *idealistic* views (not political views in general, as has standardly been assumed). (Note: In a published work, "intended for the public domain," not just a letter "written in old age to colleagues in the socialist movement" [contra McCarney 1990, 459].) If this causal relationship became known, "all ideology would be finished" (or, in the more familiar translation, there would be "an end to all ideology") because people's idealistic beliefs, assuming that they are rational agents, would not survive the exposure of the nonevidential character of their causal histories. Similarly, in his October 27, 1890, letter to Conrad Schmidt, Engels describes the "new, independent field" of law, whose ultimate economic determination is not recognized by the jurist; so he "imagines he is dealing in a priori principles [not in any deep Kantian sense, obviously, but "a priori" simply in the sense of independent of an economic genesis], whereas they are, in fact, no more than economic reflections—and thus the whole thing is the wrong way up. . . . [T]his inversion . . . in as much as it is not recognised, constitutes what we call an *ideological view*" (CW 49, 60–61).

Finally, this theme is repeated in Engels' famous July 14, 1893, letter to Franz Mehring: "Ideology is a process accomplished by the so-called thinker consciously, indeed, but with a false consciousness. The real motives impelling him remain unknown to him, otherwise it would not be an ideological process at all." And in the next paragraph, "ideological conceptions" are glossed as "this appearance of an independent [as against materially/economically determined] history of state constitutions, of systems of law" (MESC, 511). As can now be appreciated, McCarney has utterly misunderstood Engels' point by transforming this passage into a psychological account of the genesis of political ideas (McCarney 1980, 95–97) when it simply needs to be read as a reiteration of the aforementioned claim. In addition, he says falsely of my interpretation that I *assimilate* "idealism" and "false consciousness" (McCarney 1990, 458–59). I didn't do that in my original paper (Mills 1985), nor am I doing it now. My claim is not that they're the *same*, but that "false consciousness" *accompanies* "idealism," since for Engels "false consciousness" just means unawareness of the epistemically subversive material causation of the idealistic beliefs. A "true consciousness" of their actual genealogy, by implication, should lead to their rejection, which is why there would be "an end to all ideology."

Here now is some evidence for the nonideational, "superstructural" sense of "ideology," which poses further problems for McCarney's interpretation. In his reply, McCarney argues that Engels' "aberrant usage" is a "subordinate element" even in his late writings, offering as evidence some passages from *Ludwig Feuerbach* that he thinks conform to the neutral ideational reading (see CW 26, 395–96). But in this very same text, only a page or two before these passages, we find Engels saying that: "The state presents itself to us as the first ideological power over man" (CW 26,

392). How can McCarney's reading make sense of this sentence? Representatives of the state will certainly use "ideology" in his sense, but why should that make the state the "first ideological power"? On my reading, however, there is no such interpretative difficulty, for in the context (a discussion of the determination of the juridico-political by the economic) "ideological" clearly means "superstructural."

A few paragraphs on, Engels gives the pejorative characterization ("aberrant," according to McCarney) of "ideology" earlier quoted ("occupation with thoughts as with independent entities"). In this very paragraph, the putative *neutral* ideational usage cited by McCarney occurs, yet, astonishingly, McCarney does not inform the reader of this. So Engels was presumably so oblivious to any requirements of theoretical consistency that he could casually switch the meaning of a central term in the middle of a paragraph! On my reading, by contrast, it is not necessary to suppose any such implausible theoretical contradiction, since the sentence in the paragraph that McCarney takes to support *his* view can be read as supporting my own: "The Middle Ages had attached to theology all the other forms of ideology—philosophy, politics, jurisprudence—and made them subdivisions of theology" (CW 26, 395). I suggest that here too "ideology" means "superstructure," which is why it readily subsumes "politics" and "jurisprudence" as well as the ideational "philosophy." (The same can be said for another passage McCarney cites as evidence for his view [1990, 460]. See also the letter to Mehring, where, in a discussion of the superstructure's relative autonomy, "ideological spheres" seems best read as "superstructural spheres" [MESC, 512]. And in another letter, Engels refers to "a mass of ideology deriving from feudal times, such as English common law, religion, sectarianism" [CW 47, 491].) So Engels has simply moved from the ideational "ideology-as-idealism/superstructuralism" to the related macrosocial (given his and Marx's analysis) "ideology-as-superstructure." In several places in Engels' writings, such seemingly abrupt semantic transitions take place (for a particularly dramatic example, see the letter to Mehring [MESC, 511–12]); and as readers can confirm for themselves, the neutral ideational reading, unlike my own interpretation, undergoes fatal strain in trying to account for them.

The Posited Neutral Ideational
Sense of "Ideology" Does Not Exist

A standard measure of the superiority of one theory to another is that (a) it can explain everything the other theory can and (b) it can explain things the other theory can't. I think I should now have demonstrated the latter of these. Let me therefore now turn to what McCarney takes to be the positive textual evidence for the neutral ideational meaning of the term, showing how it too can be more convincingly reinterpreted from this new perspective.

The main piece of evidence he cites, which is also that cited by Mc-Murtry and by the supporters of position *c* who see this as one of *two* senses of the term, comes from the 1859 preface to *A Contribution to the Critique of Political Economy*:

> Then begins an era of social revolution. The changes in the economic foundation lead sooner or later to the transformation of the whole immense superstructure. In studying such transformations it is always necessary to distinguish between the material transformation of the economic conditions of production . . . and the legal, political, religious, artistic or philosophic—in short, ideological forms in which men become conscious of this conflict and fight it out. (CW 29, 263)

The standard argument is that this appearance of the term has to be epistemologically *neutral*, since Marx must obviously anticipate that class struggle will be "ideologically" fought out with his own theory among others. Given the central theoretical status of the preface, it has then seemed reasonable to infer a general commitment of Marx to a nonpejorative conception. But this textual "datum" is, in a sense, "theory-laden," in that commentators have taken for granted as a background theoretical presupposition the *ideational* reference of "ideology." Once the existence of the broader "ideal/superstructural" sense of "ideological" has been conceded, however, it should readily be appreciated that it fits better here than the supposed "ideational" sense. This is why the "legal, political, religious, artistic, or philosophic" can be glossed ("in short") without qualification as "ideological": they are all (including juridical changes and political struggles) subsumed by the superstructure. By contrast, McCarney and others have to make the additional assumption that Marx means to refer here to legal and political *ideas*. Thus it turns out that McCarney's strongest piece of evidence only seemed unequivocally to support his theory so long as the debate was confined to a choice between *ideational* references of the term.

The other pieces of evidence he cites are much weaker. A reference from *The German Ideology* to capitalism's destruction of the proletariat's "entire ideological superstructure" (CW 5, 372–73), which he sees as indicating a *positive* view of "ideology" (McCarney 1990, 452), can be interpreted along the "ideal/superstructural" lines. Mention in the same work of ideological "theories" and "postulates," or to "the thoughts and ideas of the ideologists," which McCarney takes as indicating a neutral tone (McCarney 1990, 452–53), cannot, it should be obvious, constitute evidence *either* of neutrality or negativity on the part of Marx and Engels. In the absence of any further characterization, these references are underdetermined, consistent equally with either a neutral or a pejorative ("idealist") reading. Finally, to describe as evidence for a "positive" view of "ideologists" (McCarney 1990, 453), the *Manifesto*'s line about the "portion of the bourgeois ideologists, who have raised themselves to the level of comprehending theoretically the historical movement as a whole" (CW 6, 494) is really grasping at straws. Obviously Marx and Engels' implication is that these individuals' being "bourgeois ideologists" has been an *obstacle* to such comprehension, which is precisely why "raising themselves" has been necessary.

The Posited Generically Pejorative Sense of "Ideology" Does Not Exist Either

Finally, we need to look briefly, but crucially, at the claim (not McCarney's) that "ideology" is pejorative and *general* in scope, referring not just to "idealism" but to "mystification" of *all* kinds. As indicated at the start, this has in fact been the dominant view among commentators (position *a*). Thus in Marx's later economic writings—the *Grundrisse, Capital, Theories of Surplus Value*—where he excoriates those economic theorists whose views he sees as fetishistic and as involving a dehistoricizing collapse of the socioeconomic into the natural, it is taken for granted in most of the secondary literature that he is critiquing these views *as* "ideology." But the virtue of what might seem to be my tedious and scholastic listing of appearances of the term in endnote 7 is that it shows the conventional interpretive wisdom to be quite wrong, unsupported by the texts: *nowhere in the scores of pages of the polemics against the "vulgar" economists does Marx describe their fetishistic/naturalizing theoretical errors as "ideology."* And if my foregoing analysis has been correct, this conclusion is quite unsurprising, since fetishism is *not* a variety of idealism but rather an example of vulgar ("unhistorical") materialism.

Moreover, my reading is able to explain what the conventional reading cannot: why it is that far and away the greatest number of appearances of the term are concentrated in *The German Ideology*. If "ideology" were a generically pejorative term for Marx and Engels, we would expect to find it used wherever they are attacking "bourgeois" and "mystificatory" views—which they certainly continued to do over their entire intellectual lives! But in fact the distribution of the term over the tens of thousands of pages of these forty-nine volumes is, with overwhelming disproportion, focused largely in just one work: *The German Ideology*, their main discussion and critique of sociological–historical idealism. It is used here ad nauseam; it is *not* used in the critique elsewhere of fetishism. Surely this is prima facie evidence that, contra the dominant interpretation, it was never intended by them to be a generically pejorative term.[19]

SUMMARY OF THE NEW
POSITION'S INTERPRETIVE ADVANTAGES

Since this discussion has been lengthy, let me now sum up the respects in which I believe my interpretation is superior to McCarney's and, where the points are applicable, to the conventional reading, position *a*.

McCarney's univocal, neutral reading is either unable to explain or has significant difficulty in explaining the following facts:

1. There is substantial textual evidence that Marx viewed "ideology" and "ideologists" negatively (McCarney denies this for "ideology").
2. Engels clearly had a pejorative conception of "ideology" (conceded by McCarney), a theoretical divergence (on McCarney's reading), which does not even develop consistently over time, since paragraphs can be found in which it coexists with the putative neutral conception.
3. In *The German Ideology*, Marx and Engels offer an analysis of the connection between "ideology" and the division of labor that is strange for both the neutral "partisan class ideas" conception and the "generically pejorative" conception of "ideology."
4. Similarly, Engels later repeatedly gave puzzling genetic accounts and odd theoretical characterizations of "ideology."
5. Marx and Engels never refer to their own theory as an "ideology."
6. The overwhelming majority of the appearances of "ideology" and its derivatives are in *The German Ideology*, their main discussion of sociological idealism (this is also a crucial point against the conventional reading, position *a*).
7. Marx never describes the fetishistic–naturalistic errors of the economists he discusses in *Capital*, the *Grundrisse*, or *Theories of Surplus Value*, as "ideology" or "ideological" (ditto).
8. The eclecticism of the lists of "ideologists" Marx and Engels give in *The German Ideology*, and the connection with "unproductive laborers" (including "soldiers") in the economic writings, is peculiar if an "ideologist" is specifically a class thinker.

The main attraction of McCarney's interpretation is the theoretical congruity of an epistemologically neutral conception of class ideas with what one would expect the commitments of historical materialism to be. But since, on my reading, "ideology's" pejorative ideational reference is *not* to partisan class ideas in general but only to idealism, my interpretation is likewise consistent with such an epistemological neutrality. The main attraction of the conventional interpretation is its fascination as a challenging thesis in the sociology of belief and as a weapon for the Left to use against the Right. But this weapon has tended to turn against the user, generating logical problems of self-refutation, political problems of sectarianism, and intellectual problems of decades of fruitless effort trying to work out a general theory of ideology-as-mystification supposedly implicit in Marx's work. On my reading of Marx, one can theorize more cautiously about *particular* negative ideational tendencies in class society without being committed to any global macrotheory about the *wholesale* contamination of the ideational realm by something called "ideology."

THE NEW POSITION AS THE OLD
POSITION IN CLASSICAL SOURCES

I now want to show that, although this reading may seem quite eccentric to a contemporary Marxist audience, it was in fact recognized by some of those closer in time to Marx and Engels' writing.

In his 1895 work, *The Development of the Monist View of History*, George Plekhanov refers repeatedly to the "ideological superstructure": "Marx himself says that economy is the real foundation on which arise the ideological superstructures" (1972, 168; see also 169, 172, 173, 199, 201). Lest it be thought that he might be referring only to ideas, I will cite a more explicit passage:

> This law [of property] is undoubtedly the same ideology we have been concerned with, but ideology of the first or, so to speak, lower sort. How are we to understand the view of Marx regarding ideology of the higher sort—science, philosophy, the arts, etc.? In the development of these ideologies, economy is the foundation. . . . (170)

So for Plekhanov law itself is "ideology," and he recognizes that for Marx and Engels "ideology" referred to the whole superstructure. Similarly, in 1894, Lenin writes: "[Marx and Engels'] basic idea . . . was that social relations are divided into material and ideological. The latter merely constitute a superstructure on the former."[20] Finally, Gramsci, in the *Prison Notebooks* (1971, 376), states that for Marx and Engels: "'Ideology' itself must be analysed historically, in the terms of the philosophy of praxis [Marxism], as a superstructure. . . . [T]he name ideology is given both to the necessary superstructure of a particular structure and to the arbitrary elucubrations of particular individuals."

In the case of all three of these writers, I suggest that we have a recognition of the original "superstructural/ideal" sense of "ideology" in Marx and Engels. The imputed meaning that would actually become dominant in the West as the twentieth century wore on, however, is a mongrel notion that conflates the *pejorative connotation*, originally intended specifically for "idealism," and the *general denotation*, originally associated with the comprehensive "superstructural" reference but now restricted to ideas, or class ideas, in general. The internal tensions and self-contradictions in the notion have been with us ever since.

CONCLUSION

In his opening and closing paragraphs, McCarney (1990) praises my paper for helping to clarify the debate on "ideology," despite naturally disagreeing with my conclusions. Let me return the compliment by saying, without irony, that if I have arrived at the correct interpretation of what Marx and Engels really meant by the term, then to a significant extent, it is due to his own work. Of the twenty books and articles I looked at for the original paper (Mills 1985), his was one of the very few that actually developed an argument for his position, and it is this argument that accounts for the differential attention I gave it. By challenging the orthodox view, he forced me to look more closely at the original texts and thus eventually to come to my present position via discussions with Goldstick. Even if he is wrong about what Marx and Engels meant by "ideology" (and I do believe he is wrong), his book remains valuable, first, as a plausible account of how the dominant interpretation became established and, second, as a possible reconstruction of where the concept of ideology in *our* sense (which is not Marx's) would fit within historical materialism. Gripped by the valuable insight, which I think is correct, that Marx's view of class ideas is neutral, McCarney has been compelled by his conventional identification of "ideology" *with* "class ideas" into a strained and unconvincing denial of the many passages revealing Marx and Engels' clearly pejorative view of the former. Once the two are conceptually prised apart, however, as is accomplished by my interpretation, the need for these exertions of his simply vanishes.[21]

McCarney ends (writing more than a dozen years ago) with the claim that my 1985 paper is a sign that the orthodox interpretation is at last beginning to dissolve. I thought at the time that while such a dissolution would certainly be a welcome development, this view was unjustifiably sanguine; and more recent work supports my pessimism. Two full-length books on the subject from the 1990s—Christopher Pines' *Ideology and False Consciousness* (1993) and Michael Rosen's *On Voluntary Servitude: False*

Consciousness and the Theory of Ideology (1996)—show that the conventional view, with all its associated problems, is alive and well. Both writers take "ideology" to be a broadly pejorative term for Marx, whose reference includes fetishism (Pines 1993, ch. 7; Rosen 1996, 200–207), despite the fact that Marx does not use the word in analyzing fetishism. Pines critiques McCarney, arguing that while "functionalism" with respect to the class struggle is part of the conception of ideology, it is a necessary but not sufficient element:

> I would add as another necessary defining condition that the ideas must be false in some way to count as an [*sic*] ideological idea according to Marx. . . . The general point I take Marx to be making in his political writings is that the ideologies used in class struggles (whether ruling-class ideologies or the ideologies of the oppressed) are epistemologically flawed in some manner. . . . Marx believed that political actors are more or less self-deceived by their own ideologies. . . . [F]or Marx ideologies are *false* collective ideas and *false* collective modes of thinking. . . . [T]he class struggle for Marx was a political struggle conducted with a false consciousness. (Pines 1993, 70–72, 86, 158)

The obvious implication of such a position is the undermining of the cognitive validity of oppositional ideologies. Pines (71) admits this problem himself: "Surely partisans advocating nonracist or nonsexist 'ideologies' believe that there is something unreasonable and untrue about the ideology of their opponents while their own positions are reasonable and true." However, he never provides an adequate solution to it, despite claiming to be giving a sympathetic exposition of Marx and Engels' views.

Rosen's account, by contrast, is highly critical of Marxism, and his conclusion is an indictment of the consequences of (what he takes to be) Marx's theory of ideology:

> What is most pernicious, however, is the way that the theory of ideology enables those who hold it to divide the world between those who are (presumed to be) and those who are not in ideology's grip. The theory of ideology offers its holders the psychic benefits that come to those who believe that they are part of an elite or vanguard. It licenses that vanguard to ignore the actions, attitudes and even votes of those in whose names they claim to act. The Leninist party, the presumed repository of correct consciousness . . . acts *on behalf of* the working-class, rather than as its representative. . . . [T]he theory of ideology immunizes those who hold it against unpleasant reality. The history of the Marxist left shows all too clearly how such short-run benefits of belief can lead to catastrophe in the long term. (Rosen 1996, 271–72)

The burden of my argument is that these unhappy consequences—all too real—have been at least partially the result of a disastrously misunderstood idea; so my textual exegesis has not been a merely scholastic enterprise, but one with substantive implications for our understanding of a supposedly central Marxist concept. To repeat: *Marx and Engels had no all-encompassing generic concept of ideology as mystification.* Thus the main virtue of my deflationary interpretation, if I am correct, is that it liberates us from the burden of a text that was unhelpful because it was referring to something else all along. A tentative theory about social influences on belief *can* be reconstructed from Marx's writings. But the mistake has been to identify this theory—a theory that, as I have argued elsewhere (Mills 1989), assumes multiple causation and interaction rather than one-dimensional determination—with what Marx and Engels intended as much more limited claims about "ideology" as "idealism." If we want to retain the term for partisan class ideas in general (or, more broadly, group ideas), then we would need to reconstruct a Marxist theory of "ideology" since none exists. Such a reconstruction would have to be sensitive to the many criticisms of Marxism that have been made over recent decades, and would, accordingly, have to respect certain constraints.

First, it should be epistemologically neutral (I am in agreement with McCarney here), conceptualized in reference to its social function rather than its veridicality. *Particular* ideologies, thought of as group ideas, will have different elements characterized to varying extents by truth and falsity; but there will be no aprioristic categorization, guaranteed in advance, of the mystificatory nature of "ideology" *as such.* In this way, the standard accusations of inconsistency, self-refutation, or self-serving exceptionalism can be avoided (i.e., "Why are *your* views not also 'ideological'?"). At the same time, what will have to be given up is the too-tempting access to a weapon that supposedly legitimizes an aprioristic dismissal of one's opponents' views as "ideology," without actual intellectual engagement with them—a bane of the history of the Left. Correspondingly, the goal of extracting from Marx and Engels' writings a general theory of ideology as antiscience and mystification, with all its implausibilities and sweeping counterfactual claims about actual societies and people's actual beliefs, will be realized to have been chimerical all along.

Consequently, it could accommodate as cognitivist and positively valorized the ideologies of subordinate groups, in both their descriptive and normative dimensions. Throughout most of the twentieth century, Marx's judgment that all morality, even that of the subordinate classes, is "ideology" has been a central pillar of the representation of historical materialism as metaethically noncognitivist, relativist, or nihilist, and undoubtedly contributed—as a theoretical authorization—to the disdain for normal moral considerations found in the practices of many self-conceivedly revolutionary movements and parties. But as I will argue in greater detail in chapter 3, in the light of this new interpretation,

Marx's judgment would now emerge not as a general dismissal of the *content* of morality, but merely as an appraisal of its likely causal efficacy in changing society. So it would no longer be possible (at least on these grounds) to claim his authority for amoralism.

Finally, by rejecting the one-dimensional, class-reductionistic, and ultimately quite absurd polarization of (Marxist proletarian) science versus (non-Marxist bourgeois) ideology, it would redraw the map of the ideational to recognize what has always been completely obvious to non-Marxists: that the world of ideas is far too rich to be exhausted by such an impoverished dichotomization. A conceptual space would thus be opened up for the recognition of ideas fitting into neither category and of systems of domination other than class, with all their accompanying intellectual products. The ideal would be that, within this textually unshackled framework, women and people of color could develop a materialist theorization of counterhegemonic ideologies and oppositional epistemologies. The desideratum would be a multidimensional conceptualization of ideologies, both the dominating and the emancipatory kind, capable of providing an integrated account not just of class thought, but of sexism and racism on the one hand, and feminism and antiracist theory on the other. Only a Marxism capable of addressing these concerns has any hope of surviving into the twenty-first century.

NOTES

1. Similarly, two survey articles of the field, Arnold (1987) and Buchanan (1987), range over numerous topics but have nothing to say about "ideology"; and a sympathetic expository text, Mayer (1994), does not even have a subsection on it.

2. Cohen (2001). In emphasizing the forces and relations of production at the expense of the superstructural concerns that had characterized Western Marxism, Cohen largely established the framework of subsequent debate even for those who contested his "old-fashioned" (Cohen's phrase) interpretation of Marxism. One author judges that "the Age of 'Western Marxism' has apparently come to an end" (Levine 1989, 29).

3. The work by McCarney that I discussed in the original article was his book *The Real World of Ideology* (1980).

4. Sushinky's criticisms will be addressed later, since they generally presuppose the view I no longer hold.

5. This reference, with which I once would have automatically and unthinkingly agreed, is a wonderfully instructive illustration of how the weight of the received interpretation can distort our reading of a text. In fact, so far as I can tell from going through the *Collected Works* (see note 7), the phrase "ideological struggle" *never* appears in Marx's writings! It is not that it appears rarely rather than frequently, as McMurtry claims, but that it does not appear *at all*. But since we already "know"

what "ideology" means for Marx, we assume that, even if we can't find some appropriate examples where we happen to be looking, it has to appear somewhere else. One could joke that there are few examples in the real world of ideological hegemony as complete as the hegemony in the secondary literature of the received view of "ideology."

6. McCarney's disagreement with my categorization here may be attributable to my possibly infelicitous choice of phrase to summarize McMurtry's view. While the phrase ("men's conceptions of themselves") is McMurtry's own, it might suggest some kind of individualist psychological introspection rather than any sort of sociopolitical theorizing.

7. Let me also offer here some results of my research that will be valuable to anybody interested in these questions, no matter how dubious they may be about the interpretation I myself embrace. Because Marx and Engels' comments on this subject are scattered all over their work, I was always worrying that some obscure passage I had not taken into account might shed some new light on their usage of the term. I therefore decided to attempt to compile a near-comprehensive list of appearances of the term and its derivatives, which would be useful both for me and other researchers—a task made easier by the fact that the projected fifty-volume English-language *Collected Works* is now almost complete. The forty-nine volumes that are now out (as of early 2003) cover everything except Engels' correspondence from October 1892 to his death in 1895. In addition, I have used a standard one-volume collection of selected correspondence (MESC 1975) for his crucial letters to Franz Mehring (July 14, 1893) and W. Borgius (Jan. 25, 1894). (Note: In this collection, the latter addressee is mistakenly identified as H. Starkenburg.) So though I cannot claim to have gone through the entire Marx–Engels corpus, I have covered more than 98 percent of it.

The listing is, of course, subject to human error, since it was done the old-fashioned, nonelectronic way—that is, page turning, page skimming. Given fatigue, inattention, and so forth, I probably missed some appearances in the works examined. So the listing will be most useful in establishing where the term and its derivatives *do* appear, and one should be cautious about the implied negative claims. The variants include "ideology," "ideologist," "ideologue," "ideological," "ideologically," "ideologise," "ideologism," and so on. So as not to beg any questions, I have separately listed citations from Marx, Marx and Engels together, and Engels. In CW 5, *The German Ideology*, the editors have included a few passages crossed out in the manuscript; I have indicated this by an X by the page number,

Marx:

CW 1: 292, 317.* CW 4: 123. CW 5: 61. CW 6: 166, 170. CW 7: 495. CW 8: 167. CW 10: 49, 68, 85, 86, 114, 586. CW 11: 170, 375. CW 12: 274. CW 14: 242. CW 16: 160. CW 24: 87, 327. CW 28: 101. CW 29: 263, 264. CW 31: 30, 182, 184, 197. CW 34: 323, 398, 471. CW 35: 376, 449, 572, 604, 752. CW 38: 376, 455. CW 40: 419. CW 41: 333. CW 43: 123. CW 45: 23, 190, 285. CW 46: 40.

Marx and Engels:

CW 5: 24X, 27, 28X, 29X, 30, 36, 37, 42, 45, 60, 62, 73, 77, 78, 92, 99, 103, 109, 111, 133, 172, 173, 176, 177, 180, 184, 195, 196, 197, 230, 232, 237, 246, 247, 255, 274, 282, 287, 292, 295, 298, 300, 304, 311, 326, 330, 335, 341, 342, 347, 348, 351, 353X, 355, 373,

378, 379, 420, 421, 437, 447, 449, 455, 456, 457, 459, 460, 462, 466, 467, 468, 469, 471, 514, 515, 532. CW 6: 494, 503. CW 7: 112. CW 10: 500, 513. CW 11: 268.

Engels:

CW 2: 145, 284, 292, 361. CW 5: 549. CW 6: 78, 267, 275, 522, 526. CW 7: 373, 375, 377, 378. CW 9: 42. CW 10: 292, 404, 405, 411, 412, 556. CW 23: 375, 381. CW 24: 292, 432, 433, 435, 467. CW 25: 35, 38, 40, 89, 247, 459, 490, 597. CW 26: 283, 303, 376, 383, 388, 389, 392, 393, 394, 395, 396, 397, 458, 470, 477, 519, 553. CW 35: 532. CW 38: 115, 204. CW 43: 394. CW 47: 326, 491. CW 48: 452. CW 49: 61. MESC: 510, 511, 512, 518.

*In Mills and Goldstick (1989), we say, misleadingly, that the earliest reference to "ideology" is in *The Holy Family* (CW 4). This is its earliest appearance in a *jointly authored* work, but there are, as indicated, a few earlier appearances in the individual writings of both Marx and Engels.

8. For a discussion of different senses of "materialism," see Collier (1979).

9. For a defense of this claim against Cohen's alternative view (2001)—that for Marx the "material" is the "natural"—see chapter 2.

10. McCarney (1980) makes this mistake several times, referring to the Young Hegelians' "continued reliance on an idealist ontology" (11) and to "Marx's over-riding concern . . . with the persistence of the idealist ontology" (86). Whether Bruno Bauer and Max Stirner were idealists in *this* sense is highly questionable—Ludwig Feuerbach certainly was not—but in any case the important point for Marx and Engels in their polemic against them in *The German Ideology* was that they were all *sociological* idealists, since they failed to appreciate the role of material–economic preconditions in changing society. Similarly, in McCarney's later discussion (1980) of Engels' comments in *Anti-Dühring*, he suggests that his "enduring concern with the shortcomings of idealism may reflect a taste for metaphysics not sustained by Marx" (94). Again, this misses the point of Engels' critique, which is *not* primarily metaphysical/ontological at all. McCarney's conflation of the two senses of "idealism" is, I suggest, partially responsible for his incomprehension of the nature of Engels' analyses of "ideology." For a comparable error, see Parekh (note 13) and David McLellan's discussion of the letter to Mehring: "[Engels' view] was founded on a kind of metaphysical materialism to which ideology was seen as the opposite. The falsity of ideology was not so much due to its origin or function as to its ontological status, its propensity to deal with things that simply were not there" (McLellan 1995, 21). This is completely wrong; see my comments that follow.

11. It would also be logically possible to be an ontological idealist and a sociological materialist. But psychologically, this combination is obviously far less likely.

12. In section 3, McCarney (1990) criticizes the postulation of a distinct "idealist" sense as a case of "arbitrary conceptual proliferation," which "once one allows it to start, it will be difficult to know where to stop" (456–57). If one takes for granted as a starting point the existence of a neutral generic ideational sense of "ideology," capable of subsuming all others, this response is understandable. But as I shall attempt to show later, no such sense exists, so the "conceptual proliferation" has in fact unwittingly been done by others.

13. McCarney is in fact aware of this passage, since he cites it in his book (1980, 4). But he does not seem aware of how embarrassing it is for his interpretation.

How could soldiers be members of the "ideological classes," if an ideologist is just a specialist in *ideas*? Obviously, soldiers can play an ideological (in the accepted sense) role in society, but it cannot plausibly be claimed that this makes them an "ideological *class*." Since *anybody* could contingently play such a role in the right circumstances, this criterion for membership would make the term's scope all-encompassing so that it would become vacuous. By contrast, in his book, Parekh (1982) correctly recognizes that Marx uses the term ("ideological class") to refer to "the unproductive occupations," but he sees this as a "sporadic usage," unrelated to the two main meanings of "ideology" he finds in Marx: "idealism" and "apologia." Parekh fails to connect the "idealism" sense to the "unproductive occupations" sense because of his conflation of the ontological and sociological senses of "idealism." Thus he writes (230, n. 1, ch. 1; 3; 1–14): "Idealism assumes that the spirit or consciousness is conceptually and, for some, even temporally prior to matter. For matter is not and cannot be the ultimate reality, and *cannot* generate and explain consciousness." As earlier argued, this is incorrect, since one could be an ontological materialist and a sociological idealist.

14. But there is yet another alternative reading. McCarney (1980, 85–92) had argued that the original German ("*Wenn in der ganzen Ideologie...*") is poorly rendered by the standard translation "If in all ideology . . ." and would be better read as "If in the whole ideology . . ." In the light of my revised view, I now wonder whether the best reading might not in fact be "If in the whole superstructure . . ."

15. In his reply, McCarney (1990, 453–54) justifiably criticizes me for citing as evidence passages that refer only to "ideologists" and not "ideology." I remedy this error in the section that follows.

16. I have tried to choose unambiguous passages, where it is clear that "ideology" must *mean* idealism; there are a great many more passages where the context (the ignoring of material conditions) makes it obvious that "idealism" is being *referred* to, but for which McCarney could deny that there is a conceptual identity. See, for example: CW 5, 24X, 195, 247, 282, 287, 304, 330, 379, 514, 532; CW 6, 503; CW 7, 495; CW 28, 101; CW 29, 264.

17. In my opinion, the whole point of Marx and Engels' views on the social causation of belief is that material determination as such is *not* necessarily epistemically undermining, since in some cases it can be enlightening, demystifying—for example, the differential experience of capitalist exploitation afforded by the proletariat's material class position. What is crucial is the *kind* of material determination: see Mills (1988 and 1989).

18. The fact that the ideational meaning of "ideology" is "idealism" also makes sense of Engels' elevational metaphors ("higher"/"more rarefied" and "lower" forms of ideology: CW 26, 393; CW 49, 61). Being "closer" to the economic base, juridico-political varieties of "idealism" are "lower" than the "pure abstract ideology" (MESC, 518) of religion and philosophy. The link with idealism in the broader sense of neglecting material realities also explains, I would claim, two otherwise mysterious passages in *Anti-Dühring* and *Dialectics of Nature*, where Engels uses the term in discussions, respectively, of geometry and biology (CW 25, 38, 490).

19. Sushinsky writes that my identification of the pejorative sense of "ideology" with "idealism" restricts "the theoretical usefulness of the concept" (1990,

473). But we can now appreciate that this simply presupposes what has to be proven—that is, that Marx *did* in fact have a concept with a generic ideational reference. The fact that he was hostile both to idealistic and fetishistic bourgeois thought doesn't prove that he had a unitary term subsuming both of them, any more than the fact that his own concept is not very useful proves that it is *not* his concept.

But could McCarney not insist just the same that fetishistic theories must clearly be "ideological" for Marx? Not if he follows his own eminently reasonable, non-question-begging methodological principle, announced on the first page of his book: "It will be assumed that where [Marx] wishes to use the concept he will generally be prepared to do so under its own name" (1980, 1).

20. V. I. Lenin, "What the 'Friends of the People' Are and How They Fight the Social-Democrats," in Lenin (1963, 151). The Marxist source Lenin cites as authorizing this interpretation is in fact the 1859 preface (cf. my reading in the previous paragraphs).

21. Similarly, the *theoretical* (as against textual) arguments for this neutrality, cited by Costello and Sushinsky as well as McCarney, can now be seen to establish at best the neutrality of Marx's conception of "class ideas." They can't on their own show the neutrality of "ideology," since it needs to be independently demonstrated (rather than just assumed) that this is indeed the term's reference.

2

Is It Immaterial That There's a "Material" in "Historical Materialism"?

Everybody knows that the Marxist theory of social evolution, which came to be called (though not by Marx himself) "historical materialism," was regarded by Marx and Engels as being in some sense *materialist*. A more difficult task would be to specify exactly what this sense is. That the task would also be a relatively unrewarding one, no more than a pedantic exercise, may be suggested by the paucity of discussion of this topic in the dozens of books and articles in Analytical Marxism published over the last two decades.[1] However, I think that such a conclusion would be premature. In this chapter I will argue that the terminological clarification on this point produced by a close examination of Marx's writings revealingly (if obliquely) illuminates the *substantive* claims of what is widely perceived to be the foundational text of the movement, G. A. Cohen's *Karl Marx's Theory of History: A Defence* (2001). In particular, I will argue *(a)* that Cohen's interpretation of Marx's use of "material" is mistaken and *(b)* that this misreading has implications for the soundness of Cohen's important retrieval and updating of the "technological determinist" reading of Marx.[2]

G. A. COHEN'S TECHNOLOGICAL DETERMINISM

Cohen's book sets out to defend what he describes as "an old-fashioned historical materialism" (2001, x), in which the productive forces—means of production (i.e., instruments, raw materials, and spaces) and labor power—have explanatory primacy. He attributes to Marx a three-tiered

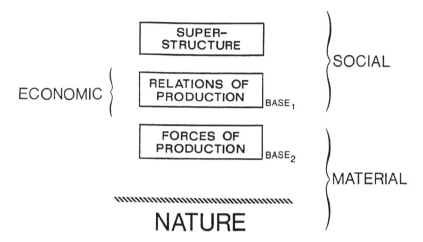

Figure 2.1. G. A. Cohen's technologically determinist model of Marxism

model of society, which, in order to assist the discussion, I am going to illustrate with a diagram (see figure 2.1). The forces of production constitute the "external" underlying material base of society (base$_2$) and are in
themselves asocial, or, respecting the architectural metaphor, *infra*social
(Cohen 2001, 28–31).[3] Society itself can be partially divided into an "internal" economic base (base$_1$) made up of the relations of production (relations of effective power over persons and productive forces: 28–31, 63)
and a superstructure (those political and juridical institutions whose character can be explained by the relations of production: 216–17). The division is only partial because, Cohen suggests, the base–superstructure distinction should not be seen as exhaustive (31). However, to avoid
unnecessary complexity I will not bother to represent these other social
areas on the diagram. Note also that Cohen, with some taxonomic idio-
syncrasy, does not include ideology in the superstructure (216).

   Two important asymmetrical relationships link these levels: the character of the forces of production functionally explains the character of the relations of production (ch. 6), and the character of the relations of production functionally explains the character of the superstructure (ch. 8). As
already indicated, then, explanatory primacy is vested in the forces of production and their autonomous tendency to develop throughout history.[4]
This interpretation is what makes Cohen's reading of Marx a technologically determinist one so that, as he points out in his foreword, "unusually
little discussion" is given in his book to such topics as class conflict, ideology, and the state (x). But he denies, against possible misconceptions,
that such an interpretation should be seen as in any way "demeaning to

humanity," since—far from "the agencies of history" being "subhuman powers"—human nature and human rationality (albeit in their "thin" contractarian versions) play a crucial role in explaining this tendency to develop as a result of their confrontation with natural "scarcity": "Given [people's] rationality, and their inclement situation, when knowledge provides the opportunity of expanding productive power they will tend to take it, for not to do so would be irrational" (Cohen 2001, 147–53).

It turns out, then, that for Cohen the "contradiction" between forces and relations of production is merely the most prominent instance of a *general* overarching polarity in Marx's thought, in which the *material* (nature/ the forces of production/the human/the real) is systematically contrasted with and opposed to the *social* (society/the relations of production/the historical/the economic) (2001, 47; ch. 4, esp. 98). Thus as he summarizes his position in a later paper authored with Will Kymlicka (Cohen and Kymlicka 1988, 171): "the fundamental explanation of the course of social change lies in facts that are in an important sense asocial, and, in one sense of the word, material." Schematically, then, Cohen's reading of the overall pattern of explanation in Marx can be depicted as in figure 2.2: the material/natural (including human nature and rationality) explains the social, while within the realm of the social, in a subordinate explanatory scheme, the base₁ explains the superstructure.

Cohen's recommended classification therefore has the following implications:

1. the forces of production are in no way inherently social;
2. the relations of production, and the economic level of society generally, are not material;
3. the material is opposed to the social rather than the ideal;
4. historical materialism is a theory about the determination of the social by the material, where the material is essentially a category of the natural ("socioneutral" facts about society and human beings).

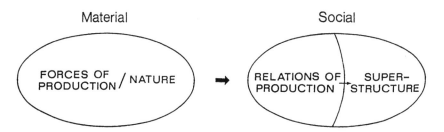

Figure 2.2. G. A. Cohen's overall explanation scheme

Now what I want to suggest is that, as an interpretation of Marx's intentions, all of these points are mistaken. A secondary issue is that they also diverge quite radically from the "old-fashioned" interpretation of Marxism offered by Marx's literary partner for four decades, Frederick Engels. While this consideration should of course in no way be taken as decisive, I think the anti-Engelsian operating principle in much of the secondary literature is mistaken in its dismissal of Engels as the main source for whatever is taken to be dogmatic, vulgar, and generally misguided in the Marxist legacy. Therefore, I will accordingly feel justified in sometimes citing Engels' views as supporting evidence.[5]

The conventional interpretation (and Engels') of the significance of Marx's choice of the word "materialism" to describe his theory of history, which can be found in any standard intellectual biography,[6] is that Marx is drawing some kind of implicit analogy between the materialism–idealism dichotomy in philosophy and two opposing positions in sociohistorical theorizing.[7] The comparison is between the ontological primacy of matter and the explanatory primacy of the economic—which is referred to as "material," which includes both the forces and relations of production (sometimes jointly dubbed "the mode of production"), and which is opposed to the explanatorily subordinate ("ideal") superstructure.[8] As emphasized in chapter 1, "idealism" in this context, of course, has no ontological implications (it does not, for example, commit one to the *nonphysical* character of ideas); but it does indicate a set of possible "superstructuralist" mistakes about the actual ordering of causal hierarchies in society—for example, the belief that society is held together by values, or that the rise of capitalism is to be attributed to the growth of the Protestant ethic, or that major juridical changes can be given a purely internalist explanation. Thus far from its being the case that the material for Marx is to be contrasted with the social, the whole *point* of his famous "inversion" of Hegel—and of his polemical battles with the Young Hegelians (which occupy so many hundreds of arid pages in *The Holy Family* and *The German Ideology*)—is that society has *both* "material" and "ideal" elements, which Marx saw himself as putting in their correct causal relationship.

Retaining the same three tiers, then, we get a somewhat different picture of their interrelation and respective categorization, which is shown in figure 2.3. The forces and relations of production cannot be as sharply separated from each other as on Cohen's model, and together they constitute a single material–economic base. However, two levels of "materiality" have to be distinguished, corresponding to *natural* and *social* materiality (respectively, material$_1$ and material$_2$).[9] Thus, as earlier indicated, the "material" does not have the same sense as it does for Cohen: let us call it the MATERIAL to register this difference. A more complex explanatory

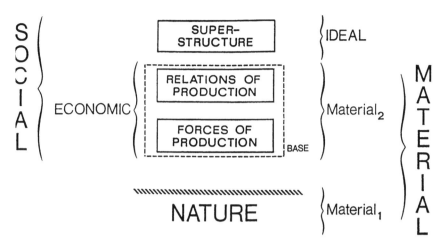

Figure 2.3. **Alternative model of Marxism**

picture is therefore entailed. The MATERIAL, in the comprehensive sense, explains the ideal, but the MATERIAL is also internally differentiated into the natural and the economic, which are in an interactive dynamic with each other. The following metaphor may bring the distinction home. For Cohen, explanatory primacy can be located in a single battlefront, the confrontation of abstract classless humans with nature, employing their rationality to overcome scarcity. By contrast, this approach assumes two fronts on which (post-"primitive communism") simultaneous interlocking (and mutually affecting) engagements are taking place: the confrontation between human beings and nature, and the conflict between human beings themselves. Thus class struggle—and, for those seeking to synthesize Marxism with other theories, other kinds of group struggle—is theoretically central in figure 2.4, whereas it is not in figure 2.2. It is not the case, then, that historical materialism is asserting the determination of the social by the infrasocial, for the social, in the form of the economic, appears within the general category of the MATERIAL.

What I must now attempt to do, of course, is to show that it is this picture rather than Cohen's that is true to Marx's intentions. Since this textual exercise will be tedious (albeit in different ways) for both writer and reader, it may be worthwhile to recapitulate its justification, and to answer some possible objections. The main justification is simply the importance of Cohen's book: the author of a 1987 survey article describes it as the "most influential work on Marx's theory of history in the last ten years (and perhaps the last twenty-five)" (Arnold 1987, 277); and it is, as indicated, seen as the foundational text of Analytical Marxism. Thus if Cohen

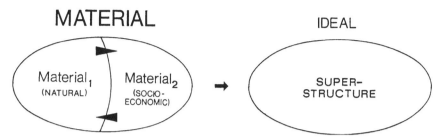

Figure 2.4. Alternative overall explanation scheme

can be demonstrated to get this question illuminatingly wrong, the effort of wading through thousands of Marx's pages will not have been
wasted. It might be objected, though, that the extensiveness of Marx's
writings, and possible fluctuations in his usage, mean that a definitive
case cannot be established anyway—or at least not at chapter length. I
think there is some truth in this, and my sights will accordingly be set
lower by showing that, at the very least, a strong presumptive case can
be made against Cohen's reading via the citation of references from a
wide range of works composed at different periods. Since the 1859 preface to *A Contribution to the Critique of Political Economy* is taken by him to
be the canonical text for his interpretation, unfavorable quotations from
this work will obviously carry a special significance. In addition, I will
try to demonstrate that my interpretation has the conceptual resources
to account for passages that, prima facie, seem to support Cohen's reading, while the converse is not the case. Finally, once the terminological
evidence for an alternative interpretation has been accumulated, I will
argue that this interpretation independently supports some of the major
critiques of Cohen.

TEXTUAL EVIDENCE AGAINST
COHEN'S TECHNOLOGICAL DETERMINISM

Some of the Forces of Production Are Inherently Social

Cohen does not deny, of course, that the forces of production usually
have "social relational, economic properties" and that they are "standardly" social; but his point is that they "are *not by nature* or 'in themselves' . . . or 'as such' . . . social" (2001, 92). Machines, for example, can
be characterized without reference to the network of social relations in
which they are embedded, which may make them alternately capitalist
or common property. And it is in *this* asocial aspect that the forces of

production are causally determining and explanatorily fundamental. By contrast, I want to argue that at least *some* of the forces of production are instrinsically social and that, even where abstraction can be made from the social characteristics of others, it is questionable whether it was really in this desocialized guise that Marx saw them as determinative.

To begin with, let me show that Marx *did* often refer to the "social" nature of the forces of production and that he did so in contexts that would suggest that their sociality is in fact ontologically central to their causal role. (Due to space considerations throughout, I will simply have to *refer* to many passages rather than actually cite them.)

The productive forces are explicitly characterized as "social" in *Theories of Surplus Value* and *Capital* (CW 32, 243, 303; CW 34, 124; CW 37, 864). Particularly noteworthy passages are those in the 1859 preface, when Marx—in describing the processes that give rise to the "era of social revolution"—refers to "the conflict existing between the social forces of production and the relations of production" (CW 29, 263); and in *Capital*, where he writes: "Centralisation of the means of production and socialisation of labor at last reach a point where they become incompatible with their capitalist integument. Thus [*sic*] integument is burst asunder" (CW 35, 750). Similarly, in *Theories of Surplus Value*, he emphasizes the historical importance for capitalism of "the development of the social productive powers of labor and the transformation of labor into social labor" (CW 31, 83). He attributes "the deepest and most hidden cause" of capitalist crises to the fact that "bourgeois production is compelled by its own immanent laws, on the one hand, to develop the productive forces as if production did not take place on a narrow restricted social foundation, while, on the other hand, it can develop those forces only within these narrow limits" (CW 32, 274). He later argues that because of the centralization of capital, "production loses its private character and becomes a social process" in which "the means of production are employed as communal, social means of production" (CW 33, 368). Also noteworthy is his emphasis that, past the "first animal state," man's "relationship to nature" is "mediated" by "his relationship to other men" (CW 33, 301), which puts into question the viability as an *explanans* of Cohen's picture of an abstract humanity confronting nature (figure 2.2). Finally, in what I think is a very significant passage, Marx says that "the VULGARIAN cannot *conceive* the social productive power and the social character of labor developed within the framework of capital as something separate from the capitalist form" (CW 32, 498). I infer from Marx's scorn that certain social aspects to the productive forces and labor *are* separable from "the capitalist form," and I suggest on the basis of the aforementioned quotes that these aspects enter into the conflict *between* the productive forces and the relations of production.

The obvious candidate for such a role is the social division of labor. But Cohen expressly excludes these relations (what he calls material/technical work-relations) from the productive forces, though he concedes they do "belong alongside" them (2001, 113). Many critics have pointed out that this position seems to run directly counter to Marx's intentions.[10] In *The German Ideology*, for example, Marx and Engels say directly that "a certain mode of production, or industrial stage, is always combined with a certain mode of co-operation, or social stage, and this mode of co-operation is itself a 'productive force'" (CW 5, 43; see also 48). Comparable passages on the role of the division of labor can be found in *Wage Labor and Capital* (CW 9, 222–24); the *Grundrisse* (CW 28, 452–53); and *Capital* (CW 35, chs. 13 and 14; CW 35, 752; CW 37, 85, 637) (the latter reference, interestingly, is to the "*social natural* forces of labor arising from co-operation, division of labor, etc." [my emphasis]). And in *Theories of Surplus Value*, Marx singles out as one of "two *cardinal* FACTS about capitalist production" the "[o]rganisation of labor itself as social labor brought about by co-operation, division of labor and the linking of labor with the results of social domination over natural forces," which leads to the "elimination" of "private labor" (CW 33, 342–43).

What these quotations suggest is that the conflict between forces and relations of production is in at least certain respects intrasocial, the conflict between a particular *social mode* of organizing labor (extensive division of labor and socialization of the work process), that is developed *by* capitalism but is more "appropriate" to socialism, and an intrinsically capitalist *social mode* of appropriation of the products of this labor. It is worth pointing out that Engels unequivocally viewed the situation in these terms. Thus, in *Socialism: Utopian and Scientific*, he claims that the central conflict of capitalism arises out of the "*contradiction between socialised production and capitalistic appropriation*," which manifests itself as "*the antagonism of proletariat and bourgeoisie*" (CW 24, 311). The "rebellion of the productive forces . . . against their quality as capital," then (Cohen's striving of the *asocial* material "content" against the *social* "form"), consists for Engels in the demand for the "*practical recognition of their character as social productive forces*," so that the "modes of production, appropriation, and exchange" can be "harmon[ised]" with "the socialised character of the means of production" (CW 24, 316–20; Engels' emphases throughout).

In effect, then, Engels is providing an explanation sketch connecting (at least for capitalism) the two main "contradictions" highlighted—with apparent contradictoriness of another sort—in Marxist theory: that between the forces and relations of production and that between classes. Insisting on the sociality of the forces of production makes this connection intelligible. By contrast, for Cohen, the class struggle is theoretically marginalized because the human powers drawn upon in the conflict of forces and relations of production are asocial, unmediated by class. I will elaborate on this point's significance later.

The Relations of Production—and the Economic Level of Society—Are Material

A complicating factor here is that, as noted, Cohen does see *work-relations* as being material relations of production. By contrast, what we are looking for is textual evidence that Marx considers social relations of production— the power-relations that underlie property relations—to be material.

In *On the Jewish Question*, Marx links the "egoistic life" of "civil society" with "material life," and he refers to "material elements, such as private property" (CW 3, 153–54). In the *1844 Manuscripts*, he says that political economy expresses "the *material* process through which private property actually passes" (CW 3, 270). And he later describes as one of Feuerbach's "great achievements" the "establishment of *true materialism* and of *real science*, by making the social relationship of 'man to man' the basic principle of the theory" (CW 3, 328).

In *The Holy Family*, Marx writes that for "old political economy," "the decisive factor was the material power of capital and of landed property" (CW 4, 49). In *The German Ideology*, using the conceptual precursors (*Verkehrsform*) of the "relations of production," Marx and Engels refer to men's "material production and their material intercourse" and the "materialist connection of men with one another" (CW 5, 37, 43). They assert that: "Civil society embraces the whole material intercourse of individuals within a definite stage of the development of productive forces" (CW 5, 89). Correspondingly, they say that each stage of history "contains a material result, a sum of productive forces, a historically created relation to nature and of individuals to one another," so that the "material elements of a complete revolution" require *both* "the existing productive forces" and "the formation of a revolutionary mass" (CW 5, 54). They describe the ruling class as "the class which is the ruling *material* force of society" and claim that the "ruling ideas are nothing more than the ideal expression of the dominant material relations," "the relations which make the one class the ruling one" (CW 5, 59; see also CW 5, 42, 176, 195, 235, 318, 329, 330, 355, 395).

Later writings confirm this pattern. In *The Communist Manifesto*, "changes in the material conditions of existence" are associated with "abolition of the bourgeois relations of production" (CW 6, 514). In *The Eighteenth Brumaire of Louis Bonaparte*, the "material conditions of existence" refer to "two different kinds of property" (CW 11, 128). In the 1859 preface, the "material conditions of life" are associated with Hegel's concept of "civil society" and assigned explanatory primacy vis-à-vis "legal relations" and "political forms" (CW 29, 262). Marx refers to "the material transformation of the economic conditions of production" and says that "the contradictions of material life" are "the conflict existing between the social forces of production and the relations of production" (CW 29, 263). (Note that this is an explicit statement, contra Cohen, of both the materiality *and* the sociality of this conflict.) *Wage Labor and Capital* begins with a statement about "the *economic relations* which constitute the material foundation of the present class struggles and national struggles" (CW 9, 197). Similarly, in Marx's famous Dec. 28, 1846, letter to P. V. Annenkov, he says that man's "material relations form the basis of all his relations" (CW 38, 96).[11] In the *Grundrisse*, the "relations of production" are later referred to as "those material relationships" (CW 28, 101; see also CW 29, 92). This usage can also be found in: CW 35, 90, 335, 611, n. 1; CW 37, 762–63, 817; CW 32, 514. Finally, "material" and "economic" are themselves often used interchangeably; for example, in *The German Ideology* (CW 5, 81), "Moralising Criticism and Critical Morality" (CW 6, 319–20), and *The Communist Manifesto* (CW 6, 513–14, 515).

My claim is that what this shows overall is that the reference of the "material" is *broader* than the forces of production and that this is obviously germane to the question of what "material determination" amounts to.

The Material (in the Broad Sense)
Is Opposed to the Ideal, Not the Social

The opposition of the material and the social is, as noted, one of the main pillars of Cohen's technological determinist interpretation of Marx. Since the material is part of the natural, this distinction is equivalent to a statement of the contrast between the natural and the social. Now I am not for a minute denying that such a contrast exists in Marx, nor that in his critiques of other theorists he frequently excoriated them for conflating the two. My claim is that this opposition does not play the central role Cohen attributes to it and that, in particular, it does not support an explanatory scheme in which the social is the *explanandum* and in which (part of) the natural is the *explanans*. What historical materialism really signifies, I am arguing, is a theory about the determination of part of the social by the MATERIAL, which is *both* social and natural.

Let me now try to explicate and defend this position, and at the same time provide an alternative account of the real import for Marx of "material." The significance of this terminological choice, in my opinion, is that Marx and Engels regarded a particular sector of society (the economic sector) as having a causal autonomy, an independence of collective human will, which was similar to the nomic independence that, as ontological materialists, they saw in *natural* laws. The latter are paradigmatically "material," being neither created by us, ontologically dependent on us, nor causally dependent on us. By contrast, the "materiality" of social laws is weaker since *(a)* they are created *by* human activity and *(b)* they are ontologically dependent on us in the sense that, if all humans were to disappear, society and social laws would disappear with them. But what they do have in common with natural laws is a *causal* independence of us, in that, as long as class society exists, we are in a sense being constrained by our own creations. (Thus conceptual links can be made here with the notion of "alienation" and the idea of human products' becoming causally refractory.)

What makes the relations of production *material*, then, is this coercive character, this "independence of our will," in contrast with that realm of greater human freedom Marx designated as the *ideal*, but which he warned could not be taken as explanatorily fundamental. Thus the basic opposition in his thought is not that between the material/nature/the human/the real and the social/society/the historical/the economic, but that between the material/the "objective"/the causally independent/ the economic and the ideal (sometimes "spiritual")/the "subjective"/the causally dependent/the superstructural.[12] This analysis, it should be noted, is completely congruent with Marx's own account of his intellectual history (e.g., in the 1859 preface): that his theory, "historical materialism," developed as an "inversion" (following Feuerbach's "transformational method") of Hegel's "historical idealism," in which an objectified Mind/Spirit is taken as the explanatory foundation.

Throughout Marx's writings, then, we find a systematic opposition of the material and the *ideal*. In *On the Jewish Question*, the "preconditions of the political state" are sorted into "material elements, such as private property" and "spiritual elements, such as culture or religion" (CW 3, 154). In the introduction to the *Contribution to the Critique of Hegel's Philosophy of Law*, Marx writes, "As philosophy finds its material weapons in the proletariat, so the proletariat finds its *spiritual* weapons in philosophy" (CW 3, 187). In the *1844 Manuscripts*, "subjectivity and objectivity" correspond to "spirituality and materiality" (CW 3, 302). In *The Holy Family*, the Bauer brothers' "Absolute Criticism" is lampooned for its mastery of the Hegelian "art of converting *real objective* chains that exist *outside me* into *merely ideal*, merely *subjective* chains, existing merely *in me*," and this is contrasted with the "mass" who "must not wish to abolish material estrangement by purely *inward spiritual* action" (CW 4, 82; see also CW 4, 95). *The German Ideology* is a sustained polemic against the idealism of the Young Hegelians, who "consider conceptions, thoughts, ideas . . . as the real chains of men" (CW 5, 30), to which Marx and Engels oppose their "materialist" understanding of history, which requires a focus on individuals "as they work under definite material limits, presuppositions and conditions independent of their will" (CW 5, 36). Thus, unlike the "idealist view of history," "it does not explain practice from the idea but explains the formation of ideas from material practice," recognizing "civil society in its various stages, as the basis of all history" (CW 5, 53–54). For the "fundamental form of [individuals'] activity is, of course, material, on which depend all other forms—mental, political, religious, etc." (CW 5, 82), so that this "material intercourse" "forms the basis of the state and of the rest of the idealistic superstructure" (CW 5, 89), whereas the Young Hegelians transform "the idealist symptom into the material cause" and so depict "material history to be produced by ideal history" (CW 5, 136–37). (See also: CW 35, 19, 375, n. 2; CW 31, 182.)

The association between materiality and causal constraint/domination is also evident at several places in Marx's writings. In *The German Ideology*, Marx and Engels describe how, as a result of the division of labor in class society, "man's own deed becomes an alien power opposed to him, which enslaves him instead of being controlled by him"; and in the next paragraph they refer to this "fixation of social activity, this consolidation of what we ourselves produce into a material power above us, growing out of our control" (CW 5, 47; see also CW 5, 77–79). A particularly illuminating passage is their statement that in class society "we have a totality of productive forces, which have, as it were, taken on a material form and are for the individuals themselves no longer the forces of the individuals but of private property" (CW 5, 86). Since the productive forces are presumably already *ontologically* material, this "materiality" is clearly conceptually separate. Similar or related passages can be found in CW 5, 93, 245, 329, 330, 363, 436–37, 438, 479.

In the *Grundrisse*, Marx describes how the "social character of the activity [of individuals]" appears as "something alien to and existing outside the individuals; not as their relationship to each other, but as their subordination to relationships existing independently of them" (CW 28, 94; see also CW 28, 98–99). In *Capital*, Marx says that men's "relations to each other in production assume a material character independent of their control and conscious individual action" (CW 35, 103). He later describes how "production relations are converted into entities and rendered independent in relation to the agents of production," thus taking on the appearance of "overwhelming natural laws" (CW 37, 818). Another revealing passage can be found in *Theories of Surplus Value*, where he says: "with the development of the specifically capitalist mode of production, not only do these directly material things . . . stand on their hind legs vis-à-vis the worker and confront him as 'capital,' but also the forms of socially developed labor, co-operation, manufacture (as a form of the division of labor), the factory. . . . [These] are all things which confront the individual workers themselves as *alien* and *objective*" (CW 34, 123). The implicit contrast here is presumably with the *"indirectly* material," the division of labor, whose "materiality/objectivity" arises out of its causally constraining character in the context of capitalist production relations. See also CW 32, 405, 484.

Finally, I want to point out that this interpretation is, ironically, most clearly vindicated in the 1859 preface itself, a passage from whose central paragraph forms one of the two epigraphs to Cohen's book. In the course of a brief intellectual autobiography, Marx traces the genesis and development of his own theory, and he gives the most famous and most quoted synopsis of it. As readers can verify for themselves, the key paragraph that begins "The first work which I undertook . . ." has running *systematically* through it a polarity between the ideal/superstructural and the material/economic.[13] Thus in the first category are "legal relations" and "political forms"; "the human mind," "a legal and political superstructure," and "forms of social consciousness"; "the general process of social, political and intellectual life," "ideological forms," "[social] consciousness," and "what [an individual] thinks about himself." In the second category are "the material conditions of life," "civil society," "relations [of production] which are independent of their will," "the economic structure of society," the "mode of production of material life," "social existence," "the material transformation of the economic conditions of production," [what an individual really is], "the contradictions of material life" (CW 29, 262–64). This opposition is not peripheral to the paragraph's theme but conceptually central to it, since Marx is not only setting out "the general conclusion at which [he] arrived" but also explaining how historical materialism developed out of his rejection of Hegelian idealism.

The Material Must Be Internally Differentiated

In the preceding sections, I argue that two levels of materiality in Marx have to be distinguished and that Cohen's conception of the material as simply a category of the *natural* is mistaken. Now I suggest that further confirmation for this claim can be found by considering the evolution of Marx's thought in relation to previous materialisms, specifically Feuerbach's. From the start, what Marx applauded in Feuerbach was the latter's perception that (part of) the social was "material," "determining" (i.e., not causally subordinate as in Hegel's perception). Thus in the *1844 Manuscripts*, Marx praises Feuerbach for establishing *"true materialism," "real science,"* "by making the social relationship of 'man to man' the basic principle of the theory" (CW 3, 328; original emphasis). But what he eventually came to reject was Feuerbach's *naturalistic* (abstract, unhistorical) conception of the social, so that by the time of the "Theses on Feuerbach," Marx was complaining about the "previous," "old," "contemplative" materialism, which conceives humans in terms of an inner, natural species essence rather than as social creations (CW 5, 3–8). This point is later made explicit in *The German Ideology*: "As far as Feuerbach is a materialist he does not deal with history, and as far as he considers history he is not a materialist" (CW 5, 41; see also CW 5, 38–41, 57–59). Similarly, in the *Grundrisse*, Marx makes a note of a point to be explicated later (though unfortunately it wasn't): "*Reproaches about the materialism of this conception. Relation to naturalistic materialism*" (CW 28, 46; original emphasis). Whereas previous materialisms had seen only *nature* as "objective" and "determining" (or if society had been seen as material, it was in a naturalistic unhistorical fashion), Marx believed that the (historically variable) forces and relations of production could *also* be viewed in this way. The terminological and conceptual point at issue here has been aptly summarized by Sebastiano Timpanaro:

> It might be said that in the expression "historical materialism," the noun was a polemic against Hegel and a whole philosophical tradition which affirmed the primacy of the spirit over any economic structure, whereas the adjective was a polemic against Feuerbach and English classical economics, in short against any statically naturalist conception of human society. (Timpanaro 1996, 40)

A good statement of the material duality that has to be theoretically acknowledged is given by Marx in CW 31, 182: "from the specific form of material production arises in the first place a specific structure of society, in the second place a specific relation of men to nature. Their State system and their intellectual outlook is determined by both." (Cf. figure 2.4; see also CW 35, 90, where "the social relations within the sphere of material life" apparently include both those "between man and man, and between man and Nature.") Correspondingly, the mistake is to collapse the two levels together. Thus Marx gives the Physiocrats qualified praise for recognizing the bourgeois forms of production "as physiological forms of society: as forms arising from the natural necessity of production itself, forms that are independent of anyone's will or of politics, etc. *They are material laws*" (CW 30, 353; my emphasis). But the theoretical *error* of the Physiocrats is that "the material law of a definite historical social stage is conceived as an abstract law governing equally all forms of society" so that "the bourgeois forms of production necessarily appeared as natural forms" (CW 30, 353). Economic materiality is assimilated to a natural materiality: material$_2$ is collapsed into material$_1$.

Cohen does appreciate, of course, that one of Marx's concerns is to warn us against the conflation of the social and the natural (Cohen 2001, ch. 4). But what he does not see is that, for Marx, this temptation arises precisely because both the socioeconomic and the natural are *material*.[14] Once we recognize their homology for Marx, we necessarily get a different picture of the theoretical commitments of historical materialism than if the material is *restricted* to the natural.

COHEN'S TEXTUAL EVIDENCE

Let us now turn to the examination of the evidence Cohen offers for his own interpretation. His most detailed case for the material/social contrast is set out in chapter 4, where he cites four passages from, respectively, *Wage Labor and Capital; The Poverty of Philosophy;* the *Grundrisse;* and *Capital,* volume 3. In these passages, a systematic distinction is established between, on the one hand, a Negro/a cotton-spinning jenny/machinery/men/means of production; and, on the other hand, a slave/capital/an economic category/slaves or citizens/capital. Cohen sees this as the statement of a general rule: "[Men and productive forces] have material and social characteristics, but *no social characteristics may be deduced from their material characteristics*" (2001, 91).

Now, as indicated, it is no part of my argument to *deny* that Marx frequently emphasizes the necessity for distinguishing between the natural and the social, and that in some contexts—though not, ironically, in any of the passages Cohen himself cites—he employs the word "material" to signify the natural. (A good example of such usage: in CW 36, 227, fetishism is described as involving the metamorphosis of "the social, economic character impressed on things in the process of social production into a natural character stemming from the material nature of those things." See also: CW 36, 204–5, 222–23, 356; CW 31, 13; CW 32, 399; CW 31, 248.) But my claim is that these and similar passages—which, prima facie, might seem to constitute something of an embarrassment for my reading—can be readily accounted for on the supposition that Marx was implicitly relying on *one* of the subdivisions of the MATERIAL, without (because of his lamentable lack of training in analytic philosophy) spelling out for the reader the desirable terminological clarification. In other words, the same contrast could be drawn by explicitly distinguishing, as I have done, material$_1$ (natural) and material$_2$ (social). All the aforementioned passages could then be rewritten in this terminology, with "fetishism" thus emerging clearly as the methodological failure to *differentiate* the two varieties of materiality and their (analytically) separable causal chains.

My claim, then, is that my recommended categorization can account for both the passages in Marx that Cohen has pointed out and the passages in Marx that I have pointed out. In the first set, the material (material$_1$) is contrasted with the social (i.e., the secondary opposition, in my view, which constitutes the internally complex *explanans* of figure 2.4). In the second set, the material (in the comprehensive sense: MATERIAL) is contrasted with the ideal (i.e., the primary opposition, in my view, between *explanans* and *explanandum* themselves). Note that it is *not*, however, open to Cohen to reply in kind that the material–ideal distinction can correspondingly be accommodated on his explanation scheme (figure 2.2). For in the first place, nothing in his book indicates that the superstructure is "ideal"; in fact, his exclusion of ideologies (paradigmatically ideal) from the superstructure underlines his repudiation of such a categorization. And in the second place (and more important), Cohen's exclusive identification of the material with the natural logically precludes categorizing the relations of production as material so that the base$_1$–superstructure relationship cannot for Cohen be a relationship of "material determination." A strength of my interpretation, then, is that it offers a possible reconceptualization of the passages Cohen cites to support his reading, while it also is able to explain many passages that would be problematic for him.

This also seems like a convenient place to mention two verbal incongruities generated by Cohen's reading. First, Cohen's separation of the relations and forces of production into internal and external bases means that one can no longer speak of *the* base and the superstructure, for there are supposedly two bases, though Marx only refers to one. (See, for example, CW 35, 92–93, n. 1, where the base is clearly described as unitary, material, and economic.) Second, Marx's theory of history has been called (hostilely) "economic determinism," or more sympathetically (for example, by Engels), "the economic interpretation of history." But, for Cohen, since the forces of production are infrasocial and therefore infraeconomic, and since explanatory primacy is vested in them, it follows that this description has been fundamentally mistaken all along and that Marx's collaborator for forty years did not even grasp the *central* theoretical claim of historical materialism!

CRITIQUES OF COHEN

Finally, I want to demonstrate that this terminological and conceptual revision—that is, if it has been found independently convincing on textual grounds—can also be shown to support recent critiques of Cohen's technological determinism.

The basic line of argument is as follows. For Cohen, as we have seen, the restriction of the material to the infrasocial underlies a conception of historical materialism as the determination of the social by purely "natural" human capacities and faculties. The "thin," transclass human desire to increase productivity and the equally emaciated "rational" perception of how to achieve this are in a sense the fundamental dynamo of the whole process. By contrast, the theoretical recognition of the necessary *sociality* of the material rules out such a simply naturalistic interpretation. It points us toward socially "thick" accounts of the forces of production in general, and human motivation and rationality in particular, with all the accompanying problems and complexities that characterize such accounts. Here I will simply cite, without discussion, some representative examples of such interpretations of Marx. My claim is not that they are in complete agreement with one another, but that they implicitly share a common explanatory framework that is congruent with that illustrated in figures 2.3 and 2.4.[15]

First, Henry Laycock, arguing against Cohen's material–social dichotomy in favor of the traditional interpretation, concludes that: "[I]f Marx's materialism does not require a contrast of the social and the material, it does not require a contrast of the social with the forces of production" (1980, 340). Similarly, Roger Gottlieb writes: "For Cohen's position, there must exist in Marx a rigid separation between society . . . and the forces of production," whereas in actuality, Gottlieb suggests, the "existence of each is always mediated by that of the other" (1985, 4). Laycock and Richard Miller argue that this social aspect is in fact central to the "determining" role of the forces of production. Marx's own practice as an economic historian, Miller claims, shows that it is changes in *work-relations*, rather than simple technological innovation, that are regarded by him as stimulating the transition from feudalism to capitalism (1984, ch. 5). And Laycock argues that it is precisely the *socialization* of the forces of production under capitalism that Marx thought would ultimately undermine it, since increasingly "planned, socialised production conflicts with the overall irrationality of unplanned, private appropriation" (1980, 351).

For these writers, then, the famous "contradiction" between forces and relations of production is not, as Cohen would have it, the conflict between a socioneutral human rationality and the "general" constraints exercised on social productivity by fettering economic structures. There are in fact no agents or agencies for the *channeling* of such an abstract rationality into efficacious causality: it is an analytical abstraction without any practical empirical bearers.

Second, what is required therefore is a "thick" account that focuses theoretical attention on the configuration of social circumstances that affect the likelihood of human rationality being employed in a transformative and revolutionary way. It is no longer a case of a "natural" rationality confronting a "natural" scarcity, and thus "externally" determining society (as in figure 2.2); but, as Andrew Levine and Erik Olin Wright have emphasized, rather a confrontation *itself* deeply mediated by the social so that it would be more appropriate to speak of "class-specific rationalities and forms of scarcity." Whether or not the "objective" fetters of capitalism are *experienced* as such by the working class, whether or not the "objective" potentiality of an alternative system is *perceived* by them, and whether or not they will have the *ability* to bring it about, will depend not just on abstract considerations of class interest and productivity, but on such factors as labor market segmentation, job hierarchies, and racial and ethnic divisions—all of which make next to no appearance in Cohen's book, but which may significantly retard the development of proletarian "class capacities" (Levine and Wright 1980, 47–68).

Moreover, as Joshua Cohen has pointed out, another problem produced by locating a theoretically pivotal "rationality" within a social context is that G. A. Cohen offers no plausible candidate for the facilitating role played in Hegel by "the ruse of reason": "there seems no reason to expect 'invisible hands' to predominate over 'prisoner's dilemmas' or other structural arrangements that generate undesirable outcomes from individually rational actions." Thus the "coordination problems" familiar from rational-choice theory will necessarily arise so that "interests and powers" may be so well organized that progress is "blocked" (Joshua Cohen 1982, 256–57).

Third, we should not be surprised, then, if the actual historical record is full of examples of stagnation and even regression in the development of the productive forces. Joshua Cohen cites some of the traditional examples: the collapse of the Roman Empire, the "second serfdom" in Eastern Europe (1982, 266–70). In addition, Roger Gottlieb points to the effects of imperialism and colonialism on India in particular and on the Third World in general, where indigenous productive capacity was destroyed or had its development distorted through the imposition of production relations designed to benefit an external bourgeoisie (1985, 9–14). For G. A. Cohen's technologically determinist reading, as Joshua Cohen stresses, such cases of blocked development must count as *counterevidence* to the basic thesis of historical materialism. By contrast, an alternative conception that "incorporate[s] the productive forces, and classes/class struggle" might be able to account for "blocking" via an expanded *explanans*, which would attribute it either directly to the relations of production or to "something explained by the production relations" (as against "independent political-structural facts" or free-floating "economic spirits") (Joshua Cohen 1982, 271–72). Such a conception would, of course, be consistent with the explanatory picture of figure 2.4.

Along similar lines, Richard Miller explicitly advocates what he calls the "mode of production" interpretation, which would make the mode of production *as a whole* the complex, internally differentiated determinant of social change:

[B]asic, internal economic change arises . . . on account of a self-transforming tendency of the mode of production as a whole, that is the relations of production, the forms of cooperation and the technology through which material goods are produced. (Miller 1984, 172)

Thus in his view "the relations of production and the processes they generate play a basic, independent role in explaining the most important changes in productive forces" (190).

They are, in short, part of the "material" in "historical materialism."

CONCLUSION

Cohen's interpretation of Marx has been a major advance in clarifying central terms, relationships, and issues in Marxist theory—not to mention providing an unprecedented stimulus for Anglo-American philosophical debate on the subject. But I think a strong case has emerged that its understanding of the basic dynamic of historical materialism is fundamentally flawed, even if, following orthodoxy, we focus just on class alone. If the account in this chapter has been plausible, then this case actually has Marx's terminological backing.[16]

Moreover, a quarter-century after the first publication of Cohen's book, in a largely post-Marxist (theoretical and political) world, it is—more than ever before—evident that *nonclass* structures of domination would need to be incorporated into an account of social change that is going to be adequate for the task of theorizing the modern world. As I will discuss in greater detail in chapters 5 and 6, Analytical Marxism, like Western/First World Marxism in general, has been a "white" Marxism, with little or no interest in the realities of imperialism, racism, and white supremacy, which have fundamentally shaped the lives of people of color. But the embedded and embodied human agents socially interacting with one another will be raced, and they will have their rationalities and senses of value shaped by the relations of domination molding them—not just as bourgeois and proletarians, but as men and women, as whites and nonwhites. Endorsers of a technological–determinist interpretation are likely to be disappointed if they assume that a "thin" rationality's rising above these divisions can be a significant, socially transformational force. When Marxism was still thought to be viable, socialist feminists argued for the expansion and reconceptualization of the material social "base" to include the relations of *reproduction* in what would be a synthesizing "dual-systems theory" (Jaggar 1988). Those seeking to salvage Marxism and bring race into a "multiple-systems" synthesis could argue, similarly, that insofar as race in the modern period is deeply tied up with benefit and disadvantage, with structural privilege and exploitation, it needs to be theorized as "material" also. The model adumbrated here could then provide the framework for an expanded historical materialism that incorporates the (social) materialities of gender and race in a way that Cohen's model, which restricts the material to the (asocial) forces of production, arguably cannot. The resolution of the significance of the "material" in "historical materialism" would have then proven to be a very material issue indeed.

NOTES

1. See the sources cited in chapter 1, note 1. Laycock (1980) is one of the few exceptions to the pattern of disregarding the issue of Marx's use of "material." I have greatly benefited from Laycock's review essay, and my argument is partially indebted to it.

After reading the original version of my paper, G. A. Cohen and Alastair Hannay kindly brought to my attention an article specifically on this topic by George L. Kline (1988). (An earlier version had appeared in *Annals of Scholarship* 3, no. 2 [1984]: 1–38.) Kline distinguishes seven meanings (two being subdivisions of the first) of "material" in Marx:

1. physical/spatiotemporal; 1a. technological,
2. biological,
3. sensuous/empirical,
4. economic,
5. acquisitive,
6. nonformal.

Since his major concern is to deny that Marx was an *ontological* materialist (the "Myth" of the title), he has comparatively little to say about *historical* materialism; however, he does remark parenthetically that Cohen is seriously in error to ignore sense 4, the economic (Kline 1988, 162–63; 178–79, n. 15).

My distinctions are not as finely drawn as Kline's (though he admits that some are of marginal significance), but for my purposes they don't have to be. In effect, I subsume senses 1, 1a, 2, and (perhaps) 3 under the natural, and I set this in primary contrast with sense 4, the economic, which, as Kline points out, is the "key sense" that "appears in all of Marx's writings, beginning with *The German Ideology*" (Kline 1988, 162). Thus I am in complete agreement with Kline on the seriousness of Cohen's denial of this sense of *materiell*. Unlike Kline, however, I think Marx was an ontological materialist (though I do not try to defend this here) and that his designation of both the natural and the economic as "material" was not just terminological sloppiness, as Kline implies, but theoretically motivated, even if the reasons for this choice of terms were not explicitly articulated: see the section of this chapter on the material versus the ideal, 46–49. Finally, Kline concludes that, while not sharing Cohen's "generally 'technological' interpretation of Marx," he recognizes it as both "plausible and as supported to some extent by the texts" (Kline 1988, 180, n. 27); however, for reasons that I explain in the following sections, I see the implications of Cohen's denial of the "material"/"economic" sense as more damaging for Cohen's interpretation.

2. In later work—for example, Cohen 1988 and some of the new essays in the expanded edition of the book (Cohen 2001)—Cohen would somewhat modify his original position. However, my critical focus in this chapter is on his original formulation.

3. In a paper authored with Will Kymlicka, Cohen offers the following amplification: "The relevant fundamental facts are asocial in that no information about social *structure* enters into their formulation." See Cohen and Kymlicka (1988, 171).

4. This must be distinguished from a tendency to develop *autonomously*: see Cohen and Kymlicka (1988, 177–81).

5. For some recent discussions on the subject, see Steger and Carver (1999).

6. See, for example, Robert C. Tucker's introduction to Tucker (1978).

7. See, for example, Engels' account in his popularizing pamphlet *Socialism: Utopian and Scientific* (CW 24, 281–325).

8. For a useful discussion of different senses (ontological, epistemological, explanatory) of "materialism" in Marx, see Collier (1979).

9. See note 1.

10. For example, Laycock (1980), and Miller (1984, ch. 5).

11. Cohen interprets this as a statement about (material) work-relations underlying (nonmaterial) *social* relations, and thus as further support for his interpretation (2001, 113). But the context is a critique of Proudhon's idealism, his "appeal[ing] from the state to civil society," his confusing of "ideas and things" (CW 38, 96). Thus I suggest it is better read as Marx's reiteration of the point that material (socioeconomic/basic) relations underlie *superstructural* (social, but noneconomic) relations—that is, juridical and political relations. Compare with *The German Ideology*, where Marx and Engels criticize Max Stirner for not seeing that "relations of right," "juridical relations," arise from "the material relations of people and the resulting antagonism of people against one another" (CW 5, 318, 343, 355): "The hitherto existing production relations of individuals are bound also to be expressed as political and legal relations" (CW 5, 363).

12. Scare quotes are obviously necessary, since the state, for example, is hardly "subjective" in the usual sense of the word, but rather the "head" of the body politic.

13. This was first pointed out to me by Danny Goldstick.

14. Note that it's not the social *simpliciter*, but the socioeconomic: there's less chance of this conflation's occurring with superstructural phenomena, which are more saliently human creations; and Marx's examples (such as those cited by Cohen [2001, ch. 4]) are standardly economic ones.

15. For Cohen's response to some of the critiques of his position, see his later collection of essays, Cohen (1988).

16. Cohen does, of course, have other textual grounds for claiming that Marx assigned explanatory primacy to the forces of production (see Cohen 2001, ch. 6); but as indicated at the start, I have focused in this chapter on the terminological question. See Miller (1984) and Gottlieb (1985) for discussions of the kinds of passages Cohen cites as further evidence for his view.

3

Marxism, "Ideology," and Moral Objectivism

We turn now to the vexed question of morality and Marxism. For most of the twentieth century, it was taken for granted that the theoretical commitments of historical materialism are difficult, if not impossible, to reconcile with any kind of objectivism in ethics, whether realist or constructivist.[1] In the heyday of metaethical noncognitivism, this would hardly have singled Marxism out from other social theories. But with the restoration of respectability to the notion of realism in ethics,[2] and with the exponential growth of Anglo-American philosophical interest in Marxist theory in the 1970s through the 1980s, an increasing number of attempts were made to represent Marx as either a moral realist or a cognitivist of the constructivist Rawlsian/Habermasian kind.[3] Such an enterprise faces numerous hurdles, though none of them is necessarily insuperable: Marx's apparently negative attitude toward morality in general, as revealed in numerous passages in his writings; the destructive implications for the sphere of personal responsibility of what is sometimes construed as an inevitabilist theory of history; the putative dependency on the mode of production of the validity of juridical ethical concepts in particular, such as justice; and the presumably anti-objectivist conception of morality implied by Marx's categorizing it as "ideology."

For this chapter, I am concerned with the last of these hurdles, though what I have to say will also have implications for some of the other issues. I am myself sympathetic to an objectivist view of Marx, and I want to show that what is usually taken to be a major obstacle to this interpretation is less formidable than it has traditionally seemed. As argued in my first chapter, I believe that an apparently central concept in historical materialism, "ideology," has been widely misconceived for decades in the secondary literature. My claim is that my new reading does the following:

1. It significantly weakens the case for the anti-objectivist (noncognitivist, error theorist, relativist) or metaethically inconsistent interpretations of Marx, insofar as such a case rests crucially or partially *on* the standard view of "ideology."
2. It clears a conceptual space for the objectivist interpretation in a more convincing way than its defenders have usually done.
3. It constitutes additional support for the long-standing alternative theory of pro-objectivists that the real target of Marx's hostility was "moralism" rather than "morality." As such, it helps to bolster the argument for viewing Marx as a moral objectivist whose real criticism of morality was not that it was cognitively void, but that it was causally secondary.

OVERVIEW

I begin by surveying fifteen writers in whose conclusions about Marx's views on ethics the concept of "ideology" plays a role, whether central or supporting.[4] Their respective conclusions—spanning three and a half decades—are, I suggest, jointly exhaustive of the spectrum of major possible positions on this question.

The standard argument they employ as anti-objectivists or must grapple with as pro-objectivists can be simply expressed as follows:

P1: For Marx, all morality is "ideology."
P2: "Ideology" is a pejorative term in historical materialism, denoting illusory ideas of some kind.
Therefore: Morality for Marx is itself illusory and cannot have the kind of cognitivist bite that moral objectivists, whether realist or constructivist, want to attribute to it.

Anti-objectivists, pro-objectivists, and those who see Marx as simply inconsistent have generally interpreted P1 as a metaethical statement about the metaphysics of value and, correspondingly, about the truth/falsity of moral propositions.[5] A mapping of positions can then be produced according to writers' responses to this argument and the different readings they give of the specific kind of illusion that ideology involves (see figure 3.1).[6]

Marx as anti-objectivist: Marx has been categorized variously as a noncognitivist (moral judgments are not actually propositional, and so are neither true nor false); a sort of "error theorist" (moral judgments are all false); or a global ethical relativist (moral judgments are true or false relative to class or the mode of production). This anti-objectivism has been seen as an important insight into the nature of morality by his defenders and as a major deficiency of the theory by his critics. Other commentators have put forward a compromise position that could be termed a partial (or partitioned?) relativism, the claim being that for Marx some ethical values are historically relative while others are not.

Marx as objectivist: Marx has been categorized by some writers as a global objectivist—whether moral realist or ideal constructivist; or, by implication, he has been categorized as a partial objectivist for some ethical values and as a relativist for others. (For both global and partial objectivists, it is obviously necessary to challenge either P1 or P2.)

Marx as confused: Finally, some philosophers have argued that no consistent metaethical position can be extracted from Marx's writings and that his theses on the illusory character of morality simply *contradict* his statements (or his implicit views) elsewhere.

Having mapped out the basic positions, let us now examine the individual writers' arguments in detail.

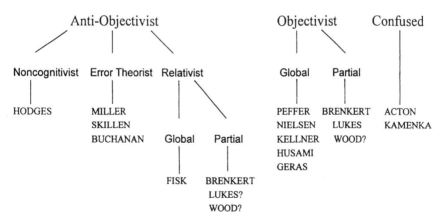

Figure 3.1.   Different interpretations of Marx's metaphysics of value

THREE MAIN POSITIONS ON
MARX'S METAPHYSICS OF VALUE

Marx as Anti-Objectivist

An article from four decades ago by Donald Hodges (1962) states a classic noncognitivist interpretation. Criticizing what he sees as the foolish attempt of some Marxist philosophers "to resurrect the dead dog of normative ethics," Hodges argues for a "scientific" approach to ethics that would abandon "the conviction that normative judgments can be true or false" and recognize instead "the ideological character of ethical theory"—which implies that "[s]trictly speaking, normative judgments are neither consistent nor inconsistent since, not being propositions, they are neither true nor false" (5, 1, 2, 4). Hodges cites as his main textual authority Marx's *Critique of the Gotha Program*, and he argues that "[h]aving cleaned the Augean stables of moral and ideological rubbish, Marx left open only one refuge for ethics—a sanctuary in the temple of historical materialism," said sanctuary being no more than the object of sociological study (6 7).

A more recent variation on this theme is offered by Richard Miller (1984), who clearly sees Marx as an error theorist. (Miller uses the *term* "noncognitivism," but his Marx regards moral judgments as false rather than nonpropositional.) His basic argument does not rest on the ideological status of morality, but on the failure of class society to meet (what Miller regards as) the necessary prerequisites for morality to be applicable: equality of concern for others, generality of norms, and universal rationality (ch. 1). Nevertheless, he does cite as supporting evidence Marx's attacks on morality as "ideology": "Marx sometimes summarizes his rejection of morality in the statement that morality . . . is ideological. An ideology, for Marx, is a system of beliefs and attitudes that distort reality. . . . Ideology is *false* consciousness" (45–46, 15, 47–48).

Similarly, Anthony Skillen (1978) denies that Marx argued for a "socialist morality": "For him, morality was an historically fairly specific ideological institution, functioning to mystify and discipline people in accordance with the oppressive needs of class society. . . . Marx regarded morality as he regarded religion, as inherently ideological, mystifying and repressive" (130–33).

A globally relativist interpretation (rather than noncognitivist) is defended by Milton Fisk (1980). Fisk argues for "a relativist ethics," which "means that the ethics valid for one class or group need not be valid for some other class or group" (xv). Using the term "a sum group" to stand for a complex of different interrelated groups in which some dominate others (e.g., classes, races), he suggests that a Marxist understanding of society leads to the conclusion that:

> The ethics of a sum group is . . . part of the "ideology" of the sum group. An ideology is a set of claims that serve more or less well to perpetuate the domination within a sum group. Those claims are in general neither valid nor true whether considered relative to that sum group or as absolute claims. (42, 45)

However Fisk does not see this relativism as problematic; rather, he urges that we simply recognize this implication of Marxist theory and thus identify with the true interests of our own group.

For all four of these writers, then, Marx's views represent a theoretically laudable *demystification* of morality. Allen Buchanan (1982), on the other hand, is critical of what he sees as Marx's anti-objectivism. His fundamental line of argument is that Marx thought justice would not be applicable to communist society, since the circumstances of justice (moderate scarcity, egoism, class conflict) would be transcended. But he also offers Marx's views on ideology as supplementary evidence for his analysis: "Marx's claim is that talk about rights and justice is obsolete ideological nonsense" (1982, 82; see also Buchanan 1986, 129, 140–41). And Buchanan goes on to critique Marx for this perceived deficiency of his theory.

George Brenkert (1983) also sees amoralism as a problem, and his position is a compromise that tries to salvage some notion of moral objectivity for Marx: a *partial*, but not global, relativism, that distinguishes the metaphysical standing of different ethical concepts. Brenkert accepts the standard definition of "ideology" as "false consciousness," and he uses this as a central underpinning of his argument. He claims that Marx's views on ideology "effectively prohibit an appeal to justice which is transcultural and transhistorical" (27, 150). Thus a "relativist interpretation" of Marx on justice is correct, though he sees this as a "Pickwickian" relativism, rather than the traditional kind, since societies at an objectively similar stage must have the same principles of justice (Brenkert 1980, 89–93). But there is, he claims, "an underlying asymmetry between freedom and justice in Marx's views." So "freedom can be used, whereas justice cannot be used, for transcultural appraisals," since freedom is "not simply ideological" (Brenkert 1980, 93, 102, 101). If Marx is a partial relativist, then he is also a partial objectivist.

Steven Lukes (1985) as well makes extensive use of the conventional understanding of "ideology" in his well-known critique of Marxism's normative deficiencies. He argues that the Marxist view of morality is paradoxical and apparently contradictory, since Marx seems to not only criticize morality but make moral judgments himself. He says that Marxism claims that "morality is a form of ideology, and thus social in origin, illusory in content, and serving class interests" and that "there are no objective truths" of morality (3). Similarly, he cites Engels' claim that justice is "but the ideologised, glorified expression of the existing economic relations" and is like "social phlogiston" (13). Overall, Lukes concludes: "Objectivity, in the sense of perspective-neutrality, was for [Marx], an illusion, indeed an ideological illusion" (59). His proffered solution to the paradox is something like Brenkert's, involving the drawing of a distinction between the morality of *Recht* (justice, rights, the deontological), which was "inherently ideological" for Marx, and the morality of *emancipation* (ch. 3). Unlike Brenkert, however, Lukes does not formally designate this as "relativism," so it is uncertain whether his interpretation of Marx should be classified as partial relativism or partial noncognitivism.

I have also had difficulty in categorizing Allen Wood's work, and I am unsure whether this reflects the challenge Marx's views pose for conventional metaethical distinctions or the possible eccentricity of Wood's own understanding of his position. In his seminal essay on Marx and justice (1980a), Wood's essential focus is on what he sees as the nonjuridical character of Marx's condemnation of capitalism—a necessary consequence (for Wood) of Marx's mode-of-production view of concepts such as justice. But he also says that "Marx in fact regarded all attempts to base revolutionary practice on juridical notions as an 'ideological shuffle' " and that Marxists who appeal to a concept of justice "are at best only translating Marx's critique of capitalism . . . into what Marx himself would have consistently regarded as a false, ideological, or 'mystified' form" (30–31). "Ideology" thus plays an important, if subsidiary, role in his argument, which becomes more salient in his later reply (1980b) to Ziyad Husami's criticisms of his article. Here Wood repeatedly cites Marx's "ideological" conception of justice and morality as textual evidence that cannot, he thinks, be accounted for by Husami's alternative realist interpretation (111, 112–13, 119, 130, 131, 132).[7] He differentiates what he sees as moral and nonmoral goods (such as self-actualization, community, and freedom), and he represents Marx as critiquing capitalism in terms of the latter rather than the former (119–26). For him it remains true, then, that Marx wanted people "to disenthrall themselves of ideological illusions"; and to attempt to create a "proletarian morality" would be to remain prisoners of this "ideological shuffle" (Wood 1985, 140).

This position is clearly anti-objectivist, but of what kind? The natural inference is that it is a kind of relativism, whether global or partial. But the problem is that Wood expressly denies that it is a relativist position: On his understanding of the term, relativism implies that there is no correct normative judgment when fundamental moral disputes between cultures and epochs are involved; however, Marxism *does* have an objective criterion (playing a certain kind of role in the mode of production) for what constitute just practices.[8]

My suggestion is that Wood, *malgré lui*, should be classified with Brenkert as a relativist, where it is stipulated (as with Brenkert) that this relativism is of a peculiar kind: it is differentiated from ordinary relativism in that moral codes are not viewed as merely conventional intersubjective creations (i.e., on a cognitive par with one another); rather, such moral codes are ranked by their "objective" appropriateness to economic systems. Following other critics, I would also suggest either that Wood's distinction between moral and nonmoral goods is questionable or that at the very least the demarcation cannot be drawn where Wood wishes; therefore, to claim that Marx condemned capitalism in the name of freedom *is* effectively to endorse the position I have characterized as partial relativism/partial objectivism.

Marx as Objectivist

We turn now to (globally) objectivist interpretations, whether realist or constructivist. For the writers in this category, it is obviously crucial to challenge the argument outlined at the beginning of the chapter.

Rodney Peffer's (1990) major attempt to reconstruct Marx's ethic argues for a cognitivist and objectivist analysis of Marx's moral views, by which he means "a theory or model of moral objectivity based on *intersubjective agreement*"—that is, a modified Rawlsian theory, informed by the work of Left thinkers such as Habermas (285). Denying Marx was a normative relativist, Peffer acknowledges that: "On most interpretations of the Marxist concept of ideology, to say of some X that it is ideological is to impute to it the characteristic of being somehow illegitimate and constitutes at least a prima facie case for the conclusion that it cannot be part of a true theory or of a correct worldview" (236). But he has a solution to "this paradox of Marxist ethics," which is to challenge the premise identified as P2. Peffer distinguishes what he sees as a global (neutral) and a nonglobal (pejorative) conception of ideology, and he then argues that morality is *not* ideology in the nonglobal pejorative sense.[9]

Kai Nielsen (1989) also defends an objectivist interpretation of Marx (ch. 1). While conceding the "tension and ambivalence" in Marx's view of morality, he claims to be able to show that "in reality there is no conflict here" and that Marx's views on morality as ideology should be seen as a thesis about the "sociology of morals," rather than any kind of deep metaethical epistemological or metaphysical claim.

The problem in summarizing this prolific philosopher's views is that, as he admits in his introduction, he seems to say different things at different times. But I think two main kinds of solution are presented. The first solution (Nielsen 1) is to grant the standard pejorative conception of ideology and then challenge P1, denying that all morality is ideological (5, 34–36, 53–54, 127–28, 146–50). The second solution (Nielsen 2) is to challenge P2, to contest the standard pejorative conception of ideology, arguing that, while ideology may be "distortion-prone," it is not necessarily conceptually distortional (5, ch. 5, 122–24, 257–60). In this way—or in these two ways—it becomes possible to rescue Marx from noncognitivism and relativism.

A similar, if less detailed, move is made by Douglas Kellner (1981). As other authors have done, Douglas Kellner finds there to be "two conflicting conceptions of Marxism and morality," one that tends "to dismiss morality as mere ideology . . . . morality is conceived of as part of the ideological superstructure: false consciousness, containing lies and illusions," while the other tradition "openly affirms that Marxism contains a moral critique of capitalism" (93–94). As with Nielsen 1, Kellner claims to reconcile the two by challenging P1, arguing that morality is only "ideology" if certain conditions are met; therefore, it is possible to envisage a "non-ideological human morality" (114–17).

Another approach is taken by Ziyad Husami (1980) in his well-known critique of Allen Wood's article. Husami's main argument is that Wood's characterization of juridical concepts as "superstructural," and therefore relative to particular modes of production, misses an essential point of Marx's "sociology of morals," the multicausal determination of the superstructure: "According to Marx, elements of the superstructure . . . have *two* levels of determination. One is the mode of production (or type of society) in which they occur; the other is the class interests which they represent. Moral outlooks change as modes of production change" (47–56). Thus the mere fact that a given concept is superstructural does not necessarily mean that it is part of the justificatory (and mystificatory) outlook of a ruling class, since it could also represent the outlook of a new emerging class; and for the working class, this outlook need not be illusory. However the retort could obviously be made that such an outlook and morality are still, by Marx's own words, condemned as necessarily "ideological." But here Husami makes another revisionary move, challenging P2: "If the spokesmen for a class justify their views by maintaining that their moral outlook is independent of historical development or of class interests, then they maintain false beliefs about their morality. Such false beliefs are called 'ideological illusions.' The moral outlook itself, on that count alone, is not considered illusory" (47–48). So we are being offered alternative conceptualizations of not only the determination of the superstructure but also of "ideology." As I will later explain in greater detail, I think Husami is in fact on the right track here. But unfortunately he weakens his case against Wood by not providing the necessary substantiation of his revisionary view of "ideology."

We move on now to Norman Geras' (1989) magisterial review article of the secondary literature on Marx and justice. Geras cites the issue of "ideology" as one of the standard obstacles in the way of believing that Marx endorsed a normative critique of capitalism:

> Moral norms and notions come within the compass of Marx's theory of ideology. Not only, therefore, do ideas about justice, but so does morality more generally, belong to the superstructure of any social formation. . . . It is not consistent with his views on ideology that Marx should have found capitalist society to be unjust by reference to historically quite general norms of justice. (217)

(Like Kellner, but unlike Nielsen and Husami, Geras seems to assume that belonging to the superstructure necessarily entails cognitive deficiency; the conceptual ambiguity in this notion is itself partially responsible for the problems in clarifying the debate.) After summarizing the positions of the anti-moralist and the pro-moralist camps, Geras himself ultimately endorses the latter position, albeit with criticisms of particular details. But the interesting thing is that, though he addresses various claims made by the anti-moralist camp, the point on "ideology" is one that remains unanswered. It is perhaps one of the clearest indications of the central nature of this sticking point: that what is widely regarded as a classic summary of the secondary literature could not find an answer to it.

Finally, Brenkert, Lukes, and Wood should also be mentioned under this heading, since, as noted earlier, their interpretation makes Marx only a *partial* relativist (or noncognitivist/error theorist); so that with respect to other than juridical values, such as freedom, Marx was presumably an objectivist (though as pointed out, Wood sees this as a nonmoral value and so would contest my categorization). Insofar as "ideology" played a role in their denial of the possibility of objectivist evaluations of "justice," the implication would be that these other values are not so affected.

Marx as Confused

In conclusion, there is the third category. These two critics are less charitable in their assessments: rather than seeing "tensions," "conflicts," or "paradoxes," they see simple confusions.

In his polemic *The Illusion of the Epoch*, H. B. Acton (1955) regards Marx's judgments on morality as an unresolvable problem in the theory. Acton accepts the standard view of ideologies as "systems of misleading or illusory ideas," "forms of 'false consciousness'" (127, 130). Since "morality" too is an "ideology," it likewise is "false consciousness," involving "valuations" that are "superstructural forms of 'false consciousness' which Marxist social science enables us to 'see through'" (130, 191). But Acton denies that Marx should be seen as a relativist, since Marxist ethics also makes "a claim to absoluteness" (193–95). Thus Acton suggests that the theory contradicts itself, since it simultaneously claims that morality is class-relative and that moral progress is possible: "Marxists inconsistently hold both that morality is mere ideology and that it is capable of real improvement" (192–201).

Another hostile account is offered by Eugene Kamenka (1969). Kamenka suggests that Marx really had no coherent position on ethical questions and that, in his writings, one finds a conflation of different views. The major conflicting strands are, on the one hand, the "critique of objectivism in ethics," a "crude relativism"; and, on the other hand, the commitment to an "eternal, immutable, non-relativistic standard by which historical moralities are judged," a contradiction that Kamenka sees as particularly flagrant in Engels' writings but which he argues Marx would have to be committed to also (4–6). His reading of "ideology" plays a role in this argument. Thus, commenting on *Anti-Dühring*, he observes: "But how a series of *relativistic* moralities (expressions of interests, not truths) can suddenly become *truths* . . . is not shown. . . . Surely the whole point of Engels's preceding paragraph had been that each morality is *not* a branch of knowledge, but an ideology" (46). And elsewhere he refers to "the Marxist exposure of all normative morality as mere ideology" (61).

"IDEOLOGY" AND OBJECTIVISM: STANDARD SOLUTIONS

I now want to examine the various argumentative strategies deployed to deal with the problem of "ideology" by those writers who do defend a partially or globally objectivist conception of Marx's moral views. I suggest that these strategies fall straightforwardly into three basic categories (two ways of challenging P1 and one way of challenging P2): strategy S1, the claim that Marx's views on "ideology" apply only to some kinds of moral *concepts* and not to others; strategy S2, the claim that Marx's views on "ideology" apply only to the morality of some *classes* and not to others; strategy S3, the claim that the standard interpretation of "ideology" is mistaken, so that being ideological does not necessarily entail metaethical anti-objectivism. Obviously, each of these strategies faces particular problems of its own. Although my own position is that S3 is correct (to be argued later), the actual arguments utilized by the authors under consideration are fundamentally flawed by their failure to adduce the appropriate supporting textual evidence.

Strategy S1

Strategy S1 is that adopted by Brenkert and Lukes. The basic problem with it, as critics have pointed out, is that since Marx and Engels explicitly characterize *all* morality as "ideological," there seems no good reason to think that some moral concepts are exempt. It is true that in the case of juridical concepts, such as justice and rights, the anti-moralist conclusion is, in a sense, overdetermined: not only are they ideological, but they also form part of the juridical superstructure of capitalism, thereby being arguably mode-of-production relative. Moreover, Marx does expressly polemicize against their usage in a way that he does not do for freedom. Nevertheless, the fact remains that "freedom/emancipation" is also an ideological concept, and some explanation is needed as to why being ideological is not in this case a handicap (that explanation, however, is not forthcoming from either of these two authors).

Lukes gives no answer at all to this question, a silence that I think must be attributed to the fact that his generally critical book is an explicit attempt to rescue Marx as far as possible from his inconsistencies; thus, if he were forced to confront this final inconsistency, he would probably just opt, resignedly, for the third position (Marx as confused). Brenkert (1980) does consider the objection "that Marx's views on ideology preclude *any* such moral condemnation of private property—whether stated in terms of freedom *or* justice" (86). His response draws an interesting distinction between the relationship of distributive principles to the mode of production and the link between the forces of production and the expansion of human capabilities—which means, he thinks, that freedom possesses an "ontological dimension" not shared by justice (93–102). But whatever the merits of this reply as a Marxist metaphysics of values, it does *not*, I suggest, succeed in sidestepping the simple challenge delineated earlier; namely, that whatever their ontology, *all* moral values are apparently deemed "ideological" by Marx. As Norman Geras says, simply and surely correctly: "To the extent that Marx does postulate an ideological limitation or relativity of values, his theory of ideology is perfectly general in its reach, encompassing every sort of normative concept and not only ideas about justice" (1989, 232).

Strategy S2

Strategy S2 is employed by Nielsen 1 and Kellner. Nielsen 1 denies that all morality is ideological, where for him the dividing line is not, as in the previous strategy, with the kind of moral concepts, but with their class content.[10] As with S1, this approach immediately faces the prima facie problem that it runs directly counter to what Marx and Engels say. Moreover, where S1 at least has some independent textual evidence for positing a distinction between the juridical and the nonjuridical, S2 is, for the critic, likely to appear as question begging in its salvaging of *proletarian* morality from the unhappy realm of the ideological.

Consider, for example, this statement: "A Marxist sociology of morals shows that moral beliefs have a tendency to function ideologically. But it is not committed to the thesis—a strange kind of *a priori* thesis, probably rooted in some questionable moral epistemology—that they all do or all must" (Nielsen 1989, 31). What is peculiar about the wording is that it makes it seem as if the necessarily ideological view of morality is some bizarre idea being foisted on harassed Marxists by their intellectual adversaries. But in fact, as Nielsen admits on the previous page, it is *Marx himself* who says that all morality is ideology, so this allegedly "*a priori* thesis" is his own. Nielsen 1 then goes on to conclude: "To accept such an *a priori* thesis about all moral beliefs being necesarily ideological and distorting of our understanding of ourselves would render all [critical remarks Marxists direct against capitalism] ideological and unjustifiable" (35). So a charitable reading requires that we reject it. But since the very point at issue in the debate with critics of Marx is whether such remarks *are* justifiable, simply to assume that they must be is to argue in a perfect circle:

A1: Ideology is illusion.
A2: If Marx thought all morality was ideology, his own normative critique of capitalism would be unjustifiable.
A3: His normative critique of capitalism must be justifiable.
Conclusion: Marx did not think all morality was ideology.

The unsatisfactoriness of this argument should be obvious. (A similarly flawed defense of Engels on morality is given later [77–78].)

Comparable problems attend Douglas Kellner's (1981) defense of his claim. Kellner begins by commenting on the "notoriously imprecise and ambiguous" theory of ideology in *The German Ideology*, and then he goes on to outline a set of criteria by which morality would or would not count as ideological (114–17). But the problem is that there is a severe dearth of textual reference to back up an essentially stipulative usage, which is in any case contradicted by Marx's generic statement about all morality. Unless one assumes that Marx and Engels' putative imprecision gives one leeway to construct any theory of ideology one likes, then, such a "solution" must clearly be regarded as inadequate.

Strategy S3

We move on to strategy S3, which is utilized by Nielsen 2, Peffer, and Husami. The claim here is not that some morality is not ideology; rather, it is that being ideological is *not* necessarily cognitively undermining, because of an alternative conceptualization of "ideology."

The problem S3 faces is in specifying the nature of the reconceptualization involved, defending it, and then showing how it is theoretically pertinent. I think that as a strategy, S3 can be carried out in three main possible ways. In decreasing order of defensibility, they are:

1. an alternative interpretation of the *actual textual evidence*—namely, reconceiving what Marx actually said about "ideology";
2. a reconstruction from the general theoretical commitments of historical materialism of what Marx's concept of ideology *should have been*;
3. a *stipulative* definition of a useful conception of ideology.

Now all three of these are perfectly legitimate enterprises, but it should be obvious that they are *different* enterprises that cannot be simply assimilated to one another. In particular, only the first two can go on to claim Marx's authority (more or less strongly) for this new conception. Since the stumbling block for pro-objectivists is the necessarily illusory character of "ideology" for *Marx*, the desired solution is a convincing reconceptualization that either *(a)* justifies the exclusion of this feature in a noncircular way on independent textual grounds, or *(b)* shows why the "illusion" is not destructive for the objective truth-content of morality. One cannot just *stipulate* a definition that happens to be convenient for one's purposes, and then represent it as Marxist—which, in my opinion, is what Nielsen 2 and Peffer come very close to doing.

Let us begin with Nielsen 2. In an essay specifically titled "A Marxist Conception of Ideology," he begins by discussing the "essentially contested" nature of the concept of ideology, suggesting that within Marx's own usage there is no *one* concept. His own aim, then, is to explicate "a tolerably Marxist conception of ideology," but he will "not be concerned with the history of this 'concept' or with textual exegesis of Marx or the Marxist tradition. . . . I shall be far less concerned with the legitimacy of its Marxist pedigree than with its adequacy as a conceptualization of ideology" (Nielsen 1989, 98). So Nielsen 2 is clearly not carrying out the first enterprise, as demarcated earlier; in fact, given his proclaimed indifference to textual exegesis and Marxist pedigree, it seems that he is carrying out the third. But, then, what authorizes the designation of this concept as a *Marxist* one?[11] And what are the criteria of "adequacy" if there is to be no control by the text, either in the form of Marx's actual pronouncements about "ideology" or in terms of rigorous fidelity to a conceptual framework? In his subsequent eleven-point list of hallmarks of the ideological, he makes no mention of the criterion conventionally *most* strongly associated with Marx's concept of ideology: that it is necessarily illusory. But it is obviously open for the critic to object that this exclusion is simply question begging and that the "adequacy" of the conceptualization has been circularly determined by what is necessary to avoid the charge of self-refutation—not by what Marx actually says, nor by what it can plausibly be reconstructed that he would have said.[12]

A similar criticism can be made of Rodney Peffer (1990). As explained earlier, Peffer distinguishes between a neutral global and a pejorative nonglobal conception of ideology, claiming that the nominal form ("ideology") subsumes both whereas the adjectival form ("ideological") always refers specifically to the latter. Simply on prima facie grounds, this claim would seem to be somewhat implausible, involving Marx in a mysteriously perverse semantics—and, in fact, it is quite false. (Astonishingly, Peffer gives not a single textual reference to back up this statement.) Throughout *The German Ideology*, as I demonstrated in chapter 1, Marx and Engels use both "ideology" and "ideological" in a pejorative way; and in the single passage most frequently cited as evidence by commentators who have argued for a *neutral* sense of "ideology" (the famous synopsis of historical materialism sketched by Marx in the 1859 preface to *A Contribution to the Critique of Political Economy*), it is precisely the *adjectival* form (putatively pejorative and nonglobal, according to Peffer) that is employed. But the substantival/adjectival issue aside, the remarkable thing about Peffer's proposed reconceptualization is, as mentioned, that he offers no textual evidence for it.[13] Like Nielsen 2, Peffer simply sets out certain criteria for a concept of ideology, and then he argues for the existence of a neutral global sense, which only has a subset of the characteristics on the list and which is not definitionally illusory. And like Nielsen 2's solution, his account is vulnerable to the obvious criticism that a convenient stipulative definition is being passed off as Marx's own without showing how it can be reconciled with the standard view of what Marx actually said.

Finally, there is Ziyad Husami (1980). As noted earlier, of the various points he makes in his critique of Allen Wood, two are of particular relevance for our discussion: the multicausal, rather than monocausal, conception of the superstructure; and the alternative view of "ideology" as meaning no more than unawareness of the role of material determination. What is missing is the textual evidence to back up this revisionary reading, a lacuna that left him vulnerable to the criticisms in Wood's subsequent reply. I try to provide this evidence and, correspondingly, a more detailed and defensible statement of this approach.

In concluding, I should repeat the point mentioned earlier: that there are many other philosophers who have defended an objectivist view of Marx's metaethics while simply *bypassing* the question of how this position is to be reconciled with his apparent views on "ideology." Regardless of my criticisms of the aforementioned theorists and the inadequacy of their attempted solutions, they must certainly be given credit for having acknowledged that there is a problem and for having tried to solve it.

"IDEOLOGY" AND OBJECTIVISM:
MY RECOMMENDED SOLUTION

I will now offer my own solution to the problem of reconciling a morally objectivist interpretation of Marx and Engels with what they say about "ideology." This position is a variant of the S3 strategy: to concede that all morality was indeed "ideological" for Marx and Engels (so P1 is true) while denying any anti-objectivist implications on the grounds of an alternative conceptualization of what "ideology" means.

The conventional view is that "ideology" is a pejorative term referring *generally* to illusory partisan class ideas. My claim, by contrast, as argued in the opening chapter, is that "ideology" has two senses, *neither* of which coincides with the standard interpretation. One sense has a nonideational reference, denoting the "ideal" superstructure as a whole—that is, "ideal" as opposed to the "material," economic base (see chapter 2). The other sense is ideational, as well as pejorative, but it refers not to illusory ideas in general, but to "idealist" views in particular—that is, "idealist," not in the ontological sense, but in the sociological, thereby indicating beliefs and theories about society that ignore or downplay the role of "material," economic factors. Thus, harking back to the set of distinctions drawn in the previous section, this reconceptualization is not a *stipulative* definition of "ideology" (the third defense), nor is it a variant of the second defense, a theoretical reconstruction of how Marx *should* have defined "ideology," with all the attendant dangers of irrelevance, question begging, or fuzzy criteria for assessment, that both of these enterprises face. Instead, it is the first defense, a reinterpretation of the *actual* textual evidence. So I am not vulnerable to the same kinds of criticisms I leveled against Nielsen 2 and Peffer since, one, my claim is that I am offering the correct interpretation of what Marx and Engels actually said about "ideology," and, two, I have, unlike both of these writers, an extensive textual defense to back it up.[14]

What, then, according to me, *are* the implications of morality's being "ideological" for Marx and Engels? In the "superstructural" sense, morality's being "ideological" just means that it is part of the superstructure. As I have argued elsewhere (Mills 1989), in agreement with Husami, this position in itself would *not* make morality automatically nonobjective, since the superstructure should be thought of as reflecting multiple causation and since only some of its ideational contents will be nonveridical. The ideational sense is admittedly pejorative (so P2 is true also), but it refers narrowly to a specific kind of illusion, "superstructuralism," which, where morality is concerned, reflects not on its normative content but on its causal efficacy. Thus the indictment is targeted at a level other than that of the moral judgments themselves. "Ideology," in the ideational sense, is a pejorative metatheoretical term for theories and beliefs that aggrandize the causal power of the superstructure—theories and beliefs that imply that global social determination takes place exclusively or primarily by "ideal," superstructural causes. Accordingly, though P1—that all morality is ideology—is a metaethical statement, it is not one in the sense conventionally presupposed by rival sides in the debate. It refers not to the truth-values of ethical propositions, but rather to their social significance. It locates morality as a social phenomenon that, for Marx and Engels, *(a)* characteristically misunderstands its own genesis, *(b)* is unrealistic about its psychological capacity to motivate, *(c)* correspondingly inflates its causal significance, and thus *(d)* systematically overestimates its actual ability to transform the socioeconomic order. *In categorizing morality as "ideology," Marx and Engels are treating it as being a descriptive theory*—or at least as having an auxiliary set of implicit empirical assumptions—*about how society works and how it can be changed.*

Since this analysis will be an unfamiliar one, let me go into some more detail. My suggestion is basically that Marx and Engels are assuming that in making a moral judgment—let us call it *M* (e.g., "Capitalism is just/unjust")—moralists, whether conservative or revolutionary, are characteristically committed to a set of metaethical propositions *(M')* about *M* and its relation to society, having to do not with its truth-value but its origins and the causal efficaciousness of its pronouncement. These metatheoretical assumptions are all predicated on a *superstructuralist* view of social causality, and as such they are all "ideological" and false. But the truth/falsity of *M'* is obviously *separable* from the truth/falsity of *M*. So one can consistently endorse ethical objectivism (the objective truth/falsity of *M*) while denying the truth of *M'*. The "illusion" of morality (the "illusion" referred to in P2), then, consists in these metatheoretical and causal claims, rather than the nonobjectivity of "Capitalism is just/unjust"—an illusion not about the truth-values of ethical judgments, but about their causal etiology and prescriptive efficaciousness. It is preeminently this point that the "ideological" characterization is meant to convey. If I am right, the debate in the secondary literature has been significantly off course from the beginning because of an initially mistaken conception of what "ideology" meant for Marx and Engels.

Marx and Engels' hostility to "morality," then, and their categorizing of it as "ideology," are in my opinion simply part of their *general* opposition to the idealistic sociological assumptions of the most prominent reformers of the time (e.g., their rivals, the utopian socialists) that voluntarized social causality, ignored or minimized natural and class constraints, and unrealistically expanded the room for prescriptive transformation. As sociological ("historical") materialists, they believed that techno-economic causes were the most important shapers of macropatterns of sociohistorical development. Now if you have such a theory of the dynamics of the social system, it means your view of social possibilities, and the means to their realization, is obviously going to be different from not only the view of those who *deny* any asymmetry (repudiating *both* materialism and idealism while asserting instead a rough parity of causal efficaciousness) but also, even more dramatically divergent, from those who view the asymmetry tilted in the *opposite*, "superstructural/ideal" direction. In the language of analytic philosophy: the conjunction of necessary conditions that jointly suffice to bring about major social change will, for Marx and Engels, be radically differentiated internally according to the degree of difficulty in manipulating its components; and at the most refractory end of this spectrum will be conditions involving the overcoming of natural necessity and oppressive economic structures (the "material"). These conditions should therefore be our primary object of focus. But sociological idealists, proponents of the primacy of *superstructural* causation, deny this position. They "turn things upside-down" by "inverting" the actual (materialist) societal causal hierarchy; that is, they ignore altogether (or at least downplay) the role of "material" techno-economic factors in social change and thereby grossly exaggerate the causal efficaciousness of superstructural changes that are unaccompanied by base/economic ones.

The point is, then, that even with the best will in the world, one will not be able to bring about radical social change that is morally desirable in the absence of the appropriate "material" prerequisites. On the macrolevel, social transformation requires technological prerequisites and appropriate class agents; on the microlevel, people's psychologies are shaped by class society. The human "will" is not floating freely, easily able to assume any desired direction in response to a moral categorical imperative; rather, it is oriented in characteristic directions, angled toward the magnetic pole of material structures. But traditional morality is a set of action-guiding prescriptions about duty, virtue, and justice: what kinds of deeds we should perform, what kinds of characters we should try to develop, what kinds of societies we should strive to build. Since "ought implies can," these prescriptions imply a certain estimate of individual and social possibilities. Absent the appropriate enabling material conditions, however, such exhortations are, in Marx and Engels' opinion, likely to be futile. Insofar as morality as a whole tends to neglect these conditions, it could be regarded as "idealistic" and as assuming an "idealistic" conception of the will. Instead, one needs to focus one's theoretical attention on the material conditions that will be necessary for the complex conjunct of variables to become jointly sufficient for change, thereby making possible the "can" that gives point to uttering the "ought."

MORALITY AND IDEALISM

Let me now try to demonstrate the textual support for the causal reading by showing both the ubiquity of causal claims in Marx and Engels' discussions of morality, and the connection between these claims and assertions about idealism/ideology.

To summarize Marx and Engels' *denials* of typical M' claims, I suggest that the evidence can be perspicuously organized under the following categories:

1. Morality is socially determined, linked to particular classes, not something that descends from a Platonic heaven.
2. Moral dilemmas and oppositions are historically bound and contingent, not eternal and necessary.
3. Moral preaching cannot overcome technological underdevelopment.
4. Moral preaching cannot overcome an unfavorable balance of class forces, and people cannot voluntaristically transform their characters.
5. In the absence of these "material" prerequisites, morality is in general "impotent" to effect radical social change.

My claim will be that Marx and Engels' judgment that morality is "ideology" and "ideological" (idealism/idealistic) is intended to point out moralists' characteristic adherence to what Marx and Engels, as materialists, are denying.

Morality Is Socially Determined

The first appearance of the judgment that morality is "ideology" is in *The German Ideology:*

> Morality, religion, metaphysics, and all the rest of ideology as well as the forms of consciousness corresponding to these, thus no longer retain the semblance of independence. They have no history, no development; but men, developing their material production and their material intercourse, alter, along with this their actual world, also their thinking and the products of their thinking. It is not consciousness that determines life, but life that determines consciousness. (CW 5, 36–37)

"Ideology" here, I suggest, should be taken in the "superstructural" sense. So the point here, in this first mature formulation of historical materialism, is to underline, against the Young Hegelians, the derivative status of the ideational, its lack of an internal dynamic of development. But even if the superstructure is so completely determined (an example of the kind of polemical overstatement Engels would later regret and seek to redress in his expository letters of the 1890s), its contents, where truth-values are involved, are not necessarily *false*. Causation is not incompatible with truth; in fact, in a passage from the previous paragraph that was crossed out in the manuscript, Marx and Engels say that individuals' ideas "are the conscious expression—real or illusory—of their real relations and activities, of their production, of their intercourse" (CW 5, 36X). So all ideas, both veridical and illusory, are materially determined—a conception consistent with the existence of true as well as false moral beliefs.

Oppositional moralities, genealogically linked to subordinate classes, could therefore constitute a part of the superstructure without being cognitively compromised (Mills 1989). But for the moralist, as Marx and Engels see her, morality is characteristically conceived of as independent of a material genesis, as "ideally" determined. Thus decades later, in *Anti-Dühring*, Engels describes Dühring as an "ideologist" (read: "idealist") because he "constructs morality and law from the concept . . . instead of from the real social relations of the people round him." As a result:

> while he thinks he is framing a doctrine of morals and law for all times and for all worlds, he is in fact only fashioning an image of the conservative or revolutionary tendencies of his day—an image which is distorted because it has been torn from its real basis and, like a reflection in a concave mirror, is standing on its head. (CW 25, 89)

The familiar "inversion" metaphor recalls the imagery of *The German Ideology*, making it clear that the defining error of *idealism* is being diagnosed: *both* revolutionary and conservative morality would be idealistic, inverting the real causal order, if the material foundation of these "tendencies" is not acknowledged.

Similarly, in *The Housing Question*—having spent some pages polemicizing against theorists like Proudhon and Mülberger, who invoke "eternal justice" as a norm—Engels writes that "justice is but the ideologised, idealised expression of the existing economic relations, now from their conservative, and now from their revolutionary angle" (CW 23, 381). Note that, consistent with my interpretation of "ideology," "ideologised" seems intended to be read as synonymous with "idealised." Engels' point is that idealistic moralists (a pleonasm for Marx and Engels), whether conservative or revolutionary, sever moral judgments from their material roots— for example, by assuming rival conceptions of "justice" to be independent of a socioeconomic genesis.[15]

Moral Dilemmas Are Contingent

Because of this lack of insight into its own materialist genealogy, moral theory also typically absolutizes and eternalizes moral dilemmas and oppositions that are actually *contingently* rooted in specific historical situations, configurations of possibilities determined by the existing socioeconomic structure. Thus, in a famous passage on Max Stirner, often cited as evidence of their moral nihilism, Marx and Engels say that "the communists do not oppose egoism to selflessness or selflessness to egoism, nor do they express this contradiction theoretically either in its sentimental or in its highflown ideological form; they rather demonstrate its material source, with which it disappears of itself. The communists do not preach *morality* at all" (CW 5, 247).

Again, what would arguably rescue them from the nihilist accusation is a sympathetic reading, which makes allowances both for the hyperbole that characterizes the whole text and for Marx and Engels' touchingly nineteenth-century faith in technological panaceas. Their point is that the opposition of egoism and altruism is not immanent in the structure of things, but a product of class society. To "preach morality" in these circumstances (to moralize without understanding this material foundation) would be to tacitly endorse the permanence of this contradiction, when in fact it needs to be transcended by a new society in which (because of the communist cornucopia of goods[!]) it will disappear. Given their view of morality as tied to an idealist sociology, a purely *moral* critique would then be inadequate because it would fail to get to the root of things—the "material source," rather than the "highflown ideological [read: idealistic] form"—and it would only address the superstructural symptom. This would be "fight[ing] against the predicates" (CW 5, 235–37). Similarly, in the discussion of another opposition, asceticism and enjoyment, Marx and Engels declare that once "it became possible to criticise the conditions of production and intercourse in the hitherto existing world" this "shattered the basis of all morality, whether the morality of asceticism or of enjoyment" (CW 5, 419). In general, for them, "moral dissatisfaction" is "an ideological [read: superstructural/superstructuralist] expression of these [existing] relations themselves, which does not at all go beyond them, but belongs wholly to them" (CW 5, 378).

Moral Preaching Cannot
Overcome Technological Underdevelopment

Theoretically, then, the important thing is to focus on the material prerequisites for social transformation, since it is they, rather than the presence or absence of suitable moral exhortations, that will determine possibilities.

The first important category of these prerequisites is natural constraint, which can only be overcome through material technological advance:

> [I]t is possible to achieve real liberation only in the real world and by real means . . . serfdom cannot be abolished without improved agriculture, and . . . in general, people cannot be liberated as long as they are unable to obtain food and drink, housing and clothing in adequate quality and quantity. (CW 5, 38)

In the absence of this technological base, the majority of humanity will be condemned to servitude, and communist revolution against class domination would just mean that "privation, *want* is merely made general" (CW 5, 49).

Moral Preaching Cannot Overcome an Unfavorable Balance of Class Forces

However, Marx and Engels believed, rightly or wrongly, that in the capitalism of their time, technological progress had now reached the point where nature no longer posed much of a barrier to the realization of the moral ideals of freedom and equality. More important now were the *social* obstacles: the "material" relations of production and the constraint they exercised over social possibilities through the consolidation of vested class interests, the crystallization of characteristic class psychologies, and the shaping of the "wills" of the human beings enmeshed in these relations. But while only the more extreme kind of idealist would think that *natural* necessity could be overcome voluntaristically, this kind of idealism—idealism about overcoming social barriers—was and continues to be the *norm* within traditional morality.

Marx and Engels can be seen as putting forward here both a sociological claim and a hypothesis in cognitive psychology: that though society is economically determined, people consistently and routinely overestimate the degree of plasticity of the social order because the structuring "material" girders—the refractory skeleton of the body politic—are less empirically visible to them. Even assuming the requisite technological base, major social change will require a certain level of economic development and a favorable balance of class forces. But on the level of common sense, people tend to explain things in terms of an atomistic psychology, the presence or absence of the "will" to do something. The "will" then becomes the target of moral exhortation: the assumption is that, with adequate persuasion, it can take any object, be directed toward any goal, and can thus be thought of as "arbitrary." However, Marx and Engels' view is that the "will" is merely the immediately accessible proximate cause and that it is largely shaped, willy-nilly ("will he nill he"), by constraining economic processes that force us to do certain things if we want to reproduce ourselves.

Thus, from the time of his earliest writings, Marx warns how, in social explanation, "one is all too easily tempted to overlook the *objective nature of the circumstances* and to explain everything by the *will* of the persons concerned," whereas the "objective standpoint" requires that we focus on the "independent" "*circumstances* which determine the actions of private persons and individual authorities" (CW 1, 337). In *The German Ideology,* this theoretical warning becomes a general antivoluntaristic contrast between the "will" and conditions "independent of the will": the former being assimilated to the category of the ideal/superstructural; the latter to the category of the material/economic, with the "material" being causally primary. Thus Marx and Engels write that our theoretical focus should be on people "as they *actually* are . . . as they work under definite material limits, presuppositions and conditions independent of their will" (CW 5, 35–36); they trace the theoretical ideas of the German bourgeoisie to "material interests and a *will* that was conditioned and determined by the material relations of production" (CW 5, 195); and they emphasize that "definite *modes of production* . . . are not dependent on the will" (CW 5, 245). Similarly, in the famous 1859 preface to *A Contribution to the Critique of Political Economy,* Marx talks about men entering into "definite relations [of production] which are independent of their will" (CW 29, 263).

Correspondingly, I think one of the clearest pieces of evidence in favor of my interpretation is that the will *itself* (and not just theories about the will) is sometimes categorized by Marx and Engels as "idealistic," "ideological." This peculiar locution is obviously hard to explain on the conventional reading of "ideology" as "illusory class ideas," since the will itself is not a *theory.* But it is readily explicable on my interpretation, since my claim is that one sense of the "ideological" is the causally secondary superstructural realm of society. So to categorize the will as "ideological/idealistic" is to indicate its position in the base–superstructure taxonomy as an "ideal" causal link that is *not* sufficient to bring about major social change; rather, it has to be conjoined with the (more refractory) economic necessary conditions. Theorists who impute this transformational power to it on its own are therefore operating on "idealist/ideological/superstructuralist" assumptions, thereby downplaying or ignoring altogether the role of material causation.

In *The Holy Family,* Marx emphasizes that "for *real* freedom [profane socialism] demands besides the idealistic '*will*' very tangible, very material conditions" (CW 4, 95). The polemical target here is the "spiritual" *idealistic* socialism of Bruno Bauer, which fails to appreciate the material/

economic/class barriers to radical social change. The "materiality" of these barriers is underlined in an explicit comparison in *The German Ideology* between natural and social determinants: "Just as the weight of [the ruling class's] bodies does not depend on their idealistic will or on their arbitrary decision, so also the fact that they enforce their own will in the form of law . . . does not depend on their idealistic will" (CW 5, 329). Similarly, in his report on the Cologne communist trial, Marx characterizes as "idealistic instead of materialistic" the "point of view" of those who "regard not the real conditions but a *mere effort of will* as the driving force of the revolution" (CW 11, 402–3). The "will" is "ideal," causally subordinate, so that treating it as explanatorily self-sufficient, as an originating rather than a proximate cause, is to be guilty of *idealism*, or, given my interpretation, *ideology*. Thus in *Ludwig Feuerbach and the End of Classical German Philosophy*, Engels criticizes the "old materialism" (eighteenth-century mechanical materialism) for its (sociologically) idealist approach to historical explanation, since it does not investigate the "driving forces," the "historical causes," which stand behind "the many individual wills active in history": "It takes the ideal driving forces which operate there as ultimate causes. . . . The inconsistency does not lie in the fact that *ideal* driving forces are recognized, but in the investigation not being carried further back from these into their motive causes" (CW 26, 388).

Since the superstructure is juridico-political as well as ideational, it will yield juridico-political forms of idealism as well as the paradigmatic ideational varieties. But what such idealist "illusions" will all have in common is, first, the severing of these causally subordinate superstructural realms from their material determinants and, second, the positing of purely, or largely, internalist explanations in terms of free-floating "wills." Thus Marx and Engels refer to "the idealistic conception of the state, according to which it is only a matter of the will" (CW 5, 334); "the [juridical] illusion that law is based on the will, and indeed on the will divorced from its real basis—on *free* will" (CW 5, 90); the "juridical illusion, which reduces law to the mere will" (CW 5, 91); and the "political illusion about the domination of arbitrariness, of ideological [read: idealistically self-determining] will" (CW 5, 335). Seeing the will as "arbitrary," free-floating, is characteristic of an idealist sociological worldview that fails to recognize the gravitational constraint of material structures. Similarly, they criticize Kant for making "the materially motivated determinations of the will of the French bourgeoisie into pure self-determinations of *'free will*,' of the will in and for itself, of the human will, and so convert[ing] it into purely ideological [read: idealistic] conceptual determinations and moral postulates" (CW 5, 195). The *general* mistake the idealist makes is therefore to transform "the idealist symptom into the material cause" (CW 5, 136) and "give the name of the cause to the effect" (CW

5, 175)—thereby voluntarizing the possibilities for juridico-political and moral change, instead of seeing it as subject to a dynamic that is primarily externalist rather than internalist.

My claim, then, is that Marx and Engels' indictment of morality as "ideological" (idealistic) is merely part of their *general* critique of historical/sociological idealism and its "upside-down," "topsy-turvy" way of analyzing society. They saw moralists as typically, or even necessarily, operating with an inverted picture of social causality, which presupposed a larger role for the "will" and a greater latitude for social transformation, as a result of superstructural causation, than in fact existed. Morality's being "ideology" in this sense implies the idealistic belief that this particular superstructural element could either causally override unfavorable material conditions, or substitute for political organization and class struggle. Any approach that "[takes] consciousness alone as its point of departure, [is] bound to end in moral philosophy" (CW 5, 366).

Moreover, their skeptical view of the restricted possibilities for radical change resulting purely from moral exhortation applies not merely to the macrolevel of society but even on the *microfoundational* level of individual psychology. Moralists, say Marx and Engels, assume "Kantian self-determinations of the will" (CW 5, 196), and these moralists put forward "the moral demand of [people's] changing themselves and thereby changing their society" (CW 5, 215). So the assumption is that people can drastically alter the psychologies that have in fact crystallized in them as a result of their shaping by class society, producing a particular internal moral economy of desire and interest (CW 5, 250–51). But the reality is that "Whether a desire becomes fixed or not . . . depends on . . . material circumstances" (CW 5, 255). Thus to expect people to embark upon radical behavioral change would just be an "impotent moral injunction about self-control" (CW 5, 255), since their psychology "by no means depends on consciousness or 'good will'" (CW 5, 262). The communists, by contrast, recognize this causal asymmetry:

> Since they attack the material basis on which the hitherto inevitable fixedness of desires and ideas depended, the communists are the only people through whose historical activity the liquefaction of the fixed desires and ideas is in fact brought about and ceases to be an impotent moral injunction, as it was up to now with all moralists. (CW 5, 255X)

Absent "Material" Prerequisites, Morality Is in General Impotent

The recurrent theme in Marx and Engels' writings is therefore the "impotence" of morality, the causal inefficaciousness of moral preaching absent appropriate material conditions. "Oughts" not grounded in objective historical possibilities are empty. In *The Holy Family*, Marx says (quoting

Fourier): "*Morality* is '*impuissance mise en action.*' Every time it fights a vice it is defeated" (CW 4, 201). This is repeated in Engels' notes on Feuerbach (CW 5, 11). In *The German Ideology*, Marx and Engels write that Christianity "does not go beyond mere moral injunctions, which remain ineffective in real life" (CW 5, 254); they refer to an "impotent moral injunction" (255); they say that unless individuals' circumstances are changed, "no moral preaching avails here" (262); they contrast "an impotent moral injunction" to "material forces" (342–43); and they deride not only "the moral postulate that competition and the relations on which it depends *should* have consequences other than those inevitably arising from them" (376) but also "the pious wish" that individuals "*should* behave *in such a way* . . . that their behavior does not acquire independent existence as a social relationship independent of them, and that their differences from one another should not assume the material character (independent of the person) which they have assumed" (437). In *Herr Vogt*, Marx describes how "moral indignation . . . rebounded off the realities of economic conditions" (CW 17, 93). And in *The Housing Question*, Engels refers to "moral sermons whose emotional effects immediately evaporate under the influence of private interest" (CW 23, 341).

Finally, it is in this light that I think we should read the notorious and frequently cited passage (e.g., by Wood, Lukes, Hodges, Buchanan) from the *Critique of the Gotha Programme*. Criticizing the Lassalleans' programmatic demands for "equal right" and "fair distribution," Marx indicts them for their "perverting . . . the realistic outlook, which it cost so much effort to instil into the Party but which has now taken root in it, by means of ideological, legal and other trash" (CW 24, 87). On the standard interpretation, a reader would infer a paradigm statement of Marxian realpolitik, in which an amoral "realistic outlook" is contraposed and prescribed as a desideratum to the "ideological trash" of morality. But once "ideological" is read as "superstructuralist" or "idealistic," the sense shifts dramatically from a critique of the *content* of these ideas to a critique of the view that they are *causally primary* and should be given theoretical center stage. The contrasting "realistic outlook" can then be simply seen as the *historical materialist* perspective on the differential causal efficacy of different regions of society (which is why "legal," as superstructural, is included with "ideological," as a target for him). So this infamous passage, far from being the "smoking gun" that confirms Marx's amoralism, would merely be a restatement of his familiar claim that the moral is causally subordinate in social change and an inappropriate programmatic starting point.

Marx and Engels would later retreat from the somewhat epiphenomenalist view of the superstructure they advanced in *The German Ideology*. And in the last few years of his life, Engels wrote a series of letters deploring the one-sidedness of his and Marx's earlier formulations, which he attributed to the context of polemical engagement with their (sociologically) idealist adversaries: "We had to stress this leading principle ["the economic aspect"] in the face of opponents who denied it, and we did not always have the time, space or opportunity to do justice to the other factors that interacted upon each other" (CW 49, 36). In these letters, Engels explicitly repudiates monocausality: a "meaningless, abstract, ridiculous piece of jargon" (CW 49, 34). Instead, he asserts a principle of multiple, but still asymmetrical, determination, which came to be known as the thesis of the "relative autonomy" of the superstructure. The idea is to affirm interaction and contributory superstructural causation while still insisting on the greater causal influence of the techno-economic.

I think this more measured judgment would also hold true for their mature view of morality; or, perhaps better, it *would have held* true if, counterfactually, they had spent any significant time thinking about morality. In fact, they could not consistently see morality as "impotent," since "the various factors of the superstructure . . . also have a bearing on the course of the historical struggles" (CW 49, 34); but they would deny its *primacy*. A moral motivation that is independent of, or actually opposed to, people's perceptions of their economic interests is never going to be a major force of social change. A few of the privileged will always, very praiseworthily, be morally inspired to join the struggle of the oppressed, sometimes making considerable sacrifices in doing so; but the crucial *global* shifts in hegemonic normative structures will in general have socioeconomic changes and shifting power relations at their root: "if . . . morality . . . come[s] into contradiction with the existing relations, this can only occur because existing social relations have come into contradiction with existing productive forces" (CW 5, 45). Such structural shifts would include the dramatic transformations in the schedules of rights and liberties; the redrawings of the very boundaries of the moral community that accompanied, say, the rise of liberal egalitarianism; the end of African slavery in the New World; and the spread of the women's movement. Moral critique of the existing order is a necessary part of political struggle for radical change, but the extent to which this challenge is a success or failure will be largely determined by the extra-ideational factors that shape people's consciousness.

To resolve the apparent "paradox" (Lukes) of Marx and Engels' views on morality—that is, the apparent hostility to "morality" together with the apparently moral denunciations of capitalism—all we need to do is to recognize that for Marx and Engels being a moralist commits you to the M' set of metatheories, the idealist theses that *(a)* morality is independent of a material genesis; and *(b)* moral agitation is sufficient to bring about—or, less strongly, is causally predominant in bringing about—major socioeconomic change. This is to see morality "ideologically"—that is, idealistically. But as Engels underlines in *Anti-Dühring*, "moral indignation, however justifiable, cannot serve economic science as an argument but only as a symptom" (CW 25, 138), since, as he later claims, "the final causes of all social changes and political revolutions are to be sought, not in men's brains, not in man's better insight into eternal truth and justice, but in changes in the modes of production and exchange" (CW 25, 254). Moral indignation may be "justifiable" (and thus arguably cognitivist), but on its own it just doesn't make the wheels turn.

CONCLUSION

I am by no means claiming that this reinterpretation solves all of the problems of the debate on Marx and morality; as I indicated at the beginning, other kinds of problematic passages in Marx and Engels' work exist and other kinds of theoretical difficulties have to be faced. But I think that the standard reading of "ideology" has been one major obstacle to an objectivist analysis, which for the most part has been unsuccessfully negotiated by commentators. Moreover, my revisionist reading of "ideology," through making the conceptual connection with "idealism," has the virtue of establishing a link between what have usually been seen as two *separate* pro-objectivist claims: that there is an interpretation of "ideology" that permits metaethical objectivism; and that the real target of Marx and Engels' hostility was "moralism" rather than "morality." If these are joint implications of the new reading (since "ideology" for me refers not to moral truth-values but to the illusion of causal primacy), the case for both is arguably strengthened.

Marx and Engels believed (P1) that "morality" standardly misconceives its own autonomy and causal significance, an assessment of continuing validity even today. But for the purposes of metaethical clarification, if nothing else, we can point out that this is a contingent rather than conceptual truth; we can separate what Marx and Engels have conflated; and we can detach M from M'. An objectivist oppositional morality is not logically or conceptually precluded when it self-consciously *recognizes* its material roots in the economic situation and when it has no propensity to exaggerate its likely causal efficacy. Such a morality would be doubly "realist," in the metaethical sense of being objectivist and in the politically informed sense of facing the uglier facts about how the world really works.[16]

NOTES

1. Unfortunately, moral philosophers show considerable variation in the terminology they use to discuss these issues. Contrast, for example, David Brink's characterization of "realism" as a metaethical theory "committed to moral facts and truths that are *objective* in some way," "independent of the evidence for them" (and thus *excluding* moral constructivism and relativism), with Geoffrey Sayre-McCord's more latitudinarian conception of "realism" as just successful cognitivism, "*not solely the prerogative of objectivists*" (and thus *including* moral constructivism and relativism). See Brink (1989, 14, 17–18) and Sayre-McCord (1988, 16, 5). To eliminate ambiguity, I will henceforth use "objectivism" stipulatively to include both realism (in Brink's sense) and constructivism (idealized intersubjectivist cognitivism). Theories in the opposing, *anti*-objectivist camp would therefore include moral nihilism, noncognitivism (emotivism, prescriptivism), error theories, individual subjectivism, and ethical relativism. For our purposes, though, the important metaethical contrast is simply that between the umbrella positions of objectivism and anti-objectivism.

2. See the very useful discussions in Sayre-McCord (1988) and Brink (1989).

3. I refer here to Rawls (1971), who was widely interpreted to be putting forward a constructivist metaethical position (Brink [1989, 303–21]), rather than the later Rawls, who claimed to be staying away from such "metaphysical" issues.

4. In alphabetical order: Acton (1955); Brenkert (1980; 1983); Buchanan (1982; 1986); Fisk (1980); Geras (1989); Hodges (1962); Husami (1980); Kamenka (1969); Kellner (1981); Lukes (1985); Miller (1984); Nielsen (1989); Peffer (1990); Skillen (1978); Wood (1980a; 1980b; 1985). Of course, many other authors have taken positions on Marx's metaethical views, but my focus is on those writers in whose arguments the concept of ideology has played a role, whether as a support or as an acknowledged obstacle to be overcome.

5. One important exception is Husami (1980). In my opinion, Husami's claims about the real significance for Marx of the "ideological" nature of morality have received insufficient attention in the secondary literature. This chapter is in part intended to retrieve, supplement, and develop his interpretation.

6. As indicated in note 1, this diagram draws on Brink's categorization, rather than Sayre-McCord's. The taxonomy is meant to be a mapping of interpretations of Marx's views, but not of all the possible metaethical positions; therefore, I have not included views that could obviously never plausibly be attributed to Marx, such as (individual) subjectivism.

7. Neither of these two articles, which originally appeared in 1972 and 1979, indicates that Wood has anything but the standard pejorative conception of "ideology." In Wood (1985), however, he argues that "ideology" has *three* senses for Marx and Engels: historical idealism, functional thought, and illusion in the sense of unawareness of "its own economic basis" (117–20). Wood suggests that morality is "ideology" in all three senses (143), but he does not seem to believe that this position requires any modification of his earlier position. My own interpretation of "ideology," as explained in chapter 1, partially overlaps with his (and interestingly enough, so does Husami's, despite their differences); and I will argue that my view necessitates rethinking the orthodox interpretation.

8. Wood (1980a, 18–19).

9. Because of his bifurcation of the senses of "ideology," Peffer could alternatively be regarded as challenging P1, since all morality is ideology in the global sense but *not* in the nonglobal sense.

10. The idea here, Nielsen 1 suggests, is that "while all ideological conceptions are superstructural, not all superstructural conceptions are ideological" (Nielsen 1989, 5). So the aim is to carve out a conceptual space for *some* morality as superstructural but nonideological. But the puzzling thing, as earlier noted, is that at more than one point in his book, Nielsen follows this strategy with that of Nielsen 2, arguing that "ideology" is only distortion-*prone* and not necessarily distortional (see, for example, 122–27, where both strategies are in evidence). But if "ideology" is indeed epistemologically neutral, there is simply no *need* for the ideological–superstructural distinction, so why bother to draw it? A further source of confusion is that, in endnotes to several chapters (e.g., ch. 1, n. 3; ch. 2, n. 29; ch. 7, n. 36), Nielsen cites John McMurtry's work (1978) as evidence for the ideological–superstructural distinction, claiming that "It is important to recognize, McMurtry claims, that, for Marx, for beliefs to count as 'ideological,' they must be social mystifications" (149). But this is a complete misunderstanding of McMurtry's position, since McMurtry is noteworthy for being one of the few contemporary Marxist commentators (the most active being Joseph McCarney; see chapter 1) who defend an epistemologically *neutral* conception of "ideology": "[W]e are going to interpret Marx as regarding scientific and unscientific conceptions of human affairs as distinct subclasses of ideology" (McMurtry 1978, 131). So to cite McMurtry as authorizing an S2 strategy misses the whole point of his book, which is that being ideological does *not* imply cognitive defect so that morality could be ideology *without* any negative implications.

11. To avoid possible misunderstandings, I should emphasize that I am *not* here prescribing that some kind of reverential bibliocentrism should determine what a useful concept of "ideology" would be. In fact, as I made clear in chapter 1, I think Marx's conception of "ideology" is of little use to us and should be abandoned. But the point is that it is *his concept*. In other words, one does not solve textual problems and clear up apparent inconsistencies and contradictions by ignoring the body of textual evidence but by confronting it and showing why it doesn't have the implications standardly attributed to it.

12. The only evidence Nielsen gives to support this clearly crucial exclusion is a reference to the work of McCarney.

13. In a footnote (Peffer 1990, 241, n. 1), Peffer cites numerous theorists who have written on "ideology"; but these citations can hardly authorize *his* (or, actually, any) preferred usage of the term since in many cases their views are sharply conflicting. At the start of the book (4, n. 1), he endorses Allen Wood's recommendation that responsible exegesis must distinguish textual facts, textual interpretations, and "speculative extensions that cohere with the texts." Peffer says he will call the last of these "rational reconstructions," and his treatment of ideology is supposed to be an example of such a reconstruction. But, in the absence of textual evidence to provide this "coherence" test, what prevents his putative "reconstruction" from degenerating—as I have suggested it does—into a mere stipulation?

14. For an oddly hybrid position, similar to my own in some respects but different in others, see Edgley (1990). (I was unaware of Edgley's piece when I wrote the original article on which this chapter is based.) Edgley endorses McCarney's analysis of "ideology," which I reject; and on this basis he denies that, for Marx, *morality* is "illusory in content" (26). But he does agree that "what Marx is rejecting in morality is its idealism": "there are certain ideas closely associated with morality that *are* implied to be illusory in content by Marx's characterisation of morality as ideological. . . . For these ideas constitute a central part of *idealism*. . . . The general character of idealism is that it elevates ideas above material reality." And it is *these* idealist claims that "are for Marx illusory in content" (27). While I would support such a reading, my criticism would, of course, be that McCarney's analysis of "ideology" is refuted by the texts. (Edgley gives no independent evidence himself.) But additionally: if "ideology" is in fact "not a critical concept," as Edgley claims, then whence the connection with "idealism"?

15. Compare with Ziyad Husami (1980, 48): "If the spokesmen for a class justify their views by maintaining that their moral outlook is independent of historical development or of class interests, then they maintain false beliefs about their morality. Such false beliefs are called 'ideological illusions.' The moral outlook itself, on that count alone, is not considered illusory."

16. Compare with Norman Geras on a specifically Marxist "moral realism" (Geras 1997, 3–19).

4

The Moral Epistemology
of Stalinism

A standard criticism of academic Marxism in general, and Analytical Marxism in particular, has been its failure to examine actual political practice. Therefore, I want to end part I with a look at the practice so deeply embarrassing to so many Marxist theorists throughout the twentieth century: Stalinism.[1] The question I want to ask is: How was it possible for people of intelligence and good faith to give their uncritical support to the now-collapsed Stalinist regimes once pragmatically described as "actually existing socialism"?[2]

Of course, in the case of those in the East, the concomitants of state power suggest little mystery: the carrot of the luxury *dacha* in one hand, and the stick of the Gulag in the other.[3] But what about Communist party members and fellow travelers in other countries who, far from benefiting from their support, often suffered for it—from loss of employment to actual execution. What made it possible for *them* to believe?[4] It is a question that has been repeatedly asked, not just from the Right, but also from the Left: by social democrats seeking to draw a clear demarcation between their socialism and "Marxism–Leninism"; and by, perhaps most revealingly, repentant ex-Stalinists themselves, trying to make sense of their own now-baffling pasts, at once denied and undeniable.

One strategy of explanation widely employed in the 1950s solved the problem by dissolving it into psychopathology. Communism and fascism were both totalitarian systems that attracted a certain abnormal personality type, so that moral deviance was hardly surprising. (This approach was neatly summarized in the portmanteau term of the time, *communazi*.)[5] As Paul Lyons (1982, 139) writes of this literature: "To stomach Stalinism and

mouth Comintern lies, one had to be a knave or a fool, an authoritarian personality, a true believer." The revisionist New Left scholarship of the 1970s
and 1980s has largely rejected this moral teratology, producing sympathetic
social histories of Communist activists and their work, though naturally decrying their political subservience to Moscow (Isserman 1993; Naison 1983;
Schrecker 1999; Kelley 1990). The contrasting tone—divergent, indeed, almost to the point of caricature—is paradigmatically illustrated by Vivian
Gornick's claim (1983, 22) about the American Communist Party (CPUSA):
"It seems to me the real point about the Communists is: they were like
everybody else, only more so." More average than average, then: not the
alien body-snatched Other, but the genuine folks next door, Beaver Cleaver
at the Young Communist League summer camp (Mishler 1999). Similarly,
in the memoirs of many ex-Communists, even those now fiercely hostile to
communism, it is usually precisely the moral appeal of the theory that is
stressed. Thus, in his account of his Stalinist past in the French Communist
Party (PCF), Maxime Rodinson (1983, 25) observes that most members
"joined because they dreamed of devoting themselves to an admirable
ideal, and . . . most of them were neither scoundrels nor imbeciles." Likewise, the once-leading Yugoslav Communist Milovan Djilas (1973, 92–93)
writes: "The great majority of us young people became revolutionaries in
the hopes of realizing brotherhood and equality, of freeing our working
people from exploitation, of giving them a happier life. . . . In my early experience I didn't know a single man who had become a Communist out of
ambition or hope of material gain."

What, then, were the psychic mechanisms that made it possible for this
moral impulse to become so perverted as to permit, indeed mandate,
complicity in the construction of systems of oppression more crushing
than those overthrown? And how might these mechanisms be linked to
the specific features of Marxist theory itself? The severing of academic
Marxist theory from the political practice of self-described Marxist parties
and states during their existence, which Perry Anderson (1985) regards as
defining of "Western Marxism," was so complete during much of the
twentieth century that, for many, these questions never even arose. Unsurprisingly, conservative critics in the period saw the erection of these
conceptual barriers as self-serving and (a cruel blow) un-Marxist. Thus
John Gray (1986, 160–61), writing before the fall, comments ironically on
what he sees as the "Platonism" of these accounts: "For Marx and Lenin,
historical practice is not conceived as a degenerate form of theory but, instead, as theory's only legitimate source. Neither Marx nor Lenin could
have endorsed the insulation from the criticism of history which the
Marxian system is accorded in the conventional academic interpretation
of twentieth-century Marxist regimes and movements."

In this chapter, I tentatively want to explore some of these possible connections between theory and practice in order to show how, as Paul Lyons

(1982, 18) puts it, "in seeking forms of sainthood, [Communists] tragically and inexorably produced its opposite." My "microfoundational" explanatory strategy will be to bring together, in what I hope will be a fruitful encounter, texts usually thought of as quite disparate and unrelated: on the one hand, some of the distinctions and discussions from contemporary analytical ethics, involving issues of self-deception and moral dilemmas; on the other hand, as resource material, writings by and about Communists and ex-Communists themselves.[6] So this reconstruction of a Stalinist moral epistemology will be in part analogous to an exercise in "naturalized" epistemology, and as such it will be clinical rather than hortatory. The idea is that by following the logic that Communists actually did tend to employ in making their normative judgments, we can illuminate a trajectory of epistemic decay that avoids demonizing them, since, in significant measure, it is attributable to the peculiar difficulties of their situation as moral agents.

COMMUNIST CONVERSION AND SELF-TRANSFORMATION

Let us begin with a stage-setting psychological sketch of the recent Communist convert. Through some combination of personal experience and exposure to Marxist ideas (one's own reading, encounters with proselytizing activists, a radicalizing intellectual climate), one has become convinced of the essential truth of the Marxist vision of the world and has thus joined a Communist party. Perhaps, as with Arthur Koestler (Crossman 2001, 23) and many others, this revelation has had the character of a secular epiphany: "To say that one had 'seen the light' is a poor description. . . . The new light seems to pour from all directions across the skull; the whole universe falls into pattern like the stray pieces of a jigsaw puzzle assembled by magic at one stroke." But even where the experience is less dramatic, there is no doubt that a fundamental paradigm shift is involved. Unlike the case of natural science, though, where such conceptual revolutions are usually fairly localized in their practical consequences for the individual, this transformation is an understanding of reality that has global ramifications for one's everyday life: one's self-concept, one's view of the world, and one's interactions with others. Gornick quotes an American party member:

> Now, I was a Communist. . . . I felt that *weight* of responsibility. . . . Everywhere. Always. Under all conditions. You see, it wasn't a matter of *conditions*. The world in which we lived was the condition. . . . Being a Communist was a condition. Your life as a Communist was everywhere: in the shop, at home, at meetings, in the neighborhood. You were always being a Communist. There was never a time when you weren't a Communist. You were a Communist when you went to the store to buy a bottle of milk, when you went to a movie, attended a party or a meeting, voted in the shop. . . . It was all one. The life was of a piece. (Gornick 1983, 113)

And this new life imposed duties that were both moral and epistemic. For the problem immediately raised by becoming a Marxist revolutionary, of course, is that one is then faced with the challenge of interacting with a world where the vast majority of people are not Communists and where in fact many of one's empirical and normative views are regarded with incredulity and odium. This challenge, I suggest, can be regarded as having two main aspects, the theoretical and the practical.

The *theoretical* aspect is the epistemological problem of accounting for the divergent beliefs of others. Here the theory itself will be called in to explain the frequently radical discrepancy between what Communist and conventional views are about social facts and which actions should be judged right and wrong. By virtue of its overarching theses about the social determination of belief, Marxism has a particularly rich array of such metatheories, including the specification of both "hot" and "cold" mechanisms of cognitive distortion (the distinction being that the former rely crucially on motivational processes).[7] These factors—class interest, class-determined ignorance, social-structural "appearance," "false consciousness," the ubiquitous pernicious influence of bourgeois ideology—can all be cited to undermine the force of criticism, explaining not only why others are wrong but why one's own spontaneous judgments and responses might be mistaken.

Second, the *practical* aspect is the psychological and moral problem of developing a character structure that will be strong enough to withstand both the hostility of others and one's own resulting self-doubts and tendency to backslide. Intellectually, the recent convert may be epistemically forearmed against the hostile environment in which he or she must operate, with theoretical explanations for the disdain and outrage with which Communist views are treated in the established ("capitalist") press and traditional ("bourgeois") scholarship; and for the fact that the door is too often slammed in one's face by the workers themselves. But a set of intellectual tools is one thing; what is also required is the *will* and *strength of character* to utilize them. The moral struggle against capitalism is not merely a battle against the external bourgeois enemy, the ruling class; it must also be waged on a second, internal front against one's own unreliable conscience, the untransformed bourgeois self, which is like a fifth columnist within one's own psyche. This struggle is, of course, merely another instantiation of the familiar paradox that the revolutionary is herself a product of the society she is trying to transform. But it implies that the Communist must engage in a process of self-reconstruction and character formation in order to successfully fulfill her task. Djilas writes:

> Our truths were daily confirmed by the misery and suffering of millions of people. . . . This in turn intensified our moral and spiritual obligations to the

movement. There was no greater and more shameful betrayal than abandoning this Communist world. . . . [W]e built up not only an external party
discipline, but a much more profound internal one as well. Implementing decisions was not sufficient; anyone could do that. One had to transform oneself so that at any time all of one's actions could be measured in terms of the
interests of the revolution. (Djilas 1973, 229)

Similarly, Gornick (1983, 110) quotes an American Communist who
dreaded her weekly task of selling the party paper, but she forced herself
to "push down the gagging and go do it. You know, people never understand that. They say to us, 'The Communist Party held a whip over you.'
They don't understand. The whip was inside each of us, we held it over
ourselves."

In understanding the dynamics of this character transformation, I suggest that recent literature from mainstream ethics may prove helpful. For
what is involved is arguably just a special case—admittedly more dramatic because of the radical divergence in beliefs—of a project usually encountered in more mundane ethical settings. All moral theories will have
an ideal of the moral agent, whether primarily as an end in itself, as with
virtue theories, or primarily as an instrument for realizing the right or the
good, as with act-centered theories. Correspondingly, and depending on
the model, the conscientious moral agent learns to cultivate certain
traits—temperance, obedience to God's will, respect for universal law,
sympathy—and to discourage others—intemperance, rebelliousness, giving in to inclination, self-centeredness. What I want to show is the radical
implications that are likely to follow from this familiar prescription in the
case under consideration: the transformation necessary for the good Communist moral agent.[8] My argument is that, to guard *against* the hazards of
moral error and self-deception (which are likely to be particularly acute in
this tectonically shifted ethical landscape), defenses will need to be
erected against those factual and normative perceptions whose etiology is
judged to be epistemically suspect. Then, in a likely second, degenerative
stage, this originally defensible pattern of cognitive filtering and exclusion will itself ironically facilitate, and itself become increasingly driven
by, a self-deceiving dynamic.[9]

MORAL DILEMMAS AND REVOLUTIONARY OBLIGATIONS

Since Harry Frankfurt's classic paper (1971) on the concept of a person, it
has been standard practice to distinguish between first- and second-order
desires: the latter have other desires as their object. In Frankfurt's terminology, second-order volitions are that subset of second-order desires that

the agent wants to be effective in modifying her first-order desires, so as to reconstruct her self. The model is of general applicability; but in the case we are considering, of course, the targeted first-order mental contents are envisaged by the agent as being socially generated, rather than peculiar to her. The new revolutionary, then, wishes to transform what she now sees as her old bourgeois self, so as to become a unified personality with a single consistent set of beliefs, values, and moral intuitions. At present, she is a divided self whose old psychology is still manifesting itself in various ways; so she has desires not only to *spontaneously* believe certain things but also to *spontaneously* evaluate and will in a certain way, when some of these reactions are book-learned, rather than "natural." (Of course, she now has an elaborate metatheoretical account that claims that these ostensibly "natural" reactions are really socially manipulated, capitalist creations.) In terms of achieving an Aristotelian *hexis*, a dispositional characteristic, she wants to be "not simply one who behaves in a certain way, but one who behaves that way out of a certain character"; so she needs "a theory not only of how to *act* well but also of how to *feel* well," a character that enables her "to exhibit the right kinds of emotions as well as the right kinds of actions" (Kosman 1980, 103–5). Becoming a better Communist implies not merely deepening one's understanding of Marxist theory, but spontaneously reacting in a Communist way, having the moral intuitions a revolutionary would have. Thus Gornick (1983, 137) describes a recent recruit who "always felt vaguely ill at ease," but: "He kept telling himself that these doubts were the residual effects of his bourgeois background and in time, as his inner merger with the Party became more complete, they would evaporate."

Now the kinds of situations in which this problem of incomplete Communist transformation will become especially acute are, of course, moral dilemmas—or apparent moral dilemmas. Failing to have what (she is told) are the correct intuitions, being unable to "feel" the rightness of the action the party prescribes for her, or disagreeing with what she sees the party doing or endorsing (e.g., some aspect of Soviet policy), the new party member may begin to wonder whether these actions are actually morally justified after all. But she then faces the problem of second-guessing, identifying the character of her doubts. Is she hesitant because of objectively repellent features of the action, or is this her unreconstructed bourgeois self speaking? If she opposes the action, is she displaying moral character or weakness of will? Is her reflexive examination of the resultant structure of her own motivations and intuitions veridical or mistaken, possibly self-deceived? And if it is quite possibly the latter (given the theories she now has about social influence on character formation), shouldn't she compensate by withholding assent to these intuitions, deliberately alienating herself from her spontaneous moral judgments?

For the peculiarities of her situation mean that an unusual kind of self-deception is a ubiquitous danger. What differentiates self-deception from ordinary error is the presence of a causal link between the mistake and *motivation*. A large literature is dedicated to the subject (Mele 1987; McLaughlin and Rorty 1988; Dupuy 1998), with philosophical work focusing on apparent problems in the concept—for example, the paradoxes, both static and dynamic, involved in modeling intrapersonal on interpersonal deception.[10] But let us assume that some viable model can be found for what appears to be a genuine psychological phenomenon: for example, as the philosopher Alfred Mele argues, by rejecting "isomorphism" with interpersonal deception; and by concentrating instead on straightforward cognitive processes of negative and positive misinterpretation, selective focusing, and selective evidence gathering (Mele 2001, ch. 2).[11] Our interest then is in showing the particular form its dynamic may assume in the case of the Communist convert: the standing danger of self-deception that is *morally* motivated.

Let me try to explain how this possibility could come about. The standard kind of case where self-deception might enter as a factor in moral decisions is, of course, when self-interest is in conflict with our moral duty, D, and when we are in danger of our persuading ourselves, in defiance of the evidence, that D is not really our duty. Correspondingly, the conscientious moral agent routinely admonishes himself to be wary of such snares, to be objective, to look at the situation from the perspective of the ideal observer, and so on. Thus, in that case, straightforward human selfishness is the threat to our seeing and doing the right thing. But the situation we are concerned with here is a more complicated one, where self-deception may be *morally* motivated. Consider the case of moral dilemmas, specifically those that involve "dirty hands," that is, where it seems that doing the all-things-considered right thing requires us to do wrong—for example, torturing the terrorist to find out where the bomb has been hidden. In mainstream moral philosophy, the debate regarding dirty hands is as follows: one side argues that if we do the all-things-considered right thing, then we have no dirty hands and no cause for shame or guilt; the other side argues that our hands are still dirty and that these emotions are appropriate, indeed morally mandatory for us to retain our integrity as moral agents (Stocker 1990). Now my concern here is not to contribute to this debate, but rather to show how its terms are transformed for the Communist moral agent. For in being asked to do something for the revolutionary cause that he would normally regard as wrong or to morally endorse something others have done, the convert is facing a dilemma whose structure is more complicated than the examples routinely discussed. The problem of deciding on the right course of action is exacerbated for the Communist moral agent because, first, he is trying to work out and adjudicate the prescriptions of *two* moral codes—traditional morality and the revolutionary new morality—and not just assess two actions by one code; and, second, he is simultaneously being forced to second-guess himself, to wonder whether his feelings (say) of moral revulsion are veridical or just the responses of his deceiving bourgeois self, which should normatively be ignored.

Some clarification of the conceptual geography may be useful here. We have a moral terrain, and we have two overlapping and conflicting maps of its features: commonsense morality and the revolutionary Marxist morality.[12] These maps will not be mutually exclusive; if the revolutionary morality is supposed to be a comprehensive moral code, then, presumably, for many issues, its prescriptions will be the same as conventional morality—for example, keep your promises, take care of your children, rescue drowning strangers when you can, and so forth. But, because of divergent empirical/theoretical assumptions, some actions will be condemned by conventional morality that are actually prescribed by the revolutionary morality. However, there will also be actions that will be condemned by *both* moralities. In other words, a plausible revolutionary morality will not (I claim) countenance *every* action that advances the revolutionary cause; rather, it will place constraints on what is permissible to do. So the mere fact that an action is condemned by traditional morality does not prove that by revolutionary standards it is in fact right, since there can be actions that are, or should be, condemned by *both*. Excluding for the sake of simplicity the categories of the permissible and the supererogatory, then, we have four categories of action: *(a)* actions required by both traditional and revolutionary morality; *(b)* actions required by traditional morality but forbidden by revolutionary morality; *(c)* actions condemned by traditional morality but required by revolutionary morality; and *(d)* actions condemned by both traditional and revolutionary morality. Now one simple way of restating what I have been saying is to point out that the uncertainties of the geography of these categorizations mean that people will be unsure where some of the boundaries are. In other words, it will not always be clear—perhaps it will almost always be *un*clear—where, in particular, the boundary between classes *(c)* and *(d)* is—that is, between the kinds of actions that would only be proscribed by traditional morality and the kinds of actions that are objectively wrong by the standards of both.

The difficulty of monitoring and correctly identifying one's motivations and intuitions, as well as normatively assessing their character and force, is far greater (I suggest) under these circumstances than in the case of self-interested versus moral motivation. The divergent phenomenological character of prudential and moral motivations in the latter case is epistemically quite clear. Here, by contrast, an unavoidable fuzziness is produced by the mutual interference of two kinds of *moral* motivation, generating an epistemic murk in which self-deception is significantly easier. The danger here is that we may be tempted into self-deception for *"moral"* reasons and that we may be tempted to categorize as *(d)* what really belongs to *(c)*—not because of prudential, but altruistic, motivation. The old morality under which we were brought up will obviously continue to exert a certain attraction for us. In many situations, we will recognize abstractly that a certain action, X, is judged right by the new standards, but is wrong by the old ones; in addition, we will *feel* this wrongness. In fact, it might well be the case that this feeling is stronger than the feeling that it is right; or it might be even that we have *no* feeling of the rightness of X, but merely an intellectual apprehension—one guided by our knowledge of the precepts of the revolutionary morality and our recognition of certain (putatively) morally relevant facts. Depending on the seriousness of X's divergence from what we had previously thought of as right (X may range from merely telling a lie for the cause to torturing and killing for it), we are likely to experience major moral discomfort at the thought of having to do it. It will be psychologically easier for us *not* to do X, to tell ourselves that it is *not* our duty, D.

So there will be a motivation of a nonprudential, apparently moral kind to refrain from doing X, and this will be phenomenologically experienced by us, based on our past moral education, as the voice of conscience. But, we will simultaneously be aware, by virtue of our (intellectual) acceptance of the superior revolutionary morality, that this phenomenology is suspect, indeed treacherous, and that this moral claim may need to be normatively recategorized as the voice of the old morality, the normative buttress of the very system of exploitation we are morally required to overthrow. As Stephen Spender (Crossman 2001, 238) writes: "My arguments [with myself] were re-enforced by feelings of guilt and the suspicion that the side of me which pitied the victims of revolution secretly supported the ills of capitalism from which I myself benefited." A metaethical distancing—a conscious, willed disregard of our moral intuitions and spontaneous feelings—is therefore called for here, since epistemically we do not know which of these are reliable and which are just the unreliable remnants within us of the old system. As a general moral metaduty, then, one may need to cultivate within oneself, first, the second-order disposition to override some of one's moral intuitions, one's feelings of duty, rightness, and wrongness; and, second, the strength of character not to be deterred by some of one's own countervailing feelings of moral repugnance, since one now has a metatheory revealing the possible epistemic deficiencies of these intuitions and feelings.

In the standard applications of coherentist moral epistemology, such as Rawls' "reflective equilibrium" (1971), one strives to achieve equilibrium between principles and intuitions, seeking to resolve inconsistencies and disagreements. In David Brink's words:

> If a theory has counterintuitive implications, then this is evidence against the theory. If the counterintuitive implications of the theory are fairly common and widespread, especially if the apparent counterexamples share important features, then this is reason to abandon the theory for another, or at least to modify the theory in significant ways. (Brink 1989, 130–31)

What I am claiming is that in the case of the revolutionary convert, this standard approach has to be revised, given the dramatic deviation from a conventional understanding of the world and the powerful array of undermining metatheories about people's perceptions, including our own. Counterintuitive implications can be widespread; and it can still be legitimate to *retain* the theory and override the *intuitions* instead, since, as noted, the theory has a theory that explains why one *will* experience certain ("fairly common and widespread") unreliable intuitions.

Discussions of this kind of problem have usually taken place in arguments with utilitarians, who have long pointed out the following: that if the theory is correct, many of our moral intuitions—instantiating as they do a deontic patchwork of heterogeneous moral traditions, not to mention plain old prejudices—may simply be *wrong*; therefore, they cannot be regarded as foundational or necessarily indefeasible. As J. J. C. Smart (1973, 68–69) puts it: "We may therefore feel inclined to reject an ethical methodology which implies that we should test our general principles by our reactions in particular cases. Rather, we may come to feel, we should test our reactions in particular cases by reference to the most general principles." In his critique of Smart, Bernard Williams (Smart and Williams 1973, 104) says that the implication of such a view is the loss of "a sense of one's moral identity . . . one's integrity. At this point utilitarianism alienates one from one's moral feelings." The fact of this alienation is therefore supposed to constitute a prima facie case against the legitimacy of such an ethical strategy.

But one can readily imagine situations where such a distancing, such an alienation, is not morally culpable, but indeed laudable. As with the situation of the Communist revolutionary (by hypothesis, anyway), the crucial background conditions are a systematically and horrendously unjust social structure; a cognitive awakening that requires the recognition and repudiation of one's past socialization in the "normalcy" and "naturalness" of this structure; and the corresponding rejection of many of the values, beliefs, norms, reflexes, and feelings one spontaneously has. In other words, it is to a certain extent a rejection precisely of one's previous moral identity. Consider, as a presumably uncontroversial example, the case of a white person's traditional racist upbringing of the American Old South or (to make it more contemporary) recent apartheid South Africa. The feelings of antipathy, disgust, and fundamental *wrongness* that such people will have at the prospect of racial intermixing (particularly interracial sexual relationships) are undoubtedly completely heartfelt and sincere; they are of a depth and intensity that might seem, if anything would, to qualify them as genuine moral intuitions. Of course, we do not regard them as such, but as the products of a racist socialization process.

If one has been raised in such an environment and has later, because of self-education or changing mores, come to see the wrongness of this response, he may still continue to have such feelings while recognizing their nonveridicality. In reeducating himself, in transforming his moral sensibility, such a person will have to school his feelings, suppress his reflexes, and purge his intuitions, since those spontaneous responses may continue to be far more authoritative and viscerally convincing than abstract intellectual pronouncements about racial equality. To this extent, such a person will be alienated from his self, or from part of his self, and we would in fact regard him as more *praiseworthy* the more he refuses to give in to this self and the more he acts *against* it. Correspondingly, we would be disappointed if he were intimidated by the hostility and moral outrage of his unreconstructed friends and relatives into abandoning his new views. Given the description of the situation, doing what is objectively the right thing (opposing Jim Crow, apartheid, and segregation) will evoke fury and moral condemnation so that his moral duty is clearly not to capitulate, but to thicken his skin and psychologically inure himself to such denunciations. Thus he will have to be on guard against surrendering to conventional opinion through simple battle fatigue, while continuing to recognize its wrongness; and, more subtly and insidiously, he will have to be on guard against convincing himself that his original enlightenment was illusory, because conventional opinion was not wrong after all. His previous "moral identity," far from being a foundational touchstone by which to reliably adjudicate what is morally right, will *itself* seem to be a tainted source of morally dubious desires, intuitions, and feelings. Thus to realize the imperative of moral transformation, they will require second-order scrutiny, sorting, and in some cases disposal, so as to avoid moral relapse. The new higher self will have to learn to resist the lower self.

SEEING THE WORLD ANEW

My point, then, is that the revolutionary convert is likely to see herself in a parallel situation, convinced that her socialization has been such that many of her spontaneous reactions will be epistemically suspect; so that, in the absence of reliable internal guides, the safest moral thing to do may be to follow the (sometimes abstract and unfelt) directives of the theory. Quite apart from the metaethical pronouncements sometimes imputed to it, the factual claims of the Marxist reconceptualization of the world are themselves sufficient to generate a radical challenge to conventional morality. For, certainly, one of the central implications of the Marxist analysis of capitalism is its dazzling revelation (arguably the fulfillment of the Enlightenment project) that: what had been thought to be tragic intrinsic features of the human condition as such, either as an outgrowth of nature or as an ultimate manifestation of God's will, are really contingent and changeable consequences of a particular social system, which could be eliminated under a different order. And this new vision means a dramatically expanded view of the role of human causality in shaping the world and, correspondingly, of the realm of the moralizable and justicizable. With respect to the internal divisions of rich and poor in First World nations, and with respect to the global chasm between the First and Third Worlds, the central claim repeatedly made is that there is a causal relationship between these divergent fates.[13] So it is not merely that some happen to be rich and some happen to be poor, and that we have existent but weakish and overridable moral obligations of a charitable kind. Rather, the much more radical thesis is that this inequitable distribution of wealth and poverty is not contingent: it is a structural outcome of a *common* system in which both are enmeshed, and it reproduces the conditions of wealth and poverty at these two poles. This new view of the role of human causality implies that it is not the defeasible duty of charity that is involved, but the much more stringent duty to end present *injustice* and compensate for past injustice. It would mean that the annual death by starvation of millions and the wrenching misery of the lives of hundreds of millions more are not only preventable, but they are in some appropriately attenuated sense categorizable as a *human* crime, the long-distance result over time and space of ruling-class causality.[14] Thus a radical transformation of our mapping of the moral universe and of our own moral responsibilities would be called for.[15]

From such a perspective, mainstream moral theory, predicated on a social ontology of individual actors, may suddenly seem quite deficient. Indeed it might then seem to the convert that the focus of much moral theory is simply misplaced, that the really important issues escape attention. They are located in a theoretical space that is usually regarded as, at best, the realm of benevolence, the charitable, the supererogatory. But once the trail of human causality has been uncovered, it becomes clear that they really need to be brought under the category of justice. Our "considered moral beliefs," the intuitions and principles that we are seeking to bring into maximal coherence with one another, would then have been revealed to be startlingly deviant from what they should have been because of these theoretical blinders.

I suggest that this reconceptualization will have several implications for the convert's thinking on the issues of moral dilemmas and Marxist dirty hands. As mentioned, the simple dramatic fact is that these hundreds of millions of lives must now be placed on the moral scales. Far from being seen as people who are suffering and dying in an unfortunate yet dikai-logically neutral way (i.e., bad, yet neither just nor unjust), they must now be categorized as people to whom a great *injustice* has been done, whose fundamental *rights* have been violated. Moreover, because of the view of Marxism as a *science* of history, particularly in the naively positivistic version that would have prevailed in these circles, largely absent would have been any uncertainty and hesitation about exactly how to assign probabilities to outcomes, whether in paradigmatically consequentialist reasoning, or as a subordinate but crucial part of another, nonconsequentialist kind of moral theory; and how to balance positives and negatives against one another. Historical materialism had proven that global socialism would bring the millennium, thus rescuing capitalism's victims; and faced with this momentous set of choices, one had to decide whether to advance or retard this (preordained) outcome.

Second, the reflective convert is likely to be struck by the epistemological aspect of the whole affair, the fact that all along she has been taking these horrors for granted as unfortunate but inevitable; however, now she sees—and is agonized that others do not see—that they are really the preventable result of the workings of capitalism. How could she have been so blind? she may wonder. And how can others go on being so blind? Gornick writes:

> [F]or all of my growing-up years "us" and "them" were socialists and non-socialists; the "politically enlightened" and the politically *un*enlightened; those who were "struggling for a better world" and those who, like moral slugs, moved blind and unresponsive through this vast inequity that was our life under capitalism. (Gornick 1983, 4–5)

Alarmed by her previous unawareness, the convert is likely to be particularly self-conscious about the need not to fall back into the old way of seeing things, the spontaneous intuitions of traditional morality that, in this respect in particular, are so clearly epistemically deficient. Commenting on the outcry over the violence of the French Revolution, Mark Twain observed that: "There were two 'Reigns of Terror,' if we would but remember it and consider it; the one wrought murder in hot passion, the other in heartless cold blood; the one lasted mere months, the other had

lasted a thousand years."[16] As part of the distancing from her spontaneous bourgeois self, the revolutionary convert must make it an essential
part of the schooling of her new sensibility that she *does* "remember it and
consider it." So whenever in the future the morality of an action is in question and she feels hesitation, she will sternly remind herself of the ongoing devastation produced by capitalism, which it is in the interests of the
bourgeoisie to represent as "natural," "inevitable," and therefore conceptually protected from moral condemnation.

Finally, the third implication for Marxist dirty hands is to put into question our criteria for cleanness. In standard analyses of the subject, such as
Steven Lukes' (1985) discussion of Sartre's famous play *Les Mains Sales*
(Sartre 1949), this aspect has not, I think, been sufficiently taken into account. Communists are simply depicted as arguing that the end justifies
the means within a framework in which political effectiveness is contraposed to retaining one's moral integrity. But I would suggest that a neglected contributory factor to the development of a Stalinist epistemology
is the Communist perception that because the present order is *not* neutral,
but an engine of oppression, it is not the case that doing nothing *does* keep
your hands clean. In other words, there would be an argument to deny, or
at least diminish, the moral distance between acts of omission and acts of
commission. As Ted Honderich writes, in his analysis of the moral justification for political violence by the Left:

> [The claim] is that we [in the West, and of the privileged classes] who are
> law-abiding, contrary to common belief, do not live lives which are anything
> like right on the whole. *Our conduct is wrong.* The argument for this is that by
> our ordinary lives we contribute to certain terrible circumstances. We make
> essential contributions to the shortening of the lifetimes of whole peoples
> and classes, and to many kinds of suffering and distress and degradation,
> and to denials of autonomy and of freedoms. In fact we *ensure* by our ordi-
> nary lives that multitudes of individuals die before [their] time. (Honderich
> 1989, 64–65)

Doing nothing will therefore mean being complicit in ongoing injustice.[17] To guard against the temptations of self-deception in a moral guise,
then, a strict personal regimen will be necessary. The Communist
"knows" in advance, from the theory, that the revolutionary struggle will
bring about a society where the injustice and suffering of the present order will be eliminated. She also knows that this struggle will on many occasions require her to do things that are condemned by traditional morality. Thus she can anticipate that there will be times when she will be
hesitant, unsure of herself, self-doubting—and that these vacillations will
serve capitalist interests. Her moral duty, then, like Ulysses' binding himself, may appear to be the hardening of her heart in advance and the steel-

ing of herself against the intuitions that will seem quite convincing at the time but that she "knows" now are the lures, the siren calls, of the bourgeois self, capitalism's agent within her. Coolly, abstractly, not yet immersed in the situation, she is better able to take up the objective moral posture of the ideal revolutionary observer. Duty therefore requires that she be prepared to ignore what will *seem* like duty in the thick of battle.

Moreover, she knows the situation is likely to be repeated; that is, it will routinely be the case that she, unlike those moral agents who take the background social structure for granted, will be faced with apparent moral dilemmas in the course of her activism. Therefore, the attitude she will have toward "regrets" and the concession of the existence of moral "remainders" (Stocker 1990) will be significantly different. The metaduty whose architectonic structures our appropriate moral responses may be interpreted by her as implying that she should preemptively fortify herself against regrets and deny remainders, even if the act itself seems to require them. For the argument would be that: given our likely psychological weakness as agents and given the dangers of falling short of the demands of the revolutionary self, the iterated character of our encounter with such dilemmas implies that to consistently do the right revolutionary thing, we should act as if *no* regrets are appropriate. If we allow ourselves to feel regrets each time, the likely long-term cumulative effect of this moral residue will be to incapacitate ourselves for doing what is objectively right. In Spender's words:

> One ceases to be inhibited by pity for the victims of revolution. Indeed one can regard pity as a projection of one's own [counter]revolutionary wish to evade the issue of revolution. . . . It is "humanitarian" weakness to think too much about the victims. The point is to fix one's eyes on the goal, and then one is freed from the horror and anxiety—quite useless in any case—which inhibit the energies of the liberal mind. (Crossman 2001, 237–38)

THE WILL TO BELIEVE

I hope I have now said enough to make it seem plausible that, given Marxism's empirical and normative claims, the Communist convert will need to be on his cognitive guard against both the world and himself; so that a character and belief transformation is called for that is intrinsically (at least initially) neither irrational nor morally contemptible, but indeed, on the contrary, rational and morally praiseworthy. What we now need to do is examine the specific techniques employed and show how a cognitive posture originally adopted in part to *guard against* self-deception would itself *facilitate* self-deception.

Belief modification via doxastic voluntarism (i.e., willing yourself to believe something) has traditionally seemed to many philosophers both implausible as a possible psychological process and, in any case, normatively indefensible from an epistemic point of view, since it implies making yourself believe via an effort of the will in defiance of the evidence. The assumption has been that if the evidence were really such as to support the belief, you would already have the belief; and if you don't, then this shows, ipso facto, that you should not.

But on both counts, this is too summary a dismissal. J. Thomas Cook (1987) has argued that it is indeed possible to "decide to believe." One does not, of course, actually make oneself believe by an act of will; rather, one sets up processes by which one is exposed to certain stimuli that one knows will help to generate and sustain the belief, and, correspondingly, avoid stimuli with the opposite effect. These stimuli can themselves, of course, produce the belief through evidential or nonevidential causal chains. For example, the Pascalian model: go to church, associate with religious types, drop your atheist friends, read the Bible every night, and eventually you will come to believe in God (Lycan and Schlesinger 1996). Similarly in one sense, though conversely in another, Cook's example involves a student who knows his creationist beliefs will obstruct a biology career, and so he deliberately sets out to induce in himself beliefs that he regards as false through going to Harvard, associating with adherents to an evolutionary viewpoint, reading scientific texts, and so on.

In these kinds of examples, our rationality is engaged only instrumentally: our initial attitude to the desired belief set is that it is false; however, we have good prudential, nonevidential reasons (eternal salvation, a successful career) why we should make ourselves believe it. However it is also possible to devise examples where the process is epistemically defensible, where an effort of will is required to believe what we have reason to think is *true*. The problem is that the belief does not come spontaneously, or is not stable, because we are resisting ("hot") motivation and/or ("cold") appearance. Here rationality is engaged both instrumentally and epistemically. We are not believing against what we believe to be epistemically convincing evidence (as in the two cases just illustrated); rather, we are believing against prima facie evidence that we believe to be illusory, one-sided, or in some other way epistemically inadequate, but that nonetheless exerts a certain doxastic pull on us, either for some motivational reason or because of its intrinsic features.

Now as argued, the revolutionary convert is in a similar position. He wishes to generate or preserve what he thinks (from Marxist theory) are the correct empirical and normative beliefs, in an environment where he knows he will be under constant pressure to abandon them; he also wishes to unify his belief system, thereby reducing cognitive dissonance, because at a lower level (or, in the language of partitioned selves, with his bourgeois self), he continues to be prone to beliefs and intuitions he now regards as false. For example, if he is himself from a privileged background and leading a comfortable life, he may have to keep reminding himself that the capitalist system is indeed an unjust and exploitative one in which prosperity and material wealth are purchased at the cost of great misery elsewhere. So it may seem reasonable to adopt an epistemic strategy in which he ignores and avoids reports and stories negative to the cause (exposés of the conditions in socialist countries, celebrations of the achievements of capitalism) and in which he is even wary about his own observations, intuitions, and reactions. The formidable array of hostile ideational influences—conservative scholarship; the corporate press; popular culture; the attacks of relatives, former friends, workmates; his own socialization—will constitute an ongoing cognitive besiegement. Moreover, there will be, in many cases, a remarkable confluence of mutually reinforcing epistemic, moral, and prudential reasons to change his views: appeals to his rationality (the apparent evidence), his moral sense (the conventional condemnations of Communists), and his self-interest (the consequences to him of his continued allegiance). But the very ferocity of these attacks, the very ease with which one could give in to them, may be taken by him as a sign of a temptation to be resisted. *Precisely because it would be so easy, it would be wrong.* Some of the reports he hears may be disturbing, but he will be able to tell himself (at least initially) that, if one had the time and resources to do the necessary investigatory work, these stories could be refuted or defused. The Left is perpetually embattled, outgunned in the propaganda wars by the bourgeoisie. So it may genuinely seem that it is rationally defensible to ignore them or even actively avoid them, with the confident expectation that at some stage the truth will come out; but, until then, to give them one's attention would only weaken one's resolve, and to do so would be morally culpable. The convert erects a concentric series of defenses, with successive fallback positions prepared:

1. One can avoid reading negative stories in the first place, or one can read them with an aprioristically dismissive attitude;
2. one can redescribe them in such a way as to defuse their impact;
3. one can morally justify them.[18]

To begin with, the convert may simply enclose himself as far as possible in the world of the party press. Maxime Rodinson (1983, 33) comments on "the refusal even to examine any document, any argument, that could imperil the delicate balance one has achieved in one's inner being. How many party militants have I known who refused to read an opponent's texts, the expositions of divergent points of view, or even neutral studies, often stating quite flatly that it was a matter of preserving their mental tranquility!" Similarly, Ellen Schrecker (1999, 37) describes the behavior of U.S. academics in the 1930s and 1940s: "Such ignorance was largely deliberate. Convinced that the CP, despite its problems, was the most effective political organization around, many academic Communists simply avoided informing themselves about these problems, and stifled their doubts about the Moscow purge trials."

Because of the press's past record, this policy seemed rationally justified. Dorothy Healey, for many decades a leading member of the Californian branch of the CPUSA, says (Healey and Isserman 1993, 153): "We had read so many lies about our own Party in the capitalist press that we felt we could dismiss reports of cruelty and repression in the Soviet Union as just so much propaganda." Paul Lyons writes:

> Communists assumed that the press was biased against the Soviet Union and all working-class peoples; they experienced media deception and hypocrisy almost every day in their own work; lies about strikers, sensationalism about outside agitators, and selective reporting. It is understandable, therefore, that Communists mistrusted press reports and relied on their own Party media. . . . The Bolshevik code, which visualized all struggles through military metaphors, argued that there are times when the revolutionary cadre has to simply maintain discipline and have faith that information will eventually be revealed to clarify seemingly compromising situations. *Such moments were tests that comrades had to pass.* (Lyons 1982, 140–41; my emphasis)

We see here a clear statement of what I have argued the psychology of the situation will produce: a perception of the fusing of moral and epistemic duty. Significantly, Rodinson (1983, 51) draws an explicit parallel between the self-conceptions of the PCF and the Catholic Church, both morally and epistemically besieged by temporal sin: "But ultimately, the party knows best, the church knows best. Especially since the thought of each individual is dulled by original sin and the insinuations of Satan, or by the weight of bourgeois ideology, which seeps in through our every pore." In such a framework, considering giving credence to hostile reports will, under one's psychological introspection, bear the phenomenological stigmata of giving in to temptation.

But even where the epistemic sorting was less Manichean, the simple fact of such radically divergent accounts, conjoined with a metatheory about the class bias motivating them, produced a state of cognitive confusion and uncertainty in which the convert was likely to decide that the best strategy was to stick with the party. Stephen Spender goes so far as to suggest that the very virulence of the accusations would in some cases have the counterproductive result of *confirming* belief:

The fanatical propaganda directed by counter-revolutionaries on the whole helped Russia very much, by producing a dense fog of prejudice in which it became impossible for a detached observer to accept what was said against Russia. (In parenthesis, I suggest that anti-Communist propaganda has proved the most reliable and best propaganda, working in the long run in favor of Stalin, since the Revolution.) (Crossman 2001, 243)

Second, where outright evasion/denial of critical stories or apparently disconfirming experiences was not possible, the fallback defense was that of reconceptualizing them in some way as to be less threatening. The general strategy here is just a variation on the familiar Duhem-Quine thesis: that any core hypothesis can be preserved from refutation simply by making suitable adjustments in the surrounding auxiliary beliefs. Because of Marxism's epistemically layered view of the social structure of capitalism and its corresponding set of metatheories about cold mechanisms of cognitive distortion, it is, as earlier argued, particularly—or dangerously—well endowed for such approaches. Thus Arthur Koestler writes sardonically about his early initiation into the 1930s German CP:

Gradually I learned to distrust my mechanistic preoccupation with facts and to regard the world around me in the light of dialectic interpretation. It was a satisfactory and indeed blissful state; once you had assimilated the technique you were no longer disturbed by facts; they automatically took on the proper color and fell into their proper place. (Crossman 2001, 34)

For example, he recounts how on a 1932–1933 visit to the Soviet Union he was initially shocked by the economic backwardness of the country. But he was able to explain it to himself as the consequence of beginning from a much lower level of industrialization than the Western nations, so that—given a long-term historical view—appearances were misleading. He developed an "automatic sorting machine" to handle problems: "I learnt to classify automatically everything that shocked me as the 'heritage of the past' and everything I liked as the 'seeds of the future'" (Koestler 1954, 53).

Finally, for those reports with moral implications that could neither be denied nor convincingly reconceptualized, there were justificatory strategies that made essential reference to capitalism's present victims and socialism's future millennium. Louis Fischer (Crossman 2001, 205) writes, in an illuminating metaphor, "The future was Bolshevik capital," on which the Soviet government could issue "promissory notes" and "postdated checks." Koestler (1954, 88), denying the putative "single-mindedness" of communists, talks about the "recurrent crises comparable to the periods of temptation and doubt in the case of religious believers," the frequent desire in "moments of disgust with Russia or the Party . . . to turn back":

"And on every occasion it was some repellent aspect of capitalist society which put [us] back again on the road." Above all, it was the theoretical analysis that uncovered the "grey agency" (Honderich) of capitalism behind the suffering and premature deaths of millions, thus making them admissible weights in the moral scales, which repeatedly helped to tip the balance. Rodinson (1983, 27, 31) describes the "general moral indignation leading to a commitment to self-sacrifice," "to put an end to a system that permanently produces poverty and crime, that subjugates and condemns millions of people throughout the world to an atrocious life, or even to death." And Stephen Spender delineates the standard pattern of argument:

> [I]f communism produces victims, capitalism produces far more. What are the millions of unemployed in peacetime, the millions killed in wars, but the victims of capitalist competition? Capitalism is a system based on victimization, in which the number of victims increases all the time. Communism is a system in which, theoretically . . . there will be no victims. . . . The Revolution was the beginning and the end, the sum of all sums. Someday, somewhere, everything would add up to the happy total. (Crossman 2001, 238, 255)

If socialism really would eliminate the unjust sufferings of millions, was the apparently moral hesitation about taking the steps necessary to bring it about not really properly categorizable as some other, more disreputable motive?[19]

LENINIST VANGUARDISM

The intrinsic difficulties of adjudicating the moral identity of one's reactions were, of course, compounded by the need for the strength of character to resist the pressures from the particular organizational form dominant in the Communist movement throughout the twentieth century: the Leninist vanguard party.[20] As classically stated by Lenin in his 1902 *What Is to Be Done?* the vanguard party is supposedly required because of the need to guide the workers with the "science" of Marxist theory, necessitating a clean break with a workers' consciousness corrupted by "bourgeois ideology" (this is somewhat qualified elsewhere in the text, but the caveats are, literally, marginal: occasional footnotes).[21] Moreover, it is not merely that the party as a whole is the vehicle of science as against the bourgeois ideology of the masses, but that internally, within the party, there are gradations of knowledge and a corresponding hierarchy of power and wisdom, atop which sits the central committee. What would obviously not have been greatly encouraged within such an organizational framework—particularly at the lower, less "scientific" levels—

would be any personal soul-searching and agonizing over the morally correct thing to be done, as well as any worries about the exact location of the boundary between what was merely conventionally morally unacceptable and what should be proscribed by any morality. In addition, as Lukes (1985) has pointed out, Lenin's own attitude toward morality was fairly clearly instrumentalist, without the nuances that can (arguably) be found in Marx, so that no answer is given to the equally important question "What is not to be done?"

The apparent success of the Bolsheviks meant that this particular organizational form, which could be seen as a defensible response to the specific conditions of Czarist absolutism, became officially canonized as the global model to be followed. Contingency was frozen into necessity. Worldwide Communist identification with the fate of a backward peasant nation, represented as the future that worked, would henceforth imply—within the militaristic metaphors of local and global class struggle—the mandatory theoretical endorsement of every tactical shift of the Soviet government.

Some might therefore argue that it is here that the real blame lies. Nevertheless, it is obviously open for critics to reply that this attempt to displace some of the responsibility onto a particular organizational form is disingenuous and simply raises the same problem at a different level: it avoids the question of why this form found such widespread acceptance within Marxist circles and whether there is not a possible organic connection between it and the ideology itself. Thus Leszek Kolakowski (1977, 284), himself an ex-Communist, asks the question: "Was every attempt to implement all basic values of Marxian socialism likely to generate a political organization that would bear marks unmistakably analogous to Stalinism?" He answers it with an affirmative. The problem for the Left is to devise an organizational structure appropriate to a theory predicated on an epistemic disjuncture (of a greater or lesser sharpness, depending on one's Leninist or Gramscian sympathies) with "common sense" and mass consciousness while avoiding cognitive authoritarianism and sectarian politics. Thus, at the other end of the political spectrum from Kolakowski, even a writer as sympathetic as Roger Gottlieb describes "The Dilemmas of Leftist Social Differentiation"; and, based in part on his own experiences with the American New Left, he argues that:

> The personal identity of leftists separates them from the rest of society. Socialist politics faces a dilemma because socialists meet their personal needs in ways alien to the majority, nonsocialist, culture. . . . A community of leftists develops its own exclusionary form of life. . . . Socialist politics becomes contradictory because socialists are driven, consciously and unconsciously, by two incompatible imperatives: meet your needs as persons, *and* create more and more socialists. (Gottlieb 1987, 215–16)

A tension exists between constituting a subcommunity to provide epistemic and moral support for one another and reaching out to the world, and the danger will be a gradual and unnoticed deterioration into a sect with self-confirmatory modes of apprehending reality.

THE WILL TO DISBELIEVE

For all the reasons outlined—the intrinsic difficulties of mapping this new moral topography, the fears that one's own moral hesitations might really be some other kind of motivation, the constant pressure from a party leadership taking its orders from a besieged foreign power—the convert increasingly begins to be less critical in her judgment, or she suspends it altogether, suppressing or banishing her doubts. If the first time is hard, the second time is easier, and the third easier still. She tells herself that the boundary between what is politically justified and what is inexcusable under any circumstances is much farther away from traditional morality than she had originally thought. She experiences a callousing of the sensibility, a calcification of the heart. Actions she would originally have questioned she now goes along with or performs herself without hesitation. But as the deeds accumulate, a strange new dynamic begins to assert itself. For if the party has been *wrong*—a terrifying thought that occasionally flits across her consciousness—then she does in fact stand condemned. Thus she would now have a motivation for denying this possibility, given the depth of her involvement. The greater the number of morally questionable actions she has performed or endorsed, the more important it will be to insist on their justifiability. So an eerily inverted transition takes place. The same set of cognitive postures originally adopted to minimize empirical and moral error begins to facilitate them; the very psychological transformation required of us to avoid self-deception begins to encourage it.

In a paper on the subject, David Jones (1989) distinguishes what he calls *episodic* and *pervasive* self-deception, suggesting that although most commentators have focused on explanations for the former, it is the latter that is perhaps most challenging. He offers an account of pervasive self-deception that he thinks lays the basis for "a more unified theory of human psychology," since the various patterns of human irrationality can be located on a single spectrum, with no need for the positing of a radical distinction between normal and abnormal psychology. For what is involved is "the unforeseen and unintended cumulative result of a largely unplanned incremental process of psychological development," which, through feedback loops and the responses to others, gradually develops into "a vicious downward spiral" (Jones 1989, 232–34). As indicated at the beginning, I am sympathetic to such an analysis, since it obviates the need of having to postulate a fundamentally deviant personality type to explain Communist belief patterns. Instead, it is the situational dynamic that is crucial. First, one inculcates in oneself a general skepticism about countervailing factual and moral claims, developing a behavioral infrastructure to support this pattern of cognition. This skepticism eventually becomes routinized and habitual, so that it is easier and easier to ignore "bourgeois" accusations, to simply dismiss them wholesale rather than discriminate among and attempt to assess different charges as one might originally have done. And then, once one has crossed a certain line, it becomes difficult to go back because of one's investment in having been right.

The diagnosis of self-deception is one that many ex-Communists have made of themselves. Thus Arthur Koestler (Crossman 2001, 71–72) refers to the "dialectical tight-rope acts of self-deception, performed by men of good will and intelligence . . . the almost unlimited possibilities of mental acrobatism." Describing the impact of Khrushchev's famous 1956 speech to the Twentieth Congress of the Soviet Communist Party, Vivian Gornick (1983, 10) suggests that "Khrushchev's report compelled millions of people to know consciously that which many of them had known subconsciously for a very long time." Dorothy Healey talks about the "false consciousness" that Communists themselves developed and the relation between it and their original revolutionary mental self-discipline:

> We ignored anything which challenged our version of the truth. What sustained us all those decades in our quest to change the world was an unreal set of notions about the world. Faith in the inevitability of history and the purity of our own cause had always been our greatest asset. Paradoxically, our illusions strengthened our commitment even as they weakened our chances of ever reaching our goal. (Healey and Isserman 1993, 156)

For it would always be possible to find reasons to stay. Since Marxism is a theory that emphasizes long-term developments, it is always possible to tell oneself that this is a temporary historical zag that will eventually straighten itself out. Moreover, one could argue that where there were problems, it was one's duty to stay to try to remedy them. Koestler (Crossman 2001, 65) writes: "Though we wore blinkers, we were not blind, and even the most fanatical among us could not help noticing that all was not well in our movement. But we never tired of telling each other—and ourselves—that the Party could only be changed from inside, not from outside." The presence of this moral motivation also meant that there was uncertainty about whether one would be leaving for morally defensible reasons, when there was such a confusing overlay of other possible reasons to be leaving. Ellen Schrecker (1999, 61) reports that for some, the persecutions of McCarthyism had an unexpected effect: "In a perverse way . . . McCarthyism seemed to have kept some people in the Party longer than they would otherwise have stayed. A historian who had joined the CP after the Second World War [recalls]: 'I would have left the party sooner . . . except that I wanted to be sure I wasn't doing so out of fear.'" Another historian stayed until 1956 because "he didn't want to be considered 'chicken.' . . . There was, another former Communist recalls, a certain amount of 'pride in not being opportunistic.'"

Let us say then, that at some point the convert begins to feel that there is something wrong that cannot be explained away as bourgeois propaganda, redescribed as superficial appearance, or morally justified as revolutionarily necessary:

> I began to feel a dreadful nagging pain developing at the edge of thought—sometimes like toothache, sometimes a sudden stab of fear, sometimes a quick wash of panic—about the "progressive" world. Its logic began to break down; injustices began to loom . . . questions arose for which there were no longer ready answers. (Gornick 1983, 11)

It is possible, of course, that the disruptive, unassimilable event will finally occur that causes the convert to put her whole system of belief, and its generative epistemology, into question. But another response is possible, which is to step up the pace of the cognitive processing machinery, machinery already oriented specifically to a skepticism about antisocialist reports and a wariness about one's own reactions to them. All one needs to do is to put it into higher gear, make it less discriminating; by now already deeply ingrained are the habits of careful inattention, the reflexive theoretical redescription, the discounting as bourgeois one's own moral intuitions, and the automatic moral justification. But for the first time a new strand manifests itself in the already complex and epistemically confusing bundle of motivations: the fear that one has been wrong about the system one has been supporting—to which one has given some, perhaps considerable, portion of one's life—and the desire to block the recognition of this. Djilas writes of how he and his comrades questioned a group of Yugoslav party members who had been to the Soviet Union:

> They saw a whole world erroneously because they couldn't grasp it otherwise. This was the world of their imagination, and they pictured it falsely to those who, in turn, didn't dare believe it different from the way they wanted it to be. If either of them had known and understood conditions in the Soviet Union, their own ideals, the whole purpose of their lives, would have been undermined and lost. (Djilas 1973, 231–32)

The deeper one's involvement has been, the more time and energy have been invested in this cause, the harder it will be to recognize it as a loss.

The greater the atrocities one fears one has been an apologist for, the more compelling the need to deny them. Far better then to persuade oneself that, even if there have been problems, things can still be made right in the end; that all will somehow be redeemed by the eventual outcome. "You see, the longer you go on believing and working for the Party, believing everything is good, the longer it takes. . . . There was always the urge to explain away the unpleasant things and to cling to every little bit of hope."[22] Leaving would make unavoidable the recognition that all their efforts had been for nothing. Instead, the machinery is accelerated. The growing hostility of others, the multiplication of adverse reports, the increasing number of defections from one's own side—they are all met by a further hardening of one's protective moral integument, a heightened perception of one's unjust capitalist persecution as the moral vanguard of the new society. By this stage one has a cognitive, affective, and moral stake in one's picture, not just of the present, but of the past as well; one needs not to know. Dorothy Healey (1993, 156) points out that many members of the CPUSA refused to read the 1956 Khrushchev speech, even when it was reprinted in the party press, because they recognized that its terrible implication was that "the sacrifices they had made during those years were in vain." Similarly, Maxime Rodinson comments:

> [T]he deeper reason for the delay in registering disillusionment is simply the visceral need not to renounce a commitment that has illuminated one's life, given it meaning, and for which many sacrifices have often been made. Hence the reluctance to recognize the most obvious facts, the desperate paralogical guile to which one resorts in an effort to avoid the required conclusions, the passionate and obstinate blindness. (Rodinson 1983, 33)

In the same way that the original conversion to Marxist theory implied a revolution in seeing the world, so this revelation of the true Stalinist character of the system one had been supporting meant a revolution in one's conception of socialism, one's own past activism, and, ultimately, oneself. Gornick (1983, 12) describes her bitter nightly debates with her Stalinist aunt after the 1956 Khrushchev revelations: "And we stared at each other, each of us trapped in her own anguish. I, in the grip of that pain and fury that I can feel to this day . . . and she, my aunt, her strong peasant face ashen with grief and survival, the world inside her and all around her dissolving in a horror of confusion too great to bear, too annihilating to take in." The double horror lay not just in the acknowledgment of the despotic nature of the system, the incredulous realization that the bourgeois press had been right all along; rather, what it also implied was the shattering retrospective reconceptualization of *oneself*, of one's own moral history. For one would then be forced to confront the fact that one had oneself been complicit in the crimes of Stalinism, denying them, explaining them away, defending them to others—the agonized but in-eluctable recognition of the bloody-handed figure in the mirror as oneself. After such knowledge—after such ignorance—what forgiveness?

CONCLUSION

As argued at the beginning, then, a virtue of this account is that it does not need to postulate any aberrant psychological profile to explain the puzzling pattern of continuing Communist fidelity to an exploded dream. While it may be the case that morally deviant psychological types were attracted to such parties in greater numbers than to mainstream parties (though the remoteness in many cases of any real chance of attaining political power might well imply the converse), there is no necessity for supposing that they must constitute the majority of Communist membership. Instead all we need to do is to follow through the degeneration of a moral epistemology constructed for the very difficult circumstances of revolutionary struggle. If the account has been persuasive, it illustrates a set of standing dangers of which the Left needs to be aware and against which any ethically responsible socialist project must somehow find a way to safeguard itself.

NOTES

1. An exception would be the early Frankfurt School, for example, Marcuse (1985). See also the thoughtful retrospective assessment of William McBride (1999).

2. The term "Stalinism" was first used pejoratively in the 1930s by those, most notably Leon Trotsky and his supporters, who argued that Stalin's policies represented not a fulfillment but a betrayal of Marx's original socialist vision. Subsequently it would become a general term of opprobrium, employed narrowly in the internecine battles of the Left and more broadly by critics on the Right, dubious that any fundamental distinction could in fact be sustained between Marx's theory and Stalin's practice, so that "Stalinist socialism" would actually be a pleonasm. (For different perspectives on this, the "continuity thesis," see, for example, Robert Tucker [1977], especially the essays by Stephen Cohen, Robert McNeal, Leszek Kolakowski, and Mihailo Markovic.) The reference is correspondingly fuzzy, ostensively indicating at least (obviously) the politico-economic system in the Soviet Union under Stalin's actual rule; but, for some, it continues to be applicable beyond Stalin's death in 1953 down to the period just before the Soviet Union's breakup, and it includes (depending on one's politics) most or all of the self-described "socialist" nations (the former East Bloc states, China, North Korea, Vietnam, Cuba, etc.). Likewise, theoretical definitions and explanations continue to be contested, with differing criteria being invoked as definitive (the party-state

dictatorship, the deification of the leader, the collapsing of civil society); with conflicting etiologies being offered (the general dynamic of "Marxist totalitarianism"; the specificities of Russian, and later East European, economic and cultural backwardness; the consequences of capitalist encirclement; the party variously as a parasitic stratum/a "state-capitalist" ruling class/a bureaucratic oligarchy); and, as mentioned, with opposing relations to Marxist theory posited (Marxism as realized/betrayed).

Fortunately, it will not be necessary for us to enter into these frequently esoteric debates (although my own sympathies are with the Left, who argue for at least partial discontinuity), since my main focus here is not on Stalinism as a politico-economic system, but rather as political culture, as a state of mind. As such, the reference is to the willingness to perform or endorse grossly immoral actions under the banner of establishing or preserving socialism. This chapter is an attempt to explain the development of a Stalinist psychology in people of ordinary decent—or even superior—moral character, where it is at least prima facie puzzling. (I take it that there is nothing at all mysterious about monstrous people acquiescing in monstrous deeds; so that for those party members who fell into this category, there is nothing to explain.) For further qualifications and clarifications in response to criticisms, see note 9.

3. The contrast is doubtless overdrawn, since, especially in the earlier stages of social reconstruction in these countries, there would have been many participating individuals inspired by a genuine moral idealism; while on the other hand, material and psychic rewards would not have been entirely lacking for certain levels of party membership in the West, particularly where the party was a significant national presence (e.g., France, Italy). But where Communists actually *rule*, the overdetermination of belief by other possible motivations—careerist opportunism, simple fear—makes the disentangling of the pertinent factors more difficult. In that sense, the situation of Communists in opposition in the West is more interesting and constitutes more of an ideal case for the phenomenon under examination.

4. Orthodox Communist Party [CP] members are a convenient reference point; they are the paradigm examples of Stalinist psychology; and they are the main source upon which I draw in the following pages. Obviously, though, CP membership would itself have been neither a necessary nor a sufficient condition for being Stalinist: one, because of the case of fellow travelers and members of nonorthodox revolutionary groups and sects (Maoist, Hoxhaist, etc.); and two, because of the case of principled anti-Stalinist party members—though (depending on the times and the particular party) the latter's stay in the organization would have been unlikely to be greatly prolonged.

5. One interesting consequence of the collapse has been the revival of the "totalitarian" model, which had fallen into disfavor in the Western academy by the 1960s, but which many Eastern European and former Soviet scholars, now given a voice to speak freely, claimed did indeed resonate with their experience. The overnight disintegration of the regimes certainly underlined their utter lack of legitimacy, but the problem remains of explaining how the model—famous precisely for its prediction of unreformability and increased repressiveness in response to dissent—could account for a largely bloodless transition and a willing yielding-up of power. For a range of different perspectives on this question, see Siegel (1998).

6. See Lyons (1982); Gornick (1983); Schrecker (1999); Rodinson (1983); Djilas (1973); Healey and Isserman (1993). Though now more than fifty years old, *The God That Failed* (Crossman 2001 [1949]) remains unsurpassed in many ways. See also Koestler (1954).

7. The terms originally come from cognitive psychology, from the work of such theorists as Leon Festinger and Amos Tversky. Their introduction into Marxist theory is largely due to Jon Elster (see, e.g., Elster 1983; 1985). Explaining away bourgeois opposition to socialist views in terms of "hot" class interest is easily enough done, but obviously accounting for working-class hostility requires another kind of account (at least it would have when socialism was still thought to be viable); hence, the crucial role played by theories of "cold" distortion. For a discussion, see Mills (1989).

8. As discussed in chapter 3, an amoralist interpretation of Marx has long been dominant, though recently it has come under challenge. But my primary concern is with the moral beliefs of the ordinary (nonacademic) men and women who became political activists and who would, I think, have seen themselves as moral agents. To the extent that they did not—that is, to the extent that they adopted a posture of amoralism—then, to repeat what I said at the beginning, there is no mystery about their behavior.

9. In the redrafting of the original article that became this chapter, the editorial board of *Politics & Society* (where it originally appeared) asked me to clarify the following: First, what is the scope of the following explanation supposed to be (i.e., what exactly is the behavioral pattern I am trying to explain)? Second, am I advancing it as the *only* account (once psychopathology has been dismissed as a contender), the *main* account, or one of *several* possible complementary accounts? Pertinent to this question is the reaction of an ex-Communist, here named *A*, to whom I showed the original draft of the paper, which I should mention here in the interests of truth, if not (perhaps), in the interests of promoting my own theory. He told me that the description that follows did not ring phenomenologically true to his own experience and to the experience he believed many other Communists of his (recent) generation had had. Joining in the 1960s and 1970s, they were relatively clear-eyed about the true character of the Soviet Union and official communism, but felt they had to support it, *faute de mieux*, as "the only game in town," the main countervailing force in the global arena against U.S. imperialism.Thus the event, or series of events, that ultimately triggered their departure (Czechoslovakia, Afghanistan, Poland, etc.) did not lead to agonized soul-searching and the shattering of illusions—as had the 1930s purges and show trials, or Khrushchev's famous speech to the 1956 Twentieth Congress of the Communist Party of the Soviet Union and the later Soviet invasion of Hungary—because there had been few illusions left to lose to begin with. "A healthy and, evidently, correct skepticism about the SU and the extent to which it had de-Stalinized was pervasive" (personal communication from April 16, 1992).

I believe I can reply, without begging the question, that my thesis was not primarily intended to explain this sort of pragmatic, lesser-of-two-evils support in the first place (in which, one could say, you hold the red flag with one hand and your nose with the other), but rather the phenomenon of uncritical support coupled with genuine belief, in the face of the evidence, that all was well with existing socialism. So one would have to distinguish (with respect to the first question) different cases: (1)

initial commitment to existing socialism when available information was scarce and hostile sources were not to be trusted, eventually shading over into (2) continuing commitment to existing socialism, even when more and more negative information from reliable sources became available, and distinct from (3) pragmatic, "cynical" signing-up in a situation of restricted choice, in the hope that proclaimed reforms were genuine and presaged systematic and permanent change. The temporal dimension of this listing is obvious, and another of *A*'s points was that a more detailed and empirically oriented study would really require a periodization of different generations of Communists and a cross-comparison of the differential salience over time of varying kinds of motivation. The extent to which my account is illuminating and useful, then, would depend on the synchronic and diachronic pattern of distribution of party members in one or another of these categories, being most valuable for (2). But I would claim in response that neither (1) nor (3) pose any particular explanatory problems; the interesting and challenging case *is* (2).

Regarding the second question, I would say that I am advancing this as at least *a* major, and perhaps *the* major, explanation within the category of (2); since though I do concede that "vanguardism" and Soviet domination of CPs were contributory causes, one would still need to explain why people accepted these organizational structures and this control in the first place.

10. A "static" paradox arises because it would seem that one must simultaneously believe that *p* and *~p*; and a "dynamic" paradox arises because of the apparently self-defeating character of the project of getting oneself to believe what one knows is false. Responses have included skepticism about the phenomenon, strategies for partitioning the mind (either in terms of levels of awareness or in terms of discrete selves), and the modification or rejection of interpersonal models.

11. In these four cases, which Mele calls "garden-variety instances of self-deception," the subject's desire that *p* be true leads him respectively to

> misinterpret as not counting . . . against *p* data that [he] would easily recognize to count . . . against *p* in the desire's absence . . . to interpret as *supporting p* data that [he] would easily recognize to count against *p* in the desire's absence . . . to fail to focus attention on evidence that counts against *p* and to focus instead on evidence suggestive of *p* . . . [and] both to overlook easily obtainable evidence for *~p* and to find evidence for *p* that is much less accessible. (Mele 2001, 26–27)

12. I do not really think it is necessary for the argument to spell out what the theoretical underpinnings of this revolutionary new morality are. Marxism has often been represented as a kind of super-consequentialism, and certainly at the popular level, this would probably have been the most frequently adopted interpretation in Communist circles. But a revolutionary morality could, in principle, be some kind of rights theory, or a modified deontology, which is dramatically divergent from conventional versions because the empirical–theoretical assumptions about the world are radically different (e.g., that because workers are compelled to sell their labor power, their rights are violated by capitalism; or that because Third World starvation is caused by the workings of the global capitalist economy, we have a duty to overthrow it). My claim is that the set of problems at issue is, to a significant extent, *independent* of the choice of moral framework, inhering rather in the implications of

Marxism's radically divergent *factual* assumptions that, when conjoined even with conventional normative theory (utilitarianism, contractarianism, natural rights theory, some kind of deontology), will yield revolutionary prescriptions.

13. This claim was sometimes reflected in the very titles of these works, which explicitly proclaimed the role of human (colonial and neocolonial) agency. For example, Andre Gunder Frank, "The Development of Underdevelopment" (1966); Walter Rodney, *How Europe Underdeveloped Africa* (1972); Teresa Hayter, *The Creation of World Poverty* (1987).

14. I have focused here on the (more controversial) argument for moral reconceptualization that follows from the putative consequences of the structural economic causality of capitalism and its (indirect) responsibility for human death and suffering. But it should, of course, be noted that arguments can be, and were, given for a responsibility of a far more direct and less philosophically contentious kind. The categorization of the European colonial powers as capitalist meant that the great crimes of the colonial period—the genocide of the natives of the Americas, the death toll of the African slave trade, plantation slavery, colonial forced labor (ten million in King Leopold II's Congo alone), the punitive expeditionary missions in Asia and Africa—were also to be charged to capitalism's account. Similarly, in the colonial and neocolonial wars of the postwar period—Kenya, Vietnam, Algeria, Angola, Mozambique, Guinea-Bissau, Namibia—and in the ebb and flow of insurgency and counterinsurgency, conflict and coup—Guatemala, Brazil, Indonesia, Chile, East Timor, Argentina, Nicaragua, El Salvador, South Africa—the notorious tortures and massacres (notorious on the Left, anyway) committed by the metropolitan powers and their client states would likewise have been ultimately attributed to the repressive logic of the global capitalist system. And the European fascism of World War II, with its body count in the millions, was, of course, categorized as "capitalism with the gloves off." In the grim arithmetic of atrocity (it would have been claimed), the Left were by no means blameless; but from the long perspective, it was the Right whose balance sheet was overall in the red.

15. A debate in mainstream ethical theory pits those like Samuel Scheffler (1992), who think morality should be moderate and not too demanding, against those like Shelly Kagan (2002), who argue that commonsense morality's belief in agent-centered options (which leave us considerable latitude to indulge our self-interest) really has no defensible basis; so that the (apparently) counterintuitive "extremist" position on what morality requires of us is actually correct. Combining Kagan's metaethical view with Marxist assumptions would produce the paradigm case of the moral transformation that I am trying to describe here, though even the weaker (moderate) position would still generate a significantly different moral cartography.

16. Cited by Geras (1997, 21).

17. For a more recent and far more detailed statement of this case, see Unger (1996).

18. One point made by several critics of the original version of this chapter is that the general techniques I go on to describe are (apart from the necessarily local specificities) common to the repertoire of any cult's trying to preserve belief in the face of disconfirming evidence; there is nothing distinctively Marxist or Communist about them. My response (although this may reflect my own Enlightenment and secular

humanist prejudices) would be that epistemic and moral degeneration are *more* surprising in this case; and reconstructing their trajectory is more of a challenge, since (unlike, say, religious fundamentalism) Marxism is explicitly committed to a scientific worldview in both the natural and social realms, and since it (unlike, say, fascist and racist ideologies) begins from widely shared moral assumptions about human equality. It is not in the least remarkable, in other words, that given their starting point, fideists, fascists, and racists should end up endorsing irrationalist belief structures and immoral practices. It is at least somewhat more remarkable that a commitment to reason and humanism should (under certain circumstances) end up in the same place. I see the interest of my chapter as lying in the explanation of how rationality and morality can themselves lead to this paradoxical outcome.

19. Everybody will have their own favorite anecdotes, of course, but I cannot resist citing here two personal encounters from a decade or so ago that demonstrate the remarkable robustness of these strategies of response. Around Christmas 1989—that is, roughly halfway through the reverse domino effect (after Poland, Hungary, East Germany, and the fall of the Berlin Wall, with fighting ongoing in Romania)—I ran into an orthodox CP member, whom I had not seen for about a year. "So," I naturally asked him, "what do you think about what's going on?" "What's going on?" "You know—the collapse." "What collapse?" "What collapse do you think? The collapse in Eastern Europe!" "Is there a collapse in Eastern Europe?" This dialogue, with its strangely vaudevillian who's-on-first character, continued for some time. Eventually he conceded that there did seem to be a few minor problems, but explained that these were "superstructural"; basically, "It's just the bourgeois press making a big fuss over nothing. In a year's time, they'll have gone on to something else."

This response is perhaps—to quote a French magazine headline from the distant seventies, from the period of the union of the Left—*"plus gauche que sinistre"* (more gauche than sinister). For an entry on the *sinistre* side of the ledger, I am indebted to a militant from one of the nonorthodox sects, who generously took time out from his busy schedule in the class struggle to read and comment on an earlier version of this chapter. As he patiently explained to me, among the (innumerable) things wrong with it was that I seemed to be using *Stalinism* pejoratively, as if I thought Stalin should be morally criticized in some way, whereas the real problem had apparently been insufficient diligence of application: "The real criticism of Stalin is not that he killed too *many* people, but that he killed too *few*." (!) (To be fair, he also believed that the number of Stalin's victims had been greatly exaggerated.) Thereby, it turned out, his actions allowed capitalism to be later restored under Khrushchev.

20. Ex-Communist *A* himself felt that the real explanatory weight should be put here rather than on the individual psychological dynamic: "Were I to attempt a generic explanation, I think I would turn to the political culture associated with vanguardism, central [traits] among which are elitism, moralism, suspicion of democracy (even in the name of democracy), and a we–they social psychology" (personal communication: April 16, 1992).

21. Lenin (1969). For a discussion of vanguardism, see Lustig (1977).

22. Czech Communists Marta and Edward Goldstucker, quoted in Healey and Isserman (1993, 222).

II

RACE AND CLASS

The second part, on race and class, marks the bridge between my previous and my present work, and as such it is most obviously and explicitly transitional. To strike an autobiographical note: I went to graduate school in Canada in the 1970s in the hope of finding a philosophical framework for making sense of the struggles around race, class, and imperialism then taking place in my native country, Jamaica. But I found philosophy very frustrating, very "white." (As one may imagine, however bad things are today, they were far worse then.) The body of theory that came closest to providing the kind of framework I was looking for, which made oppression central, was Marxism. So I became a Marxist. There was that sense of revelation, of scales falling, that many others have experienced and that has been crucial in understanding the theory's appeal to intellectuals. But I nonetheless found many aspects of the theory problematic, including its treatment of these very issues of imperialism and race.

Moreover, on coming to the United States to work after graduation, my dissatisfactions deepened. I have never been as conscious of race as I have been in this country. (The Canadian style of racism—at the time anyway—was somewhat different, more oblique.) These two chapters express this unhappiness. In chapter 5, I look at the then ongoing debate about the so-called underclass, which is disproportionately black and Latino. While arguing from a Left perspective against mainstream liberal and conservative conceptions, I also argue against traditional Left theory. The paper expressed my frustrations, in a way that would later become more pronounced, with orthodox Marxism, which claimed to be historical but ignored white

121

supremacy as a major historical structure. Though still identifying myself as a Marxist, I make a case for the need to develop a modified Marxism that takes race into account in a deep, rather than superficial, way. In a phrase dropped for this revised version, I commented on the paucity of analyses of "whiteness"—little did I know what a growth industry this would become over the course of the decade! By analogy with the attempt to develop a dual-systems approach, like "socialist feminism," I argued for the need for a black Marxism that would synthesize the approaches of the Marxist and black nationalist traditions. (The phrase "critical race theory" had not yet been widely established at the original time of writing.)

An invitation to be on a "Rethinking the Left" panel some years later provided me with a forum for exploring and airing my emerging new view. Bracing myself in advance for the reaction, I boldly argued that in the United States, race was the "primary contradiction." My presentation outraged many in the audience. But after people had calmed down somewhat, and with subsequent e-mail exchanges, at least some of those who had been present developed a greater appreciation of (if not necessarily agreement with) the point I was trying to make. I later incorporated this presentation into a paper invited for a special journal issue on Marx and Marxism, which would become chapter 6. In this chapter, I flesh out and defend the claim in greater detail in order to make a case for the *asymmetric* significance of race in the United States versus gender and class. Moreover, I had begun to believe that race could legitimately be conceptualized as "material" even within a Marxist framework, indeed in a sense more deeply material than class. Whereas previously (for example, at the time of writing the original of chapter 1) I would have thought of race as purely superstructural, a matter of ideological construction, I now saw it as located within the base. However, I have not subsequently pursued this line of argument in my later work. Five years after the underclass paper appeared, this article was to be my last paper explicitly within the Marxist tradition.

5

Under Class Under Standings

I want to turn now to the issue of race and the question of whether, or to what extent, race can be conceptualized within a class (i.e., Marxist) framework. As a convenient reference point, I will use the debate about the "underclass" and what (if anything) to do about it. Certainly, few social issues of the last decade have generated as much acrimonious popular and academic debate. The problem has, in effect, become a kind of ideological touchstone for sorting different domestic agendas—liberal, conservative, radical—for the future of the country and the place envisaged in it for the nonwhite poor.[1] Given the large literature on the subject, I will pay particular attention to Bill Lawson's edited philosophy collection (1992a). Based on papers originally given at a 1989 conference at the University of Delaware, his book—a set of essays by African American philosophers addressing various conceptual and normative questions in the debate—is particularly noteworthy, since, as far as I know, it is the first collective written intervention on a specific topic by black philosophers in U.S. history. (Since so much of the controversy has centered on William Julius Wilson's work *The Truly Disadvantaged* [1987], he has written, appropriately enough, a brief foreword.) As such, it represented at the time a welcome sign that African American philosophers were starting to make the difference in helping to reconceptualize the discipline and contributing to the national dialogue that women philosophers have done with feminist theory.

My own philosophical perspective in this chapter is doubly minoritarian: first, as an African American in a largely white profession, I am concerned to make a case along with my fellow black philosophers for the sociopolitical importance of race; second, as somebody sympathetic to

Marxism, I wish to relate this importance to class forces. So I will be attempting to bring out the possible insights provided by a "black," or at least racially informed, Marxism.[2] My claim will be that race is much more central to the American polity than is usually recognized in philosophy; that it should accordingly be much more central to our theorizing than it currently is; and that this situation can be explained by (a modified) historical materialism. I will focus on the following four topics: the "underclass" as a category; race and class; moral obligation and motivation; and the political spectrum of diagnoses and solutions. Accordingly, my title is meant to be read three ways: in general reference to different "understandings" of the "underclass"; in specific reference to "understandings" arrived at through, or "under," a class framework; and in pointed reference to what is sufficiently acknowledged neither by Marxism nor liberalism, the subordinate moral–racial standing of the "underclass."

THE "UNDERCLASS" AS A CATEGORY

What's in a name? A great deal, as it turns out. "Naming the Underclass makes the Underclass, nominates it into existence, and constitutes it at once as Other," says David Theo Goldberg (1992, 17). The Left standardly argues that concepts carry hooks, theoretical and (frequently) political commitments that link them up to particular understandings of the world and the way it works—often condensing questionable existential assertions, normative judgments, and substantive presuppositions about causal connections. And for many radicals, the "underclass" is itself already a loaded category, being judged to be inherently biased, racially coded, and methodologically vacuous.

Inherently Biased

The objection here is that the term mystifies and stigmatizes, begging crucial questions about causation and agency.[3] It is internally divided, in that, at one and the same time, a human collectivity (a "class") is identified—which presumably, in good Aristotelian fashion, is being seen as a constituent of society—while simultaneously, by the quarantining and threatening adjectival preposition (suggesting the "disreputable, dangerous, disruptive, dark, evil, and even hellish" [Peterson 1991–1992, 617]), it is being removed from it. So this is a class that is not a class, a social entity that is asocial. And, of course, a long line of historical precedents exists for such a notion—the eighteenth-century "mob" and "rabble," the "undeserving" poor, the "dangerous classes"—that fills what could be regarded as a permanent theoretical niche within class ideology of those systemically marginalized by the economy, with social-structural causation then being reified and moralized as psychological traits.

Racially Coded

Moreover, the inherently suspicious nature of the category is exacerbated by its racial cryptography. Intrinsically, the term is a race-neutral one, and it could theoretically be used in an ethnically and racially homogeneous society. In the U.S. context, however, it necessarily acquires a racial subtext that is fused (whether through straightforward biological determinism or more attenuated ethnocultural attribution) with the characteristics of personalized causal responsibility, as just indicated. The long history, embedded in popular white consciousness, of awareness of the black threat—whether from slave rebellion or, in the postbellum period, unruly free blacks—creates a conceptual space for a term whose referent remains essentially constant, though its name may change. With the shift from explicitly racist public discourse to the more sanitized language of the post–Civil Rights Act struggles, a vocabulary of euphemism and indirection becomes necessary, in which one can refer without pointing, and many Left critics see the "underclass" as the latest entry in this old semantic shell game, a way of talking about blacks (and, increasingly, Latinos) without talking about blacks.[4]

Methodologically Vacuous

Finally, the underclass category involves problems of operationalism. One urban geographer demonstrates that—in New York, for example—one can get a variable count of "underclass" census tracts that ranges from 131 all the way down to 6, depending on the threshold and standard deviation norms one takes to be plausible candidates; thus, it leads him to conclude that the concept is "too volatile an organizing principle" (Hughes 1989; Sawhill 1989). Somewhat similarly, Christopher Jencks (1992, ch. 5) shows that even answering a presumably simple question like "Is the underclass growing?" is hampered by the multiplicity of criteria for determining its boundaries. He examines the pertinent statistics under four possible characterizations: the impoverished underclass (income level); the male and female jobless underclass (income source); the educational underclass (cultural skills); and the violent and reproductive underclass (moral norms). Overall, Jencks concludes that from these diverse characterizations no simple vector outcome results, with some problems getting worse and some getting better; thus, it raises questions about how useful the "underclass" actually is as a synthesizing social category. For Left commentators like Adolph Reed Jr. (1990), these difficulties arise unsurprisingly from the fact that the concept has no real theoretical content, that it is a politically driven empiricist construct that amalgamates neighborhoods and peoples with no real connection with one another, under a questionable behaviorist rubric.

As a result of objections like these, Jennifer Hochschild (1991) proposes the term "estranged poor." Wilson himself (1991) now prefers to speak of "ghetto poor," arguing that Hochschild's phrase fails to capture the dual dimensions of economic marginality and social isolation. Goldberg (1992), criticizing both, suggests the "racially marginalized," though the obvious objection to this phrase is that it excludes the *white* underclass. These locutions, it is argued, better facilitate a nontendentious discussion of moral responsibility and public policy. However, since all the authors being considered do use the term, I will follow suit, scare quotes being taken as read.

RACE AND CLASS

Race, as indicated, is central to discussions of the underclass, which is disproportionately, though not exclusively, black and Latino. The "race and class" (or, sometimes, "race versus class") debate, which in one form or another has been going on in the black intellectual community for decades, is really a broad umbrella, by now covering at least four related (but different) debates, some of older, some of more recent, origins:

1. the general theoretical question of the extent to which a convincing class (i.e., Marxist) account can be given of the centrality of race, racial self-identification, and white racism to the polities of the New World;
2. the old nature–nurture, or hereditarian–environmentalist, dispute over the causes of the social ills (e.g., high unemployment, poverty, and crime rates) characteristically associated with blacks;
3. the "culture of poverty" controversy between those who read underclass culture as, in part, racially–ethnically linked and significantly contributing to underclass perpetuation, and those who would redescribe its character and dynamic in Marxist terms;
4. the question arising more recently, especially from Wilson's work (1978; 1987), of whether ongoing (as against past) white racism continues to be a significant social barrier for blacks.

The General Theoretical Question

I want to spend some time on this question, since, unsurprisingly, I see it as the key to the whole tangle of issues.

It would not seem prima facie unreasonable to expect that a purportedly global theory of history would view the project of explaining white racism as important, since it has been a central reality of the planet for the past several hundred years, with a major historical impact on a large proportion of the earth's inhabitants. Unfortunately, First World Marxism, being largely white Marxism, has historically (following the founders) had little useful to say about race. In part, this characteristic is a corollary of the general weakness of Marxist theory on issues of national identity and ethnicity, "backward" local particularisms that Marx and Engels envisaged as being swept aside in the universalizing drive of a progressive globalizing capitalism, thereby producing a workingman who had no country (Munck 1986). But the pattern of neglect has been perpetuated, more culpably, by subsequent generations of white Marxists, who have tended to write off race consciousness and black nationalism as an obfuscatory digression from the necessary focus on class (Outlaw 1990).

Understandably, then, many black intellectuals discussing Marxism have tended to contrapose race to class, seeing a commitment to Marxist theory as excluding a theoretical focus on the causal significance of white racism. Accordingly, any Marxism that is going to survive in an increasingly nonwhite United States needs to be able to demonstrate that this polarization can be transcended. In Bernard Boxill's contribution to the Lawson collection, for example, he distinguishes two main approaches to analyzing black problems in African American political thought: a "race school" and a "class school," with the former blaming white racism, the latter black disabilities. (Wilson's views on the underclass are assimilated by Boxill to the second.) Boxill says that the "class school is not necessarily inspired by Marxism," though "[n]o doubt a Marxist could subscribe to its main tenet" (1992b, 19).

The response, to begin with, would be that this characterization appears to presuppose a Weberian, rather than a Marxist, conception of class—that is, "class" as cashed out in conservative stratification theory in terms of income, attitudes, behavior, culture, education, and so forth, rather than by relationship to the means of production. It would certainly not be true for Marx that the working class's, or any other class's, social position would be attributed primarily to their personal disabilities; this account was precisely the kind that earned his special derision. So Boxill's mapping of the conceptual geography is really a bit misleading, and a Marxist reply to him would be that his dichotomization of theories into a "race school" versus a "class school" might better be cast as a "racism school" (which should be expanded to encompass both Marxist and non-Marxist theories of racism) versus a "group disability school" (including both biologically determinist and culturalist accounts of this putative disability). The question would then be—that such a formulation would leave open rather than foreclose—whether plausible Marxist accounts of racism can be developed. (I am not sure in any case how fair Boxill's categorization of Wilson is, since Wilson explicitly distances himself from accounts that emphasize present-day white racism and from the culture-of-poverty argument. So he would presumably reply that the alternatives for explaining the perpetuation of the underclass are not exhausted by Boxill's dichotomization, since he should include the "race-neutral"—in character, if not in social impact—structural transformation of American capitalism.)

What would a convincing Marxist theorization of race be like? The challenge that such Left accounts (as have been given) have generally failed to meet is the capturing of the *phenomenological* dimension of a racialized existence, the centrality of racial identity, the extent to which race both structures one's life and penetrates to one's ontic bones. Race has been seen as epiphenomenal, the tool capitalists use to divide the workers, the "false consciousness" that needs to be demystified so that the underlying proletarian identity can assert itself and so that we can all get on with the important thing, the class struggle. A successful account would have to synthesize the insights and recognize the theoretical failings of black separatists and the traditional white Left: the essentialism, ahistoricism, and frequent biological determinism that mystifies race, thereby lumping all whites and blacks into single undifferentiated categories; but also the deficiencies of an ostensibly colorless Left universalism that, like its liberal counterpart, fails to see that white supremacy needs to be understood as a sociopolitical object with its own contours, internal dynamic, and associated normative rules—an object not simply reducible to class.

In fact, from the 1970s onward, more theoretically sophisticated Marxist treatments of race have begun to emerge, emphasizing both the reality and the historicity of racial identity.[5] The impulse toward racial identification based on phenotype; the membership rules for partitioning the polity into race R_1, race R_2, . . ., race R_n; the decision where to locate new arrival, or biracial, offspring R_x; the character of the relations between "races." For such a theory, all are inadequately explained by the invocation of "primordial" sentiments of exclusionary solidarism and "natural" human divisions. Rather, racial identities are seen as historically constructed over time in response to historically variant political projects and shifting constellations of economic interests. But this "construction" is not arbitrary and purely "discursive"; it is motivated, materially enabled, and objectively rationally intelligible, contra postmodernism, precisely by the facts of a particular "metanarrative," the expansion of colonial capitalism, or (as otherwise described) the European conquest of the world. It is because of this sequence of historical events that "whiteness" itself emerges as the preeminent racial category,[6] through which the radical class and ethnic differences between Europeans are submerged into a common identity as a global *Herrenvolk*, rulers of colonies and founders of colonial settler states inhabited by an aboriginal and slave population. White supremacy is then established as a system in which one's identity as a settler, a member of the *Herrenvolk*, generally overrides one's identity as a worker (Fredrickson 1981; Kiernan 1996; Anthony Marx 1998; Winant 2001).

To speak in the abstract of "capitalism" and its laws in this context, as white Marxists have traditionally done, is then fundamentally mistaken, for it presupposes a colorlessness and intrinsic race neutrality that does not in fact obtain. Rather, in the "New World," one has to speak almost from the beginning of a white-supremacist capitalism, the capitalism of white-ruled colonies and white settler states.[7] And particularly for polities of the latter kind, like the United States—*Herrenvolk* democracies, in the sociologist Pierre van den Berghe's (1978) illuminating phrase—the moral psychology, sentiments of political solidarity, and potentialities for empathic identification of the white workers will necessarily be shaped by racial identity in a way not explored by Marx in *Capital* (Roediger 1994, 1999; Allen 1994–1997).

Correspondingly, the normative moral and political theories, as well as the juridical rules, that assign moral standing to, and codify the legal status of, the inhabitants of this society cannot be understood in terms of an abstract liberalism, even a flawed one. Instead they must be seen as the organic outcome of this peculiar hybrid system. Here, it seems to me that what black philosophers in moral and political theory need to do is to follow the example of the pioneering feminists of three decades ago, who constructed "patriarchy" as a central theoretical notion to understand a hitherto unnamed system of domination, with multitudinous ramifications throughout the social/economic/legal spheres and their accompanying ideational universe. Black philosophers need, analogously, to start speaking bluntly of a historic system of *global white supremacy;*[8] and, correspondingly, of a white-supremacist liberalism, a racialized legal theory; and even, remarkably but only apparently oxymoronically, of a *Herrenvolk* ethics, *Herrenvolk* Kantianism and Lockeanism. (Idealized Kantianism has a moral universe divided simply between persons and everything else; *Herrenvolk* Kantianism, on the other hand, has a more complex internal structure, a social ontology partitioned, on the basis of qualitative differentials in rationality, between persons and racial subpersons [*Untermenschen*], with the central moral notion of "respect" reconstituted accordingly. Similarly, the *Herrenvolk* Lockeanism of white-supremacist American capitalism restructures property rights along color-coded lines, with "whiteness" itself then becoming property, and with full self-ownership restricted accordingly to racially demarcated persons and denied to those humanoid entities characterized, on the basis of their phenotype, first as chattel and later as subordinate citizens.)[9] The task for philosophers of race, whether black or white, would then be to investigate and elucidate the dynamic and evolution of these intellectual formations (particularly the crucial transition from de jure to de facto white supremacy), demonstrating their internal logic (i.e., showing that it is not a matter of "accidental," "contingent" deviations from an abstract liberal ideal), and the characteristic silences, conceptual maneuvers, and double bookkeeping by which color-coded particularistic exclusion is systematically reconciled with proclaimed universality.

In philosophy, such an investigation will be made more difficult by the discipline's traditional abstraction, that has often been problematic for conceptualizing the experiences of oppressed groups—not because abstraction itself is suspect, but because hegemonic abstractions have typically idealized away from the specificities of their situation (O'Neill 1993). In addition, with the shift from de jure to de facto white supremacy, accounts by white scholars will tend to be deficient: whether because of embarrassment or ignorance about the past, or because of contestable theoretical judgments about what is central and what are unimportant "deviations," unworthy of attention. Anita Allen, for example, gives an interesting analysis of the plight of the underclass from the perspective of the philosophy of law, specifically the historic American drawing of the boundaries of the rights-holding population. She argues that the standard mainstream texts on this subject are flawed: In their abstract positivistic insistence that "in principle, legal rights can be ascribed to anything" and that "all normal adult human beings are paradigm rightsholders" (Allen 1992, 121–24), they elide the obvious historical fact that—not just during, but also after, slavery—blacks were *not* seen as equal rightsholders (e.g., the "sixty percent solution" of the Constitution; the 1857 *Dred Scott v. Sanford* decision that blacks in America had no rights that whites were bound to respect; the 1896 *Plessy v. Ferguson* decision that formally legitimated Jim Crow). So an adequate philosophical understanding of U.S. juridical history, and its implications for shaping the characteristic exclusions and cognitive blindnesses of the racialized moral consciousness of the white majority, would require the frontal recognition of this (a "naturalized" ethics), not its evasion.

The general claim is that race—like gender—provides an illuminating prism for reconceptualizing moral/political philosophy and that this needs to be appreciated even by those hostile to Left theory. My additional, Marxist claim would be that it *is* possible to develop a historical materialist account of this tectonic partitioning in the social ontology of the planet, explaining why race and racial identity then become central to the polity, so that, in W. E. B. Du Bois' famous 1903 prediction, "the problem of the Twentieth Century [and, on current trends, the twenty-first also] is the problem of the color line" (1996).

The Nature–Nurture Dispute

Against this theoretical background, let us look at the other debates. As mentioned at the beginning, conservative strategies for personalizing subordinated groups' causal responsibility for their own subordination can be divided into two main categories: the more recent cultural–attitudinal approach; and the old-fashioned, straightforwardly biologistic line. The latter was once thought to have been definitively refuted in the postwar revulsion against Nazi *Rassenwissenschaft*, but it is now a live issue again with the resurgence from the late 1960s onward of an aggressively refurbished biological determinism. A Marxist critique is useful here not merely from the perspective of a sociology of science—that is, a thesis about the extrascientific engines driving this research agenda—but also from a politicized cognitive psychology, which offers the valuable reminder that there is a spontaneous cognitive tendency for the social-structural to be fetishized, to be read as "natural," "biological."[10] Indeed some of the explanatory tropes now deployed against blacks have been applied in the past in Europe to subordinated ethnic groups and peripheral, undeveloped European nations like the Irish, who are *now* elevated to full-fledged "whiteness" but were previously "raced," seen as beyond the pale, with the familiar implied *Untermenschen* characteristics of hereditarian taint and biological predestination (Ignatiev 1995).

The issue arises in connection with current controversies about violence and underclass crime. Jencks (1992, ch. 3) compares the hereditarian analysis of James Wilson and Richard Herrnstein (1998) with the socioeconomically oriented explanation of Elliott Currie's far less publicized work (1985). Liberals, and even more so radicals, have been very hostile to hereditarian explanations because of their apparent continuity with earlier discredited biologically determinist theories, such as phrenology, craniometry, or (most apposite here) Cesare Lombroso's "criminal anthropology," which characterized criminals as evolutionary throwbacks identifiable at birth by their apish body type.[11] But though Jencks is more sympathetic to Currie's environmentalist approach, he argues that Left/liberal political opposition to genetic theories is actually misguided, since "heredity and environment are not mutually exclusive explanations of human diversity" (1992, 100). Current U.S. statistics show that "blacks are five to ten times more likely than whites to commit most violent crimes" (Jencks 1992, 98), and this fact stands in need of explanation, calling for research that looks at both genetic effects and cross-national variation.

The first point to be made here is that minority criminologists have long challenged the process by which such statistics are constructed. They argue that methodological flaws mean that the racial differential is much less than standardly claimed and that, where it exists, it can be situationally explained

(Mann 1993). But an additional criticism would be Jencks' apparent naïveté about the likely direction of such research and the political employment of such theories in a country whose tradition has been to preempt (by an ostensibly neutral "bio-logic") claims for social justice from structurally subordinated groups categorized as "races." The past history of biologically determinist theories documented by critics such as Chase (1980); Gould (1996); Rose, Kamin, and Lewontin (1984); Tucker (1994); and others is an astonishing record of outright fraud, "unconscious" massaging of data to fit preconceived conclusions, breathtaking logical gymnastics—for the most part uncritically accepted by the supposedly "objective" scientific establishment of the day—and creating at least a presumptive inductive case for suspicion about their latest avatar. (And indeed, Richard Herrnstein and Charles Murray's [1994] racist best-seller *The Bell Curve* would appear only two years after Jencks' book.) Jencks argues that the impact of negative environmental determination on individuals can be no less "irreversible" than having "wrong genes" (1992, 110), but the point is that on the socially meliorist level, the prescriptive implications of environmentalist theories are for progressive social reform. At a time of increasing concern over underclass crime and the challenge it poses for social policy, the role of sociobiology will be to foster either neglect or actively suppressive measures for the policing of what will be perceived as biologically driven miscreants—more SWAT teams, prisons, and mandatory sentencing; fewer social programs; no job creation—with any preventative intervention likely to take the ominous form of biotechnological "fixes," such as sterilization, psychosurgery, or preemptive genetic screening and engineering, as facilitated by the human genome project.

The "Culture of Poverty" Controversy

The influential "culture of poverty" thesis, on the other hand, takes the more respectable psychological–attitudinal route. Originally advanced by anthropologist Oscar Lewis (in a form more tentative than its current version), this thesis posits the notion that a subculture of dysfunctional attitudes and values can acquire an almost purely autonomous and self-sustaining dynamic (Lewis 1975; 1966; Valentine 1968; Leacock 1971; Steinberg 2001a). Conservatives will tend to describe this culture as *(a)* extensive and easily identifiable, *(b)* peculiar to the underclass, and *(c)* morally pernicious (henceforth: *a*, *b*, *c*, etc.) The term often used—and increasingly adopted by liberals also—is "pathological." (One thinks readily of the truly scary young black men of the inner cities, of the world cinematically depicted in John Singleton's *Boyz N the Hood*, or the Hughes brothers' *Menace II Society*.) The idea is that the culture of poverty has been produced by *(d)* forces long past (e.g., in the case of blacks, the experience of sharecropping) and is now *(e)* the sufficient condition, or at least a major cause, of the perpetuation of the underclass; so that the prescriptive solution is attitudinal and cultural reform to take advantage of the opportunities present in a market economy where the old racial barriers (for those who even admit them) either no longer exist or are minimal.

Traditional liberals and the Marxist Left will in general, of course, be far more skeptical about assigning such a central role to culture, with the latter in particular being committed to a sociological materialism that lays primary explanatory emphasis on socioeconomic structure rather than attitudinal deficiency. The claim is that if good jobs and training *were* actually to become available, then people's norms and practices would change; so the real fault lies in the institutional arrangements. However, Howard McGary seems to suggest that this dichotomization is a mistaken one. He criticizes both conservatives and liberals for their "doctrinaire commitments," while simultaneously arguing that their apparently competing *explanans* of the underclass's plight—the underclass's "mindset," as opposed to "the design of social institutions"—are both correct (1992, 57–58). He resolves this seeming paradox by arguing that the underclass's legitimate feelings of injustice at their lack of full citizenship—produced by an unfair social structure, and not their alleged "laziness"—debilitates their motivation and self-confidence. But even if this diagnosis is right, it is certainly not one lifted above the political fray; rather, it is consistent with a standard Left/liberal account, which anybody on that wing of the political spectrum would accept as a supplementary, noncompeting cause. The conservative conception of the crippling underclass mind-set involves fatalism, poor impulse control, lack of a work ethic, and so forth—that is, not a mistaken moral perception ("mistaken" since conservatives would deny that the basic structure of the United States is unjust). So though McGary gives a good (liberal) analysis of the psychological handicaps the underclass have, which would need to be addressed by any policy of social reform, it seems to me that he is misled if he thinks he has transcended the terms of the debate; in other words, he has merely shifted the terms and endorsed one side.

The radical critique of the conservative position, and of those liberals who since the 1960s have increasingly moved in that direction, is represented by Tommy Lott's contribution to the Lawson collection (1992). On *a*, this critique questions the extent of this alleged culture, or redescribes it altogether, pointing out the possible methodological circularity in identifying the target group by the culture and the culture by the group (with similar traits in *other* groups being conceptualized as categorically distinct on what may turn out, under examination, to be ad hoc rather than principled grounds). On *b* and *c*, two moves are possible. One would be to accept the negative moral judgment of underclass culture, but to dispute the conceptual separation, the *tu quoque* reply that pejoratively characterized underclass values (or some subset thereof: e.g., alleged criminal proclivities) are by no means *sui generis*, but are related to the larger society (cf. Hochschild 1991). Lott, for example, argues that what is represented as the culture of poverty is in many ways just a recoding of mainstream values under different circumstances, "pathological social conditions" (1992, 82–84). The background assumption is then one of a structural indictment, *d*, of the society at large, usually conjoined with a claim about the greater (and ongoing) causal responsibility of those in high places for this character. Black underclass crime, then, has to be seen in the larger historic context of white ruling-class criminality—the past and ongoing crime in the suites that has created the environment producing the crime in the streets, but which (conceptually and morally laundered, its causality obfuscated) is not seen as responsible. So one thinks far *less* readily of the truly scary old white men who, motivated by the "culture of wealth," put the pathological systems of chattel slavery and Jim Crow into place to begin with. Moral condemnation would not then—as in the standard mystificatory delinking—be separated from the requisite parallel, and greater, condemnation of structural apartheid, and the state and federal complicity with the creation of the ghetto in the first place. Finally, as Frank Kirkland points out, this "desiccated" ghetto cultural life is not an "epiphenomenon"; so it needs to be addressed via a "bilateral and serially ordered" policy of social reform, involving both economic transformation and the restoration of "the meaningfulness of institutions and practices" (1992, 153–55). Radicals, however, would deny *e*, that the latter can substitute for necessary structural change or that it is of equal causal significance. Too often conservative demands for such "cultural" changes from blacks are simply ways of denying the need for job creation and radical economic measures.

The other approach, which may be complementary, would be to accept the separation of underclass culture, or at least elements of it, as distinctive, but to dispute the moral characterization. Lott takes this approach also, arguing that black urban culture represents "notions of affirmation and resistance" (1992, 72). So this is the argument for the reconceptualization of ghetto culture, or at least certain elements of it, as "revolutionary." However, the moral and political problem such a Marxist analysis faces, of course, is how to demarcate justifiable resistance and cultural self-assertion (e.g., antiracism, Afrocentrism, exposés of police brutality) from values and practices in gang activity and "gangsta rap" that are immoral by any standards (e.g., the glorification of violence, women as "bitches and ho's"). It would clearly be absurd, and morally irresponsible, to take the position of some elements of the white Left in the late 1960s to early 1970s that all black criminal activity is somehow "revolutionary." (I am not saying Lott does this.) Moreover, capitalism's protean capacities for recuperating resistance and commodifying everything have led to the ironic situation where a significant proportion of ostensibly "revolutionary" inner-city rage is really calculated posturing being marketed for suburban white kids to get off on.

Ongoing White Racism as a Significant Social Barrier for Blacks

Finally, to what extent is continuing motivated white racism responsible for the plight of the underclass—that is, as against the "natural" structural functioning of a self-transforming capitalist economy? William Julius Wilson's earlier book, *The Declining Significance of Race* (1978), was controversial for its claim that race was of diminishing importance in determining black Americans' fate. (It was, in fact, denounced by the Association of Black Sociologists.) However, Wilson has repeatedly insisted that his argument has been misunderstood; he is not, he says, claiming that racism has declined but that it is "less important than economic class in determining black life chances" (1991, 604, n. 21). In *The Truly Disadvantaged* (1987), Wilson continues this theme, arguing that while past racism played a historical role in the underclass's formation, present-day racism is a minor factor, as shown by the emergence of a large black middle class. But if the modified Left argument above is plausible, then the white-supremacist character of U.S. capitalism is organically related to its nature, central to the structuring of the polity and its citizens' identities, and thus not to be shuffled off so readily.

Some of Jencks' (1992, 120–42) criticisms of Wilson's etiology in his fourth essay are consistent with this skepticism. Wilson argues that the important causes of underclass perpetuation are *(a)* structural unemployment resulting from shifts in the nature of the U.S. economy and the consequent "spatial mismatch" between inner-city residents and the jobs that have moved to the suburbs; *(b)* a diminishing number of "marriageable" black men, because of unemployment, imprisonment, or premature death; and *(c)* the physical isolation of the underclass in deteriorating neighborhoods deserted by the black middle class. On the "spatial mismatch" hypothesis, Jencks argues that it works for teens but not for adults, who usually don't hear about jobs in the first place because of the racial exclusiveness of the communication networks involved and who could, if necessary, drive to the jobs. Jencks thinks that the slack labor market is more important and that, given a choice between white and black job applicants, employers will tend to choose the white applicant, with the blacks being seen as more likely to be unskilled, assertive, and belonging to an alien and inferior culture. On single motherhood, Jencks asserts that the statistics don't confirm Wilson's claim and that the spread of this phenomenon needs to be related to broader cultural shifts toward more liberal attitudes. Moreover, somebody who disputes Wilson's thesis could obviously argue that the shortage in the demographic cohort of "marriageable" black men is not an independent variable but itself the product of the racist denial of economic opportunities to black men and a criminal justice system that has historically been stacked against racial minorities (Mann 1993; Cole 1999). Jencks thinks the argument from neighborhood effects is the most important, and potentially Wilson's most valuable, contribution; but it remains unproven.

Even on Jencks' somewhat cautious reading, then, racism continues to play an active role. A far stronger statement of this case, however, comes from Douglas Massey and Nancy Denton's devastating book, *American Apartheid* (1993), which probably represents the most sustained and statistically detailed critique of Wilson to date. Some of their criticisms, it is true, have been made before. For example, many whites would like to believe that systematic white racism is a thing of the past; but Federal Reserve studies of denial rates of mortgage applications, residential patterns more than three decades after the 1968 Fair Housing Act, and income comparisons when controlled for education, show

- that even middle-class blacks are turned down at higher rates than their white peers;
- that U.S. housing continues to be grossly segregated, with millions of anti-minority fair-housing violations annually (according to the Department of Housing and Urban Development); and
- that educated blacks' salaries continue to lag behind whites who have comparable or inferior credentials.

Ellis Cose's book, *The Rage of a Privileged Class* (1993), summarizes moving personal testimony from middle-class blacks about everyday discrimination, slights, pigeonholing, professional ceilings, and (depending on the circumstances) both *hyper*visibility and invisibility in their lives in the corporate world. In addition, some critics have argued that the size of the black middle class is overestimated by Wilson, as is the extent of its suburbanization; and the crucial statistic is really the racial wealth differential between blacks and whites in general (Fainstein 1986–1987; Inniss and Feagin 1989; Willie 1988; Oliver and Shapiro 1995).

The provocative title of Massey and Denton's book is deliberately chosen to reflect their claim for the global significance of these facts, that "racial residential segregation is the principal structural feature of American society responsible for the perpetuation of urban poverty and represents a primary cause of racial inequality in the United States" (1993, viii). Moreover, it is by no means a matter of "impersonal" social forces, as in Wilson's decolorized description of a race-neutral process of residential dynamics; rather, it is a deliberate policy of racially motivated decision making, "maintained by ongoing institutional arrangements and contemporary individual actions," and with the support or connivance of the federal government. So while they acknowledge the value of Wilson's points on the importance of the transformation of the U.S. economy in creating the urban underclass, they argue that "what made it disproportionately a *black* underclass was racial segregation" (1993, 136–37). The conclusion, then, contra Wilson, is that "blacks are segregated no matter how much money they earn" (1993, 11), so that both race and class continue to affect the life chances of blacks, as one would expect in a white-supremacist capitalism.

MORAL OBLIGATIONS

We turn now to the moral issues posed for both blacks and whites by the underclass: First, do the relatively privileged black middle class have differential racial obligations to their less fortunate brothers and sisters? Second, to what extent is it realistic to think that the white majority is going to be morally able to perceive, and be morally motivated to initiate and stick with (the Rawlsian "strains of commitment"), the radical socioeconomic changes that would be necessary to incorporate the underclass if the Left analysis were indeed correct?

Moral Obligations of the Black Middle Class

Bill Lawson is himself a native, as he tells us in his preface, of what is now an underclass neighborhood in Philadelphia. In his chapter, he looks at the interesting question of whether middle-class blacks, who in recent years have been fleeing to the suburbs, have a special racial obligation to stay and build up poorer ghetto neighborhoods. Some have historically argued that all African Americans should be considered as one's extended family, so that differential racial obligations would be analogous to, or perhaps literally be, family obligations. Following a discussion of Anthony Appiah's, Lawson argues that such a position is incompatible with Kantian universalism, that it is not one blacks would want whites to adopt (or, perhaps better, to continue with!), and that such putative obligations would in any case be outweighed by those to one's immediate biological family (1992b). However, I am not sure the issue is so easily settled. It might be possible to work out a nonfamilial deontological rationale not in terms of the inherently differentiated *moral* status of "races," a position Appiah calls "intrinsic racism," but through special *situationally* arising obligations—that is, the situation of a group oppressed by racism, and one's corresponding responsibilities as a group member.

Moral Obligations of the White Majority

Perhaps more important (given their power), consider the moral obligations of the white majority. The problem here involves epistemic and motivational aspects that have implications not only for whites' moral decision making and for blacks' estimate of realistic social possibilities, but also for any consequent political strategies. What kinds of circumstances are favorable or unfavorable to the recognition of right and wrong and the development of the motivation to act on this perception? If the foregoing analysis is plausible, then the existing structure of white-supremacist American capitalism is systemically unjust; so that it is not just a question of addressing local anomalies—that is, deviations from a Rawlsian "ideal" state—but, rather, of confronting the necessity for fundamental change. But this system will itself (at least tendentially) socialize individuals into acceptance of the naturalness and rightness of the existing order. As argued in chapter 3, Marxism can be interpreted as making the "realist" claim that people's moral psychologies are shaped by their social situation in such a way as to make it generally unlikely that, of the privileged, any but a few will perceive the necessity for antisystemic change of a fundamental kind. So there will be a *general* conservative bias, by which dominant moral norms will tend to adjust themselves to material structures, rather than vice versa. In addition, in the United States, the white majority's moral psychology will be shaped not merely by class but by racial structure; and this racialized identity and psychology ("*Herrenvolk* ethics") will be characterized by "settled expectations" of racial privilege as a baseline (Harris 1993) and by a blurred moral vision and diminished affect where the plight of blacks is concerned. Thus it is doubly unlikely that they will recognize, and be moved purely by, considerations of justice—as, in fact, the history of the black civil rights struggle has shown.[12]

(The reader, who is most likely to be a professional philosopher, indeed a professional ethicist, is asked to submit herself to the following simple test. Make a list of what you consider to be the ten most important works in ethical theory and political philosophy of the last three decades. Now ask yourself: How many of them have even as a *subordinate*, let alone a major, theme the achievement of racial justice and what would be necessary to redress the legacy of slavery in this country? The point is that this issue is simply *not* a major concern to whites, even in the cases where one would think that there is the highest probability of finding some systematic reflection on the subject—that is, among professional intellectuals whose subject matter is questions of justice. And if so little reflection can be found at this level, then there is hardly going to be much more in the mind of the average white citizen hustling to get by and worrying about her and her children's future in a problematic economy.)

The issue is not merely one of cognition, of course, but of vested interests in the established order, the material and psychic payoffs of whiteness in a white-supremacist system. Contemporary ethical theory pits ethicists like Shelly Kagan (2002) against ethicists such as Samuel Scheffler (1992): the former argue that commonsense morality is simply *wrong* in thinking that deeds that would require great sacrifices of us are morally optional; the latter argue for a restricted role for morality, with a "moderate" content, making demands that would not be too burdensome. But whatever the merits of their respective cases, the commonsense view is clearly the more likely to prevail. Imagine a scenario where the prescriptions of the Left for incorporating the underclass were somehow convincingly vindicated, but where—given the existing size of the deficit—the costs would mean a freezing or an actual deterioration of the standard of living for most other Americans for the next twenty years or so. How many people would in fact be motivated to accept and stick with this program? I suggest that an honest answer is: very few. People are sometimes willing to give up part of their growing share of an expanding pie to meet considerations of justice; but when it is static, or shrinking, there is little chance of this happening. And in real life, of course, we do *not* have such epistemic authority to draw on, but only the opinion of conflicting experts in a highly charged debate where people tend to line up on ideological and racial lines, and where the possibilities are obviously very great for self-deception, weakness of will, racist denial and indifference, or a genuine but mistaken conviction based on a limited selection of evidence.

The issue of finding plausible candidates for motivation appears in Boxill's (1992b) discussion of Wilson. Boxill criticizes Wilson for basing his solution on people's self-interest (a stimulation of the economy from which all will benefit), arguing that this appeal to self-interest is characteristic of (what Boxill calls) the "class school" and that it "implies an unjustified contempt for the moral powers of the average person" (31). Instead, one should say up front that the plight of the underclass is the outcome of past and present white racism, thereby appealing to people's sense of justice as a motivator.

First, according to Wilson's version of the causal story, white racism's *present* role in maintaining the underclass in existence is minimal, since it is more a question of the unfortunate consequences of a changing capitalism. So while, as earlier seen, I am sympathetic to Boxill's critique here, it needs an auxiliary empirical–theoretical discussion of Wilson's story.

Second, at least from the point of view of the Marxist Left, I am not sure that this position commits one to "contempt" for the average person; it's more a grudging respect for the power of bourgeois and racial socialization, and the habituation to racial privilege. Boxill has claimed elsewhere (1991; 1992a), I think rightly, that it is morally important for blacks' self-respect and whites' moral education that policies to remedy black problems be publicly perceived to be rooted in justice. But one could agree with this claim while simultaneously being skeptical that such motivation will be causally significant. Some commentators have argued that the riots of the 1960s were in fact critical in advancing the civil rights struggle, in that white concessions would not have been made except for the genuine conviction that national race war was a possibility (Button 1978). And Boxill himself concedes that the "race school" "does not suggest that moral suasion alone is sufficient to achieve this end" (1992b, 29), but must also appeal to other motivation (e.g., Frederick Douglass' threat of slave rebellion). (N.B.: the text says "class school" at this point, but this is clearly an error.) So the gap between the two competing positions on the motivational question is not as great as it might originally have seemed.

THE POLITICAL SPECTRUM OF
DIAGNOSES AND SOLUTIONS

Finally, we arrive at the practical issue of public policy and the underclass. On the traditional political spectrum (before the proliferation of prefixes: "*neo*conservatives," "*neo*liberals," "market socialists"), one would have distinguished liberal and conservative prescriptions, which basically accept a capitalist economic framework; and radical accounts, which do not. Capital L liberals, also known as Left/"progressive" liberals, assumed that social problems such as racial injustice were to a significant extent governmental responsibilities; so that an activist state was called for, a tradition that reached its high point in Johnson's "War on Poverty" (Manley 1990; Greenberg 1990). Conservatives, also known as Right/"corporate" liberals, argued that such problems were largely a matter of personal responsibility, that racism (if it ever existed) was essentially a thing of the past, and that blacks (insofar as they were addressed at all) needed to remedy their situation through market mechanisms like everybody else. This framework puts the Right in an enviable win–win position ideologically, since their personalized account enables them to not only take credit for black success ("See? The system works"), but also wash their hands of black failure ("See? They don't want to work").

Jencks makes some effective empirical–theoretical criticisms of representative conservative figures Thomas Sowell (1981a; 1981b) and Charles

Murray (1995). Against black conservative Sowell—the bête noire (or perhaps bête blanche) of majority Left/liberal black opinion—Jencks argues in his first essay (1992, 24–69) that there were qualitative distinctions in the kind of socioeconomic discrimination blacks faced in the United States; so the fact that *some* previous victims of discrimination are now better off than the average doesn't prove (as Sowell infers) that antiblack racism cannot be responsible for black poverty. He also develops a useful schema of economically rational and economically irrational types of discrimination, aimed at undermining Sowell's claim that discrimination is *always* expensive for the perpetrators and so will automatically be eliminated by market mechanisms. White conservative Charles Murray's influential *Losing Ground*—a precursor to his later coauthored *The Bell Curve*—had claimed that Federal social-welfare programs actually make the poor worse off (1995). Characterizing this view as "Social-Darwinist," Jencks cites in chapter two (1992, 70–91) an array of statistics that convincingly refute it, since net poverty declined between 1965 and 1980.

For traditional liberals, of course, negotiating the ideological terrain is much more difficult. The perceived failure of the "War on Poverty," and the backlash against the movements of the sixties, has led to a national shift to the Right; so that "liberal" has long since become a term of odium. Black Americans are in the politically awkward position of being taken for granted by one party and written off by the other. An increasing number of commentators argue that race is a divisive issue and that Democratic "concessions" to black demands have been a major factor in driving away blue-collar white voters, that is, those who became "Reagan Democrats" in the 1980s (Sleeper 1990; Edsall and Edsall 1991). As another sign of the times, race is barely mentioned at all by the two contributors to a symposium on the future of liberalism who call for a *renewal* of the progressive Jeffersonian tradition to meet the challenge of the twenty-first century (which is, of course, fully in keeping with the Jeffersonian tradition in another way).[13] The eight-year Clinton presidency of "new" Democrats would then represent the "new," "moderate" liberalism of the future, highly convergent if not identical with traditional conservatism; and the plight of the underclass would essentially be ignored, left to a new "benign neglect" increasingly malign—as illustrated by Clinton's own role in dismantling welfare. Wilson's proposed remedy for the problem of the underclass is a Keynesian national stimulus to the economy to promote economic growth and a tight labor market, combining "universal" programs, as well as job training and apprenticeship programs targeted at the most disadvantaged. Thus, it is seriously out of step with the times and would be seen by the Right, old and new (i.e., yesterday's liberals), as a pointless attempt to resurrect the discredited solutions of the past.

From the Left, both liberal and radical, Wilson's program invites several lines of critique.

First, one of the virtues of Wilson's proposal is his linking of domestic problems to macroeconomic global changes—that is, transformations of world capitalism. But by the same token, the increasing mobility of capital and jobs in a globally interconnected economy raises problems for the viability of his solution. Boxill points out that the decline of the United States from the economically hegemonic global position it enjoyed in the post–World War II period imposes serious constraints and that illegal immigration from Latin America ("browns," who are often preferred by U.S. employers to native "blacks") is likely to make a tight labor market impossible (1991). More generally, as Richard Barnet presciently argued a decade ago, "we are swimming in a global labor pool": "[A]n astonishingly large and increasing number of human beings are not needed or wanted to make the goods or to provide the services that the paying customers of the world can afford" (1993, 47). From a Marxist position, then, the likelihood is that a large section of the world's workforce is simply going to be written off by capitalism as expendable, a surplus labor population. And, indeed, a January 2003 report from the International Labor Organisation pointed out that world unemployment had hit a record high of 180 million, 6.5 percent of the global labor force (Foulkes 2003).

Second, Wilson's remedy is a classic social democratic solution, the ideal of "capitalism with a human face," predicated on the assumption that distribution patterns are largely detachable from production relations and that the latter set no objective limits to the possibilities for state reform. But this assumption, Marxists would claim, is simply false; so that the general criticism Marxists have always had of the social democratic Left is that they misunderstand, or are naive about, the nature of the capitalist state, and so have illusions about the extent to which it is going to be responsive to popular demands. (Of the black philosophers in the Lawson collection, only Frank Kirkland says directly [1992, 164–68] that Wilson's corporatist conception of the state blurs over labor's structural subordination as an "interest group" to the priorities of capital investment.) For Marxists the state is not a neutral arbiter standing above different lobbying constituencies, as in classic postwar pluralist theory; rather, it is an institution basically responsive above all to capitalist interests (whether via conscious ruling-class strategy or because of structural constraint). So the argument is that possibilities are significantly restricted by "material" imperatives of capital accumulation. Social democracy's historic zone of success—Western Europe—has long been experiencing economic conditions that have led to the rolling back of many of those workers' gains earlier made, and to a convergence of the former Left with more centrist parties. Moreover, where this success (even if temporary) has been achieved, it has been as a result of the militancy and activism of strong labor movements and social demo-cratic/communist parties. The United States, by contrast, has notoriously been the despair of the Left because of so-called American exceptionalism: the fact that in this seemingly ideal, "pure" capitalist state, with no feudal legacy of status and deference to muddy proletarian consciousness, no ef-fective mass workers' movement or social democratic party has ever de-veloped (or as the title of Seymour Lipset and Gary Marks' recent book has it, *It Didn't Happen Here* [2000]). Race has also been cited as explanatory here: white workers' "vertical" cross-class ethnocultural identification with white settlerdom—in opposition to the native reds and the enslaved blacks—militating against class consciousness.

Finally, the third set of criticisms arises out of Wilson's denial or un-derestimation of the continuing importance of racism, or—where he does concede it—his failure to draw the appropriate theoretical conclusions. As indicated above, liberal commentators like Jencks, Boxill, and Massey and Denton would argue that continuing white racism is far more causally significant than Wilson seems to admit; that is, it is not merely a matter of systemic processes with "accidentally" racially differentiated conse-quences. But this position has implications for the feasibility of the politi-cal alliance Wilson, and indeed some of these same commentators, pro-poses, as well as the probability of white opposition to the preferential treatment for blacks within "universal" programs that Wilson (softly) calls for. And if Massey and Denton's argument is correct, residential seg-regation would on its own have been causally sufficient to perpetuate the underclass even without the structural transformations on which Wilson focuses. So even if his policies were implemented, a massive program of desegregation, requiring the confrontation of racism, would be necessary for its success. (From the hybrid Left position I have sketched above, the even stronger conclusion follows that: since race is *central* to the polity, and since the state is not just the bourgeois state of classical Marxism but also historically a white-supremacist state, then the full inclusion of blacks is going to require whites to rethink and give up their whiteness—that is, whiteness is less a color than an oppositionally defined power relation-ship. However, such a divestiture is obviously improbable, since present and future economic problems make the clinging to racial privilege far more likely.)

But—it will naturally be asked, perhaps with some irritation—what positive remedies do *Marxists* have to suggest? Here, in a world where a socialist alternative seems to have collapsed, there is, admittedly, an em-barrassing disarticulation between analysis and prescription, with the discrediting and/or dissolution of many national Left groupings, and with the diminished entryist hope of influencing a Democratic party moving steadily rightward. There are, of course, the perennial calls for a third party (or, if you accept Gore Vidal's analysis, a second party); but in general the national Left is disheartened, demoralized, and in disarray. The working class, the traditional countervailing force against capital, are, apart from being racially divided, now at unionization levels (13 percent) that are the lowest in six decades. Other agencies are hardly credible. Aging '60s radicals with long memories might want to remember (or then again, might prefer to forget?) that Eldridge Cleaver—before he found God, the Republican party, and a (mercifully brief, so presumably not divinely inspired) calling to bring back the codpiece—had argued, contra Marx, that it was the black lumpen proletariat of the inner cities who were the *really* revolutionary class. Leonard Harris, whose chapter is focused on a conceptual analysis of the underclass, looks again at this question, asking whether the underclass is a "serial entity" or a collective agent; and he concludes, I would think uncontroversially, that it is "serial," an "impotent actor," structurally disorganized and so incapable of acting on its own (1992, 51, 37). So in the absence of any plausible candidates as vehicles for radical change, the Left is caught in a situation where both avenues seem blocked: on the one hand, a socialist solution that seems improbable, and for which no attractive models exist; and on the other, a capitalist economy whose workings, at least according to Marx, will continue relentlessly to grind out these conditions. A grassroots movement for social change would, *inter alia*, require the class overcoming of race so that, in an ironic inversion of the old Left slogans: it would not be that socialism is needed to eliminate the problem of racism, but that antiracism is needed to eliminate the problem of capitalism.

What inevitably happens under these politically unfavorable circumstances, of course, is that one is psychologically pulled rightward by the fear of political marginalization and irrelevance; so that one then puts forward recommendations in the odd spirit of hoping that one is wrong in one's analysis. Doffing my Marxist hat, then, let me assume what I believe to be false: that is, that moral motivation can be a social prime mover. What would be needed is a job creation and training program of the kind Wilson describes. In this program, however (following Boxill; Inniss and Feagin; Massey and Denton), race and race-specific policies (above all, desegregation) would not be a "hidden agenda"; they would be the first item on the agenda, *foregrounded* via a national debate on race, initiated at the highest levels of society, as the unfinished business that white America needs to confront before this nation can be redeemed of the historic crime (as yet unapologized for) it committed against blacks. In this debate, white Americans would somehow have to be made to understand that their color has historically given them a massive systemic advantage quite independent of their personal degree of liberalism on race and the Negro best friends they may (or may not) have; and that—as

Cheryl Harris (1993) has argued—whiteness has been (stolen) property, a collective agreement to share in the illicit booty of racially structured exploitation and its proceeds. Only in this way can the necessary reconstitution of the polity, and the transcendence of its *Herrenvolk* character, be achieved.

NOTES

1. William Julius Wilson (1987) legitimized the term, giving it the irreproachable imprimatur of a black liberal (or self-described "social democrat"); and it is Wilson's work that has been at the center of most recent discussion. But there are many earlier appearances, for example Glasgow (1980) and Auletta (2000). (Credit for the modern coinage is sometimes attributed to Myrdal [1962].) Discussions in the mass media have, of course, been more important in shaping public discourse, usually with a conservative slant—for example, Lemann (1986), Hamill (1988), and Herrnstein and Murray (1994). Critical replies from the Left include Fainstein (1986–1987), Willie (1988), Inniss and Feagin (1989), Gans (1990), Reed Jr. (1990), Goldberg (1992), Jencks (1992).

2. See Cedric J. Robinson's unfortunately neglected *Black Marxism: The Making of the Black Radical Tradition* (2000).

3. Paul Peterson (1991–1992) says that "underclass is a word that can be used by conservatives, liberals, and radicals alike"; but I think most radicals would disagree—see, for example, Goldberg; Inniss and Feagin; Gans; Reed Jr.

4. See Gans (1990) and Goldberg (1992). Inniss and Feagin (1989, 15) point out that the notion of a dangerous urban "rabble" of "freed blacks" can be found as far back as de Tocqueville's *Democracy in America*.

5. For an overview, see Omi and Winant (1994).

6. In the original version of this chapter (1994), I had the parenthetical comment "though least analyzed" after "preeminent," which was true then, incredible as it may now seem, given the exponential growth of the "whiteness" industry over the last decade.

7. There is an obvious parallel here with the socialist–feminist debates of the pre-postmodernist 1970s—the notion of a "dual-systems" theory, "capitalist patriarchy," which would recuperate the insights of both Marxist and radical feminists. (For a classic exposition, see Jaggar 1988.) A crucial difference, however, is that patriarchy predates capitalism, whereas global white supremacy (as against simple white ethnocentrism) is established *by* colonial capitalism.

8. Black philosophers *recognize* that white supremacy exists, of course, but have not, for the most part, constructed it as a theoretical object, a political system in its own right, like "absolutism," "fascism," "patriarchy."

9. For rival perspectives on whether Kant and Locke themselves were *Herrenvolk* Kantians and Lockeans—that is, the significance of their racial views for their own theories—see, for example, the following. For Kant: Eze (1995), Louden (2000), Bernasconi (2001; 2002), Hill Jr. and Boxill (2001). For Locke: Glausser (1990), Tully (1994), Welchman (1995), Uzgalis (1998; 2002). Harris (1993) develops the provocative case for whiteness as functioning in the U.S. context as "property."

10. "The most general and encompassing lay theory of human behavior—so broadly applied that it might be more aptly termed a 'metatheory'—is the assumption that behavior is caused primarily by the enduring and consistent dispositions of the actor, as opposed to the particular characteristics of the situation to which the actor responds" (Nisbett and Ross 1980, 31).

11. For an illuminating, and often hilarious, discussion, see Gould (1996). Sometimes, as Gould points out, it was necessary for Lombroso to go even further back up the evolutionary trail—with cattle, pigs, lemurs, rodents, and even flatfish occasionally being pressed into service as immanently reassertive ancestors (156–60).

12. Some scholars have argued that national "crises of conscience" had little to do with the postwar federal push to initiate de jure desegregation, the far more important cause being Cold War competition with the Soviet Union for Third World hearts and minds, somewhat discommoded by the discrepancy between "Free World" posturing in the international arena and domestic apartheid at home. See, for example, Klinkner and Smith (1999) and Dudziak (2000).

13. Manley (1990), Greenberg (1990).

6

European Specters

Accelerating into the new millennium, more than a century and a half after the publication of the *Communist Manifesto*, we live in a world simultaneously Marxist, post-Marxist, and pre-Marxist. If the old man were to rise up from his uneasy sleep in London's Highgate Cemetery and hurry over to a newsstand to check on the global situation, he would in certain respects find a world instantly familiar to him—indeed the world of the *Manifesto*. Globalization; megamergers; transnational supercorporations; economic meltdown of entire countries; chasms between rich and poor; commodification of everything possible and of some things one would have thought impossible; the desacralization of all relations; the planetary interconnection of stock exchanges and the corresponding flow of capital, investment, information, and panic around international circuits, in a market that never closes; so that if it is time to shut up shop in New York, it is a new day in Tokyo; if there are tremors in Kuala Lumpur, there will be rumbles in London. . . . How could he resist crowing: "I told you so!"

But the celebration would, of course, be mistaken. For—apart from his surprise at finding that capitalism was near ubiquitous—he would also discover, to his greater astonishment, that the gravediggers he had confidently expected to be attendant at the funeral had themselves been interred: communist parties globally dissolved and discredited; self-styled socialist states either defunct and dismembered unions or strange "market Stalinist" hybrids; oppositional workers' movements largely impotent or integrated into capitalism; his own ideas universally derided and disgraced as nineteenth-century anachronisms. It would be a world he recognized, but a world that no longer recognized him: Marxist in the politico-economic domination by capital he had so presciently delineated; post-Marxist in its ideological domination by neoliberalism and free-market theory. Expecting to be able to toast the demise of class society, he would find instead that he and revolutionary communism were the ghosts at the bourgeois banquet—and not even respectable bogeymen anymore, but pathetic shades incapable of frightening anyone.

How did this come about? There are, of course, numerous explanations, some competing, some complementary. What I want to suggest is an important contributory cause that has not, I think, received sufficient theoretical attention. I will suggest that if the world we inhabit is both Marxist and post-Marxist, it is also in crucial respects pre-Marxist. I do not mean this in the sense of the discredited teleology of a secular predestinarianism, according to which a brave socialist future is still somehow just around the corner. Rather, I mean that one central set of the "objective conditions" Karl Marx presupposed to exist in his time has even now, a century and a half later, not really materialized; and in its absence it is questionable how successful socialism as a global movement could ever have been. For in the gathering of ghosts above, one specter remains unmentioned and unexorcised: the European specter that we know as race.

THE SOCIAL ONTOLOGY OF MODERNITY

Those who come to Marx's texts for the first time are often surprised at how little he actually has to say about socialism. Expecting political manuals on how to bring about the classless future, they find instead analyses of the class-dominated past and present. For what Marxism is, above all, is a way of analyzing society and a theory of history: historical materialism. Changing the world was to be made possible by an interpretation of the world superior to those previously advanced. And as a theory of history, Marxism was for generations an illuminating holistic paradigm for intellectuals who sought to discern and explain global patterns of social evolution. The "materialism" promised a realism, a revelation of what actually mattered, a cutting through surface appearances to the underlying causes. Some things were just more fundamental than others, and Marxism knew what those things were. Thus the theory provided a *social* ontology,[1] in the sense of a mapping of the basic determining social existents: the central political actors—classes; the real forces motivating them—class interests; the nature of humans, and what kinds of concerns and identities were fundamental to their existence—class membership and class being, the relation of the worker to his product, alienation and the hope of self-realization through labor.

Now one way of situating this theory is as a particular account of modernity. Indeed Marshall Berman's well-known book on the subject, *All That Is Solid Melts into Air* (1988), takes its title directly from the *Manifesto*. Marxism could be seen to be offering an account of modernity that, while opposed to the Whig theory classically associated with liberalism, is nonetheless still part of the larger European Enlightenment narrative. So there is the mainstream Enlightenment and the radical Enlightenment, but from a broader perspective they are in certain respects still operating within a common framework of assumptions.

The respectable mainstream story will talk about the impact of new ideas and values—liberty, equality, fraternity, personhood; the radical story will admit the force of ideas and values but stress the underlying "material" changes that generated and made people more receptive to them. The orthodox narrative will speak unqualifiedly of the American and French Revolutions; the Left narrative, more picky, will qualify them as bourgeois revolutions. The mainstream account will describe an inspiring egalitarian transition from ascriptive hierarchy to meritocracy, from birth-to-death membership in feudal estates to a world of free and equal self-making individuals; the Marxist account will contest this picture, arguing that actually one kind of class society is overthrown by another in which class no longer announces itself. For both stories, then, modernity is intimately tied up with the end of the status distinctions of the ancient and medieval world. But for Marxists, the new moral and juridical egalitarianism that exists at the level of exchange is systematically undercut by the economic compulsions and domination existing at the level of production. Modernity's promise can only be fully realized when these material, nonnormative barriers—largely unacknowledged by the atomic ontology of classic liberalism—are also removed.

A familiar tale, then, whether in its orthodox or radical version. What I now want to point out is how Eurocentric this narrative is.[2] I don't just mean the obvious and trivial sense that it focuses on Europe (and Europeans in the "New World"). Nor do I mean the less trivial sense that it involves assimilating all the world to a basically unilinear path of development, with other nations destined to be impressed into the European line of industrial march: "traditional" and "modern" societies for the mainstream view; "slave," "feudal," and "capitalist" for the Marxist view; with some awkward, ad hoc categories like the "Asiatic mode of production" stuck on. Rather it is Eurocentric in a deeper, more theoretically important sense. It projects as a global model of tectonic normative change and moral transition what is really true only for Europe and Europeans (and not, of course, true for women). And it ignores the emergence and consolidation of a new normative structure of moral inequality that is equally fundamental to the making of modernity. I refer to race, the specter that, emanating from Europe, comes to haunt the modern world.

Consider, for example, Will Kymlicka's well-known introduction to political philosophy. In the opening chapter of this book, Kymlicka says that: "[T]he idea that each person matters equally is at the heart of all plausible [modern] political theories" (1990, 5). So the thesis is that: though liberalism, conservatism, libertarianism, communitarianism, socialism, and so forth, will differ on other points, they will all have this commitment to moral egalitarianism in common. Kymlicka does not in the least mean this as a controversial claim. It is rather a liberal shibboleth, a banality, an obvious point that one makes as a preliminary to discussing more important matters. Yet if one thinks about it for a moment, one should see that for the classic ("modern") political theorists of the seventeenth, eighteenth, and nineteenth centuries, it is—far from being axiomatic—patently false. The reflexive, automatic, knee-jerk assent it evokes in us (if I may locate myself among the "us" here) derives from our considering only the European context. It is here, on this continent, and among its representatives on other continents, that it becomes "obvious" in the modern period that all men are normatively equal. But these theories of liberalism—whether Lockean, Humean, Kantian, or Millian—are being put forward by thinkers who did *not* believe all people mattered equally. John Locke's proscriptions in the *Second Treatise* against hereditary slavery seem, strangely, not to apply to the captured Africans in whose enslavement he was earlier an investor (Glausser 1990; Welchman 1995). Hume says explicitly that: "There never was a civilized nation of any other complexion than white, nor even any individual eminent either in action or speculation. . . . Such a uniform and constant difference could not happen, in so many countries and ages if nature had not made an original distinction between these breeds of men" (Hume 1997, 33). Kant's anthropology, credited by some as the first systematized theorization of modern (i.e., "scientific") racism, differentiates humanity into four tiers—white, yellow, black, and red—of which only the white European tier have the capacity to become fully autonomous persons (Eze 1995; Bernasconi 2001; 2002). And Mill reminds us in *On Liberty* that of course he does not intend that his antipaternalist harm principle, which prohibits interference with individuals for their own good, should be extended to those barbarian nations where "the race itself may be considered as in its nonage" (Mill 1989, 13; Souffrant 2000).

So the vaunted egalitarianism that supposedly characterizes the modern period is really a white one—that is, all *whites* are equal. The traditional liberal narrative of modernity is fundamentally misleading because it represents as a *global* normative change what is an *intra-European* normative change: a shift from the world of ascriptive hierarchy to a world of equal individuals that is true, at best, for (male) Europeans. In fact, a new system of ascriptive hierarchy is established by the European expansionism (white settlement, slavery, colonialism) that is the other face of modernity and that creates the material basis for European superiority to the rest of the world.

In understanding the ramifications of this system, actual Marxist theory (if not necessarily a potential, reconstructed Marxist theory) has also been inadequate. If liberals describe a transition from caste society to egalitarian individualism, then Marxists describe how bourgeois revolutions equalize normative standings but leave economic privilege intact. Formal equality has been achieved, in this society of "persons" without formal differentiation; but another kind of revolution will be required to overcome the structures of economic disadvantage that make these persons actually radically unequal. In this narrative, then, race does not officially exist. The social ontology (at least in the official narrative) is class-based, and it leaves no room for race; but no room is necessary, since the ontology is supposedly universal, colorless, and all-inclusive. Thus, in *The German Ideology*, in the first developed theoretical statement of their new worldview, Marx and Engels proclaim that they, unlike the Young Hegelians, begin from "real, active men," not "men as narrated, thought of, imagined, conceived," but "as they *actually* are, i.e., as they act, produce materially . . . as they are conditioned by a definite development of their productive forces and of the intercourse corresponding to these" (CW 5, 35–36). This statement is not supposed to be an empiricist banality, but a deep theoretical claim about what is putatively most "real" and "actual" about these "men." And what is ostensibly most fundamental about their situation is their level of technological development and the production relations in which they're enmeshed, which shape their being in a profound way and from which all the basics of their existential situation can be read off.

Yet the characterization offered implicitly makes it plain that Marx and Engels' colorless, raceless workers are actually *white*. Only for them have ascriptive hierarchy and caste distinction been abolished. The significance of the French Revolution is appreciated; the significance of the Haitian Revolution—and why there had to be a Haitian Revolution—is not (James 1989). If we were to give Marx and Engels the benefit of the doubt, it is clear, then, that at best there was no perception on their part that the peculiar situation of people of color required any conceptual modifications of their theory. And if we are less charitable, we must ask whether their contemptuous attitude toward people of color does not raise the question of whether they too, like the leading liberal theorists cited above, should not be indicted for racism and the consignment of nonwhites, particularly blacks, to a different theoretical category. It is a familiar criticism, as

pointed out in the previous chapter, that, following Hegel's distinction between world-historic and non-world-historic peoples, Marx and Engels
were Eurocentrists who sometimes spoke about "barbarian" nations
(Munck 1986). But in addition, in their more unguarded moments in the
correspondence, we sometimes find them talking about "niggers." Thus,
Marx, on a trip to Algiers, describes a "dancing grinning nigger," and he
observes of his mixed-race son-in-law Paul Lafargue that he "has the blem-
ish customarily found in the negro tribe—*no sense of shame*, by which I mean
shame about making a fool of oneself" (CW 46, 225, 231–32, 374). Engels casually refers to "amusing" "nigger waiters"; he remarks jocularly of Samuel
Moore (translator of volume 1 of *Capital*) that in taking up the post of Chief
Justice of the Territories of the Royal Niger Company, he has "consented to
become Lord Chief Justice of the Niger Niggers, the very cream of Nigrition
Niger Niggerdom"; he suggests that Lafargue is "in his quality as a nigger,
a degree nearer to the rest of the animal kingdom than the rest of us"; and
he speculates about some alleged political blunder of Lafargue's that he
"can only suppose that it's the eighth or sixteenth part of negro blood
which flows in Lafargue's veins and occasionally gains the upper hand that
has led him into this quite inexplicable folly" (CW 48, 209, 337, 52–53; CW
49, 302). So even if there is no explicit articulation and defense of racist ideology as such in their work, it can be seen that they shared the commonsense conviction of their time of European racial superiority.

I have argued elsewhere (Mills 1997; 1998), following the feminist example on gender, that it is a mistake, as the mainstream secondary literature
too often does, to bracket and segregate such passages from the philosopher's thought, as if they had no implications for the actual boundaries of
the population covered by his [sic] theory. If the philosopher in question really meant white males when he said "men," he likely had somewhat different descriptions and prescriptions in mind when it came to women and
people of color. My focus in those writings was on the normative apparatus of personhood and rights utilized by liberal theorists, and on the question of where nonwhites really fitted in this moral topography. But a parallel analysis could obviously be done of the Marxist apparatus of
sociohistorical agency and determination, with its supposedly colorless
workers. Consider, for example, this revealing passage from an 1882 letter
of Engels to Karl Kautsky on the prognosis for the anticolonial struggle:

> As I see it, the actual colonies, i.e. the countries occupied by European settlers,
> such as Canada, the Cape [South Africa], Australia, will all become indepen-
> dent; on the other hand, countries that are merely ruled and are inhabited by
> natives, such as India, Algeria and the Dutch, Portuguese and Spanish pos-
> sessions, will have to be temporarily taken over by the proletariat and guided
> as rapidly as possible towards independence. How this process will develop

is difficult to say. India may, indeed very probably will, start a revolution and, since a proletariat that is effecting its own emancipation cannot wage a colonial war, it would have to be given its head, which would obviously entail a great deal of destruction, but after all that sort of thing is inseparable from any revolution. . . . Once Europe has been reorganised, and North America, the resulting power will be so colossal and the example set will be such that the semi-civilised countries will follow suit quite of their own accord. . . . What social and political phases those countries will then have to traverse before they likewise acquire a socialist organisation is something about which I do not believe we can profitably speculate at present. (CW 46, 322)

The set of contrasts in this passage speaks volumes: on the one hand, the "civilized" white settler states; on the other hand, the "semi-civilized" countries that are inhabited by natives. The former are already fit for independence; the latter are not, and ideally they should be guided to independence ("when they become ready"—a familiar colonial trope) by a "proletariat" whose color is not indicated but, by the logic of the passage, are clearly the *white* European working class. "A colonial war" is ambiguous: Surely Engels couldn't possibly mean a war of counterinsurgency *against* Indian independence? (That would be a remarkable interpretation of proletarian internationalism!) But even on the more charitable reading, it is obvious that Europeans must be in charge to make sure things go right. Using Marxism's own famous contrast between what a theorist says and what he means, then, we could conclude that: if classes are the sole, or main, existents in Marxism's *official* social ontology, it would seem that nonwhite races nonetheless have a being that, in Marx's *actual* ontology, definitely involves a somewhat different dialectic of social emancipation.

So, I would support that the subsumption of the experience of the colonized and the racially subordinated under orthodox Marxist historical materialist categories is doubly problematic. These raceless categories do not capture and register the specificities of the experience of people of color; and though they are now deployed race-neutrally, they were arguably not intended by the founders to extend without qualification to this population in the first place.

This conceptual opacity, or at least insensitivity, is reproduced by Marx's intellectual heirs: for example, in Lenin's classic booklet on imperialism (1996), originally published in 1916. Though Lenin does describe "a world system of colonial oppression" divided between the advanced capitalist nations and the "subjected countries and peoples" (5, 83), the very word "race" is mentioned only twice (104, 114), once in reference to J. A. Hobson's work, and it certainly gets no theoretical treatment. Since class exploitation is the central form of domination, subordinated nonwhite peoples have their situation characterized in terms of national oppression and superexploitation. That is, whereas the abstract colorless (but actually white) worker, as a "wage-slave," has surplus value extracted from him during "normal" free wage labor, the literally enslaved and those carrying out forced labor in the colonies do not even get the chance to sell their labor power. But while such differential exploitation is certainly part of the story of racial subordination, it is not remotely the whole story. The distinctive reality of race and the profound shaping effect it has on one's life, for both the privileged and the subordinated, are not explored. The benefits to the metropolitan white working class are conceptually cashed out in terms of payment from "super-profits" to a "labour aristocracy" (7), but not in terms of joint stockholding benefits in whiteness itself. So though this may be a "new capitalism," its newness essentially inheres in "the domination of finance capital" (43, 58); and racial oppression makes no appearance on the list of its "five essential features" (90). Racial domination and racial struggle can have no reality of their own, since while "the *forms* of the struggle may and do constantly change in accordance with varying, relatively particular, and temporary causes . . . the *essence* of the struggle, its class *content*, cannot change while classes exist" (75). Even when the significance of race seems to be admitted, as by Oliver Cromwell Cox (2000), where race is linked as a global formation to imperialism, it is still ultimately reduced to class.

So with a few laudable exceptions, such as Victor Kiernan's work (1996), the orthodox white Marxist tradition has been impaired by a general theoretical failure in appreciating the reality of race as itself a system of oppression. Not accommodated within the terms of the theory is the idea that European expansionism and European imperialism bring race into existence as a global social reality, a structure of domination in which, on the planetary scale, Europe dominates the other continents; and within these continents, whites dominate nonwhites. Racial domination is not itself seen as a system of political oppression because it is not viewed as *racial* oppression, but rather as "really" something else, as class oppression in one of its many manifestations, or as national subordination. Typically, racism has been seen as a set of ideas and values imposed on the working class by the bourgeoisie, a particular variant of bourgeois ideology. Since the worker (defined by relationship to the means of production) is essentially raceless and has no country, the fact that the United States, for example, has historically been "a white man's country" has no bearing on his class being. In the classic Marxist social model of (materialist) base and (ideal/ideological) superstructure, class is in the base, and race is ideal. So in terms of a social ontology, class is metaphysically "deep," but race is not. A social ontology of class, certainly; a social ontology of race, no.

Moreover, these omissions and evasions are not just features of the past, but the recent present. As an example, let us turn again to the five representative anthologies in Analytical Marxism cited at the start of chapter 1: Ball and Farr (1984); Roemer (1986); Callinicos (1989); Ware and Nielsen (1989); Carver and Thomas (1995). (Anthologies are more useful in illustrating the point, since omissions in a single-authored book can always be attributed to the shortsightedness of the individual author.)

Together these five books run to sixty-five chapters and seventeen hundred pages. (I am counting the long introductions in Callinicos, and Ware and Nielsen as chapters.) One might expect, then, that in all these words looking at a global theory of history, there would be some treatment of a subject, race and racism, that has obviously been pretty central to that history—especially when the pretensions of Analytical Marxism are to have jettisoned the dogmatism and Left catchphrases of the past; to be examining Marxism critically; and to bring it up to date in the light of modern sociology, economics, and political science. But the actuality is that: not only is it not the case that several chapters are dedicated to the subject, not even one chapter is dedicated to the subject; not only is it not the case that several sections in different chapters focus on the subject, not even one section in one chapter focuses on the subject. There are two brief discussions and some scattered sentences in a few chapters, but there is no systematic treatment.[3]

So this is an indication of the state of affairs in what could be regarded as a "white" Marxism: neither in the founders' original work nor in the subsequent elaborations of (most of) their intellectual heirs has sufficient attention been paid to race. The understanding of the growth of capitalism is not crucially linked—as it would be in a "black" Marxism—to imperialism's role in establishing a world-system of racial domination (Cedric Robinson 2000). And the political conceptualization of particular countries, such as the United States, is inadequate in that the significance of structural white privilege for their makeup is not appreciated. Since the workingman has no country, even less does he have a race. There is no need, then, to develop a theorization of the significance of race in a general theory of history and society, despite the centrality of race to that history and despite the fact that most of the authors in the anthologies are Americans, and thus citizens of what is one of the most race-conscious societies in the world, with a history hundreds of years old of white supremacy (Fredrickson 1981; Anthony Marx 1998).

"RACE AS THE PRIMARY CONTRADICTION"

In 1996 I was invited by the Radical Philosophy Association (RPA) to participate in one of those "after the fall"/"rethinking the Left"/"which way forward" panels that were so prevalent in the post-1991 period.[4] Having been musing for some time on the issues discussed in the previous section, I decided that—instead of the usual ritualistic Left genuflections and pieties—I would raise the question of whether there might not be some deeper problem not addressed in white American Left theory. Originally, I had meant to complete a paper, as well as a handout to go with it; but in the end, pressed for time, I simply expanded the handout to become the paper. I here reproduce in full that handout (only slightly edited), distributed to the jaw-dropping consternation of the panel organizer and most of the audience, not to mention the outrage of many present:

RACE AS THE PRIMARY CONTRADICTION
Or, "Does White American Radical Theory Rest on a Mistake?"
Or, "Why Is There No Liberalism in the United States?"
Or, "Why White Marxists Should Be Black Nationalists"[5]
Or, "Socialism in Our Time: A 500-Year Plan"

BASIC THESIS: The original white radical orthodoxy (Marxist) was that: (i) there is a primary contradiction, and (ii) it's class. The present white radical orthodoxy (post-Marxist/postmodernist) is that: there is no primary contradiction. My radical thesis is that both of these orthodoxies are wrong. Instead, the truth is that: (i) there is a primary contradiction, and (ii) it's race.

1. Prelude: A Short Brechtian Exercise for the White Radical Reader

Look at yourself in the bathroom mirror (other mirrors can do as well, but it may be best to do this in private), and ask yourself the following question: What am I doing here? After all, I am not Apache, Cheyenne, Kiowa, Pueblo, Navajo. The tribe of which I am a member is the European tribe, the white tribe. What entitles me to be here is that I am a descendant of white settlers in a white settler state established by taking this land by force from its native inhabitants. The structure of moral and political entitlements that legitimated this taking was condensed in "race." This is not ancient history, like the Fall of Rome, or even more recent history, like the Norman Conquest. The last battles were still being fought little more than a century ago. Yet this structure remains largely unexamined, ignored, naturalized, taken for granted, in white radical theory. What does this say about white radical theory? What does this say about me?

Do this once every morning for a week, or at least until you start feeling worse.

2. Race as the Primary Contradiction: What I Don't Mean

Here are some possible misunderstandings of my claim: (i) Race as the oldest oppression—obviously false (gender has that honor), since race only comes into existence over the last five hundred years or so. (ii) Race as the progenitor of all other oppressions (gender, class, etc.)—obviously false, given that it's not the oldest. (iii) Race as involving the highest rate of exploitation (in the technical Marxist sense)—not necessarily; the metropolitan white working class may be more exploited than nonwhites in the Third World. (iv) Race as biological, transhistorical, transworld—no (see [i]), race is constructed. (v) Race as exhaustive of the political—no, the political is broader than race. (vi) Race as the only important oppression—no, other oppressions are important also.

3. Race as the Primary Contradiction: What I Do Mean
Race as the central identity around which people close ranks (no transracial gender bloc; no transracial class bloc; but transgender and transclass racial blocs). Race as the stable reference point for identifying the "them" and "us" which override all other "thems" and "us's" (identities are multiple, but some are more central than others). Race as the best predictor of opinion on a myriad public issues. Race as what ties the system together, and blocks progressive change.

4. Why Gender Isn't the Primary Contradiction
White women are oppressed, but gain at least a virtual personhood/ personhood-by-proxy through their appropriate relation to the white male (father, husband, brother, etc.), and share materially in white male wealth through family and racial group relations in a way that nonwhites do not. Straight white women (the vast majority of white women) routinely hang out with, date, sleep with, marry, have kids with "the enemy" (this is the truth in lesbian separatism)—obviously not a basis for systemic opposition. The "enemy" are their fathers, brothers, cousins, friends, workmates, children. (White lesbians are a tiny minority and in any case generally hook up with other white lesbians.) Thus at the end of the day, when the consciousness-raising sessions and the feminist demonstrations are over, white women return in the main to the white-male-centered household.

5. Whites as a Cognitively-Handicapped Population
Whites as multiply handicapped in seeing this system because (i) *motivationally*: whites benefit from the existing order, and so have a vested interest in not seeing it; (ii) *experientially*: whites don't experience racial oppression themselves, and live in a largely segregated white lifeworld—raised in white families, growing up in white family/school/social circles, hanging out with other white people, dating and marrying their fellow whites—thereby having little opportunity to gain access to nonwhites' divergent perceptions; (iii) *discursively/ideologically/conceptually*: whites inhabit a white cognitive universe, whose dominant categories block apprehension of the centrality of race.

6. White Radicals as (Sorry Guys, No Hard Feelings) a Subset of the Above
White American radicals import their radical categories from across the Atlantic, the theories following the same immigrant route as their bearers. But European models of radicalism, predicated on a system where race is much less domestically/internally important (race as the external relation to the colonial world), operate with a basically raceless (at least nominally) conceptual

apparatus. Race then has to be "added on." What white radicals fail to realize is that European expansionism brings into existence in the United States and elsewhere a *new* kind of polity—white supremacy—and that it cannot be conceptualized within the orthodox left frameworks. "Empirical observation must in each separate instance bring out empirically, and without any mystification and speculation, the connection of the social and political structure with production," and "Not only in its answers, even in its questions there was a mystification" (Marx and Engels, *The German Ideology* [CW 5, 35, 28]). But instead white radicals start with white people (differentiated from red natives and black slaves) conceived of merely as abstract "workers" and "capitalists" in a white settler state conceived of simply as "capitalism." They then ask (when they deign to notice it at all) where "racism" comes from. Better question: where do "white" people come from?

7. Why White Marxists Should Be Black Nationalists

Imagine you're a white male Marxist in the happy prefeminist, prepostmodernist world of a quarter-century ago. You read Marcuse, Miliband, Poulantzas, Althusser. You believe in a theory of group domination involving something like the following: The United States is a *class* society in which class, defined by *relationship to the means of production*, is the *fundamental* division, the bourgeoisie being the *ruling* class, the workers being *exploited* and *alienated*, with the state and the juridical system *not* being neutral but part of a superstructure to maintain the existing order, while the *dominant ideology* naturalizes, and renders invisible and unobjectionable, class domination.

In other words, you believe a set of highly controversial propositions, all of which would be disputed by mainstream political philosophy (liberalism), political science (pluralism), economics (neoclassical marginal utility theory), and sociology (Parsonian structural-functionalism and its heirs). But the irony is that all of these claims about group domination can be made with *far greater ease* with respect to race, relying not on controversial Marxist notions, but undeniable (if embarrassing) and well-documented (if usually ignored) facts from mainstream descriptive social theory, and on conventional liberal individualist values from mainstream normative social theory. As demonstrated below:

CLASS	RACE
FOUNDATIONAL CATEGORY (Genealogy/Origins/Meta-Narrative)	
Class society—capitalism	European expansionism—white settler state—white supremacy
Class as the fundamental social division	Race as the fundamental social division
Class as the relationship to (ownership of/dispossession from) the means of production	Race as the relationship to (entitlement to/exclusion from) full personhood

Base (relations of production) supposedly determines the superstructure (state, legal system, ideology)	Racial "base" (relations of personhood) definitely does determine the superstructure (state, legal system, ideology)
State ostensibly a bourgeois state, dominated by the capitalist class, owners of the means of production	State clearly a racial state, dominated by whites, the full persons
Bourgeoisie as the ruling class— polity supposedly a bourgeois democracy even with universal suffrage	Whites as the ruling race—polity obviously a *Herrenvolk* democracy even with universal suffrage
Legal system establishes and consolidates capitalism, though it undergoes changes over time (laissez-faire to state interventionist)	Legal system establishes and consolidates white supremacy, though it undergoes changes over time (de jure to de facto)
Hegemonic bourgeois ideology naturalizes/justifies class domination	Hegemonic white settler ideology naturalizes/justifies racial domination
Workers as alienated from their product, supposedly affecting their being fundamentally	Nonwhites as alienated from their personhood, unquestionably affecting their being fundamentally
Workers as exploited (labor theory of value) at the point of production; transfer of surplus to the bourgeoisie, who benefit from class exploitation	Nonwhites as exploited through slavery, land expropriation, market discrimination, rent, lower wages, general denial of equal opportunities; net transfer of wealth, land, surplus, opportunities in general to the white population, who benefit from racial exploitation
Class interests—notion of privileged classes having vested group interest in class order	Racial interests—notion of whites having vested group interest in racial order
Sociohistorical trends are supposed to lead (but haven't) to workers' becoming "class conscious," so that the system can be changed	People are already (and have been for hundreds of years) "racially conscious," with the white majority intent on retaining the system unchanged

So if—despite the manifold theoretical obstacles—you were able to believe the claims in the left-hand column, you should have no difficulty believing the claims in the right-hand column, which are far better substantiated. (You can pick up your Malcolm X cap at the door.)

8. Gee, Thanks for Explaining Everything; But Now That You've Pointed It Out, It All Seems So Obvious—How Come I Didn't Realize All This Before?
    You're welcome; see (5) and (6) above.

9. Socialism in Our Time: A 500-Year Plan
    As pedants know, if nobody else, the new millennium doesn't actually start until the year 2001, so this gives RPA members several years to prepare a 500-year plan, to be passed on to their grandchildren:

    2001–2100: Struggle against white supremacy/majoritarian domination
    2101–2200: Struggle against white supremacy/minoritarian domination
    2201–2300: Struggle for social democracy
    2301–2500: Struggle for socialism

    Get your black diapers now!

THE OPPRESSION SYMMETRY THESIS

Now one can appreciate that with such a handout I was bound to get myself in trouble in many ways, with many different sectors of the audience. For the unreconstructed Marxists, it was, of course, heretical that anything but class could be central. For the post- and never-Marxists, it was, of course, heretical (that quasi-Maoist title!) that anything at all could be central. Who after all, in these postmodernist times, believes that anything, let alone race, can be "primary"? But what I was trying to capture, however inadequately expressed, was my sense, first, of the reality of race as itself a system of domination and, second, of the *a*symmetry between race and other systems of domination in the United States. In other words, it is not merely that, as a black philosopher talking to a predominately white audience, I was saying that "this is an issue that has received insufficient theoretical attention from you white folks" (in the kind of scene that has taken place with black intellectuals many times over the decades). I was also making a more radical claim: that actually, in a way I found hard to tease out, race might well be of *greater* importance. (In subsequent weeks, I suggested in correspondence with various attendees that a more accurate title might have been "Race as of Differential Causal Significance in a Society of Multiple Systems of Oppression," especially since I didn't mean "primary contradiction" in the original Maoist sense of that term. Not quite as catchy, perhaps.)

The first point was itself noteworthy enough. Once I sat down and started to compile the list (under the seventh item in the handout) I was struck by how much more easily the argument for racial domination can be made. There is, once one thinks about it, a kind of obviousness to it—the obviousness of the natural, of the purloined letter. Why had I not seen it before? Because it is there in plain sight and so is not seen. For it should not be thought that I had had these ideas worked out clearly in my mind all along and that I was chafing at orthodox white Left theory's refusal to recognize them. Rather, though I was uneasy with the myopias of Left theory, my account is in part about my discovery as a black person from the Third World of the scales on my own eyes (an unnoticed layer beneath the previous, already fallen scales). In part, I was wondering at myself, at my failure to register what was so "obvious" once it was written down. Why had I not seen this before? Because of the categories of orthodox Left theory, which here had served as ideological blinkers. Whites and non-whites don't really exist, because race is not real. So the exploitation involved is the exploitation of capital. Capitalists exploit everybody, though nonwhites may be somewhat more exploited. And exploitation is what takes place in the factory. So in a sense, I had not seen what was there because I did not have the apparatus to see it. Mentally colonized in my own way by the orthodox Left narrative, I had not discerned what was now "obvious" to me: that white supremacy was itself a system of domination, that whites in general (and not just capitalists) were advantaged by it, and that whites benefit from this system not merely at the point of production but much more broadly.[6]

But the second point, that racial domination could in any sense be "primary," is obviously the really controversial one. There are two lines of response here: first from the (few) unreconstructed Marxists who would insist on the continuing primariness of class; and, second, from the much larger audience who would deny the primariness of anything. I want to begin with the latter.

I think that many radicals nowadays subscribe to what could be termed (I hereby dub it) the "Oppression Symmetry Thesis." In other words, there is supposed to be a symmetry about all oppressions, or at least the Big Three: class, race, gender. I don't mean a structural or experiential symmetry; people are not necessarily assuming that class, racial, and gender domination are all structured the same way or experienced the same way. I mean a moral and/or causal symmetry: the moral claim that all oppressions are equally morally bad; and/or the causal claim that all oppressions are of equal causal significance for determining the overall workings of the society.

In my opinion, the "Oppression Symmetry Thesis" (henceforth, the OST) has several confluent sources:

The reaction against Marxism. Marxism claimed, or was standardly interpreted to be claiming, that class was the primary oppression and that other oppressions could be understood in terms of class, or at least traced to class (if not always reduced to it). So Marxism, especially in the base–superstructure model of society, was classically committed to the fact of asymmetry, which in part is the significance of "materialism." The theoretical and political–practical failure of this analysis, manifested in the rise of the so-called new social movements of the 1960s and 1970s (though some, such as black American struggles, were actually much older, long predating this period), led to a backlash against any such claims, whether made by Marxists or others.

The failure of the grand synthesis. In the heyday of socialist feminism, the hope was that a "dual-systems theory" could be synthesized from the insights of Marxist and radical feminists so that a synoptic view of "capitalist patriarchy" could be developed. (See, for example, Eisenstein 1979.) But socialist feminism has largely collapsed with the decline of Marxism, and the most important contemporary feminisms are not influenced by class theory.

Poststructuralism. As we all know, the whole point of the rise of postmodernism, as classically expressed in Lyotard (1984), was an "incredulity" toward metanarratives. So claims about causal priority, objective truth, global pictures, and so forth, are seen as illegitimate.

Politeness. Finally, the simple but important point: that people who are trying to organize radical, or any kind of, political movements do not want to alienate groups that they're trying to ally with; and announcing a hierarchy of moral and causal priority seems a pretty sure way to do this.

So there are many obvious causes for people believing in the OST (or at least tacitly operating as if they believed in the OST). But obvious causes need to be distinguished from good reasons. I suggest that the OST is false, at least as a general truth valid for all societies for all times, and that, in fact, only a moment's thought should be necessary to demonstrate its obvious falseness.

Apply a good old-fashioned taxonomical philosophical apparatus, and ask yourself the following question: What is the status of this thesis supposed to be? Is it an analytic a priori truth, guaranteed by the meanings of words? Obviously not; nothing is conceptually inherent in the definition of "oppression" that necessitates symmetry of all oppressions. Well, is it a synthetic a priori truth then, such as those Kant thought he had discovered? But Kant's candidates had a much stronger claim, and even they have not survived later philosophical judgment. Then it has to be an a posteriori statement, an empirical generalization about the world; and as such it needs to be based on empirical investigation, cross-comparisons of differ-ent societies, and so forth. But no such investigation has been done; rather, it *is* held basically as an a priori truth. Yet its obvious falseness can be shown most simply by the fact that not all the oppressions even *exist* in all societies, so clearly they could not then be equally significant. Gender oppression comes closest to being universal, but class oppression is not a feature of hunting and gathering societies; and, as earlier noted, racial oppression has been argued by many to be a feature distinctively of the modern world.

Why then should the OST have such acceptance in radical circles? Apart from the reasons outlined above, there is also a kind of wrongheaded moralism that, on the normative issue, works like this. To deny equal moral significance to all oppressions shows a lack of respect for the group in ques-tion and only adds to their oppression. But this is a simple confusion: that all oppressions are morally bad does not imply that the extent of their moral badness is the same. Some things are worse than others; and though con-struction of a metric is not always straightforward, because of possible problems of incommensurability, one good test is one's own ranking of them in a list of dispreference. Being kicked in the shin is bad, but it is not as bad as suffering a broken leg, which in turn is not as bad as having one's leg amputated. Or on a less personal scale, consider Nazi Germany. The Nazis set out, and in many respects succeeded, in absorbing the German working class into the fascist corporatist state; confining women to *Kinder*, *Kirche*, and *Kuche*; and committing the genocide of Jews, Romani, and Slavic peoples. So the Nazis imposed class, gender, and race oppression. But surely it would be absurd to say that it is just as bad to have surplus labor extracted from you and to be restricted to traditional gender roles as it is to be herded into ghettoes, medically experimented upon, starved, tortured, shot, and gassed. So the point is that the relative badness of oppressions in a given society is in part an empirical question, to be settled by looking at its structure. It is *not* an a priori truth to be determined in advance.

My real interest here, however, is the causal question, that is, the possi-bility of some structures of domination being of greater causal significance than others in shaping a particular society's overall dynamic. As noted, this position was always the central, distinctive claim of the Marxist tradition: class oppression was the most important; and not just the oppression of any class, but the oppression of the working class in particular. So Marxism is overtly committed to the Oppression Asymmetry Thesis: some oppressions *are* more important than others. One could try to cash out this claim in var-ious ways: that other oppressions are brought into existence by the most important one; and/or that they can be reduced to the most important one. But both of these moves are problematic. Even if one form of oppression is brought into existence by another—as modern racism can plausibly be ar-gued to have been brought into existence by imperialist capitalism (at least

as a systematic set of theories and practices)—this genealogy does not necessarily translate into continuing causal preeminence. And class, gender,
and racial oppression all have distinctive features of their own that would
seem to rule out a reductionist program, regardless of their respective ge-
nealogical relations. So if the claim of differential causal significance is to be
defended, it will have to be on other grounds.

RACE IN THE UNITED STATES

What could these grounds be? Let me now turn specifically to racial domination in the United States and at least gesture in what I think is the right
direction—but first, a preemptive, anticipatory clearing up of possible
misunderstandings. Saying that, because of the peculiarities of U.S. history, race is of differential causal significance here does not, it should be
obvious, commit me to generalizations about all societies throughout history (though I do think my claim is valid for many other "New World"
and postcolonial societies). Nor does it commit me to saying that other
oppressions are of zero causal importance; the claim is comparativist, not
absolute. Nor does it imply the obvious falsehood that racial domination
precedes and/or generates class and gender oppression.

Well, what does it mean? To begin with, it is a claim about group self-
identification, about who and what we are, and what interests we correspondingly have or take ourselves to have. We all have multiple hats, multiple identities, because of both group membership and social roles. But if
one hat tends to remain in place, if one identity tends to trump others in
cases of conflict, that seems to me to constitute a good prima facie case for
regarding it as in some sense more important. And race does in general
have this characteristic; that is, it *is* the white hat that historically has been
most firmly fixed on the head. As I have written elsewhere: "[W]hite racial
identity has generally triumphed over all others; it is race that (transgender,
transclass) has generally determined the social world and loyalties, the lifeworld, of whites. . . . There has been no comparable, spontaneously crystal-
lizing transracial 'workers' world or transracial 'female' world: race is the
identity around which whites have usually closed ranks" (Mills 1997, 138).
Because it is only comparatively recently that the perception of race as *socially* constructed has become widespread, this obvious truth has been read
naturalistically; and it has been deprived of its appropriate sociological significance. But once we look at race as a social structure like class and gender, how can it be denied that, in the United States, it overrides the others?

Consider America's original "primary colors" of red, white, and black.
Do the wives and daughters of the invading male white settlers, in what
is a white settler state, identify either with the wives and daughters of the

Native Americans with whom they are locked in conflict for over two hundred and fifty years, or with the women of the Africans they have enslaved? Do white workers reach out across racial lines to form class alliances with expropriated Native Americans and with blacks subordinated first as slaves and later as the victims of Jim Crow? Obviously, the answer in both cases is in general a resounding "No!" So how can it be denied that race *is* the primary social division and that, though there are secondary intraracial conflicts of class and gender, they take place within a larger structure of white racial domination, which white workers and white women benefit from and generally support?

In cases of class conflict, for example, to address the orthodox Marxist challenge, white American workers have historically tended to identify themselves *as* white, as struggling against white capital but as retaining their own capital in whiteness by excluding blacks from unions; discriminating against them in promotions; moving to segregated neighborhoods; failing to protest when the racial state dispenses benefits to them on a discriminatory basis; and tacitly and overtly supporting Jim Crow. David Roediger (1999; 1994) points out that there has been an embarrassment about these facts on the part of white Left labor historians: they have been played down or written out of labor history; or, when grudgingly acknowledged, they have not been given the theoretical attention they deserve. And this theoretical failure is conceptually linked, I would again suggest, to an imported social ontology in which the workers cannot in the end be "really" anything other than workers. Certainly they cannot "really" be white, because whiteness has no ontological significance. But this presumption is false. White workers really are white at the same time that they are workers. The refusal to recognize and theorize white supremacy as a system in itself leaves a theoretical hole that drains Marxist understanding of the ways in which race can be real. Presented with the theoretical alternatives (in a class ontology) of race as biological and race as nonexistent, white Marxists have chosen the latter; and they have blinded themselves to the ways in which white workers participate in, benefit from, and reproduce racial domination, thus making race socially real.

Where racial domination has grudgingly been admitted, it has been represented as really the domination of capital. But once you admit the possibility of a society of multiple systems of domination, it is not contradictory that the bourgeoisie dominate the workers *and* that whites dominate blacks. So, as workers, they are exploited by capital; as whites, they are themselves the beneficiaries of an overlapping but distinct system of exploitation that not only secures personhood and its benefits for themselves but also denies them to others. Their being is shaped in part by thinking of themselves as superior beings; and of having this "superiority" embedded in social structures, national narratives, law, the racial division of labor, and public policy. The top-down manipulation and imposition model, by which race and racism are bourgeois inflictions on a colorless and innocent proletariat, ignores the reality that, as E. P. Thompson famously emphasized, the working class also make themselves; and in the United States, they make themselves as white (Roediger 1999, ch. 1). Indeed, the imposition model rapidly becomes a kind of self-parodic puppetry in which causality and agency are selectively vouchsafed to and withdrawn from the workers according to a circular agentic logic: when they do good things, they are acting on their own; but when they do bad things—organize lynch mobs, participate in race riots, have hate strikes to exclude black workers from factories, sign restrictive covenants to maintain segregated neighborhoods—it is at bourgeois behest. (One wonders how socialism was ever to be brought about by so capriciously causal a set of people!) Seymour Lipset and Gary Marks remind us that:

> Fierce and prolonged discrimination against African-Americans produced a distinct underclass that was regarded as a race apart from white workers and their unions, and which, as a result, was excluded from their political projects, including socialism. Those who were the most exploited and who had the least to lose in militant class struggle—namely blacks—were distant from the political concerns of the working class as a whole. White workers were often as motivated to keep African-Americans out of their job territories as to battle employers directly for better conditions. (2000, 130–31)

Yet the grip of Marxist orthodoxy has been so great—and the categories, despite their being so illuminating elsewhere, have been so blinding here—that no absurdity or incongruity has been perceived in writing, as if these white American workers stepped straight out of the pages of *Capital*. What has not sufficiently, or at all, been recognized and thought through theoretically have been the implications of their being not the proletariat of a nineteenth-century England largely racially homogeneous, but participating junior partners in a white supremacist state.

Unsurprisingly, then, it takes a black theorist—W. E. B. Du Bois (1998)—to do the conceptual innovation necessary to point out the existence of a distinctive "wages of whiteness," a payoff that is multidimensional in character and far broader than that received by Marx's European wage laborers. To begin with, they have a straightforwardly material benefit—which is part of the reply to an orthodoxy that would see race only as "ideal," "superstructural." Insofar as whiteness translates into guaranteed nonenslavement; entitlement to participate in the homesteading of the West; the racial reservation of certain jobs and opportunities (with correspondingly differential chances of employment, promotion, and good wages); residence in better neighborhoods; a prerequisite for full political membership; superior resource allocation for one's children's education;

increased access to local, state, and federally provided benefits; and the general return on one's investment in the social surplus produced by slavery and racial discrimination; in addition, insofar as whiteness tendentially underwrites the division of labor and the allocation of resources, with correspondingly enhanced socioeconomic life chances for one's white self and one's white children—it is clearly "material" in the classic economic sense, and it should have been long since recognized as such. If, referring back to chapter 2, we follow G. A. Cohen's gloss of *relations of production* as relations of effective power over persons and productive forces, then even by this orthodox criterion a case can be made that "whiteness" is part of the production relations—"whiteness is property," argues Cheryl Harris (1993)—and so race would indeed be part of the socially determining "base" (in my broader, rather than Cohen's, narrower sense: see figure 2.3, p. 41).[7] One way to develop a specifically Marxist critical race theory, then, would be to follow up what the ramifications of this conceptual synthesis would be and what it would imply for the rethinking of orthodox Marxist categories. (Cf. the socialist–feminist innovation of "relations of reproduction" [Jaggar 1988].)

But there is an additional, deeper point I want to make about the need to reconceptualize Marxism properly to take race into account, which goes back to the issues raised at the beginning of the chapter. Du Bois spoke of other benefits also: a "psychological" wage linked with the status of whiteness. I prefer to think of this as "ontological," linked with personhood, and arguably more profoundly "material" than the economic. If, as earlier emphasized, personhood is central to the emergence of the modern world, then the reality that has to be faced is that whiteness has historically been a prerequisite for full personhood, recognition as a full human being. In a medieval Christian world of lords and serfs, a higher community of souls exists in which independent of estate membership, all have their humanity guaranteed. But in a more secular modern world, where these tiers have been collapsed into "persons," there is less temporal consolation for the racially inferior, whose subpersonhood lowers them to proximity to the animal kingdom. In his recent short history of racism, George Fredrickson points out that:

> What makes Western racism so autonomous and conspicuous in world history has been that it developed in a context that presumed human equality of some kind. . . . If equality is the norm in the spiritual or temporal realms (or in both at the same time), and there are groups of people within the society who are so despised or disparaged that the upholders of the norms feel compelled to make them exceptions to the promise or realization of equality, they can be denied the prospect of equal status only if they allegedly possess some extraordinary deficiency that makes them less than fully human. (2002, 11–12)

So race then becomes tied up with our human dignity, our sense of ourselves as beings of intrinsic equal moral worth (or not). Being white is being fully human. Being nonwhite is not being fully human. One has an ontological stake in racial hierarchy because it is linked with one's sense of oneself as a human being, someone superior to lesser nonwhite beings. So even though the white working class are on a lower rung of the social ladder, the fact that they are on the ladder at all historically raises them normatively above blacks and Native Americans. The inadequacy of the Marxist thesis about social being is that, presupposing the European background, it can talk about the foundational shaping of the being of persons by the relations of production, of the psychological centrality of alienation from one's product and so forth, because it is the person population (whose full being is *already* ontologically guaranteed) that is being presupposed. But for those who are not in this population to begin with, their being will be shaped far more fundamentally by their *exclusion* from personhood.

Now what I want to argue is that Marx's own categories can be developed to accommodate this position as a variety of materiality. In chapter 2, I claimed that for Marx the material includes both the natural and (part of) the social, since the material is what is causally independent of us. Now apply this to race. If race is socially constructed, as we now know, then it is not itself biological; and so it is not an example of what I called there material$_1$, but rather material$_2$, like class. But unlike class, it is a social structure and social identity that roots itself *in* the biological, insofar as its identifiers move us to invest the physical with social significance. Thus Linda Alcoff (1999) has emphasized the centrality of the *visual* to race. We see others, we see ourselves, as raced, in a way that we do not see others or ourselves as classed. And this follows, of course, from the fact that it is on the body that race is inscribed. We can escape the workplace, we can come home from the factories; but our bodies are always with us. So one looks in the mirror and sees oneself preeminently as somebody of a certain race, since the criteria are, after all, written all over us, on the ineluctable physical part of ourselves. And this ineluctable racialization, I would submit, is not, of course, a naturalistic, biological materialism, arising from the intrinsic properties of these bodies (material$_1$). Rather, it is a social materialism, through which political domination *becomes* incarnated (material$_2$). It is because of the hovering European specter, the ghost inhabiting these fleshy machines, that we come to see these bodies as raced. But once these houses are so haunted, once this ghost is so incarnated, the spirit, the word, becomes flesh; so that it is as the material beings that we are that the body then shapes our self- and other-understanding. Not originally biological/natural, it becomes biologized/naturalized, the European specter penetrating the skin, incorporating our vision of ourselves and of others. Who am I? What am I? Who are you? What are you? We learn to see whiteness and blackness, seeing ourselves in our own eyes, and in the eyes of others, as equal, as superior, as inferior, but in all cases ineluctably (given a racialized social order) as a human of a certain racial kind. And this ineluctable racialization, I would further submit, is "material" in Marx's own sense—indeed at a deeper, more foundational level of his own sense—even if he himself did not develop the implications of his ideas in this direction because of his own racism and because of his focus on the class-disadvantaged, but racially privileged, white proletariat.

And this ontological stake, whether or not we want to think of it as "material," will shape interest calculations also. The economic payoff is usually coincident with the ontological one; but if they diverge, one may choose (as a white) to hold on to one's status of racialized privilege and thus may pass up the opportunity of certain economic benefits, in fear of being dropped to the level of those racial inferiors "beneath" one. The United States notoriously lags behind most other Western nations in crucial social indicators, and in recent decades in particular the country has experienced a massive transfer of wealth upward: "[The United States] is the only developed nation that does not have a government-supported, comprehensive medical system and it is the only western democracy that does not provide child support to all families. . . . No western democracy has as unequal a distribution of income as the United States once tax and transfer payments are included into the calculation" (Lipset and Marks 2000, 282). Similarly, Micaela di Leonardo cites research that shows "We now have the most poor and the smallest middle class, proportionately, in the First World" (1999, 57). Yet these growing inequalities have attracted little protest or political activism. Werner Sombart's (1976) old, turn-of-the-century question (originally posed in 1906) as to why there is no socialism in the United States has now become, with the rightward shift in the political center of gravity and the corresponding restriction of possibilities, the question of why there is not even any (Left) liberalism, any social democracy, in the United States. (In the 1970s, Rawls' welfarist *A Theory of Justice* [1971] was seen by many on the Left as bourgeois reformism, a book to be militantly critiqued and exposed. Now, of course, it represents a radical vision far outside the spectrum of political respectability.) And though white socialists for most of the century have generally ignored or downplayed it as a factor,[8] black intellectuals, from Du Bois in the early twentieth century to Derrick Bell in our own time (Du Bois 1998; Bell 1987; 1992), have long argued that race constitutes a major explanation for this seeming anomaly, with white workers' preferring incorporation in white domination, even as junior partners, to their joining a transracial class struggle that might endanger their privileged status.

Thus the reality—the reality that most white Marxists have not wanted to face—is that it is (perceived) *racial* group interests, not class interests, that have been the most important motivator in shaping people's decision making. Racial self-identification and group solidarity have generally trumped other identities and group belongings. If this has been hard to see, it is in part because racial choices have been so readily biologized that they have seemed natural, not even showing up on the conceptual radar screen. We do not question the fact—it does not strike us as a *political* fact—that race is the most important shaper of whites' lifeworlds, that as Thomas and Mary Edsall (1991) have documented, "many whites structure nearly all of their decisions about housing, education, and politics in response to their aversions to black people" (cited in Lipsitz 1998, 19). The failure to see racial domination as a political system has conceptually blocked a categorization of these as political decisions; yet in a profound sense they are political decisions—whites are making life choices in a way that generally maintains and reproduces their domination and privilege. Similarly, Donald Kinder and Lynn Sanders' recent book, summarizing numerous attitudinal studies on racial issues, points out that "Among postindustrial democratic societies, the United States tends to finish near the bottom on measures of class polarization" (1996, 90); racial division, by contrast, eclipses any other kind of social differentiation:

> Political differences such as these [i.e., on race] are simply without peer: differences by class or gender or religion or any other social characteristic are diminutive by comparison. The racial divide is as apparent among ordinary citizens as it is among elites. It is not a mask for class differences: it is rooted in race itself, in differences of history. (287)

And this attitudinal divergence turns out to be tied not to a perception of individual self-interest but *racial group interest*, in that, even where whites do not have racist views, they regard their group interests as threatened by the advance of black interests. The irony, then, is that in the United States the Marxist materialist model of group identification in a society does not work for class but works very well for race: that is, people are highly conscious of themselves as members of opposing groups; they feel the need for group solidarity; and they see their group interests as antagonistic to one another.

In a country where race has been so central, then, it seems to me dubious that socialism was ever really on the agenda, quite apart from factors of state repression of the Left and its stigmatized association with existing Stalinist regimes. To reply that socialism is the solution to racism is doubly problematic. In the first place, racism and white supremacy can continue under socialism. (The saying in the black community during the

1930s high period of Left activism, which I used as my epigraph, was: "Even after a revolution, the country will still be full of crackers.") And in the second place, the rational-choice decision making of white workers will itself be shaped by their racial privilege (a perspective not typically gleaned from the 1980s literature on the subject). I think that this judgment holds for many other countries also. And more generally, I would claim that on the international level, the underwriting of imperialism and its postcolonial legacy by race provided, first, an empathic barrier to First World (white) working-class identification with (largely nonwhite) Third World poverty and, second, a set of mystified schemas for explaining that poverty—both of which inhibited and continue to inhibit the solidarity that would have been necessary for a genuinely internationalist movement.

So one could say, only half-jokingly, that Marx was somewhat premature in his call to arms. If we detach the concept of a "bourgeois revolution" from class, and think of it, more generally, as a revolution against ascriptive hierarchy of all kinds, then one could say that this normative leveling has yet to be fully carried out. In a sense, Eurocentrism is written into the concept itself, in that it takes for granted that the main or only system of ascriptive hierarchy is that of feudal estates, while ignoring the significance of the system of racial estates. It is white domination, not the rule of lords and ladies, that is in many parts of the world the real *ancien regime*. And the political projects of those subordinated by this regime will be significantly divergent from those privileged by it. So the Marxist timeline—primitive communism, slavery, feudalism, capitalism, socialism—really has to be rewritten to take this actuality into account, with white supremacy (in particular nations and as Western domination) added to the list: primitive communism, slavery, feudalism, racial/white supremacist/Euro-dominated capitalism, capitalism, and only then (if at all) socialism. A socialist revolution has to await the completed revolution against the socially pivotal form of ascriptive hierarchy remaining, the exorcism of the European specter haunting the planet. If we want to retain the term for the sake of irony and paradox, then we could say that Marxist revolutionary socialists now need (and in fact needed from the start)—disdaining to conceal their views and aims—to persuade white proletarians to lose their chains of whiteness and inscribe on their banners: "Toward the bourgeois revolution!"

NOTES

1. Though the term is now ubiquitous in radical theory, it is Carol Gould who deserves the credit for first bringing it into English-language usage: see Gould (1978).

2. See, for example, Goldberg (1993), Gilroy (1993), Dussel (1995).

3. The closest thing to a sustained analysis is Allen Wood's discussion of "other forms of social oppression, such as racial and sexual oppression" (Wood 1986, 298–300). See also G. A. Cohen (1989, 157–58). There are one- or two-sentence references in Callinicos (1989, 34, 43, 60); Roemer (1986, 159); and Carver and Thomas (1995, 25–26, 63, 303). (Carver and Thomas also have a whole chapter on feminism, the only one of the five books to do so.) Unless I have missed some reference, there is nothing at all (i.e., not even a sentence) in either Ball and Farr (1984), or Ware and Nielsen (1989).

4. The panel was "Envisioning the Next Left," at the second national conference of the Radical Philosophy Association, Purdue University, West Lafayette, Nov. 14–17, 1996.

5. The term "critical race theory" was not at the time as well-established as it is now; today I would say "Why White Marxists Should Be Critical Race Theorists" (and also in paragraph 7).

6. Since that time some years ago, more and more work has been published on the subject, so that the case has become far easier to make. See, for example, Oliver and Shapiro (1995); Lipsitz (1998); Brown (1999); Conley (1999).

7. Note that since Cohen's definition is explicitly nonjuridical in character ("effective power"), it would also be extensible to the de facto white supremacy of the present.

8. See Lipset and Marks (2000, ch. 1): "[Racial heterogeneity] was generally ignored as a source of socialist weakness by socialist writers" (29).

III

CRITICAL RACE THEORY

The focus of the third and final part, accordingly, is race. As emphasized in the previous two chapters, this shift in focus should not at all be taken to imply a complete repudiation of Marxism, since I do think that attempting to incorporate whiteness-as-property into an expanded conception of the relations of production would represent a promising line of research for the necessary transformation of historical materialism. But interesting and fruitful as such an undertaking might be, it is not one that I myself pursue here or have explored in my other writings. Rather, my strategy has been to leave bracketed the question of whether such a theoretical synthesis is possible and to treat white supremacy as an at least semiautonomous system, on the assumption that important and interesting things can still be said about it without necessarily seeking to resolve these other questions. Whether or not an adequate Marxist account can be ultimately developed of the logic of race, racial oppression has a reality and specificity that need to be investigated in their own right. In a post-Communist world, the struggle for socialism is not currently on the agenda, even if it may revive in the distant future; and if capitalism is the present reality that limits our horizons, then surely both Marxists and non-Marxists alike should be able to agree that a non-white-supremacist capitalism is morally and politically preferable to the white-supremacist capitalism we have had for hundreds of years. (A similar argument applies, of course, for gender.) Moreover, if the analysis of chapter 6 is correct, the trumping of class by race in the white-supremacist capitalism of the United States has itself been one of the major obstacles to the development of a more equitable society for *whites* also. Both on intrinsic and instrumental grounds, then, the achievement of racial justice should be a priority for the Left.

For old critical theory, of course, class society was the central category, and this analysis has informed the perceptions and writings of generations of theorists in the Left tradition. My argument implies that new critical theorists should (*inter alia*) be critical race theorists and should recognize in their work the historic and differential importance of race in the modern world in general and in the United States in particular. In keeping with the systemic approach of critical theory, I argue (as I have done elsewhere) that "white supremacy" should be the overarching category for critical race theory. Note that this does not foreclose theoretical options. In the same way that *feminism* today covers a wide range of different approaches (liberal, socialist, poststructuralist, psychoanalytic, ecological, etc.), which are nonetheless in agreement in seeing male domination/patriarchy as crucial, so critical race theory can accommodate a comparable divergence of political and theoretical perspectives while working with the idea of white supremacy as the central reality.

In chapter 7, then, I make a case for conceptualizing white supremacy as political, in the same way that Marxists see capitalism as dominated by a "ruling class" and that feminists see patriarchy as male political rule. I then sketch out what I take to be its main dimensions. In the process I demonstrate what we should already know from several decades of feminist theory: that reconceptualizing the political necessarily gives one a different mapping of it. The chapter is more descriptive and taxonomical than explanatory, a reflection of the fact that we do not as yet have a *theory* of the deep inner dynamics and workings of white supremacy comparable to what Marx advanced for class society.

Marxists, as so-called scientific socialists, differentiated themselves from utopian and ethical socialists by downplaying or sometimes deriding demands for "justice," which, as earlier indicated, became a questionable category for many on the Left. In the hundreds of years of struggle of the racially subordinated, by contrast, the demand for racial justice was usually the central banner under which people organized. So for critical race theory, historically, there has been no ambivalence at all about making moral demands. Apart from a differing theoretical apparatus, part of the explanation for this divergence was that white supremacy (unlike capitalism) was oppressive by straightforward liberal ("bourgeois") norms themselves, once nonracially applied, whereas the Left had to make a more controversial case in terms of economic oppression, unfair constraints on proletarian freedom, and so forth. Similarly, while the Marxist concept of class exploitation relied in the traditional formulation (as against the recent work of Analytical Marxists like John Roemer) on contested theses about the labor theory of value and the extraction of surplus value, racial exploitation is wrong by conventional values. You don't need a theory of surplus value, after all, to see that slavery is unjust. Yet in the huge literature on justice generated since John Rawls' *A Theory of Justice* (1971) appeared thirty years ago, very little has been done on racial justice. In chapter 8, I argue that structural racial injustice has obviously (if not obviously to white philosophers) been central to recent U.S. (and global) history, and as such it should be central to discussions on the subject. Moreover, an adequate treatment of racial justice will require us to move far beyond the usual limited distributivist economic concerns of mainstream white theory, since people of color suffer specific race-based injustices in addition to the supposedly "general" ones that are the focal concern of the philosophical literature (Young 1990).

Finally, Jorge Garcia (2001) did a thorough and stimulating critique of my book *The Racial Contract* (1997) in the black diasporic philosophy journal *Philosophia Africana*. In chapter 9, I give my reply. Garcia's critique provided me with the welcome opportunity to clear up some possible points of misconception about the book and to make a positive case for using contractarianism the way I do. Since I am bracketing Marxist questions and focusing on white supremacy as a structure oppressive by mainstream liberal–democratic norms, I can utilize the descriptive and normative apparatus of contractarianism to map (in a general way) white racial domination and to prescribe appropriate corrective justice. Mainstream contractarianism begs crucial questions about social structure and political institutions by presuming atomic individuals in egalitarian relations with one another who give equal input into the creation of the polity. But by jettisoning the social ontology of liberalism, we can retain the valuable part of it—its normative commitments—while putting them on a more informed sociopolitical foundation. Garcia's critique of me, based as it is on his own well-known individualistic analysis of race and racism (1996), provides a useful foil against which I can elaborate a structural position drawing both on liberalism and classic Left theory.

7

White Supremacy as Sociopolitical System

How should we set about theorizing race if we are no longer going to work within a Marxist framework? And what contribution can philosophy and critical theory make to such an enterprise? Philosophy's classic pretensions—to be able to illuminate the human condition with the light of reason—have, to many critics, collapsed in a retreat to an inbred hermeticism, opaque and irrelevant to the outsider. Those in the analytic mainstream of the profession, in particular, share a reluctance to engage with the social and historical. Indeed, in an important recent book, John McCumber goes so far as to anoint analytic philosophy with the dubious honor of being "the most resolutely apolitical paradigm in the humanities today." In one famous formulation, if philosophy is "the queen of the sciences," then she has had very little to say to her subjects lately, being "strangely isolated from other fields" and playing no important role in American social life and cultural discussions. But McCumber argues that it would be a mistake to attribute this reticence to purely internal factors. On the contrary, he claims that an examination of the pre- and postwar record shows an externalist account to be far more plausible: the impact of McCarthyism, which differentially targeted philosophers, and its making philosophy, in fact, "the most heavily attacked of all the academic disciplines" (McCumber 2001, 13, 37). As a percentage of their professional membership, proportionally more philosophers lost their jobs in the 1950s through political harassment than academics in any other field. Thus, whereas in the first half of the century John Dewey's influential pragmatism had pursued a vigorous engagement with social and political problems, the postwar period saw a disciplinary (and "disciplined") retreat from such involvement—as part, of course, of a broader run for cover in the academy.

So if academic philosophy today seems to have little to say to the uninitiated, this development is by no means a matter of disciplinary necessity; for the fear quite recently was that it would say too much. Philosophy at its best does indeed have the capacity to illuminate, to challenge everyday assumptions of normalcy, to undermine the taken-for-granted, to upend the conventional wisdom—to be, in short, a highly *subversive* discipline. Moreover, by virtue of its positioning as a "meta" subject, it is strategically located to draw upon and make pronouncements about the *other* disciplines: their foundational assumptions, the location of their borders, their conceptual frameworks. Insofar as one is talking about human beings in general, philosophy is characterized (in theory, if not always in practice) by a principled openness to insights from all directions. And the grand tradition of Western philosophy has often been characterized by system building on the most ambitious scale. After all, Karl Marx's radical revisioning of society—which had implications for economic, sociological, political, historical, anthropological, and psychological areas of inquiry—was ultimately rooted in philosophy.

What I will argue in this chapter—following the Marxist and feminist examples—is that the best way to do critical race theory is in social-systemic terms, and that philosophy can make a contribution to such an understanding by its historic (if not always current) willingness to map global pictures that transgress subject boundaries. In my own work (Mills 1997; 1998), I have sought to expose the conceptual whiteness of mainstream philosophy, and I have argued that *white supremacy* needs to be taken as a theoretical object in its own right—a global social system comparable in current significance, though not historical age, to Marx's *class society* and feminist thinkers' *patriarchy*. If philosophy is about understanding the human condition, then it needs to understand the condition of humans *as* shaped and molded by these systems into capitalists and workers, men and women, whites and nonwhites. The distinctive insights of the subject—the genuinely holistic enlightenment arising from a perspective positioned at a higher level of abstraction—can then be informed by the material realities of social oppression, thereby guiding both descriptive and normative critical theory.

CONCEPTUALIZATION AND SCOPE OF WHITE SUPREMACY

Marx had to redefine "class" and "class society" in terms of ownership relationships to the means of production; feminists had to adapt the term "patriarchy" from a usage originally significantly different. By contrast, retrieving "white supremacy" from the historical lexicon has the advantage that it was already traditionally used to denote the domination of whites over nonwhites. As against the currently more familiar "white privilege," the term has the semantic virtues of signaling the existence of a *system* run by, and in the interests of, whites—thereby pointing on its face toward a conceptualization in macroterms. When the phrase is used in mainstream social theory, of course, it is usually restricted to *formal* juridico-political domination, as paradigmatically exemplified by slavery, Jim Crow, and black disenfranchisement in the United States and apartheid in South Africa (Fredrickson 1981; Cell 1982). Since official segregation and explicit political exclusion of this sort no longer exist in the United States, the term has now disappeared from mainstream white American discourse. If it is employed at all, it is only to refer to the unhappy past or, in the purely ideological and attitudinal sense, to the beliefs of radical white separatist groups (i.e., as white supremacists). That the United States could still be significantly white supremacist would, of course, be rejected out of hand.

A crucial initial step toward reviving the term, then, would be establishing the simple sociological and political truth—not exactly unknown to the Western sociopolitical tradition—that power relations can survive the formal dismantling of their more overt supports. Even for postapartheid South Africa, where whites are a minority, it should be obvious that their strategic economic and bureaucratic power will continue to give them differential influence. For the United States—where racialized and vastly disproportionate concentrations of wealth, cultural hegemony, and bureaucratic control are of course reinforced by white political *majoritarianism*—the case should, were it not for ideological blinders, be much easier to make. So the argument would be that American white supremacy has not vanished; rather, it has changed from a de jure to a de facto form. The merely formal rejection of white supremacist principles will not suffice to transform the United States into a genuinely racially egalitarian society, since the actual social values and enduring politico-economic structures will continue to reflect the history of white domination (Crenshaw 1988, 1336). White supremacy thus needs to be conceptualized in terms broader than the narrowly juridical. Frances Lee Ansley suggests the following definition: "a political, economic, and cultural system in which whites overwhelmingly control power and material resources, conscious and unconscious ideas of white superiority and entitlement are widespread, and relations of white dominance and non-white subordination are daily reenacted across a broad array of institutions and social settings" (Ansley 1989, 1024n). Though white–black racial domination has clearly been central to this system, a comprehensive perspective on American white supremacy would really require attention to, and a comparative analysis of, white relations with other peoples of color also: Native Americans, Mexican Americans, and Asian Americans (Takaki 2000; Okihiro 1994; Almaguer 1994; Foley 1997; Lee 1999).

In this more latitudinarian suprajuridical sense, white supremacy could be said to characterize not merely the United States but the Americas as a whole. For many decades a sharp contrast was drawn in the sociological literature between Anglo North America as racially exclusionary and the supposedly more egalitarian Iberian societies of Latin America. But in recent years, an increasing body of work has dismantled the promulgated myths of color-blind racial democracy, pointing out that most Latin American nations have historically stigmatized and subordinated their Afro-Latin populations. *Mestizaje* (race mixture) as an ideal has in actuality been predicated on the differential valorization of the European component and the goal of *blanqueamiento* (whitening); and, to this socially meliorist end, many Latin American nations have had white immigration policies. A color pyramid with multiple subtle steps and shadings has—when set in contrast to the crudely bipolar and explicitly exclusionary U.S. model—been falsely represented as racially egalitarian, rather than differentially hierarchical (Minority Rights Group 1995; Twine 1998).

Finally, insofar as the modern world has been foundationally shaped by European colonialism, white supremacy could be seen as transnational, global, the historic domination of white Europe over nonwhite non-Europe and of white settlers over nonwhite slaves and indigenous peoples, thereby making Europeans "the lords of human kind" (Kiernan 1996; Cocker 1998). David Theo Goldberg (2002) argues that the European and Euro-implanted state has been racialized from the modern period onward, and Frank Füredi reminds us that before World War II, most of the planet was in fact formally ruled by white nations who, on colonial questions—whatever their other differences—were united on maintaining the subordination of nonwhites. Indeed, in a (today embarrassing) episode now rarely discussed in the historical literature, a Japanese proposal to include "the equality of races" in the League of Nations' Covenant was formally defeated at the 1919 post–World War I Versailles Conference (Füredi 1998, 42–45). To the extent that this European and Euro-American domination persists into the postcolonial period, albeit through different mechanisms (military, economic, cultural), we could be said to be still living in an age of global white supremacy.

ORIGINS AND EVOLUTION OF WHITE SUPREMACY

The verdict on the origins of racism is still out; though most scholars locate its genesis in the modern period, some theorists argue for antecedents, or even full-blown versions, in the medieval and ancient worlds (Gossett 1997). But whatever the ultimate answer to this question, white supremacy as a *system*, or set of systems, clearly comes into existence through European expansionism and through the imposition of European rule via settlement and colonialism on aboriginal and imported slave populations—the original racial "big bang" that is the source of the present racialized world (Winant 1994).

But this domination need not itself have taken a "racial" form. The causes for the emergence of "race" as the salient marker of exclusion, and the corresponding growth and centrality in the West of racist ideologies, continue to be contested by scholars. What are sometimes called "idealist" accounts would focus on the role of culture, color symbolism, and religious predispositions—for example, the self-conceptions of "civilized" Europeans opposed to a savage and "wild" Other, the positive and negative associations of the colors white and black, and the assumption of a Christian prerogative to evangelize the world and stigmatize other religions as the devil worship of heathens (Jordan 1995; Jennings 1975). On the other hand, so-called materialist accounts, primarily Marxist in inspiration, would see such factors as either irrelevant or subordinate to the causally more important politico-economic projects of obtaining a supply of cheap labor, expropriating land, and imposing particular superexploitative modes of production, for which "race" then becomes the convenient superstructural rationale (Cox 2000; Fields 1990). Marxist accounts have tended to the class reductionistic (for example, in Cox), but they need not necessarily be so. The challenge is to explain the emergence of race in historical materialist terms, with appropriate reference to the interests, projects, and differential power of the privileged classes; while recognizing that—*once created*—race acquires a power, autonomy, and "materiality" of its own; so that white group interests then become a factor in their own right. Unfortunately, few theorists have been able to achieve this delicate balancing act.

Other explanations, not straightforwardly fitted into a materialist–idealist taxonomy, regard white racism either as a systematized and sophisticated extrapolation of the primordial ethnocentrism of all humans, or as linked with particular psychosexual projections on to the dark body (Kovel 1984).

Debates over origins also have implications for the conception of "race" itself and the evolution of white supremacy. Until recently, race has paradigmatically been thought of as natural, biological, the carving of humanity at its actual ontological joints. By contrast, contemporary radical thought on race almost universally assumes what has come to be called a "constructionist" theory (Omi and Winant 1994; López 1995). For this account, race is not natural but an artifact of sociopolitical decision making, so that one function of political power is deciding where the crucial boundaries are drawn. From this perspective, "whites" and "nonwhites" do not preexist white supremacy as natural kinds; rather, they are categories and realities themselves brought into existence by the institutionalization of the system. The white race is in fact invented (Allen 1994–1997), though theorists will differ on the relative significance of the role of the state (from above) in making race and whiteness (Anthony Marx 1998) as against the role of the Euro working class (from below) in making themselves white (Roediger 1999). Correspondingly, white supremacy evolves over time not merely in its transition from a de jure to a de facto form, but in the changing rules as to who is counted as fully white in the first place. Matthew Frye Jacobson (1998), for example, has recently argued that U.S. whiteness is not temporally monolithic, but it should be periodized into "three great epochs": from the 1790 law, which limited naturalization to free white persons to the mass influx of Irish immigrants in the 1840s; from the 1840s to the restrictive immigration legislation of 1924; and from the 1920s to the present. In the process, groups once recognized as distinct races (Mediterraneans, Celts, Slavs, Teutons, Hebrews) have now disappeared into an expanded white race. Similarly, other authors have argued that over time the Irish and the Jews, not originally (fully? at all?) white, *became* white in the United States (Ignatiev 1995; Brodkin 1998).

WHITE SUPREMACY AS POLITICAL

In radical oppositional political theory, such as that centered on class or gender, a crucial initial conceptual move is often the redrawing of the boundaries of the political itself and the corresponding entry of new, hitherto unrecognized actors onto the theoretical stage. What is taken for granted by mainstream theory as natural, or at least apolitical, is reconceptualized as itself problematic and political. A case can be made that "white supremacy" should play the same role in critical race theory that "capitalism"/"class society" and "patriarchy" respectively play in Marxist and feminist political theory: providing an overarching holistic reconceptualization of the polity as a system of group domination. In this way, a diverse array of phenomena can be illuminatingly conceptually integrated as constituting different aspects of what is in fact a global system.

In the Marxist model, capitalism is not seen, as in neoclassical economic theory, as a set of market transactions disconnected from societal structures. Rather it is viewed as a system dominated by a bourgeoisie whose differential economic power ramifies throughout society, making them a "ruling class," so that even with universal suffrage the polity is still no more than a "bourgeois democracy." Thus the atomistic social ontology of liberalism, most famously manifested in social contract theory, is asserted to be profoundly misleading. Moreover, the Left point out that the rigid orthodox mainstream partitioning of sociology from economics from political science tends to obfuscate the connections linking their areas of investigation—hence, the significance in the Left tradition of the term *political economy*, signaling a consciously integrated and transgressive theoretical approach.

Similarly, the radical feminists of the 1970s, who devised the use of "patriarchy," argued that men as a group dominate women as a group but that this dominance is mystified by another set of conceptual blinders: the limiting of the boundaries of the political to the so-called public sphere. The ubiquity of patriarchy as a political system is therefore obscured through the seemingly "natural" relegation of women to the apolitical domestic space of child rearing and care of the household. Male domination becomes conceptually invisible rather than recognized as itself the oldest form of political rule (Clark and Lange 1979; Jaggar 1988; Pateman and Gross 1997; Okin 1989).

In both cases, then, the challenge of class and gender theory to mainstream thought involves a revision of what counts *as* political in the first place and a focus on power-relations and manifestations of domination not recognized and encompassed by the official definition of the political (political parties, formal contests in the electoral arena, the actions of delegated representatives in parliamentary bodies, etc.). The deliberate employment of the term "white supremacy" (in contrast to the orthodox paradigm of "race relations") constitutes a parallel challenge. The idea is that it is politically illuminating to see whites in the United States as ruling as a group, thus constituting the "ruling race" of what was originally—and is in some ways still—a "*Herrenvolk* democracy" (van den Berghe 1978), a "white republic" (Saxton 2003), historically founded on a notion of racial, Anglo-Saxonist "manifest destiny" (Horsman 1986).

Obviously, such a conceptualization is radically at variance with a mainstream white American political theory that generally ignores or marginalizes race. The hegemonic "race relations" paradigm largely confines discussions of race to sociology—that is, race is not seen as *political* in the double sense of being created and shaped on an ongoing basis by political forces, and as being itself the vehicle of political power. Moreover, apart from this disciplinary confinement, the paradigm itself is fundamentally misguided insofar as it seeks to conflate the experience of assimilating, ambiguously white/off-white/not-yet-white Europeans (Irish, Jewish, Mediterranean) with the radically different experience of subordinated, unambiguously nonwhite non-Europeans (black, red, brown, yellow), the former within, the latter beneath, the melting pot. "It erases the crucial difference between the incorporation of the colonized minorities by force and violence—not only the intensity of their repression but its systematic nature—and that of the European immigrant groups" (San Juan Jr. 1992, 32). Where race has been dealt with in mainstream political theory, it has been at the local level of urban politics; or, when tackled as a global reality, it has been standardly framed as an "anomaly" to supposedly central and inclusive liberal democratic political values, and it has been conceived of in ideational, attitudinal, and individualist terms: a tragic "American dilemma" (Myrdal 1996). As such, racism is to be redressed through moral suasion and enlightenment, having no substantive conceptual implications for American political theory, which can take over without modification the (facially) raceless categories of European sociopolitical thought, in which the ascriptive hierarchy and traditionalism of the Old World are contrasted with the egalitarian and democratic liberalism of the New (Smith 1997).

White supremacy as a concept thus registers a commitment to a radically *different* understanding of the political order, pointing us theoretically toward the centrality of racial domination and subordination. Within the discursive universe of white social theory on race, liberal or radical, it disrupts traditional framings, conceptualizations, and disciplinary divisions, effecting what is no less than a fundamental paradigm shift (Blauner 2001; Steinberg 2001b).

To begin with, attention is displaced from the moralized realm of the ideational and attitudinal to the realm of structures and power, which has been the traditional concern of political theory. Correspondingly, the mainstream framing of race in terms of the facile and illusory symmetry of an individualized "prejudice"—equally to be condemned whether encountered in whites or blacks—is revealed as a mystificatory obfuscation of the clearly asymmetrical and enduring system of white power itself. It is this framing, of course, which opens the conceptual door to the later notion of "reverse discrimination" and to the Supreme Court's opting for the "color-blind" "perpetrator perspective." "The perpetrator perspective presupposes a world composed of atomistic individuals whose actions are outside of and apart from the social fabric and without historical continuity" (Freeman 1995, 30). Second, this conception blocks mainstream theory's ghettoizing of work on race through rejecting its conceptual framing of the polity as a raceless liberal democracy. Instead, the polity is conceptualized as a white-supremacist state, a system as real and important historically as any of those other systems formally acknowledged in the Western political canon (aristocracy, absolutism, democracy, fascism, socialism, etc.). Third, the notion of a global racial system with its own partial autonomy constitutes a repudiation of the too-often epiphenomenalist treatment of race in the most important Western theory of group oppression, Marxism. Instead of treating race and racial dynamics as simply reducible to a class logic, this approach argues that race, though biologically unreal, becomes socially real and causally effective, since it is institutionalized and materialized by white supremacy in social practices and felt phenomenologies through constructions of the self; proclaimed ideals of cultural and civic identity; decisions of the state; crystallizations of juridical standing and group interests; permitted violence; and the opening and blocking of economic opportunities. What is created, in the words of Eduardo Bonilla-Silva, is a "racialized social system," in which "the race placed in the superior position tends to receive greater economic remuneration and access to better occupations and prospects in the labor market, occupies a primary position in the political system, [and] is granted higher social [esteem]" (2001, 37).

Finally, it should be noted that this alternative paradigm—race as central, political, and primarily a system of oppression—is (at least in broad outline) not at all new; but it has in fact always been present in oppositional African American thought. Over thirty years ago, for example, Kwame Ture (originally Stokely Carmichael) and Charles Hamilton argued in their classic *Black Power* that, in general, white Americans "own the society," that the most important kind of racism is "institutional," and that blacks should be seen as an internal colony facing whites who, on issues of race, "react in a united group to protect interests they perceive to be theirs," dominating blacks politically, economically, and socially (1992, 21–23). From the struggles against slavery to the battles against Jim Crow, from David Walker's militant 1829 *Appeal* (2000) to Malcolm X's matter-of-fact 1963 judgment that "America is a white country and all of the economy, the politics, the civic life of America is controlled by the white man" (1989, 91), blacks have historically had little difficulty in grasping that the central political reality of the United States is, quite simply, that it is a "white man's country." But this "naive" perception has apparently been too sophisticated for mainstream white political theory to apprehend.

Moreover, as earlier noted, white domination has traditionally been seen as an *international* political system. Walker's *Appeal* is addressed not merely to black Americans but to the "coloured citizens of the world," a global racial perspective that anticipates the later anti-imperialism and anticolonialism of Pan-Africanism: Du Bois' assertion of an "international colorline" separating lighter and darker races, Marcus Garvey's message to Africans "at home and abroad," Frantz Fanon's vision of a planetary "wretched of the earth," Malcolm X's prediction (somewhat premature, to be sure!) of "the end of white world-supremacy." Paul Gilroy points out that black radical political thought is "hemispheric if not global" in orientation and scope (1993), and this perspective is fictionally dramatized in such novels of international slave rebellion and anti-imperialism as Martin

Delany's *Blake* (1859–1862), Du Bois' *Dark Princess* (1928), and George Schuyler's pseudonymously authored science fiction serials *The Black Internationale* and *Black Empire* (1991 [1936–1938]), with their pulp fantasies of a black international dedicated "to destroying white world supremacy." Current work on white supremacy in critical race theory and critical white studies is thus belatedly catching up with the insights of black lay thought, which is simultaneously disadvantaged and advantaged by its lacking the formal training of the white academy; and proper intellectual credit needs to be given to the black pioneers of this conceptual framework.

DIMENSIONS OF WHITE SUPREMACY

White supremacy should therefore be seen as a multidimensional system of domination, encompassing not merely the "formally" political that is limited to the juridico-political realm of official governing bodies and laws; but, as argued above, it should also extend to white domination in economic, cultural, cognitive-moral, somatic, and in a sense even "metaphysical" spheres. A pervasive racialization of the social world means that one's race, in effect, puts one into a certain relationship with social reality, thereby tendentially determining one's being and consciousness.

Juridico-Political

For the alternative paradigm, the state and the legal system are not neutral entities standing above interracial relations, but for the most part they are themselves agencies of racial oppression (Kairys 1998). To Native Americans, the white man's law has constituted an essential part of "the discourses of conquest" (Williams 1990). For blacks, the history has been similar. As the late Judge A. Leon Higginbotham Jr. documented in detail, blacks have consistently been legally differentiated from and subordinated to the white population, not merely with the obvious case of the enslaved, but also in the lesser rights of the free black population (1978; 1996). The Philadelphia Convention notoriously enshrined slavery without mentioning it by name through the three-fifths clause; and in 1790 Congress made whiteness a prerequisite for naturalization. The 1857 Dred Scott decision codified black subordination through its judgment that blacks were an inferior race with "no rights which the white man was bound to respect." The promise of Emancipation and Reconstruction was betrayed by the Black Codes, the 1877 Hayes-Tilden Compromise, and the 1896 *Plessy v. Ferguson* decision that formally sanctioned "separate but equal." For the next seventy years, Jim Crow was the law of the land, with widespread black disenfranchisement, exploitation, and inferior treatment in all spheres of life (Litwack 1998). Thus for most of U.S. history, white supremacy has been de jure, and blacks have either been noncitizens or second-class citizens unable to appeal to the federal government to provide them equal protection (King 1995).

While the victories of the 1950s through the 1960s over Jim Crow have led to the repeal of overtly racist legislation, and thus to real racial progress, substantive racial equality has yet to be achieved. The failure to allocate resources to implement antidiscrimination law vigorously; the conservatively narrow interpretations of civil rights statutes; the backlash against affirmative action and desegregation; and the general shift since the 1960s from the "victim" to the "perpetrator" perspective (Freeman 1995) in effect mean that further erosion of white domination is increasingly being resisted. Moreover, since the United States, unlike apartheid South Africa, has a white majority, a democratic vote guided by white group interests will itself continue to reproduce white domination in the absence of opposition from a Supreme Court committed to "veiled majoritarianism" (Spann 1995). Donald Kinder and Lynn Sanders' research shows, in contradiction to the expectations of classic postwar pluralist theory, that racial group interests are nationally the most important ones, cutting across and overriding all other identities, and that whites see black interests as antagonistic to their own (1996). Whether through legalized inferiority, electoral disenfranchisement, or majoritarian group-interest-based domination, then, blacks have been systematically subjugated for nearly four hundred years in the white American polity.

Finally, in mapping the juridico-political, the role of official and unofficial white violence in perpetuating white rule also needs to be taken into account: the sanctioned tortures and informally connived killings of slave penal codes; the "demonstration effects" of lynchings in terrorizing the local black population; the freedom given to the Klan to operate; the differential application of the death penalty; the race riots, which were basically white riots until well into the twentieth century; and the part played by the repressive apparatus of the state—slave patrollers, federal militia, police, military, the prison system, the intelligence services—in first suppressing slave uprisings and then later targeting legitimate black protest and activism to gain the rights enjoyed by white Americans (Berry 1994; Garrow 2003; Shapiro 1988; O'Reilly 1991; Dray 2002). In effect, for most of U.S. history the state has functioned as a racial state protecting white supremacy.

Economic

Marx's theorization of the dynamics of capitalism famously rests on the claim that it is intrinsically an exploitative system: even when the working class are being paid a "fair" wage, surplus value is being extracted from them. But with the discrediting of the labor theory of value, this claim is no longer taken seriously in mainstream neoclassical economics, though John Roemer has recently attempted to develop a general theory of exploitation in other terms (1982).

In the case of white supremacy as a system, however, a pervasive "exploitation" is ongoing throughout society; it is (or should be) quite obvious, and it is unequivocally wrong by completely respectable, *non*-Marxist, liberal bourgeois standards (if applied nonracially). As one classic line puts it, white American wealth historically rests on red land and black labor. What could be termed "racial exploitation" covers an extensive historical variety of institutionalized and informal practices operating much more broadly than on the backs of proletarian wage labor: the expropriation of Native Americans; African slavery; the refusal to blacks of equal opportunity to homestead the West; the debt peonage of sharecropping; the turn-of-the-century exploitation of Asian "coolie" labor; the exclusion of blacks and other nonwhites from certain jobs and trades, as well as the lower wages and diminished promotion chances within those employments permitted; the blocking of black entrepreneurs from access to white markets; the denial of start-up capital by white banks; the higher prices and rents for inferior merchandise and housing in the ghettoes; the restricted access of blacks to state and federal services that whites enjoyed; the federally backed segregation and restrictive covenants that diminished the opportunities for most blacks to accumulate wealth through home ownership; the unfair business contracts that took advantage of nonwhite ignorance, or, when recognized as such, had to be signed because of lack of an alternative to white monopoly control; and many others (Massey and Denton 1993; Oliver and Shapiro 1995; Lipsitz 1998; Brown 1999; Conley 1999).

An adequate theorization of white supremacy would require a detailed taxonomy of these different varieties of racial exploitation: they jointly and historically have deprived people of color, as a group, of billions or even (globally) trillions of dollars of wealth; correspondingly, they have benefited whites; thus, they in effect constituted the "material base" of white supremacy, the "wages of whiteness." (In 1990, black Americans, though they make up about 12 percent of the population, owned only 1 percent of total U.S. wealth [Conley 1999, 25].) And globally a longstanding black and Third World argument claims that slavery, colonialism, and the exploitation of the New World were crucial in enabling European development and producing African underdevelopment; so that racial exploitation really has to be seen as planetary in scope (Eric Williams 1994; Rodney 1981; Blaut 1993). The recently revived struggle for black reparations in the United States, and the indictment of the legacy of colonialism at the August 2001 UN conference on racism in Durban, South Africa, are manifestations of a global movement of people of color for compensation for historically stolen land and labor that has the potential—whatever its actual success in getting the West to pay up—of raising long-buried crimes, as well as forcing an official acknowledgement and (partial) reckoning of the terrible human costs of the past few hundred years of global white domination.

Cultural

Given recent debates about "multiculturalism," the cultural dimension of white supremacy at least is familiar: a Eurocentrism that denigrates non-European cultures as inferior, or even nonexistent, and places Europe at the center of global history (Amin 1988). What is not usually articulated is the role such denigration played in teleological theories of history that made Europeans the (divinely and biologically) favored race, destined either to annihilate or to lead to civilization all other races, generating a discourse that could be regarded as "fantasies of the master race" (Churchill 1992; Said 1993). Colonial peoples in general, of course, have suffered this denial of their cultures' worth, but the centrality of African slavery to the project of the West required the most extreme stigmatization of blacks in particular. Thus sub-Saharan Africa was portrayed as the "Dark Continent," a vast jungle inhabited by savage "tribes" lost in a historyless and cultureless vacuum, to be redeemed only by a European presence (Mudimbe 1988; 1994). The Tarzan novels and movies, the *Phantom* comic strip, the thousands of African "adventure" stories of pulp and ostensibly highbrow fiction of the last hundred years, are all part of this master narrative of white cultural superiority (Pieterse 1995). From north to south, from Ancient Egypt to Zimbabwe, the achievements of the continent have generally been attributed to anybody other than the black population themselves. Blacks in the United States and in the Americas generally were, of course, tainted by their association with such a barbarous origin (Fredrickson 1987). African cultural survivals were actively suppressed as part of the project of Christianizing and civilizing the slaves, and, in some cases, for fear of their possibly subversive employment. Similarly, after the defeat of Native American resistance, a policy of cultural assimilation to "Kill the Indian, but save the man" was implemented.

Finally, apart from this well-known pattern of white cultural hegemony, a related phenomenon of cultural *appropriation* without acknowledgement deserves more theoretical attention: that civilization in general seems to have an exclusively white genealogy. "You took my blues / and now you're gone," complained Langston Hughes, a form of exploitation that, again, is uneasily fitted within the categories of the best-known mainstream theory of exploitation, Marxism. Cultural white supremacy manifests itself not merely in the differential valorization of Europe and European-derived culture, but in the denial of the extent to which this culture—"incontestably mulatto" in the famous phrase of Albert Murray (1990)—has itself been dependent on the contributions of others, a "bleaching" of the multicolored roots of human civilization. Ancient Egyptian influences on Ancient Greece, Babylonian and Indian mathematics, Chinese and Arabic astronomy, Native American agriculture and forms of government are all denied or minimized so that Europeans seem to be the only people with the capacity for culture (Bernal 1987; Harding 1993; Teresi 2002).

Cognitive-Evaluative

Systems of domination affect not merely the persons within them, but their theorizing about these systems. Integral to both Marxist and feminist thought has been an auxiliary *meta*theoretical aspect, the theorizing about hegemonic theories. In Marx's analysis of fetishism and naturalization, in feminists' exposure of overt and hidden androcentrism, oppositional thinkers have mapped the various ways in which ideas, values, concepts, assumptions, and overall cognitive patterns contribute to the reproduction of group privilege and rule. White supremacy likewise will have associated with it distinctive epistemologies, factual claims, and normative outlooks, which need to be exposed and demystified.

  The clearest manifestation will be the development of racist ideology itself, in its numerous and polymorphic historical variants, theological and "scientific": from the Ham myth; through polygenesis, social Darwinism, and craniometry; to IQ theory and *The Bell Curve* (Gould 1996; Hannaford 1996; Gossett 1997; Jacoby and Glauberman 1995; Fredrickson 2002). But there will be many other kinds of examples also, sometimes not claims to knowledge so much as claims to ignorance—a nonknowing that is not the innocent unawareness of truths to which there is no access, but a self and social shielding from racial realities that is underwritten by the official social epistemology. In Ralph Ellison's classic novel *Invisible Man*, the eponymous narrator describes the "peculiar disposition" of white eyes, a blindness arising not out of physiology but socialized cognitive psychology, "the construction of their *inner* eyes"; and in *Black like Me*, white-turned-black John Howard Griffin looks back from the perspective of his newfound consciousness at the "area of unknowing" of Whitetown (Ellison 1995, 3; Griffin 1996, 41). Thus there will be characteristic and pervasive patterns of not seeing and not knowing—structured white ignorance, motivated inattention, self-deception, historical amnesia, and moral rationalization—that people of color, for their own survival, have to learn to become familiar with and overcome in making their case for racial equality.

More generally, white normativity in the factual and moral realms will involve taking whites as the normative reference point and illicitly generalizing from their experience, from Eurocentrism in models of history (Blaut 2000) to current "color-blind" denials of the reality of white American racial privilege. The original fusion of personhood—what it is to be human—with membership in a particular race will continue to shape white perception, conceptualization, and affect in unconscious and subtle ways even in apparently nonracist contexts (Lawrence 1995). Being constructed as white means, *inter alia*, learning to see and understand the world in a certain way. Differential racial advantage will not appear as such, but rather as legitimate entitlement, the history of racial exploitation having been whitewashed out of existence. In a polity of Lockean proprietors, as Cheryl Harris argues, whiteness with all that it entails will itself become "property"—a neutral baseline, any incursion upon which will be sincerely and righteously viewed as an attack on fundamental human rights and freedoms (1993). Since this system will inevitably influence nonwhite cognition also, the racially subordinated will have to think themselves out of conceptual frameworks and value systems that justify or obfuscate their subordination. Those people of color who have internalized a belief in their own mental inferiority will be cognitive cripples, deferring automatically to white epistemic authority, unable to develop theorizations and moral evaluations that challenge white supremacy, and as such accepting (not merely feigning) an "ethics of living Jim Crow" (Wright 1993).

Somatic

White supremacy also has a central somatic dimension, especially where the black population is concerned. Since this is a political system predicated on racial superiority and inferiority, on the demarcation and differential evaluation of different races, the "body" in the body politic naturally becomes crucial—and *non*metaphoric—in a way it does not in the abstract polity of (official) Western theory. A white "somatic norm" assumes hegemonic standing, serving as an important contributory measure of individual worth; and the literal lack of incorporation of people of color into the extended white macrobody of the *polis* is written directly on their flesh (Hoetink 1962). In his book simply titled *White*, Richard Dyer documents the pervasive iconography of the white bodily ideal, and he shows how over decades it has come to be constructed in movies through special photography and lighting techniques (1997). Not merely in the United States, but in its broader external cultural sphere, these images influence how people see others and how they see themselves. Thus Latin American *telenovelas*, for example, depict a Caucasoid universe far removed from the representative body types of the populations of these significantly black, indio, mestizo, and mulatto nations. The nonwhite body—red, yellow, brown, black—has been clearly demarcated as alien, as flesh *not* of our flesh. The black body in particular, being both the sign of slave status and the body physically most divergent from the white one, has historically been derogated and stigmatized as grotesque, ugly, simian: mocked in blackface minstrelsy, newspaper cartoons, advertising, animated films, memorabilia (Pieterse 1995; Turner 2002).

The young Marx made alienation from one's labor a central concept in his indictment of class society. It could be argued here that under white supremacy, one has an alienation far more fundamental; since while one can always come home from work, one cannot get out of one's skin. Nonwhites socialized into the acceptance of this somatic norm will then be alienated from their own bodies, in a sense estranged from their own physical being [read: be-ing] in the world (Russell, Wilson, and Hall 1992). Recent philosophical work on the body has generally focused on gender rather than race (Welton 1998), but some philosophers of color—for example, Lewis Gordon and Linda Martín Alcoff—are beginning to explore racial embodiment and alienation from a phenomenological point of view (Gordon 1995; Alcoff 1999). Particularly for women, for whom the (patriarchically driven) imperative to be beautiful is most important, this alienation will manifest itself in attempts to transform the body to more closely approximate the white somatic ideal, whether through makeup, cosmetic aids, or, in the extreme case and for those who can afford it, plastic surgery: eye jobs, nose jobs, dermabrasion (Gilman 1998). Moreover, there will be an inevitable racialization of sexual relations in terms of the differential social attractiveness of certain bodies (Fanon 1991). Toni Morrison's powerful and moving first novel, *The Bluest Eye*, depicts the tragic fate of a young black girl whose dearest wish is to get the blue eyes whose lack, she concludes, is what makes her unloved (2000). Necessarily, then, the resistance to oppressive corporeal whiteness has taken the form of a guerrilla insurgency on the terrain of the flesh itself (White and White 1998).

Metaphysical

Finally, let me conclude by saying something about what could be termed the "metaphysics" of white supremacy. Mainstream Anglo-American analytic philosophy tends to separate metaphysical issues of being and consciousness, identity and the self, from the social; one thinks of the classic images of the isolated solipsistic Cartesian ego, of the atomic and presocial individuals of contract theory. By contrast, the Continental tradition exhibits far greater appreciation in its numerous variants (Hegelian,

Marxist, poststructuralist) of the notion of the socially constituted self, or at least the socially shaped self. Hence the idea of a *social ontology*, a mapping of the deep structures of being (thereby legitimately "metaphysical") that does nonetheless locate them in changing sociohistorical realities. Insofar as assumptions about what human beings basically are will necessarily guide theoretical research, often unconsciously, it is obviously crucial to ensure that one brings to light and scrutinizes these underlying supports of the conceptual framework being employed.

Now as argued in chapter 6, while the mainstream narrative of modernity is nominally egalitarian—in that normative human equality is taken to have been achieved by the Enlightenment—a case can be made that most of these writers were operating with an ontology that assigned people of color a distinct and subordinate naturalistically based moral status. So whiteness was a prerequisite for full personhood: normative, sociopolitical, and "metaphysical" equality. An ontology of society and the self that accurately maps, rather than obfuscates, these realities thus needs to recognize the centrality of racial inegalitarianism. From this perspective, white supremacy could be seen as a bipolar system whose ontological underpinnings lift a white *Herrenvolk* above nonwhite, particularly black, *Untermenschen*—entities whose inferior physicality underwrites their inferior metaphysicality and lower moral standing. In this sense, white supremacy is founded on a distinctive metaphysic, which is embedded in sociopolitical realities and which in turn reciprocally shapes those realities. People of color have always recognized that racial subordination is predicated on regarding them as less than fully human, as subpersons rather than persons; so if the class struggle is central to Marxist theory, one could say that the "ontological" struggle for equal, socially recognized personhood is comparably central to critical race theory. Frederick Douglass writes: "My *crime* is that I have assumed to be a man." Sojourner Truth asks: "And ain't I a woman?" Du Bois ironically describes black Americans as this curious "*tertium quid*," this third thing "between men and cattle." Ralph Ellison recounts the fate of an "invisible man." James Baldwin complains that "nobody knows my name." And black civil rights demonstrators in the 1950s and 1960s carry placards that declare simply: "I *AM* A MAN."

CONCLUSION

The virtue of using white supremacy as an overarching theoretical concept is that it enables us to pull together different phenomena and integrate these different levels: juridico-political, economic, cultural, cognitive-evaluative, somatic, metaphysical. For the elements I have separated analytically are of course interacting with one another in reality, jointly contributing to the reproductive dynamic that helps to perpetuate the system. If race was previously thought of as in the body, it is now too often thought of as merely in the head: claims of nonreality have replaced claims of physical reality. But race is best conceived of as not primarily ideational, but as embedded in material structures, sociopolitical institutions, and everyday social practices that so shape the world with which we interact so as to constitute an "objective" reality—deriving from intersubjectivity, socially constructed. Philosophy's promise to illuminate the world requires a realization of the whiteness of that world and how it affects its residents. Theorizing white supremacy as objective, systemic, multidimensional, and constitutive of a certain reality that evolves over time can contribute to understanding the world and, ultimately, to changing it.

8

White Supremacy
and Racial Justice

Against this background, then, let us turn to the question of racial justice. As pointed out in chapter 5, the best-known books on justice of the last three decades by white philosophers have not made racial justice a central, or usually even a peripheral, concern. And in the thousands of articles inspired by Rawls (1971), very few have dealt with race. Indeed, in a five-volume collection of eighty-eight articles on Rawls from those thirty years (Richardson and Weithman 1999), only *one*—by the African American philosopher Laurence Thomas—does so.[1] Yet as the detailed analysis of white supremacy in the previous chapter should have made clear, the subject does raise numerous pressing normative questions. In this chapter, then, I want to make some suggestions for ending this relative silence.

CHALLENGING THE ORTHODOX FRAMEWORK

What challenge does the idea of racial justice pose for conventional frameworks? One way to answer this question might be to ask ourselves what a racially just society would be like. A straightforward answer is that it would be a society in which people's life chances would be independent of race, that nobody would be unfairly advantaged or disadvantaged because of race. Articulating norms of *racial* justice, then, is not the same as propounding all-encompassing criteria for justice as a whole. In this respect, racial justice differs from socialist justice and from those varieties of feminist justice that do have such pretensions (feminism as a comprehensive and self-sufficient worldview). Some Afrocentrists might argue that an African-centered ethical outlook, drawing on precolonial communitarian values, *would* be able to provide such a framework to compete with the more familiar Western ones—for example, through being predicated on a different model of the self than that familiar from liberal theory. But interesting though this challenge might be, I am not seeking to develop it here. For me, then, racial justice is only a part of justice; one could have a society that is racially just, but unjust in other ways. Racial justice is best seen as corrective justice, as remedial justice, as addressing the legacy of the past and the ongoing practices of the present.

So part of the philosophical work that has to be done in determining what racial justice requires is getting straight on this legacy. Political philosophy is sometimes represented as a purely normative subject, but in fact it also has a crucial descriptive/explanatory component. Indeed, we can regard moral judgments in general, including judgments about justice, as based on a combination of factual and value claims, as expressed in the following simple equation:

$$\text{Facts} + \text{Values} = \text{Overall Moral Judgment}$$

That is, facts (what happened, what is happening, what is likely to happen, what is the case) put together with values (what is good/right) lead to an overall moral judgment. I am using "facts" broadly enough to cover empirically discrete, localizable events and larger ongoing states of affairs that would need to be characterized in systemic terms.

People can, of course, disagree about both; but in ethics and mainstream political philosophy, the focus is usually on divergence in *values*—for example, debates among utilitarians, Kantians, and libertarians about the most defensible axiology and what its implications would be.

It is not that *no* attention at all is paid to the facts. Utilitarians, for example, will typically argue that once we take likely future consequences into account, we will be able to see why their recommended policy is the better one. Libertarians will be concerned, among other things, to trace the past factual history that, according to them, gives people normative entitlement to certain property holdings. Rawlsians will assume that we take behind the veil a certain general knowledge of society and history. And all parties may, from time to time, appeal to empirical features of the world, whether natural or social. So facts do play some role in these debates. But because a high degree of commonsensical or scientific consensus exists, or is presumed to exist, on the factual picture (the description of natural and social reality), it tends to drop out as a major factor. In other words, even when utilitarians, libertarians, and Rawlsians are tracing future consequences or past causal chains, they are doing so within a framework on which "we" can agree—they are *reminding* us of things we (putatively) already know, or they are *spelling out* in greater detail what that picture implies. So the factual component of the equation is taken to be—not exactly, but more or less—relatively uncontroversial among the different parties; and the real fight is then over what follows when different conceptions of the right and the good are linked with these facts and how well, in some coherentist process of cognitive equilibrium, the outcome matches our moral intuitions.

But for those judged to be politically "radical"—for example, socialists and feminists—the agenda is different. Usually it is precisely the factual, or the allegedly factual, picture of the social world that comes under challenge. What is seen as an uncontroversial, largely consensual characterization of sociopolitical reality by mainstream figures is exactly what is contested by the heterodox.[2] The radicalness of their challenge, then, often inheres not in a startling new axiology, but in a startling new picture of the world, which overturns the conventional wisdom and the orthodox consensus on what "we" know about social reality. Indeed, it puts into question the idea of an uncontested "we" as a cognizing agent by arguing that the "consensus" is more likely to reflect the perspective of the socially privileged (bourgeois, male) than a classless, genderless "ideal observer." Marxists claim that even what seem to be inclusivist and egalitarian liberal democracies are structured by oppressive relations of class exploitation (Peffer 1990). Feminists claim that male domination, patriarchy, has been so ubiquitous that it has been naturalized—ignored at best, when not overtly justified—by the (male) political philosopher (Okin 1989; Nussbaum 1999).

So the heart of the matter really lies here; or, to switch metaphors, it is this revisioning that does most of the work in the "challenge" to mainstream theorizing on justice. Once this divergent factual picture has been sketched, once a case has been made for the pervasiveness of class and gender domination—and the mechanisms by which they reproduce themselves and thus perpetuate systemic unfairness—even ethicists with fairly divergent value commitments should be able to agree that a given society is unjust. Susan Moller Okin's *Justice, Gender, and the Family*, for example, does a highly effective feminist job simply by going through a range of different male theorists with quite divergent axiological assumptions—Michael Sandel, Alasdair MacIntyre, Michael Walzer, Robert Nozick, John Rawls; communitarianism, libertarianism, welfare liberalism—since she shows how their prescriptions would all have to be radically revised once the real-life family (as against the mythical idealized family) and its gender structuring are examined (1989).

In this spirit, Iris Marion Young argues that from the perspective of critical theory:

> Normative reflection must begin from historically specific circumstances. . . .
> Reflecting from within a particular social context, good normative theorizing
> cannot avoid social and political description and explanation. . . . Unlike pos-
> itivist social theory, however . . . critical theory denies that social theory must
> accede to the given. Social description and explanation must be critical, that
> is, aim to evaluate the given in normative terms. Without such a critical
> stance, many questions about what occurs in a society and why, who bene-
> fits and who is harmed, will not be asked, and social theory is liable to reaf-
> firm and reify the given social reality. (1990, 5)

From the somewhat different viewpoint of mainstream analytic political philosophy, Jean Hampton strikes a similar note. She criticizes those conceptions of political philosophy that would restrict it purely to normative theorizing; she points out that descriptive/explanatory claims, though at a different level of abstraction than political science, are also crucial:

> The task of political philosophy is not any surface description of particu-
> lar political societies. Instead, the political philosopher wants to under-
> stand at the deepest level the foundations of states and their ethical justi-
> fication . . . [the] political and social "deep structure" which generates not
> only forms of interaction that make certain kinds of distributions [of re-
> sources] inevitable but also moral theories that justify those distributions.
> (Hampton 1997, xiii–xv)

Both theorists agree, then, that the prescriptive needs to be anchored in the descriptive as well as the axiological: we need to understand how the polity works and, in particular, how systemic unjust disadvantage may be continuously reproduced in order to make well-informed judgments about justice and what it requires of us in the way of social reform or transformation. And on the reflexive, metatheoretical level—where we self-consciously theorize about our theories—we need to be particularly watchful that our moral reflection does not in crucial respects simply adapt to existing background "deep structures," "given social realities," of injustice instead of putting them into question also; since such adaptation is precisely what these structures and realities promote.

So to summarize: Here, and elsewhere in radical political theory, it is often really the facts that are doing the revisionary work rather than the values. And one can mount a challenge to mainstream orthodoxy simply by contesting hegemonic but misleading pictures of social reality and by bringing the underlying deep structures of injustice to light.

CRITICAL RACE THEORY

Let us now consider race as one of Hampton's "deep structures." Socialism and feminism are well-established viewpoints in political philosophy. But because of the whiteness of the profession, both demographic and conceptual, critical race theory is still a very new and unfamiliar perspective to most philosophers. As mentioned at the start, the provenance of the term is legal theory: "critical race theorists" was the designation of racial minorities within the Critical Legal Studies (CLS) movement who, while applauding the "crits'" critique of mainstream conceptions of the functioning of the law, were in turn critical of them for their neglect of racial issues (Hutchinson 1989; Delgado 1995; Crenshaw et al. 1995). But the term is increasingly being used in a much broader sense to refer to theory that takes race to be central to the making of the modern world, and that tries to elucidate and unravel its complicated implications in various areas—cultural studies, film theory, gender studies, labor history, even (dare one say it?) philosophy.

The adjective "critical" has several different meanings here:

1. It self-consciously distances critical race theory from the *un*critical "race theory" of the past, for example nineteenth- and twentieth-century social Darwinism, Nazi *Rassenwissenschaft*. Unlike these theoretical outlooks, critical race theory is explicitly antiracist.
2. In a sense, it also self-consciously distances itself from "race" by putting the word in scare quotes to indicate its constructed, rather than biological, character.
3. Finally, it links critical race theory with the Left idea of a "critical theory," which seeks to understand structures of social oppression for the emancipatory purpose of transforming them.

What would critical race theory mean in political philosophy? I argued in the previous chapter that it would mean following the feminist and (before that) the Marxist example: looking at society as a system of group domination. Marxists talk about class society in general and, for the modern period, capitalism. Feminists use the term "patriarchy." The equivalent theoretical move for critical race theorists in political philosophy, I suggest, would be to revive the term "white supremacy." On those rare occasions when the term is used in mainstream discourse, it is employed to refer to the values and beliefs of racist fringe groups—for example, skinheads, the Ku Klux Klan, Aryan Nations, and so forth. So the sense intended is really ideational and attitudinal: the individual's subjective beliefs. The usage I am recommending, by contrast, is objective: "white supremacy" as a politico-economic system founded on white racial domination. So race would be seen as a "deep structure" that generates not only disadvantageous and unjust patterns of social interaction and resource transfer, but also moral theories that naturalize/justify/obfuscate this systemic inequity.

Now the interesting thing about this term is that—however oddly it might strike people today—originally there was nothing in the least controversial about it. By contrast with the oppositional Marxist characterization of "class society" and with the feminist "patriarchy" (which were originally, and for many still are, quite controversial), "white supremacy" was a description that the dominant group—that is, the white population—originally embraced quite matter-of-factly. There was little pretense, in other words, that the society was supposed to be racially inclusive: rather, the United States was explicitly thought of as "a white man's country." In his recent book *Trouble in Mind*, which seems likely to be the definitive history of Jim Crow for years to come, Pulitzer Prize–winning historian Leon Litwack writes: "America was founded on white supremacy and the notion of black inferiority and black unfreedom. . . . The ideology of white supremacy always rested on the arrogant assumption that white people owned the country, that this was essentially their domain" (1998, xvi, 205). Similarly, in what is regarded as a classic work of comparative history, *White Supremacy*, George Fredrickson argues that the phrase "white supremacy" "applies with particular force" to South Africa and the United States, since they, more than other multiracial societies, "have manifested over long periods of time a tendency to push the principle of differentiation by race to its logical outcome—a kind of *Herrenvolk* society in which people of color . . . are treated as permanent outsiders" (1981, xi–xii).

So the historical reality here is well documented (regardless of whether it is a closed book to contemporary white political philosophers). That the phrase now strikes us as radical, perhaps even extremist, is a tribute to an impressively successful engineered amnesia about a now embarrassing past. Penny Von Eschen pinpoints the ideological transition in the postwar, Cold War concern of the American governing elite about necessary strategies for winning over a colored Third World and the need for distancing from the ideas of the defeated Third Reich. In the interwar years, and into the 1940s, "racism had been widely portrayed not only by African American intellectuals but also in popular discourse as located in the history of slavery, colonialism, and imperialism," the product of "global processes" (Von Eschen 1997, 22, 155). So race was explicitly seen in terms of political economy: the systemic domination and exploitation of one group by another, brought about through European expansionism and racial capitalism. But the postwar ideological "consensus," recoiling from Left analyses, undertook a "retreat from explanations grounded in political economy." Race was now framed in terms of "prejudice," the problematic attitudes of individual personalities having no connection with the broader social structure: "The eclipse of historical analysis . . . in the 1950s reconstructed 'race' and 'racism' from something rooted in the history of slavery and colonialism to something seen as a psychological problem and an aberration in American life" (Von Eschen 1997, 6, 155). (This, it will be appreciated, is how "white supremacist" gets its current transformed usage.) So it is important to understand that what I am doing here is *not* conceptual innovation; this paradigm is not new, but resurrected. It is the recovery of what used to be a standard usage, which was deliberately dropped for political reasons and for the need to whitewash and sanitize the past.[3] Racial domination as a *system* vanishes, and we are left with atomic individuals, some of whom have bad attitudes.

The reality is, then, that white racial domination—white supremacy—has been central to U.S. history. Whether one wants to date the republic from 1776 or go all the way back to 1607, we have had hundreds of years of de jure discrimination—that is, discrimination backed by the force of the law and the state—followed by decades of de facto discrimination. The crucial legal decisions formally ending these practices are all comparatively recent: *Brown v. Board of Education* in 1954, the Civil Rights Act in 1964, the Voting Rights Act in 1965, the Fair Housing Act in 1968. And in some cases the practices have continued. After a brief period of (partial) desegregation in education, the country is segregating again, as the Harvard Civil Rights Project has documented.[4] In fact, in a 2000 *New York Times* article decrying "The Lost Promise of School Integration," some commentators predict that "the central premise of the Brown decision—that integrated public schools are the most important institutions in a pluralistic society—will not survive the 21st century."[5] Residentially, the country continues to be profoundly segregated, as the authors of *American Apartheid* have demonstrated (Massey and Denton 1993). And the white backlash against affirmative action, antidiscrimination law, congressional redistricting, and other race-conscious policies has imperiled those gains earlier made. Indeed, Philip Klinkner and Rogers Smith (1999) argue that substantive racial progress in U.S. history has been confined narrowly to three periods, the Revolutionary War, the Civil War (and its aftermath), and the Cold War; it has been motivated by contingent historical circumstances and perceived white benefit, rather than white moral transformation; and it has always been followed by a period of rollback and retrenchment—such as, in their opinion, the period we are living through now.

These political truths have, of course, long been recognized in the black radical political tradition. From David Walker and Martin Delaney, through Marcus Garvey and W. E. B. Du Bois, to Malcolm X and Kwame

Ture (Stokely Carmichael), blacks have had little difficulty in perceiving the central reality of white racial domination (Moses 1996; Van Deburg 1997). But these figures and their views were not, of course, seen as academically respectable. Within mainstream political science, as Rogers Smith (1997) has recently massively documented, the orthodox conception of the American polity—as represented by the classic texts of Alexis de Tocqueville, Gunnar Myrdal, and Louis Hartz—has been that of a flawed (where flaws are conceded) liberal democracy: the "anomaly" view of American racism. It is admitted (when it is admitted) that there was some racism, but this admission is at best an offhand or sotto voce concession that does not affect the dominant conceptualizations of the polity itself. In a remarkable evasion of the facts, the systemic subordination of people of color by law and custom is theoretically ignored. Thus instead of the "anomaly" view, Smith advocates what he calls the "multiple traditions" view, which recognizes that alongside the tradition of liberal inclusiveness is also the long-standing tradition of white-supremacist exclusion. An older position, more radical than Smith's, is the "symbiosis" view. It would claim that the divergent "traditions" are not in any necessary tension, as Smith supposes, since liberalism develops as a racial liberalism so that its crucial terms are really only meant to extend fully to whites (i.e., the human population) (Ture and Hamilton 1992; Hochschild 1984, ch. 1).

In deciding how to conceptualize the American polity in its present period, then, one would at the very least have to utilize, and work out the implications of, the concept of a "white privilege" that rests on the legacy of white supremacy. And as argued in chapter 7, some theorists would claim that—admittedly in a weaker sense—we are still living under white supremacy, though of a de facto rather than de jure form. But in either case, white domination in its various manifestations would need to be recognized and be taken seriously by the political philosopher concerned about justice.

WHITE SUPREMACY AND RACIAL JUSTICE

Yet, as argued, such recognition has not occurred. Instead, I would suggest, most white social and political philosophers work with the philosophical version of the anomaly view. If you think this judgment is unfair, just reflect back, as earlier recommended, on the most important works in political philosophy of the past few decades. Ask yourself, in which of them does the fact of systemic racial subordination, and what is needed to correct for it, get any sustained discussion? Can it be found in Rawls, Nozick, Walzer, Sandel? The answer is, of course, no. It is a rare piece by a white author that begins, as Amy Gutmann's article does, "Racial injustice may be the most morally and intellectually vexing problem in the public life of this country" (1996, 107). In this respect, most white political philosophy reflects its racial origins, its "whiteness"—not in the sense of overtly advocating the racial suppression of people of color, but in the weaker sense of being written from the perspective of white racial privilege; so that certain realities, certain structures of oppression, do not come into view at all, or they do so only distantly, nonurgently, so that no recommendations are made for their elimination. (Compare the pejorative Marxist term "bourgeois" theory, the feminist "androcentric" theory.) If the facts were conceded, their recommendations for justice—given their *own* value commitments—would have to be radically different.

Consider, as an example, James Sterba's recent prizewinning book on justice (1998). I am not singling Sterba out as a *bad* example—on the contrary, he is far more conscientious than most, which is precisely the point. The book is characterized by a self-conscious attempt to be comprehensive in its coverage of contemporary issues, with chapters on feminism, environmentalism, pacifism, multiculturalism, and so forth, as well as constant recourse to the empirical data that I have suggested are crucial to these matters. Moreover, at least nominally, Sterba rejects the anomaly view, since he says explicitly (e.g., 102) that whites have dominated blacks. Yet what I would claim is that Sterba's recommendations, though praiseworthy, are inadequate because they do not appreciate the multidimensionality of white supremacy. Because the details of domination are not spelled out, we do not get enough of a sense of what this means in practice; the whole discussion, especially when compared with his discussion of feminism, is somewhat cursory. In fact, a useful contrast can be drawn between Sterba's treatment of gender and his treatment of race, starting with the formal allocation of a whole chapter to the former (and part of a second chapter too) and merely a subsection of a chapter to the latter. His treatment of gender draws extensively on the impressive body of work by feminist philosophers, which has transformed the way we think about political philosophy. But his book evinces a conspicuous lack of citation of black philosophers, with only one—Bernard Boxill—even being mentioned. (To be fair, other black thinkers are cited.) The family as a main site of gender injustice, the need to reform domestic structures, the role of rape and domestic violence in forcibly subordinating women, the ideal of androgyny—all get extensive discussion in Sterba's text. The material on race, however, is brief and undertheorized. The book gives no sense of white supremacy as a pervasive system of entrenched racial advantage with interlocking manifestations in numerous spheres that tends to reproduce itself and whose elimination is a requirement for racial justice.

In the previous chapter, I suggested that white supremacy has at least six dimensions: economic, juridico-political, cultural, somatic, cognitive-evaluative, and metaphysical/"ontological." Complete racial justice would thus require eliminating white privilege/advantage in all these areas. I will focus on the economic dimension as the most salient, but I will say something, if only briefly, about the others also, as an indication of how conventional normative discussions would need to be transformed to take account of race.

Economic

Let us start with the obvious dimension, the economic, and look at Sterba's treatment. His main subject is the defense of affirmative action against its critics. In the present period of a national rollback of the policy, this position is certainly a stand to be applauded, and I do not have much to add to or criticize in what he says on this familiar topic (Sterba 1998, 105–9). The problem, however, is that because of his inadequate framing of the full dimensions of black economic disadvantage, this measure, even if it were strengthened and retained, can only go a limited way to remedying the situation.

To begin with, he gives no discussion of a training program for blacks who lack the skills to be eligible for affirmative action—for example, those in the so-called underclass (Lawson 1992a). Sterba wants to defeat the conservative objection that affirmative action will mean giving jobs to the unqualified, so his focus is on those qualified blacks who are, or are likely to be, the victims of discrimination. But nothing is said about the large number of blacks who don't have the skills, not because of personal irresponsibility but because of an unjust educational system. Historically, for example in the South, fewer resources were allocated to black schools. So children who graduated from such a program were underprepared and not able to compete adequately on equal terms. But if we ask the question of *why* they lacked the requisite skills, we do not come up against bedrock, or something impermeable to issues of justice, but rather a conscious public policy decision. Today, schools continue to be segregated—there is, as mentioned, a pattern of resegregation occurring—and schools in the inner city are generally inferior to those in the suburbs (Kozol 1991). And again, if we ask why—for example, why the suburban tax base is higher—we encounter facts that are not remotely neutral, but rather the legacy of decades of white-supremacist policies.

Moreover, segregation has broader ramifications that need to be examined. In fact, the word "segregation" does not even appear in Sterba's book, which is not, however, to say that it makes much of an appearance in the books of other white political philosophers. Indeed, as Douglas

Massey and Nancy Denton (1993) point out, the term "disappeared from the American vocabulary" in the 1970s and 1980s, a vanishing act all the more startling since "it once figured prominently in theories of racial inequality" (1, 3). But segregation today, at the start of the twenty-first century, remains a principal feature of the topography of the United States. And segregation is a key factor in the perpetuation of racial inequality—through poor housing; lack of an equal chance to acquire a good home and build wealth; substandard education; inferior access to new economic opportunities and the jobs in the new "edge" cities; and so on. In fact, Massey and Denton argue that though there are various processes of racial domination,

> Residential segregation is the institutional apparatus that supports other racially discriminatory processes and binds them together into a coherent and uniquely effective system of racial subordination. Until the black ghetto is dismantled as a basic institution of American urban life, progress ameliorating racial inequality in other areas will be slow, fitful, and incomplete. (1993, 8)

Why have whites been so reluctant to integrate society? We need, I suggest—as part of the reconceptualization of the polity—to focus on the benefits whites as a group derive from the present order, and we need to start talking about *racial* exploitation. There is an interesting comparison here with Marxism's view of group domination. For Marxist theory, the central societal relationship is class exploitation, and this exploitation—for those who do take a normative position—is what makes capitalism unjust. So the Marxist challenge inheres in the claim that what seem to be equal consensual relations between wage laborer and employer are really structured by domination and exploitation. Now the Marxist claim is, of course, not taken seriously these days, for various reasons: the rejection of the labor theory of value, the controversy over the thesis about economic constraint's narrowing proletarian choice, the seeming nonviability of socialist alternatives underlined by the collapse of the former Soviet Union and the Eastern European states. But the point is that we can all see how the argument would go through, if the premises were in fact defensible. The fact of class exploitation pervades the society; because of class exploitation, the worker is always at a disadvantage, and the result of class exploitation is an unfair net transfer of assets from the workers to the capitalists.

Now, as discussed in chapter 7, what I want to argue is that a straightforward case can be made—far more easily and uncontroversially than the Marxist case—that racial exploitation has been central to U.S. history and that it structures society as a whole, so that unjust economic transfers from the black to the white population are going on all the time. A number of illuminating contrasts can be drawn to class exploitation. First, racial exploitation takes place far more broadly than at the point of production. It certainly includes inequitable economic arrangements like slavery and the debt servitude of sharecropping that succeeded it. But I am also using the term broadly to cover things like the denial of equal opportunity to homestead the West, differential allocation of educational resources, job discrimination, promotion discrimination, blocking of union membership, segregation in housing, inequitable transfer payments by the state, and so forth. So there is a constellation of different factors whose net effect is to benefit whites as a group and systematically deprive blacks of an equal chance to accumulate material and human capital. But the second illuminating contrast is that: whereas class exploitation is the subject of a huge body of literature, racial exploitation is a topic on which there is virtual silence. Yet racial exploitation as a reality should be quite uncontroversial by conventional liberal bourgeois standards and thus condemned by a philosophical audience much broader than the political Left. One recent anthology on exploitation in a left-wing series has only one chapter out of twenty-one on the subject, and it is squeezed into a Marxist framework, with the author conceding at the start that "Race has been virtually ignored in Marxian theorizing about exploitation" (Dymski 1997, 335). And a highly praised liberal treatment by Alan Wertheimer does not even have "race" in the index (1999). Finally, whereas class exploitation (at least in Marx's conceptualization) can only be eliminated by moving beyond capitalism to communism, racial exploitation can (in theory anyway) be ended within a capitalist framework.[6]

Though undiscussed by philosophers, a growing body of literature elsewhere is beginning to map these processes in their different dimensions. There is older work that is still valuable—Lester Thurow's *Poverty and Discrimination* (1969) and Boris Bittker's recently reissued *The Case for Black Reparations* (2003). But there are also many more recent books: *The Wealth of Races* (America 1990); *Black Labor, White Wealth* (Claud Anderson 1994); *The Possessive Investment in Whiteness* (Lipsitz 1998); *Race, Money, and the American Welfare State* (Brown 1999); *Being Black, Living in the Red* (Conley 1999); and, perhaps most important and most widely read, the prizewinning *Black Wealth/White Wealth* by Melvin Oliver and Thomas Shapiro (1995).

The last undertakes a systematic survey of households and an analysis of statistics on wealth to track the processes by which wealth is accumulated, the racial disparities in whites' versus blacks' chances at obtaining it, and the consequent, overall differential impact on people's lives. What the authors conclude is that wealth is far more important than income in determining the long-term prospects for racial equality. Wealth furnishes a cushion in times of layoffs and medical emergencies; it enables one to start a small business; it can be invested for the future; it is routinely used to influence the political process; and it provides a head start for one's children through better education and inheritance. So wealth represents past history; and in the case of race, it represents a past history of accumulated illicit advantage and disadvantage. The standard practice is to use black/white family income differentials as the measure of racial inequality, and these ratios are somewhere (depending on the time period being considered) in the 50 to 60 percent range. But the figures on the wealth differential are much greater: the median white household has more than *eight times* the net worth of the median black household. This difference is not because white people are eight times as smart as blacks (even *The Bell Curve* authors limit it to one standard deviation on IQ curves), and it is certainly not because they have worked eight times as hard! What this differential reflects is systemic illicit advantage, carried out at the personal, institutional, state, and federal level, in pursuance of a policy of privileging the white population at the expense of the black population.

So original injustice is compounded by further injustice—it's not just slavery; it's not just that the freed slaves never got their forty acres and a mule; and it's not just that they were promptly resubordinated through debt servitude. It's also Jim Crow: the denial of access to white markets; the blocking from better jobs; the denial of promotions; the differential in educational funding; the diminished opportunity as a result of discriminatory Federal Housing Authority policy for blacks to own their own home; the burning down, in some cases, of successful black businesses by white mobs, as with the 1921 Tulsa Riot, where the Greenwood business district (known as the "Black Wall Street") was destroyed in the worst U.S. race riot of the twentieth century, with perhaps as many as three hundred deaths and with details of the incident suppressed until very recently (Hirsch 2002). So there's a whole set of mechanisms that an adequate theory of racial justice would need to track down and show the workings of by drawing, obviously, on research in political science, economics, and sociology. The fairy stories that white political philosophers tell one another would be blown away.

As I emphasized at the start, then, it is the facts that would be doing the real work in the argument. These would constitute the equivalent kinds of sociological points for race that, for gender, Sterba *does* talk about. The basic idea would be to show how systemic racial advantage is produced and reproduced, through mechanisms of racial exploitation that continue in somewhat different forms today. And the implication would be that these facts, put into conjunction with most mainstream values, have radical implications for how we think about justice and what our moral priorities should be. Oliver and Shapiro (1995) sum up their findings:

> This book [*Black Wealth/White Wealth*] develops a perspective on racial in-
> equality that is based on the analysis of private wealth. . . . Private wealth . . .
> captures inequality that is the product of the past, often passed down from
> generation to generation. . . . We argue that, materially, whites and blacks
> constitute two nations. . . . To take these findings seriously, as we do, means
> not shirking the responsibility of seeking alternative policy ideas with which
> to address issues of inequality. *We might even need to think about social justice
> in new ways.* (2–9; my emphasis)

Note that the claim is not that they have come up with a revolutionary new set of values; after all, they are sociologists, not philosophers. Rather, the point is that simply by documenting, tracking, and analyzing the different mechanisms that have affected the respective fates of blacks and whites, a case can be made for radical conclusions even within a conventional normative framework. As they point out later:

> The sedimentation of inequality occurred because blacks had barriers thrown
> up against them in their quest for material self-sufficiency. Whites in general,
> but well-off whites in particular, were able to amass assets and use their se-
> cure economic status to pass their wealth from generation to generation.
> What is often not acknowledged is that the accumulation of wealth for some
> whites is intimately tied to the poverty of wealth for most blacks. Just as
> blacks have had "cumulative disadvantages," whites have had "cumulative
> advantages." Practically, every circumstance of bias and discrimination
> against blacks has produced a circumstance and opportunity of positive gain
> for whites. When black workers were paid less than white workers, white
> workers gained a benefit; when black businesses were confined to the segre-
> gated black market, white businesses received the benefit of diminished
> competition; when FHA [Federal Housing Authority] policies denied loans
> to blacks, whites were the beneficiaries of the spectacular growth of good
> housing and housing equity in the suburbs. The cumulative effect of such a
> process has been to sediment blacks at the bottom of the social hierarchy and
> to artificially raise the relative position of some whites in society. (50–51)

I apologize for the length of this quotation, but I would argue that it vindicates my point about where the real challenge posed by theories of racial justice lies. In which book on justice that you have read in the last thirty years do facts such as these appear? Here we have vividly illustrated the thematic/conceptual whiteness of political philosophy—a process of massive injustice carried out over decades which is all but ignored in the most prestigious publications on the subject.

And this brings me to another way in which Sterba's treatment of racial justice needs supplementation. There is no discussion at all of reparations. This issue has never gone away in the black community, and in recent years it has gained renewed vigor because of the precedents in dealing with Native Americans; the Japanese Americans interned during World War II; the Canadian government's treaty with Native peoples; and the German reparations to Israel. In addition, the publication of *The Debt* (2000), by well-known TransAfrica activist Randall Robinson, received a lot of publicity in the black media. Since 1989, Representative John Conyers (D-Mich.) has been introducing in Congress the "Commission to Study Reparation Proposals for African Americans Act" (H.R. 3745). So far it has yet to make it out of committee, but it has the endorsement of many mainstream black organizations, such as the National Association for the Advancement of Colored People (NAACP) and the Southern Christian Leadership Conference (SCLC). There is also a national umbrella group focused specifically on this question, the National Coalition of Blacks for Reparations in America (N'COBRA); and various prominent black intellectuals and lawyers have called for a public discussion of the issue as well.[7] The argument would be that blacks have been systematically deprived of an equal opportunity to accumulate material and human capital, whereas whites in general have illicitly benefited from this; so reparations are owed on respectable Lockean grounds (McGary 1999; Boxill 2003).

No extensive opposing literature on this subject has been produced by white philosophers, since it is seen as so off-the-wall (when it is seen at all) as to not even need a reply. But the basic counterargument would probably be the point that the same persons are not involved, since both the perpetrators and the original victims of slavery are long since dead. There are two rejoinders here. The first is to argue that the descendants of the victims are still suffering the long-term consequences of these processes, even if it is just slavery that is considered. Moreover, if the indictment is directed against white supremacy more broadly, and not just slavery—through mapping the kinds of discriminatory practices Oliver and Shapiro describe—then in most cases it *will* be people still living today who have been directly affected. And certainly the "paper trail" by which subsequent generations have been disadvantaged is far more easily retrievable here, since these are twentieth-century practices. One would point to the massive disadvantage blacks suffer today in terms of inferior education, lower life expectancies, differential incarceration rates, worse jobs, confinement to unsafe neighborhoods, and so forth—all of which can plausibly be traced to the legacy of white supremacy with the help of fact-finding books like Oliver and Shapiro's. (See also, more recently, Conley 1999.) Moreover, it is not as if it would be necessary to reduce whites to penury to achieve racial economic justice; rather, all that would be required is a policy of progressive taxation to redistribute illicitly acquired wealth. Overall, then, I think that the issue of reparations deserves to be taken far more seriously by mainstream political philosophy than it has been.

Juridico-Political

Let me turn now—more briefly—to some of the other dimensions of white supremacy that would need to be discussed in any serious, racially informed treatment of social justice, beginning with the juridico-political. Whereas economic justice (if not *racial* economic justice) has been a staple topic of the discussions of the last three decades—with familiar debates among egalitarians, libertarians, and Rawlsian liberals on what a fair distributive pattern would be (or whether there should be a pattern at all)—juridico-political questions tend to be presupposed as resolved. Liberalism as a political philosophy may be divided between Left and Right wings, but liberalism in the broad umbrella sense is supposed to be uncontroversially committed to the equal personhood of its citizens, from which equality before the law and equality of citizenship rights smoothly follow. The exact strength of property rights and their normative justification are subject to dispute, but the rights to equal protection and equal democratic input into the political process are taken for granted. These were, after all, precisely the spoils of liberalism's historic victory over autocracy and (Filmerian) patriarchy. So in mainstream discussions of justice, the legitimacy of a liberal-democratic framework is usually simply presupposed, not seen as in any way problematic; and after some standard boilerplate on the subject one moves quickly on to more interesting issues.

But as argued in chapters 5 and 6, it is really only the *white* (male) population who were the beneficiaries of this historic defeat of the regime of ascriptive hierarchy. In the colonial world, and certainly in the United States, a new system of ascriptive hierarchy was established—race—and in the framework of this system, people of color, especially blacks, were subpersons rather than persons. As such, they were *not* entitled to equal rights and protections, equal treatment under the law, and equal political input. On the contrary, it is the law itself that contributed to their oppression, by helping to make race (whiteness/nonwhiteness) in the first place (López 1996) and by continuing to be deeply implicated in the maintenance of white racial domination—overtly at the time of slavery and legalized segregation, more subtly at the present. The whiteness of mainstream political philosophy is perhaps nowhere more clearly illustrated than in its failure to discuss these issues. They are not a problem for the population (of persons) who draw the discipline's map of what is important and central, as against what is residual and marginal; so they are not a problem. But once one begins from the actuality that the United States has historically been a *Herrenvolk* democracy, rather than the Tocquevillian/Myrdalian/Hartzian fantasy tacitly presupposed by most mainstream white political philosophers, it is obvious that the debates taking place in legal theory over the role of the law and race (Delgado 1995; Crenshaw et al. 1995) have to be central to political philosophy also. The paradigm shift required here is more radical than that implicit in the century-and-a half-old Marxist critique of "bourgeois democracy"; for the reality is that, for a population historically equated to three-fifths of a human being and judged by the Supreme Court in 1857 to have "no rights which the white man was bound to respect," not even the qualified equality of bourgeois democracy has been attained. To repeat my point of chapter 6: To assume that normative equality and the presumption of equal personhood and corresponding sociopolitical status have been achieved for this subpopulation is to beg all the crucial questions. Yet such a begging is precisely what routinely obtains in most texts on justice.

Moreover, it would be a serious mistake to assume that the existence of antidiscrimination laws on the books today at least demonstrates the commitment in theory to eliminating unequal treatment. One also has to ask what resources are allocated for their enforcement, what kinds of criteria must be met for violation to be established, upon whom the burden of proof falls. Consider the case of housing discrimination, for example. Massey and Denton (1993), earlier cited, have argued that the 1968 Fair Housing Act "was intentionally designed so that it would not and could not work" (195). Through a combination of the removal of enforcement mechanisms, lack of follow-up by the Department of Housing and Urban Development (HUD), widespread regional variation in enforcement, a short statute of limitations, the requirement that the plaintiff hire a lawyer and prove discrimination, and the stipulation of limited punitive damages for the very few discriminators actually taken to court and successfully prosecuted, the law can be and is routinely violated with impunity (195–200). Unsurprisingly, then, thirty-five years after its passage, the country is still massively segregated, and it remains much more difficult for blacks and Latinos to get mortgages in the first place. A front-page *Chicago Tribune* story from late 2002 cited a study that pointed out that "On a national basis, blacks were 2.3 times more likely to be refused a conventional mortgage than whites, and Latinos were 1.5 times more likely to be denied." A spokesperson for ACORN, the Association of Community Organizations for Reform Now, attributed the differential to continuing "institutional racism."[8] As a result, minority rates of home ownership have still not caught up with white rates.

Similarly, Stephen Steinberg (1999), who sees "the essence of [American] racial oppression" in the "racial division of labor," argues that despite civil rights legislation, "employment discrimination is widespread, even when candidates for a position are identical in everything but skin color." He contends that most employers have negative views of blacks as workers; that to the extent that there is a black middle class, it is "an artifact of affirmative action policy," the reflection of government intervention rather than the "lowering of racist barriers in occupations"; and that middle-class blacks in corporate management and the business sector continue to be segregated *within* these structures (216, 222, 226–29). Through employment agencies, employee networks, and informal white grapevines, through coded references to blacks as undesirables and the invocation of supposedly neutral standards often dubiously related to actual ability to do the job, white employers continue to be able to bypass supposed safeguards and reserve the best positions for whites.

But it is their status in the criminal justice system that most profoundly reveals blacks' *inequality* before the law: in effect, this is a criminalized population. In his recent book on the subject, starkly titled *No Equal Justice*, David Cole (1999) summarizes the startling facts:

> The per capita incarceration rate among blacks is seven times that among whites. African Americans make up about 12 percent of the general population, but more than half of the prison population. They serve longer sentences, have higher arrest and conviction rates, face higher bail amounts, and are more often the victims of police use of deadly force than white citizens. In 1995, one in three young black men between the ages of twenty and twenty-nine was imprisoned or on parole or probation. If incarceration rates continue their current trends, one in four young black males born today will serve time in prison during his lifetime. . . . Nationally, for every one black man who graduates from college, 100 are arrested. (4–5)

Cole goes on to discuss racial profiling, police brutality, the history of empanelling all-white juries, the differential value attached to the lives of white as against black victims (as manifested in prosecutors' seeking the death penalty more often in the former than the latter cases), the failure to provide adequate counsel for the indigent—all to make his argument that race and class inequalities are *built-in* to the criminal justice system, with double standards as the rule rather than the exception. And in the last few years, numerous high-profile national cases of police beatings and killings, as well as the Innocence Project's work in utilizing DNA testing to overturn death penalty convictions, have made it clear how often poor black defendants are doomed to *injustice* in any encounter with the criminal justice system. (The most recent and spectacular example is the 1989 Central Park jogger case, where a confession by the real perpetrator in

2003 confirmed that the five convicted Harlem teenagers—widely depicted as brutal animals in the press at the time—had been innocent all along.) But one would search in vain in most white mainstream philosophy texts on justice for any discussion of these matters.

Finally, with respect to political questions: the menu of liberal–democratic rights is standardly taken to include the right to vote and run for office, so that as a citizen one has equal political input. But historically, of course, blacks have been denied the vote, so that what is a *given* for white liberalism is a recent achievement for a population originally seen as less than persons. And even with the franchise, majoritarian white domination means that, because of the racism of their co-citizens, blacks have a harder time electing representatives. While progress has obviously been made in comparison, say, to fifty years ago, it is still the case, as Donald Kinder and Lynn Sanders (1996) point out, that blacks are "substantially underrepresented" since "fewer than 2 percent of elected officials in the United States are blacks"; and what progress has been made has "been due in large measure to the creation of favorable districts through reapportionment or court order, since it remains today not quite impossible but very difficult for black candidates to succeed outside black majority districts" (5). And nationally, as Lani Guinier (1994) has argued, it raises the general problem first discussed at the time of the founding by James Madison (though *not*, of course, in connection with race!) of "majority tyranny":

> [M]ajority rule is unfair in situations where the majority is racially prejudiced against the minority to such a degree that the majority consistently excludes the minority, or refuses to inform itself about the relative merit of the minority's preferences. This is because the claim that majority rule is legitimate rests on two main assumptions that do not hold where racial prejudice pervades the majority: (1) that majorities are fluid rather than fixed; and (2) that minorities will be able to become part of the governing coalition in the future. . . . The documented persistence of racial polarization, however, defeats both of the assumptions supporting the legitimacy of majority rule. Simply put, racism excludes minorities from ever becoming part of the governing coalition, meaning that the white majority will be permanent. Because it excludes minorities from joining the majority, racism also renders the majority homogeneous, comprised of white voters only. (103)

Again, then, we see how thoroughly liberal verities can be overturned once the difference race makes is taken seriously. Nominated in 1993 by the Clinton White House as assistant attorney general for the Civil Rights Division, Guinier was defeated amidst national controversy over some of her recommendations for remedying this patently unfair and undemocratic situation—for example, through cumulative voting or supermajority voting (Guinier 1994, vii–xx). So the problem remains for theorists of justice: What corrective measures are called for when the "democracy" under theoretical consideration does not conform to the raceless model imported from the Old World, but is instead the *Herrenvolk* democracy of the New World?

Cultural

Recent work linking culture with the "politics of recognition" has made the demand for respect for people's cultures a familiar part of overall justice. Insofar as cultural identity is intimately linked with one's self-concept, social recognition of the worth of the cultures of the racially subordinated is a central part of the struggle for social equality. The well-known exchange between Nancy Fraser and Iris Marion Young (Fraser 1998a; Young 1998; Fraser 1998b) raises the question of whether the politics of recognition is in necessary tension with the politics of redistribution; but certainly in the case of the racially oppressed, both dimensions of subordination have to be overcome, and they are interwoven with one another. The long twentieth-century struggle for black civil rights and equal opportunity always had, as a crucial component, consciousness-raising about black history, the repudiation of the imposed identity of the "white man's Negro," and the demand that blacks re-create themselves in their own image.

However, the situation is particularly complicated in the case of blacks, since the destructive legacy of slavery means that the extent of African retentions has long been contested (and in any case people were kidnapped from many *different* African groups and communities). So it is not a straightforward matter of affirming a pristinely intact Old World heritage but of at least partially "inventing tradition" (as with Kwanzaa). The adjudication of "authenticity" is thus a far more complex, if not hopelessly unresolvable, process. Afrocentrist romanticization of a glorious Egyptian past may sometimes seem absurd to the outsider, especially considering the actual national origins of those Africans captured and brought to the Americas. But is it intrinsically more absurd than a common European identification with the glories of ancient Greece and Rome? Further complications are the spread of rap and hip-hop from the American inner city to the world stage, so that in some respects the most successful form of global popular culture is black, while black Americans continue nonetheless to be oppressed; in addition, the music of genuine protest competes with celebrations of "thug" life and hyperconsumerist acquisition, which are not at all threatening to the status quo or to the huge corporations commodifying ghetto style (Tricia Rose 1994). So is ghetto culture more "authentically" black than the experience of the black middle class? And may the dancing-out of revolutionary fantasies actually displace real-life political activism? Black cultural theorists will have to continue to debate these and many other questions in the quest to turn cultural success into actual political empowerment.

Somatic

The idea of "somatic injustice" easily lends itself to parody; and, as a hostile *reductio*, the derisive challenge as to whether science fiction scenarios about preemptive genetic engineering or advanced cosmetic surgery at state-subsidized clinics to modify human appearance would be the desirable solution. It might be argued variously that beauty is in the eye of the beholder; that membership in the dominant race is no guarantee of attractiveness, since many whites would be judged "plain" or "ugly" by conventional standards; that society pays too much attention to looks anyway; and that, in any case, this is hardly an appropriate matter for public policy. But as discussed in the previous chapter, while individual variation always exists in aesthetic judgments, there is nonetheless a social—panoptical—beholding eye with fairly uniform standards; and historically these standards have been white racist ones. Essentially, the body beautiful has been the white body; it is this somatotype that, with the increasingly global dissemination of Western popular culture, is projected as the planetary ideal. A preoccupation with physical appearance is undoubtedly superficial; but even if in our society it is a trait encouraged to perverse hypertrophy by the media and the cosmetic industry, comparative research suggests it is in fact universal, transcultural, and deeply rooted in human behavior. And as such, it seems unfair that entire races, or the darker-skinned and less Caucasoid members of entire races, should be stigmatized for their physical appearance and made to feel inferior, except insofar as they can approximate the white somatic norm. (Mixed-race individuals—light-skinned blacks and Latinos, with European features—and some Asian ethnic groups are sometimes more acceptable.) The racist caricatures of the physical appearance of nonwhites, especially blacks, are no longer routine in the iconography of the West. But the absence, or the considerable diminution, of negative images, is not enough. What will also be required is the positive projection in the image industry of the full range of human physical types, thereby affirming in fashion, the movies, on television, in magazine covers, that beauty is to be found in all races, all skin colors, all phenotypes, and not just restricted to whites.

Cognitive-Evaluative

The cognitive-evaluative may seem more *instrumental* to the achievement of justice than a part of justice itself; one thinks of the "ideal observer" of mainstream monological ethical theory or the dialogical "ideal speech situation" of Jürgen Habermas. But while the substantive goal is undeniably the most important thing, a procedural aspect is also involved, insofar as we commonly speak of giving people "a fair hearing" and readily pass judgments on the injustice of *not* doing so.

What I want to suggest is that one of the most important, though most subtle and elusive, aspects of white supremacy is the barriers it erects to a fair hearing. It is not merely that people of color are trying (against vested white interests in the status quo) to make a case for the economic and juridico-political injustice of their treatment; it is that they are additionally handicapped in doing so by having to operate within a white discursive field. In other words, the framework of debate is not neutral: it is biased by dominant white cognitive patterns of structured ignorance, an overt or hidden white normativity, and a conceptual recalcitrance to accommodating certain realities. Both at the lay and academic levels—in terms of what is generally taught in high schools and the university, and what is portrayed in the media (movies, television, popular novels)— there has been a long-standing pattern of the historical suppression of the ugly realities of white domination in their full detail. Moreover, the physical segregation of the white and nonwhite populations itself leads straightforwardly to a segregation of experience and on this basis alone (quite apart from hegemonic framings and constructions of social reality) to radically divergent pictures of the world. Typically white and typically black realities—in terms of everyday experience with government bureaucracies, the police, the job market, housing, and so forth—are simply not the same. So at the basic factual level, many claims of people of color will just seem absurd, radically incongruent with the sanitized picture white people have of U.S. history. Thus, they will be viewed with an aprioristic skepticism.

In addition, the tendency to take whites as the reference group and/or the default mode; the continuing prevalence of victim-blaming stereotypes in the white population about blacks in particular, as documented in sociological surveys; and the global framing of the United States as a liberal democracy with at worst a few flaws cumulatively militate against acceptance of the picture of structural racial subordination. Descriptive concepts about the possibilities for agency and social mobility, normative concepts about freedom, equality, and self-reliance, will all be deployed not in a colorless ideational vacuum but on the basis of a racialized lifeworld that makes a neutral argumentative encounter between whites and nonwhites very difficult. The achievement of racial justice will require, in part, the recognition of how profoundly racial *in*justice reflexively affects, at the metalevel, the very ways in which we talk about justice, the silences and evasions not even heard and seen as such—as illustrated by the very fact that I have had to list them in this and the previous chapter.

"Ontological"

Finally, I want to conclude by underlining that in a sense it all comes down to the "ontological": the original injustice, of which the preceding are just different manifestations, of the failure to see people of color as full persons in the first place. At the most basic normative level, this failure of reciprocity—of an equal "I"-to-"Thou" relationship (as against the tutoying of social inferiors), of equal respect—shapes everything else. If the creation of "whites" has been the elevation of one group of human beings as superior—not merely as reflected in social structures, but as molding their own psychology and very being—then in the end, the dismantling of white supremacy will require an ontological leveling, ontological equality, the end of the differentiation, once overt and de jure, now hidden and de facto, between persons and subpersons. In this spirit, the collective around the journal *Race Traitor* have called for "the abolition of the white race": not, of course, through a conservative "color-blindness," which by refusing to see race and white racial privilege only perpetuates their existence, but through the genuine dismantling of the supports of whiteness. And, to be sure, this matter is not to be directly legislated into existence, or rather nonexistence; rather, it will be the cumulative result of social change, the eradication of the multiple social structures that underpin the social ontology of hierarchy. From the nonrecognition symbolized by the absence of a national monument to the black victims of slavery to the using of Native American figures as mascots for sports teams, the moral economy of the white nation is still comfortable with a disrespect for people of color that is not even seen and realized to be such. Only when such social "dissin'" becomes genuinely unthinkable, spontaneously rejected without the need for elaborate, or indeed any, argumentation, will one really be able to say that whites have ceased to be white. And this will require, at the profoundest internal level, the rethinking and transformation of oneself, in keeping with the classic Socratic tradition of a "justice" that requires not merely social but individual change.

The unwhitening of mainstream political philosophy has barely begun. A prerequisite is an end to the pattern of theoretical evasion by white political philosophers and their acknowledgment—at the *conceptual* level—of the historic reality and continuing significance of white supremacy.

NOTES

1. I am indebted to my colleague Tony Laden, author of an *Ethics* review essay on the collection (2003), for this useful piece of information.
2. Sometimes, of course, there is an axiological challenge also. Many theorists have seen Marxism as being anti-moralist, as discussed in chapter 3; but among

those who have sought to extract an ethical commitment from his work, it has sometimes been argued that he implicitly advocated a left-wing communitarianism. Marxists sympathetic to this line of argument would then critique the mainstream discourse of rights and justice as the contaminated superstructure of alienated bourgeois class society and would thus represent communism as a utopia beyond justice and rights. (Such claims have obviously not worn very well!) Somewhat similarly, some feminists have argued for a distinctive feminist "ethic of care," which allegedly arises out of the peculiar moral standpoint of women and its difference from the perspective of brittle male egos maintaining their distance from one another in the masculinist public sphere. But the point is that many socialists, and many feminists, have simply relied on mainstream moral values to indict capitalism and male domination. (This is admittedly less the case for deep ecologists as "radical" theorists, where the axiological shift away from an anthropocentric normative system is what is really crucial.)

3. Obviously there is no room to explore this issue here, but it needs to be recognized that the American case is just part of a *broader* process of the rewriting and reconceptualization of "race" that took place in the West in the period of postwar decolonization. For a discussion, see Füredi (1998).

4. The Harvard Civil Rights Project has mapped a consistent pattern of resegregation in education. As a result of various factors, including increases in minority enrollment, continuing white flight, residential segregation, and the termination of court-ordered desegregation plans:

> black and Latino students are now more isolated from their white counterparts than they were three decades ago. . . . [B]lack students now typically go to schools where fewer than 31 percent of their classmates are white. . . . Latino students . . . now attend schools where whites account for only 29 percent of all students, compared with 45 percent three decades ago. . . . [White children] are still America's most segregated group . . . . [going] to schools where 80 percent of their classmates are white. The consequence is a nation in which every racial group that is big enough to be described as segregated generally is. ("Schools Resegregate, Study Finds," *New York Times*, Jan. 21, 2003, A14)

5. "The Lost Promise of School Integration," *New York Times*, April 2, 2000, section 4: 1, 5.

6. The qualification is necessary since, as mentioned in chapter 6, some Left theorists have argued that the racial nature of American capitalism, originally contingent, is now an *integral* part of it, and so too deeply embedded to be eliminated without disrupting the class system itself.

7. See the cover story in *Emerge* magazine (Feb. 1997), "Righting a Wrong," by Lori Robinson, 43–49; and a "Forum" discussion in *Harper's Magazine* (Nov. 2000), "Making the Case for Racial Reparations," 37–51.

8. "Mortgage OKs Tougher for Local Blacks, Latinos," *Chicago Tribune*, Oct. 5, 2002, 1–2.

9

The "Racial Contract" as Methodology

Finally, I close by replying to Jorge Garcia's recent (2001) full-length critique of my book, *The Racial Contract* (Mills 1997), and by giving, much more briefly, rejoinders to some criticisms from other writers. Choosing this as a final chapter is appropriate for a number of reasons. Classic social contract theory has a descriptive as well as a normative dimension, insofar as the idea of a "contract" captures the idea that society is a human creation. But the atomic individualism of mainstream contractarianism obviously bears no relationship to the actual history of human societies. However, in *The Racial Contract*, and also in a later expository paper (Mills 2000), I argue that social contract theory can be put to surprisingly radical ends once we drop its misleading social ontology and use the apparatus to map *domination* instead. The theoretical framework of white supremacy and the correspondingly necessary prescriptions for racial justice that were discussed in the previous two chapters can be translated into contractarian language, thereby challenging the pseudoracelessness of the discourse of mainstream political philosophy. One would theorize white supremacy as a specific instance of what I have called, more generally, the "domination" contract (Mills 2000), and then work out what would ideally be required to dismantle it.[1] In this way, and in keeping with my declared project of turning the apparatus of liberal Enlightenment theory to radical ends, I would have shown how a transformed contractarianism could become part of the arsenal of a new critical theory to deal with race.

However, Garcia is dubious about this enterprise, in part because of his own competing understanding of racism. He is the author, among other writings, of an important and widely anthologized article ("The Heart of Racism" [1996]), which offers an analysis of racism in individualistic and volitional terms. (The title encapsulates his thesis: that racism is essentially in the "heart" and is a matter of "ill-will.") So apart from the simple need to answer what is certainly the best critique of *The Racial Contract* to appear thus far, it will also give me the opportunity to engage with an approach neatly polar to my own: a contrast not merely between Left and Right, but between social-structural accounts of racism and white supremacy, like my own, which see racial domination as normatively central to the making of the modern world, and psychological, vice-based accounts like Garcia's, which deny that the West's moral code has itself been a racialized one. And finally, doing a reply should be useful just in helping to clear up for readers some possible confusions and misunderstandings about my strategy in the book.

I will divide my reply into two sections, first answering what I take to be Garcia's major critical points, and then moving on to his long list of minor critical points.

REPLY TO GARCIA'S MAJOR CRITICAL POINTS

That Garcia misunderstands the aim of my book *The Racial Contract*, thereby vitiating his main critical points, is no more simply and directly expressed than in his title itself: "The Racial Contract Hypothesis" (2001). The title implies—what Garcia goes on to say explicitly—that the "Racial Contract" is something like a social–scientific hypothesis, and thus it is to be judged by, and live up to or fall short of, the criteria of adequacy standardly applied to such hypotheses. In a sentence: He sees me as positing the Racial Contract as a *literal* event that constitutes a *social–scientific* explanation of *white racism*. (For a comparable theoretical misunderstanding, in this case one that imputes to me a literally contractual account of the creation of the modern state, see David Theo Goldberg [2002, 37–39].)[2] And this judgment of his is not one, not two, but *three* stages removed from reality. The Racial Contract was *not* intended by me to be taken literally; I am not offering a *social–scientific* explanation of anything; and to the extent that I am offering an explanation or a perspective, it is about *white supremacy*, not white racism. Thus in a sense his entire critique, though thoughtful and provocative in many respects, is based on a series of misunderstandings, summarized in his conclusion that I would have done better to have treated the Racial Contract "as a hypothetical model" since "racism is best understood as a matter of . . . moral and intellectual vices, rather than as an

'actual historical agreement' among almost all white people to deper-
sonalize nonwhites" (Garcia 2001, 37).

The framework of the original discussion needs to be borne in mind
throughout: social contract theory. I did not invent social contract theory; I am merely trying—given its importance and centrality to Western
political philosophy—to utilize it for importing into mainstream ethics
and political philosophy the discussion of issues of racism and white supremacy. And the simple analogy for theoretically locating the "Racial
Contract" is as follows: *racial contract theory* is to the understanding of
racialized social structures and the white-supremacist polity, as *social
contract theory* is to the understanding of egalitarian social structures
and the liberal-democratic polity. This is the appropriate reference class.
Social contract theory is not in theoretical *competition* with Comte, Marx,
Weber, Durkheim, Simmel, Parsons, Foucault, and others. Someone who
finds social contract theory useful is certainly not saying that we can
now dispense with the sociological work of these authors. Rather, it is
deployed in a different conceptual space. Similarly, racial contract theory is not in theoretical competition with Comtean, Marxist, Weberian,
Durkheimian, Simmelian, Parsonian, and Foucauldian theories of
racism (if and where they exist). The "Racial Contract" is not meant as a
detailed, nuts-and-bolts account of the origins of white racism and
white supremacy any more than social contract theory (as used today
anyway) is meant as a detailed, nuts-and-bolts account of the origins of
society. So in both cases, for a detailed social–scientific account, you
would need to turn elsewhere.

Now in my follow-up expository paper that Garcia cites, "Race and
the Social Contract Tradition" (Mills 2000), I claim to "make more explicit than I did in my book" this use of contract; and I go on to distinguish three ways in which the "contract" can be thought of descriptively: as literal, as hypothetical in the "idealized reconstruction"
sense, and as hypothetical in the "useful model" sense (442–44). (Note:
because of a mix-up in titles, this paper is mistakenly identified by Garcia in his article as "White Racial Interests.") I cite Ernest Barker, Peter
Laslett, and Jean Hampton as endorsers of this third sense, and I suggest that that is the best way to think of the "Racial Contract." Any
reader will appreciate that this is the very sense that Garcia himself rec-
ommends as the only defensible one: contract as "hypothetical model"
rather than "actual historical fact." But Garcia sees my move here not
as *explication* but as "back[ing] away," a definite "repudiat[ion]" of and
retreat from what I say in the book: "Whatever the merits of this more
modest approach, it is largely new" (Garcia 2001, 38–39). And finally,
while he concedes that the idea of a Racial Contract in this sense may
be viable, he is ultimately dubious about its value and usefulness.

I want to reply to this first—major—set of Garcia's critical points in three parts. I will argue that:

1. The book itself makes clear that I meant the "useful model" way, rather than the "actual historical fact" way, of understanding the "contract," so that no later retreat is involved.
2. "Explanation" in contract theory is at a different level of abstraction than in social–scientific theory.
3. The textual passages Garcia cites have been misinterpreted by him.

"Useful Model" versus "Actual Historical Fact"

Here is the positive evidence. To begin with, in the introduction (which is, after all, where the author tells you what she is going to do), I give the rationale for using contractarianism this way—as a means of de-ghettoizing work on race—and I describe the Racial Contract as "one *possible* way of making this connection with mainstream theory" (Mills 1997, 3; new emphasis). The very fact that I use the term "possible" should make it clear that I think a number of strategies are possible and that the Racial Contract—since it is only one of them—could not be a literal fact in the sense Garcia attributes to me. Moreover, I go on to qualify this proposed employment with the conditional "*Insofar as* contractarianism is thought of as a useful way to do political philosophy" (7; new emphasis), which should make it plain that I don't necessarily think it is the most useful way to do political philosophy but that I am willing to go along with the program for the duration. In other words, *if* we're going to work within a contractarian framework (and there are arguments both pro and con doing so), then at least let's get straight on what the initial "contract" really was. Finally, the penultimate paragraph of the introduction states that the book can be thought of as resting on three claims: existential, conceptual, and methodological. And what I identify as the existential claim is not that there actually was a (literal) Racial Contract. Rather, I locate the idea of a contract under the third category: "the methodological claim—as a political system, white supremacy can illuminatingly be theorized as based on a 'contract' [and note the enclosure within scare quotes] between whites, a Racial Contract" (7).

So the introduction makes plain to the reader that the "contract" is being used as a methodological device. Insofar as—to use Garcia's phrase—there is a "Racial Contract Hypothesis," then, that hypothesis would be the *second-level* claim that "the idea of a Racial Contract is an illuminating way to theorize white supremacy." It would not be the *first-level* claim that "the Racial Contract exists." So the debate would be the methodological one over how useful a contractarian approach is—not the existential one over whether there really was a contract. The existential claim I do make is that white supremacy exists; this is the pertinent "hypothesis," if one wants a hypothesis about existents. But the "Racial Contract" isn't a hypothesis in this sense, but a theoretical strategy (which one can find more or less useful) on the level of abstraction appropriate to the conceptual space of social contract theory (not social–scientific explanation) for conceptualizing and explaining white supremacy, and bringing it into the same universe of discourse as social contract theory.

Moreover, additional evidence can be found in my second book, *Blackness Visible* (Mills 1998). (Since Garcia cites from this work as well to make his case, it seems legitimate for me to do the same.) *The Racial Contract* and *Blackness Visible* came out within a few months of each other (late 1997 and early 1998), and the final drafts were being rewritten over the same period. In two chapters of *Blackness Visible*, chapters 4 and 5, I specifically address the question of the origins of white racism, and I offer respectively the following two lists of explanations: "culturalist explanations, psychosexual explanations, politico-economic explanations" (ch. 4); and "various rival theories—ethnocentrism on a grand scale, religioculturalist predispositions, the ideology of expansionist colonial capitalism, the rationalizations of psychosexual aversions, calculated rational-choice power politics" (ch. 5) (Mills 1998, 78–79, 100). Nowhere on either of these two lists do I cite the "Racial Contract," whether as superior to the others or as at least a contender. What is the reason for this silence? A becoming modesty? Not at all (not that I'm not a becomingly modest guy . . .). The simple answer is, to repeat, that I did *not* see the "Racial Contract" in this light, as an entry in such an explanatory competition. Rather I saw it as a device compatible with a wide range of explanations, theoretically *agnostic* on these social–scientific debates and so not linked to any particular one, though at least minimally committed to seeing race as "constructed" rather than natural.

Different Levels of Abstraction

So how is the "contract" to be cashed out, if it doesn't literally exist? And how can one assert that a nonexistent contract may still in some sense be "historical," "descriptive," and "explanatory"? At the risk of tedium for the reader, I want to cite from several authorities here: one, because this is the crucial place where Garcia goes wrong; and, two, so as to underline my point that my usage is not at all idiosyncratic, but congruent with mainstream readings of the theory (though my own employment, of course, is for radical, nonmainstream ends).

First, Michael Walzer in *The Oxford Companion to Philosophy*:

> Perhaps the most significant claim of social contract theory is that political society is a human construct . . . and not an organic growth. There is no body politic but only this artefact, made in (fictional) time and in principle open to remaking. (Walzer 1995, 164)

Likewise Jeremy Waldron:

> We do not need to take contractarianism as the claim that political institutions were set up in a single dramatic event, or a small series of events, in order to take it seriously as a historical hypothesis. [Note Waldron's acceptance of what Garcia finds a contradiction in terms.] That some arrangement is a human invention or contrivance, answerable to human purposes, does not necessarily mean that it was invented *all at once*; human inventions (the arch, the water wheel) can be developed gradually over time, even over long periods of time, without losing their essentially artificial or conventional character. . . . A set of institutional arrangements may evolve by gradual steps over a period of time; but if each step involves elements of choice, deliberation and purpose, then the whole process takes on an intentional flavour, becomes susceptible to intentionalist categories, and may be evaluated in terms of human purposes in the way that contract theory requires. (Waldron 1994, 69)

Similarly, Christopher Morris, editor of a recent anthology on social contract theory:

> There may, however, be some explanatory import to the idea of states of nature and social contracts that should not be overlooked. Even if our particular societies did not result from any actual agreements, and even if we never found ourselves in any pre-political setting, nevertheless our political institutions and arrangements are, in some sense, our creations. They are brought into existence by humans and maintained by our acquiescence and support. (Morris 1999, x)

Finally, and in greatest detail, a lengthy quote from the late Jean Hampton, which makes clear at what level of abstraction and in which conceptual space the contract is intended as "explanatory":

> Philosophers hate to admit it, but sometimes they work from pictures rather than ideas. . . . [T]he contract imagery has struck many as enormously promising. . . . I will argue that social contract theorists have intended simultaneously to describe the nature of political societies, and to prescribe a new and more defensible form of such societies. . . . [T]heir invocation of a social contract among the people as the source of the state is, in part, an attempt to make one modest factual statement, namely, that authoritative political societies are human creations. . . . The contractarian's term of "social contract" is

misleading in so far as it suggests that people either tacitly or explicitly exchange promises with one another to create or support certain governmental
structures. We do no such thing. . . . Certain institutions, practices and rules
become conventionally entrenched (in a variety of ways) in a social system,
and in so far as the people continue to support them, these conventions continue to prevail, and thus comprise the political and legal system in the country. . . . [S]ocial contract arguments for the state can be interpreted so as to
provide plausible descriptions of political societies as conventionally-generated
human creations—far more plausible, indeed, than rival divine rights arguments or natural subjugation theories. (Hampton 1993, 379–83; note the conceptual space tacitly presupposed in Hampton's list of theoretical rivals, and
imagine the comparable candidates for race.)

For all these theorists, then—all well-known in the field—"contract"
can be descriptive and explanatory without being a literal event.

So it is in this sense that we need to think of the Racial Contract. The
Racial Contract is not real/actual and historical as a formal contract
signed, or formally agreed to, by the global tribe of white people. (What
would this, the literal contract, mean? That I really thought all the white
people in the world had gathered around a big table—a *really* big table—
and signed a contract to subordinate people of color? How could anybody
seriously attribute this view to me?) Nonetheless it is real/actual and historical in the sense of the intentional creation by white people of racialized
institutional arrangements and social practices. In other words, I am distinguishing the literal contract (that's *not* real) from the translation of
what "contract" comes to in this formulation (that *is* real). If the "contract"
is glossed as these theorists suggest, then it is obviously not imaginary at
all. White supremacy as a set of institutions and social practices—indeed
race itself—is a political artifact, a human construct (Walzer); an artificial
human contrivance involving elements of choice, deliberation, and purpose (Waldron); brought into existence by humans and maintained by
(some) humans' acquiescence and support (Morris)—in short, a conventionally generated human creation (Hampton). So, to repeat my initial
statement of intent in *The Racial Contract*, I would, if successful, have
shown how contract theory can provide a "global theoretical framework
for situating discussions of race and white racism."

And here we need to address a matter earlier postponed. As readers can
confirm for themselves, my declared intention throughout the book is to
elucidate *white supremacy*. Thus, nowhere do the terms *racism* or *white
racism* appear in the introduction's penultimate paragraph, where I am
setting out the "three simple claims" on which the book rests; instead, my
stated focus is on *white supremacy*. Indeed *racism* does not even have its
own index entry in the book! The reason is that, as explained in chapter 7,

I have an analysis of race according to which white supremacy is more fundamental: it is related to white racism as patriarchy is to sexism and as class society is to class prejudice. White supremacy is "objective," a politico-economic system of racial privilege; white racism is "subjective," a set of ideas, beliefs, values, and attitudes. So given my framework, it made sense for me to strategize the theorization of white supremacy through the device of a "contract," since I am seeing it as a political system.

Now Garcia brushes impatiently and dismissively past these claims (2001, 32) on the grounds that I do not adequately clarify and explain the terms (what "white supremacy" is, how it is "political"); and he proceeds for the rest of his critique to operate (for the most part) as if I had made white racism my major explanatory focus and were using contractarianism to understand that. This is a remarkably cavalier attitude toward authorial intent. Whether I have done a good or a bad job of explanation, it will obviously distort the critical and interpretive project to represent an author as trying to do something he is *not* in fact trying to do. Quite apart from any of the other critical points I have made, this misrepresentation of my textual aim must necessarily make Garcia's critique somewhat problematic, since his initial assumptions are askew. I am (primarily) trying to conceptualize race as a *political system*; he is taking me to be (primarily) trying to explain the genesis of *individuals' racist attitudes, beliefs, and values*. Given this divergence, is it surprising that, by his criteria, some of my claims will be inadequate?

Textual Passages Misinterpreted by Garcia

Let me turn now to the textual evidence (apparently) against me. In the introduction I say, and Garcia cites me as saying, things like the following: this use of contract is "naturalistic," "a reversion to the original 'anthropological' approach in which the contract is intended to be historically explanatory," so that the contract possesses "descriptive/explanatory life" (Mills 1997, 6). And more generally, "I use [the 'Racial Contract'] . . . descriptively, to *explain* the actual genesis of the society and the state, the way society is structured, the way the government functions, and people's moral psychology" (5). So Garcia sees these and similar assertions later in the book as statements of my "central realist and explanatory contentions": "Plainly, anything that correctly, genuinely, and causally explains historical events must itself be something historical, real, not a mere imaginative device" (Garcia 2001, 28).

With the help of the quotations in the previous section, I hope I have shown how the Racial Contract can be descriptive and explanatory without being a literal event. But what about Garcia's insistence that by "real" in the book I *do* mean a literal contract, so that I am now watering down my thesis without wanting to acknowledge it? The simple refutation of his claim is that I cite Hampton's article as an endnote (n. 7) to this very passage ("I use [the 'Racial Contract'] . . . descriptively, to *explain*"). Here at the very start of the book, where I am laying out how I plan to use terms, I write that "Hampton points out that the imagery of 'contract' [scare quotes in the original, yet again, and the use of a term ('imagery') clearly designed to forestall literalist readings] captures the essential point that 'authoritative political societies are human creations' (not divinely ordained or naturally determined) and *'conventionally* generated'" (Mills 1997, 136). And in the final endnote to the introduction (n. 11), I conclude: "Hampton's own focus is the liberal-democratic state, but obviously her strategy of employing 'contract' to conceptualize conventionally generated norms and practices is open to be adapted to the understanding of the *non*-liberal-democratic *racial* state, the difference being that 'the people' now become the white population" (137).

So how could I be clearer? I am stating that I am going to adapt for my own purposes the "strategy" of a writer who thinks "contract" can still be thought of descriptively, but not literally. At the very start of my book (though admittedly in the notes, rather than the text itself) I am glossing how I plan to use "contract." (Significantly, though Garcia refers to some other passages where he concedes I distance myself from a literalist reading, he doesn't refer to these endnotes at all.) Subsequent statements about the "reality" and "historical actuality" of the Racial Contract then need to be read in the light of this preliminary gloss. What is "real" and "historically actual" are the racial "institutions, practices and rules" created by one section (the white one) of the human population.

Now it *is* true that I also claim (Mills 1997, 19–21) that the Racial Contract is comparatively differentiated from the social and sexual contracts by having "the best claim to being an actual historical fact"; by being "'real'"; and by being "not just metaphorically but close to literally" true. But as Garcia himself admits (indeed, this is part of his criticism of me [Garcia 2001, 29]), *I never go all the way* on these pages: the scare quotes are in place, and the gap between "literal" and something weaker is never closed. What I was trying to capture here was two points.

First, the fact that, insofar as racial subordination (on most analyses) is a product of the modern period, a paper trail *does* exist, whereas one does not exist for an "original" social contract or an "original" sexual contract. Thus in his famous essay "Of the Original Contract," David Hume writes: "[I]t cannot be denied, that all government is, at first, founded on a contract"; but "In vain are we asked in what records this charter of our liberties is registered. It was not written on parchment, nor yet on leaves or barks of trees. It preceded the use of writing, and all the other civilized arts of life" (Hume 1960, 149). Similarly, though it is obvious that women have been subordinated for thousands of years, it remains controversial when this subordination took place. But in the case of race, we actually have the documents.

Second, we think of the iconography of the signing of a contract as a discrete, fairly sharply spatiotemporally locatable "event"; so, the "contract" imagery comes closest here, in the case of race, to the *non*-metaphoric, since formal and informal structures are put in place, accompanied by explicit discussion of the status of nonwhites (as compared to what one presumes occurred with gender), over a relatively short time period. (Think, for example, of the famous debate at Valladolid, Spain, between Sepúlveda and Las Casas on the humanity of Native Americans; or consider the pro- and antislavery debates; or the Berlin Conference to partition Africa.) So Hampton's "institutions, practices and rules" are "conventionally entrenched" in a way much more self-conscious and documented, over a period much shorter, and in a manner much more like an actual "agreement," than is the case for the other two.

It was these differences that I was trying to highlight in the kind of locutions Garcia cites, and I do concede that they are susceptible to misinterpretation. But I would claim that my original endnotes (which, in retrospect, should have been imported into the text), and my "battery of qualifications" (Garcia 2001, 29), should have made clear that I did not mean there was a literal contract.

REPLY TO GARCIA'S MINOR CRITICAL POINTS

I turn now to twelve of the more minor critical points he raises. The sequence here is roughly (though not exactly) their order of appearance in his text.

Problems with "Tacit Consent"

Garcia (2001, 30–31) warns of the dangers of using contractarian "tacit consent" to infer racist complicity: "For the reason some sixteenth-century Spaniard peasant, say, chose not to 'speak out and struggle' against royal imperialism may be not that she consented to the crown's abuse of nonwhite people, but that she saw the costs of protest as too great."

I think Garcia makes some good criticisms here. Tacit consent is admittedly a "slippery" notion, and as such it constitutes one of those many problem areas of social contract theory. Moreover, given hierarchies of power within the white population, the detailed assignment of moral responsibility would need to take into account class and gender differentiation also. The "Racial Contract" is a simplified story that treats "whites" in a fairly undifferentiated way; but in a long endnote near the start of chapter 1 (Mills 1997, 137–38), I signal my awareness that a more nuanced account would need to modify this approach. But Garcia is right that one should be wary of inferring racist complicity too quickly. (Though it should not be forgotten either that working-class whites, both male and female, *were* often directly and uncontroversially complicit in racial subordination and *were* participants in racial atrocities—as with European soldiers and settlers in the service of imperialism, for example, or as with white women who helped with the enforcement of Jim Crow.)

I should also point out that in my list of "white renegades and race traitors" (Mills 1997, 108–9), I had not meant to imply that only by carrying out such spectacular acts of opposition as a Las Casas or a John Brown could one show one's repudiation of the "contract" (Garcia 2001, 41, n. 8). By definition, the well-known cases involve the heroic figures whose names have come down to us, which is why they sprang to my mind. But I cite in that same list more low-key actions, like getting involved in "Aborigines Protection Societies," which "ordinary white individuals" (Garcia 2001, 30) could have joined. So one could do a range of useful things that are well short of the supererogatory.

More generally, it needs to be remembered that I am sketching moral issues in broad strokes, as one would expect of a theory concerned primarily with the macroissue of race as a political structure of domination, rather than the microissues of individual racism, culpable intent, and personal vice/virtue. "Tacit consent" is a blunt tool as well as a slippery one, and in the same way that one would not expect social contract theory to tease out these fine points of individual moral responsibility, one should not expect it of racial contract theory either. What I really wanted to capture is the crucial point that nonwhite subordination comes about through *collective white agency*, thereby producing a general moral complicity that needs to be theorized somehow. Writing about segregation and the making of the black underclass, for example, Douglas Massey and Nancy Denton (1993, 2) emphasize that: "This extreme racial isolation did not just happen; it was manufactured by whites through a series of self-conscious actions and purposeful institutional arrangements that continue today." And they go on to cite the 1968 Kerner Commission Report: "What white Americans have never fully understood—but what the Negro can never forget—is that white society is deeply implicated in the ghetto. White institutions created it, white institutions maintain it, and white society condones it" (4). It is this kind of racial social causality, and this kind of collective moral complicity that I was using the concept to map.

White Moral Consciousness and the "Epistemology of Ignorance"

Garcia (2001, 32) criticizes my claims about white moral psychology, and he points out the possibly question-begging pitfalls of a strategy of invoking an "epistemology of ignorance": "[T]his claim poses the danger that the RCH [Racial Contract Hypothesis] becomes nonfalsifiable. . . . Why should we believe Mills's account of someone else's psychology when his own relies for its support on the RCH, itself of dubious credibility? This smells of begging the question."

The claims about white moral consciousness are not based aprioristically *on* the "Racial Contract"; rather, the "Racial Contract" is used to conceptualize and explain (in the sense earlier glossed) these claims. The claims themselves are based on the historical evidence—namely, that most whites over the past few hundred years (i.e., modernity) have been racists and have not seen people of color as full persons. I cite numerous texts in the notes to back up this assertion. As a claim, it is a statistical generalization and so is subject to the standard problems of such generalizations; that is, it needs to be applied to individual subjects cautiously and in a probabilistic fashion. If 90 percent of the white population in a given area at a given time period are racist, then obviously the odds are that a given white person picked at random will be racist. But since there have always been antiracist whites (though historically they have been a minority), this statistically based presumption is not indefeasible and can, by the appropriate evidence, be shown not to go through in particular cases.

As for the concept of an "epistemology of ignorance": this was my attempt to express, in the simplified vocabulary of social contract theory, the crucial point that structures of social oppression will themselves have a pernicious effect on social cognition. I chose this term because—in keeping with its Enlightenment origins—accurate cognition is central to the modern social contract; so it seemed a nice ironic touch to turn this upside down to dramatize how, in a system of oppression, the socially privileged become epistemically disadvantaged in seeing the social truth. Admittedly, Garcia is right that the concept may be dangerous if abused (cf. my own points in chapter 1 about "ideology"); but this just shows that it should be used carefully, not that it should be abandoned. What needs to be avoided is an intellectual short-circuiting where, in lieu of evidence for one's case, one simply characterizes one's opponents' views as wrong and then responds to demands for proof by invoking an "epistemology of ignorance" to explain their disagreement. This response would exemplify the circularity and question begging that Garcia warns of. Instead, the proper approach is to provide the evidence first and only then bring in, as a possible explanation, the suggestion of group-based cognitive distortion. In the book, I give (part of) this evidence, which is why I draw so heavily on *extra*philosophical texts (history, political science, etc.). This evidence, I claim, shows that white racism has been the norm for the modern period and that most whites have actively supported or gone along with the various structures of racial domination central to the making of the modern world. So most whites have been "signatories" to the Racial Contract; and insofar as that involves averting one's eyes from certain uncomfortable factual and moral truths, ignoring the evidence, being blind to things they should see, they will indeed be influenced by an "epistemology of ignorance."

Finally, it should not be thought that this idea is extremist, thereby overstating the cognitive reality. Think of the fantastic distortions and misrepresentations, at both the lay and scientific levels, of the history of Africa, the conditions of slaves, the achievements of native peoples. Consider, for example, Leon Litwack's recent book on Jim Crow, and its description of typical patterns of white cognition:

> "My problems started when I began to comment on what I saw," recalled a [black] woman born into an impoverished family in Durham, North Carolina. "I insisted on being accurate. But the world I was born into didn't want that. Indeed, its very survival depended on not knowing, not seeing—and, certainly, not saying anything at all about what it was really like." . . . The happy, carefree "darkies" had become what they had always been—necessary figments of a vivid white imagination, found now mostly in the images and artifacts of popular culture, in renditions of a history whites wanted so desperately to believe. . . . To flatter their egos, as well as to assuage their doubts and apprehensions, whites during slavery had invented the figure of Sambo. . . . If whites embraced this image during slavery, they became downright ardent in their reverence for it after emancipation. They needed Sambo more than ever before. . . . Between 1890 and World War I, white Southerners went to extraordinary lengths to mythologize the past, to fantasize an Old South, a Civil War, a Reconstruction, and a Negro that conformed to the images they preferred to cherish, images that both comforted and reassured them. . . . Whether in published histories, school textbooks, or public displays, the revision of history in the late nineteenth century came to accord with the selective memory of white Southerners. . . . The fantasies of whites knew few if any restraints. (Litwack 1998, 34, 115, 184–85, 194, 197).

Doesn't this sound like an "epistemology of ignorance"?

The "Racial Contract" as Allegedly Wrong about Nonwhite Perspectives on White Racism

Garcia (2001, 32–33) disputes the "Racial Contract's" claim to capture, in a philosophical framework, nonwhite lay understandings of race: "First, the RCH is a rather novel, technical, and arcane notion. . . . Second, there is evidence that many nonwhite people, specifically African Americans, see our national situation rather differently from the way Mills does." (Garcia goes on to cite various statistical findings about black opinion and about the present situation of blacks.)

Obviously, for the layperson not familiar with contractarianism, the "Racial Contract" will not be immediately transparent, and it will need some facilitative pedagogical glossing. But once done, I would claim that the crucial ideas—whites' constructing themselves by mutual "agreement" as superior to other races, developing a racist ethic accordingly, and exploiting other races through institutionalized socioeconomic structures—do indeed resonate with the "ordinary thinking of nonwhite peoples," both historically and currently. Indeed, the latter resonance has been no more clearly demonstrated to me than by the success of the book with students of color in particular, as reported to me by many of the professors across the country who have assigned it in their courses.

The statistical evidence Garcia cites on black American opinion (Garcia 2001, 33) does not constitute a refutation of the book's claims, because he is simply focusing on the wrong question. The answer blacks give to the question of what is the most pressing problem in the black community is not necessarily the same as the answer they would give to the question of what is the most important cause of the disparities in the socioeconomic conditions of blacks and whites. The "Racial Contract" is seeking to answer the *latter* question (and it gives as an answer the history and continuing legacy of white supremacy). I am sure that the same people who are concerned about teenage pregnancy, drugs and alcohol, and crises in values would *not* claim that these factors are, for example, the main cause of the remarkable statistic earlier mentioned, that in 1990 blacks owned only 1 percent of U.S. wealth. (Similarly, an opinion poll among blacks in contemporary South Africa might well choose the AIDS crisis as the most urgent issue currently facing the black community, but surely they would not cite AIDS as the main explanation for black disadvantage; rather, they would point to apartheid and its legacy.)

And in fact I don't even have to speculate on this, since I actually took the trouble to look it up. In the latest revised and updated edition of *Racial Attitudes in America*, seen as the definitive sociological study on the subject, the authors have a section on "Explanations of Inequality," that is, endorsement of "various explanations for black disadvantage in jobs, income, and housing." They conclude that

> blacks emphasize discrimination as a cause of black economic disadvantage [66 percent, the top choice—1996 figures, then the latest] to a much greater extent than do whites: a difference of 32 percentage points. . . . Thus blacks

and whites point in different directions when accounting for black disadvantage: blacks see the main source as white discrimination, whereas whites see the main source as lack of motivation by blacks. . . . [I]t is evident that black and white Americans perceive and define the most important causes of racial inequality in American [*sic*] from quite different vantage points. (Schuman et al. 1997, 253–56)

This is the question Garcia should have focused on, and the answer given is obviously congruent with what I say in the book. Moreover, even if problematic black behavior were "a contributing cause of black disadvantage" (Garcia 2001, 33–34), as he claims, this position is not incompatible with the "Racial Contract"'s claim that white supremacy is the *major* cause.

Finally, with respect to Garcia's point (2001, 33) that black unemployment is now (or was then) down to 8 percent: Black unemployment goes up and down with the fluctuations in the economy; but the point is that at all times it is between two to three times the rate of *white* unemployment, and it is this differential that is the manifestation of systemic white advantage. (And, in fact, with the advent of the bear market and recession since Garcia wrote, blacks have been laid off at higher rates than whites, which has always been the historic pattern.)

Supposed False Dichotomies and Mistaken Claims to Explanatory Superiority

Garcia (2001, 34, 36) suggests that I present readers with a false dichotomy of "racism as random and unpredictable (an 'anomaly'), and racist acts as a manifestation of the Racial Contract," when there are clearly other explanatory possibilities; he goes on to say that in any case "traditional social contract theory does not attempt to explain what Mills wants to explain—racist incidents, structures, and so forth."

First, my use of the term "anomalous" in the book section in question (Mills 1997, 121–22), which I should perhaps have explained more, was in specific reference to the political science literature earlier cited on race: the "anomaly" theory of American racism as classically expressed in the work of Alexis de Tocqueville, Gunnar Myrdal, and Louis Hartz; and as discussed by Rogers Smith in an important 1993 article to which I refer the reader on that same page (122). And the "dichotomy" is not that between different *explanations* of racism but that between different *conceptualizations* of the American (or, more generally, Western-implanted) polity and the role of racism within it.

Smith's point, later expanded into his prizewinning book *Civic Ideals* (1997), is that the mainstream theorists of American political culture (such as the aforementioned gentlemen) have (usually) evaded the fact of—and (always) evaded the conceptual implications of—the centrality of racism and white supremacy to U.S. history. (Smith discusses gender and nativist exclusion also, but we are focusing here on race.) Instead, they have conceptualized the United States as an egalitarian and inclusivist liberal democracy, for which racism has been an "anomaly." To this—the "anomaly" view of American racism—Smith contraposes his own "multiple traditions" view. So these are standard terms in the literature. (I will here pointedly repeat the quote I use in the book itself, thereby underlining my contention that it was there all along for Garcia to read.) Thus he says: "[T]he cumulative effect of these persistent failures to lay out the full pattern of civic exclusion has been to make it all too easy for scholars to conclude that egalitarian inclusiveness has been the norm," whereas "the exceptions obviously have great claim to be ranked as rival norms" (Smith 1993, cited in Mills 1997, 160, n. 73). So the target is not the idea that racism is "accidental," to which I am contrasting the "RCH"; the target is the idea that "egalitarian inclusiveness" has been the norm and that "racist exclusion" has been the "deviation," to which I am contrasting the alternative picture of the book, in which racism is central.

Note again, then, the consistency of Garcia's misinterpretation, which runs like a red thread through his critique. I am discussing two alternative ways (why these two? because they're standard in the literature) of *conceptualizing* the American and, more generally, the modern, Western-implanted polity: one in which racism is an anomaly and one in which racism is the norm (or at least *a* norm); one modeled by the social contract and one modeled by the "Racial Contract." And I am saying that the second is obviously superior, since it corresponds to the historical reality. Garcia, on the other hand, thinks I am offering a "false dichotomy" of social–scientific *explanations*: racism as "accidental, unpredictable, random"; or racism as explained by the Racial Contract.

Second, I would claim that mainstream social contract theory's failure to explain racism—or, given my preferred analysis, failure to acknowledge/conceptualize white supremacy—is precisely the point. Modern political theory is ostensibly egalitarian, thereby denying the normative validity of ancient and medieval systems of ascriptive hierarchy. That's why the starting point is the "freedom and equality" of "men" in the state of nature. But the whole point of my critique, and the earlier feminist critique, is that while (normative) *class* hierarchy is challenged—as, for example, in Sir Robert Filmer's patriarchalism—systems of racial and gender ascriptive hierarchy are *not*; indeed, they are inscribed in the theory. That Garcia misses a point so basic to the argument of my book suggests that he has not really understood it. Or, perhaps better (though I do not have the time to pursue this point here), what blinds him to my argument is his own refusal to recognize racism as an alternative normative system—the *real* "dominant intellectual tradition" of the modern period (Garcia, 35–36). To cite a quotation I have used before, from George Mosse: "Racism as it developed in Western society was no mere articulation of prejudice, nor was it simply a metaphor for suppression; it was, rather, a fully blown system of thought, an ideology like Conservatism, Liberalism, or Socialism, with its own peculiar structure and mode of discourse," indeed *"the most widespread ideology of the time"* (1997, ix, 231; my emphasis).

"Wild" Men, Racist Moral Psychology, Anti-Nonwhite Violence, Colonial Expropriation

Garcia (2001, 34, 28, 34–35, 35) argues, in opposition to my claims:

1. that in social contract theory even the "uncivilized" are free and equal persons;
2. that the Racial Contract would be recognized as immoral by its signatories;
3. that, since white people become civilized by the Racial Contract, they would not condone violence against nonwhites; and
4. that the European seizure and colonization of nonwhites' lands can find no Lockean justification.

I will deal with these four objections together, since they are obviously interconnected; and points made in reply to one will be pertinent for the others also.

On the first issue, I am not quite sure whether Garcia is conceding that nonwhites (allegedly) in the state of nature were seen as intrinsically inferior through the eyes of the European culture of the time, while denying that *social contract theory* specifically represents them as such; or that he is asserting that they were seen as intrinsically inferior *neither* by European culture nor social contract theory. But for safety's sake, and to remind us of the cultural background, I am going to begin by establishing the former—namely, the pejorative conception of Native Americans and its link with their alleged "wildness."

In an essay from thirty years ago—long before the current boom in work on philosophy and race—Richard Ashcraft provided an account of Hobbes' views on Native Americans, which included how they were shaped by and how they would themselves go on to shape contemporary

European perceptions. He starts by summarizing the seventeenth-century view of Native Americans:

> We might begin by considering the comparative status of men, beasts, devils, and Indians, because such a comparison will disclose some of the connecting links between cosmology and natural history. In the clear light of Aristotelianism, men stood above the beasts, and, Christians added, devils were beneath the latter. The exact classification of Indians posed something of a problem, however, since they were men who lived like beasts and, generally, worshiped the devil. Traditionally, it was assumed that beasts were distinguishable from men in the grand scheme of things, because, among other reasons, the former were "irrational" creatures and therefore not subject to the law of nature. An obvious and relevant issue, then, concerned the relationship between the "wild" American and natural law. That was by no means an easily answerable question.
>
> Seventeenth-century Englishmen were raised on the belief that without religion and a notion of the Deity, men would live like "savage beasts." Naturally, this opinion easily shaded itself into the conviction that it was Christianity which rescued men from their "beastly" condition. . . . However much they extolled natural reason, and even natural religion, most Englishmen simply were not willing to place themselves, enlightened as they were by the precepts of Christianity, on a par with these "beastlike" men as obedient subjects of the law of nature. The growing store of information about America, therefore, only served to blur the "ancient landmarks" of Aristotelianism. . . .
>
> The European attitude of superiority to the Indian was part of the cultural baggage of any voyage to America. Hence, the metaphorical language of travelers' reports emphasizes the "beastial" nature of primitive life. These "new men," as Joseph de Acosta refers to them, were "like savage beasts." Throughout his *Commentaries*, Garcilaso de la Vega associates the Indians with "wild beasts" who have to be "taught" how "to live like men." Virginia, one Englishman reported in 1609, "is inhabited with wild and savage people, that live and lie up and down in troops like herds of deer in a forest." "We look upon them [the Indians]," wrote another, "with Scorn and Disdain and think them little better than Beasts in Human Shape." Indeed, others were prepared to "set aside" their human shape. In short, the Indians were regarded as being "as wilde as . . . any other wilde beast" and were only grudgingly admitted into the ranks of humanity. (Ashcraft 1972, 149–51)

It should be obvious, then, both that Native Americans were seen as inferior creatures, barely if at all human, and that their inferiority was linked with their "wildness," that is, their living in the "state of nature" rather than society. (And assessments like this are myriad: this point is completely uncontroversial and massively documented in the literature on colonialism and imperialism.) So civilized Englishmen were contrasted to savage Indians. Now is it *logically* possible that a conceptual apparatus drawing in part on these terms (read: social contract theory) could remain uninfluenced by their associations? Yes, it is—but *psychologically/ culturally/socially* it is not remotely likely. The golden age of social contract theory (1650–1800) overlaps with the imperial enterprise; and, as I document in the book, it is also shaped by it. The "men" who demonstrate their capacity for "civilization" by leaving the state of nature are (in general) white, and they are contrasted with the *nonwhite* "savages" who are incapable of leaving it.[3] "Savage," then, is by no means a neutral term, but a strongly pejorative one. Its role in what Francis Jennings calls "the cant of conquest" is to justify the European invasion of America as part of a civilizing mission:

> The basic conquest myth postulates that America was virgin land, or wilderness, inhabited by nonpeople called savages; that these savages were creatures sometimes defined as demons, sometimes as beasts "in the shape of men"; that their mode of existence and cast of mind were such as to make them incapable of civilization and therefore of full humanity; that civilization was required by divine sanction or the imperative of progress to conquer the wilderness and make it a garden; that the savage creatures of the wilderness, being unable to adapt to any environment other than the wild, stubbornly and viciously resisted God or fate, and thereby incurred their suicidal extermination. (Jennings 1976, 15)

Against this background, we can now appreciate how utterly ludicrous as a transracial generalization is Garcia's claim that "in social contract theory even precivilized people were free and equal *persons*." This statement is in general *only* true for whites (and white men at that). As I emphasize in *The Racial Contract*, the contractarian apparatus is tacitly or overtly racialized by all the major social contract theorists, with the crucial differentiation being the ability to leave the state of nature. Hobbes is sufficiently a racial egalitarian in that he conceptualizes the state of nature as bestial for everybody; but the crucial point, obviously, is that *Europeans are rational enough to take the steps necessary to leave it, while Native Americans are not.* How could this *not* reflect on their inherent rationality (Garcia), when his book (*Leviathan*) is pivoted around the rough parity of men's mental powers (as detailed in chapter 13) and its implications for "contracting" to create the commonwealth and avoid the state of war (Hobbes 1996, 86–90)? Ashcraft points out that Hobbes explicitly refers to Native Americans as examples of "men who, in his time, were living proof that such a state of nature as he describes actually existed" (Ashcraft 1972, 148). Moreover, these references appear not only in *Leviathan*, but also in *De Cive* and *De Corpore Politico*: "Clearly, Hobbes' definition of the state of nature was explicitly intended by him to be associated with the 'brutish' and 'savage' life of the Indians" (Ashcraft 1972, 154). And Native Americans are expressly singled out again in chapter 30 of *Leviathan* for their poor grasp of the "Principles of Reason" (Hobbes 1996, 232).

Evidently, then, since Native Americans do not have what it takes to leave the state of nature, they necessarily occupy a different category from whites. Because of the ahistoricity of analytic philosophy, the Eurocentrism of the tradition, and, frankly, the likely congruence of Hobbes' picture of Native Americans with that shared by most white readers (until comparatively recently anyway), this fact—obvious enough once it has been pointed out—has not been noticed and given the theoretical attention it deserves. For the clear implication is that those *not* capable of creating political society are indeed, contra Garcia, our inferiors (if I may momentarily position myself as white here!); they are not "free and equal persons." As Ashcraft concludes: "[M]en are not recognizably different from other animals by virtue of divine creation (which may leave them, as the 'savages of America,' still in the state of other animals, i.e., the state of war); they become different only because they themselves *create* a political society" (Ashcraft 1972, 157). So no rigid distinction can be sustained between inferior state-of-nature "savages" in contractarian literature and inferior state-of-nature "savages" in the general political/literary/cultural writings of the time; the conceptions come from the same source and, with some variations according to the particular theorist, are driven by the same racializing and dichotomizing logic.

And this brings us naturally to Garcia's sixth and seventh points. If, from the modern period onward, "civilization" becomes a racialized term, so that (generally) only Europeans can be civilized in the full sense; and if this "civilization" is threatened by the "savagery"/"barbarism" of nonwhites, then within this racialized normative schema, what is "reasonable" and "moral" undergoes a change. The actual code that develops is a racist one—what I called in the book a *"Herrenvolk* ethics"—which makes nonwhites in general "subpersons," lacking the moral status of whites, and thus unprotected by standard white-on-white moral constraints. Put into practice on a large scale, this code inevitably leads to differential violence against nonwhites, acts that *would* be judged atrocities by the idealized terms of the social contract, but that are perfectly legitimate by the terms of the Racial Contract. They are not "recognized as immoral according to the moral codes of its presumed signers" (Garcia 2001, 28) precisely because this moral code assigns an inferior moral status to people of color. In Jennings' words: "[T]he civilized-uncivilized distinction is a moral sanction . . . a weapon of attack rather than a standard of measurement. . . . To call a man savage is to warrant his death and to leave him unknown and unmourned" (Jennings 1975, 8, 12). Such atrocities may be "patently immoral" to us, judging from within the framework of a *nonracial* code; they are certainly not "patently immoral" to those who have used race as a device for the moral partitioning of their concern and the allocation of rights.

And under certain circumstances, atrocity moves from the permissible to the mandatory. Matthew Frye Jacobson cites a nineteenth-century American writer: "I believe that in killing the savage I performed my duty as a man and served my country as a citizen" (Jacobson 1998, 17).

This point should be so obvious, so little in need of belaboring, that I almost feel that I must be misunderstanding Garcia. It was *not* seen as wrong for white settlers to kill Native Americans or Native Australians in the "wild." It was *not* seen as wrong for Europeans to inflict massive punitive retaliations after slave and anticolonial uprisings. It was *not* seen as wrong for whites to lynch, or for white police to kill blacks judged to be threats to the social order. *In all these cases (white) civilization is being threatened by (nonwhite) savagery*; so to preserve and expand civilization, the savages have to be destroyed. Has Garcia never watched any of the hundreds of (prerevisionist) Westerns, with Indians being massacred without a qualm, as a variety of dangerous fauna that must be cleared away for white settler civilization to be safe? Has Garcia never read the accounts of lynchings, where thousands of white men, women, and children gathered (with trains sometimes being organized for out-of-towners) for the spectacle of black people being slowly burned alive, posing unashamedly for the cameras, and subsequently distributing postcards of the event? Let him read *Without Sanctuary* and peruse its photographs (Allen et al. 2000). These people were not doing anything wrong, anything "unreasonable" in their moral framework: since red/brown/black savagery is a menace to civilization, one manifests one's civilization by destroying it.

In his "Hellhounds" chapter of *Without Sanctuary*, Leon Litwack gives a grisly account of the April 23, 1899, roasting at Newman, Georgia, of Sam Hose before a crowd of over two thousand people. He comments:

> As in most lynchings, no member of the crowd wore a mask, nor did anyone attempt to conceal the names of the perpetrators; indeed, newspaper reporters noted the active participation of some of the region's most prominent citizens. And as in most lynchings, the white press and public expressed its solidarity in the name of white supremacy and ignored any information that contradicted the people's verdict. . . . The use of the camera to memorialize lynchings testified to their openness and to the *self-righteousness* that animated the participants. Not only did photographers capture the execution itself, but also the carnival-like atmosphere and the expectant mood of the crowd. . . . Many photographs of lynchings and burnings (such as the burning of Sam Hose) would reappear as popular picture postcards and trade cards to commemorate the event. (Litwack 2000, 9–11; my emphasis)

These are *not*, in other words, people in any kind of moral turmoil because of their recognition of the "patently immoral" character of what they are doing!

What made this possible? Litwack quotes a black Mississippian:

> *"Back in those days, to kill a Negro wasn't nothing. It was like killing a chicken or killing a snake. The whites would say, 'Niggers jest supposed to die, ain't no damn good anyway—so jest go on an' kill 'em .'"* . . . The cheapness of black life reflected in turn the degree to which so many whites by the early twentieth century had come to think of black men and women as inherently and permanently inferior, as less than human, as little more than animals. *"We Southern people don't care to equal ourselves with animals,"* a white Floridian told a northern critic. *"The people of the South don't think any more of killing the black fellows than you would think of killing a flea."* (Litwack 2000, 12–13; Litwack's emphases throughout)

Could the statement of a *"Herrenvolk* ethics" be any clearer? And isn't this exactly what I argue for in the book?

Finally, with respect to point eight. Garcia argues that on a Lockean theory, aboriginal peoples could acquire property rights that would have to be respected by Europeans. But as with his claims about Kant (see below), this really rests on a *counterfactual* Lockeanism, not what the real-life Locke actually said. Could one sanitize and deracialize the actual Locke to produce nonracial "Lockean" views on private property? Yes, one could, and in Mills (2000, 456–58), I argue precisely for this project as a way of justifying reparations. But it has to be recognized that one is producing a revisionist account, not the (somehow) "actual" account. The real-life Locke thought of Native Americans as so inferior to Europeans in their productive capacities that an English day laborer lived better than an Indian king; and since recognition of natural law requires one to be industrious, this has to be taken as a sign of their inferiority. Moreover, Locke's views were used throughout the white settler states (America, Australia, parts of Africa) to justify native dispossession. What does that have to do with the Racial Contract (asks Garcia)? (!) Obviously, it has *everything* to do with the Racial Contract, since nonwhites are being seen as savages, as subpersons without an equal capacity to appropriate the world, and thus as expropriatable—indeed, they are often not even there to the eyes of white civilization (hence the judgments in international law about *terra nullius,* virgin land, etc.). Again, though Garcia obviously does not recognize it, this assessment is standard and commonplace in the literature on imperialism. As James Tully points out:

> First, Locke defines political society in such a way that Amerindian government does not qualify as a legitimate form of political society. . . . Second, Locke defines property in such a way that Amerindian customary land use is not a legitimate form of property. Rather, it is construed as individual labour-based possession and assimilated to an earlier stage of European develop-

ment in the state of nature, and thus not on equal footing with European property. Amerindian political formations and property are thereby subjected to the sovereignty of European concepts of politics and property. Furthermore, these concepts serve to justify the dispossession of Amerindians of their political organizations and territories. . . . The . . . major conclusion Locke draws from the premiss that America is a state of nature is that appropriation of land may take place without consent. . . . [T]he argument justifies European settlement in America without the consent of the native people, one of the most contentious and important events of the seventeenth century and one of the formative events of the modern world. (1994, 167, 172–73)

The Supposed Murkiness of the Relationship between the Racial and Social Contracts

Garcia (2001, 36) complains that I am unclear and inconsistent on the relationship between the Racial Contract and the social contract, and that I vacillate on what is "historical" and "mythical":

Mills leaves murky his understanding of the Racial Contract's relationship to the social contract (67, 74, 93, 111, 120, 129 ff.). Is any social contract historical in Mills's view, or just "mythical" (111)? If historical, then how can the RCH replace or "supplement" the social contract? How do we replace historical facts? If mythical, then how can the Racial Contract constrain or "underwrite" the social contract (93)? And how can the Racial Contract be the social contract's "real meaning" (74)? Social contract theory, especially in Hobbes and Locke, sought primarily to justify state authority or policies by appeal to real or imagined transfers of rights. The RCH does nothing similar.

First, we need to make the elementary distinction between X itself and the theory associated with X (roughly the distinction between talk of X *de re* and *de dicto*). Thus there is the social contract as an entity, whether a literal contract/agreement/exchange of promises or, as I gloss Hampton, a set of "conventionally generated norms and practices" created with intent by humans; and then there is social contract theory, which is the deployment of the idea of (in some sense) a social contract. Similarly, there is the Racial Contract as an entity and the theory of the Racial Contract.

With this distinction in place, we can now clarify what Garcia (puzzlingly) finds so puzzling. What is supposed to be "replaced" or "supplemented" is *not*, of course, the actual (*de re*) social contract (however we cash it out ontologically) but rather the accounts (*de dicto*) in our textbooks of the contract involved. Absent a time machine, we can't go back in history and change historical events. Nor would the idea, in any case, be to "replace" the nonracial social contract with the Racial Contract, since there is no nonracial (i.e., egalitarian, inclusivist) social contract. It's mythical—that's the whole point of the book. The burden of the book is that the social contract (*de re*) is already racialized, though this is not admitted in texts (*de dicto*) about it. So if we did have a time machine, the thing to do would be to try to replace the exclusionary, inegalitarian Racial Contract with the inclusivist, egalitarian social contract. But what we can change is the mystified accounts in philosophy texts that imply that social contract theory ushers in an age where the moral equality of human beings becomes the norm, when in fact racial inequality, which (contra Garcia) makes some humans superior to others, is the actual norm. That's why my tenth thesis in the book refers to "The 'Racial Contract' as a theory" and says that it's "explanatorily superior to the raceless social contract." And that's why I say in the first paragraph of that thesis: "I therefore advocate the supplementation of standard social contract discussions with an account of the 'Racial Contract'" (Mills 1997, 120; the paperback version, which I am quoting from here, is slightly different from the cloth version). So I am arguing explicitly—and, I think, to most people quite clearly—that we need to change how we *theorize* about these processes. I am not, absurdly, arguing for an impossible alteration of the historical past, but for a change in philosophy texts in how we talk about that past.

On the other hand, when I talk about the Racial Contract's "constraining" or "underwriting" the social contract, I am speaking *de re*. I am saying that insofar as the social contract is real (see Hamptonian gloss), then it is marked by patterns of exclusion and seeming inconsistency that can be explained once we realize that the Racial Contract is the real "agreement" that determines its normative logic of inclusion and exclusion.

Finally, the claim that "the Racial Contract is the real meaning of the social contract" comes at the end of a paragraph (Mills 1997, 73–74) on the evolution (from a de jure to de facto form) of white supremacy and its implications for the moral standing of nonwhites. In context, then, it is referring to the moral rather than political dimension of contractarianism. Contractarianism, as I point out at the start of the book, is ostensibly committed to moral egalitarianism. As one author writes: "The emergence of the notion of the social contract is hence linked intimately with the emergence of the idea of the equality of human beings" (Forsyth 1994, 37). And my claim in the book, of course, and in the paragraph in question, is that in reality this equality is restricted to whites: thus my conclusion that "the Racial Contract is the real meaning of the social contract."[4]

Whiteness as a Contingent Power Construct

Garcia (2001, 36) finds my claim about the historical contingency of whiteness ridiculous: "Mills imagines that the concept of whiteness, white people, is simply a social power construct, so that in other societies, histories, and possible worlds white people may not be the 'whites,' but Asian or African or Native Americans could be 'white' (106, 124 ff.)!"

This could be termed "argument by exclamation mark." As such, it serves as a reminder of what we all smugly tend to forget, that group A's conventional wisdom is often group B's outrageous claim. Apparently in Garcia's mind, and possibly in the social circles in which he moves, this unremarkable statement—virtually a cliché to current researchers in "critical white studies"—is so self-evidently absurd as to need no discursive refutation; merely stating it constitutes a disproof.

But even allowing for our radically different politics (and correspondingly different social circles), I'm puzzled as to why. Presumably he's not attributing to me the view that Africans who are ruling over Europeans in an alternative universe would actually undergo a metamorphosis of skin color. But if not, then what's so ridiculous about the idea that in an alternative system of racial supremacy "blackness" (or "redness" or "yellowness") would become the preferred skin color—with African (or Native American or Asian) features the somatic norm, with African (or Native American or Asian) culture the hallmark of superiority, and so forth—so that black (or red or yellow) would become "white"? If he does find this concept absurd, then his reaction, I submit, is further evidence of his tacit naturalizing of "whiteness" and his failure to appreciate its historicity and contingency, which the "Racial Contract" tries to elucidate. Let us think of a system of racial supremacy in the abstract as $R_1 > R_2 > R_3$. In our actual world, the R1s have for hundreds of years been white; thus, it is cognitively easy to conflate "whiteness" with "R_1-ness," when in fact "R_1-ness" is a placeholder that, in a world with an alternative history, could have been occupied by some other racial group. So the point of my comments about other races becoming "white" was simple Brechtian "defamiliarization," aimed at conceptually peeling apart whiteness as skin color and whiteness as occupation of the R_1 slot of racial privilege.

Garcia's reaction is all the more puzzling since he himself cites (35) the practice of some Native American peoples of referring to themselves as "the human beings." Well, suppose one or more of the great pre-Columbian American empires with such a normative dichotomization had had the technology to cross the Atlantic and "discover" and conquer Dark Ages Europe. What social order might conquerors operating with such a partitioning of humanity have brought into existence?

Enlightenment Philosophers' Moral Theories as Racist

Garcia (2001, 34, 37) is dismissive of the claim that Enlightenment philosophers' theories are racist. He says (41–42, n. 20) that in any case I later retreat from this position.

I will focus on Kant, as the most clear-cut example.

The first point is that there is nothing in the least "murky and only marginally intelligible" (Garcia 2001, 34) about the claim that the *actual* (as against the counterfactual, sanitized, cleaned up, etc.) moral philosophical theory of Kant was racist. If you believe that all persons should be treated with respect, but you do *not* believe that people of color are full persons (and you provide a detailed theoretical account as to why), *then your moral theory is a racist one.* What's hard to understand about that? The elementary, circular fallacy Garcia commits, as do others who want to save Kant from himself, is to de-racialize Kant's actual views and then triumphantly present the de-racialized result as somehow the "real" nonracial Kant. Of course, I am not denying that a moral apparatus can be constructed that is recognizably Kantian in its key terms (persons, respect, the categorical imperative, the kingdom of ends), though not Kantian in its racial inclusiveness. But insofar as it is racially inclusive, I would claim, *it is not Kant's actual theory.* So what we teach our students in introductory ethics courses, what professional philosophers debate in journal articles, what is summarized in philosophical encyclopedias and handbooks is actually a scare-quoted, sanitized, and idealized "Kantianism"; but it is not *Kantianism.* In a recent article, Robert Bernasconi warns against the common practice of "editing Kant's philosophy to make it appear more wholesome" and "doctoring the Kantian corpus so that race disappears from it" (Bernasconi 2002, 160–61). Bernasconi points out that Kant viewed blacks and Native Americans as natural slaves, and he envisaged a future in which all races but whites would have perished! Is this not relevant to his cosmopolitanism, his theory of history, his moral–political theory of the *Rechtsstaat* and its obligations toward the autonomous "persons" who are its citizens—in short, his "philosophy itself"?

The second point is that the implication that Mills (2000) represents a retreat from Mills (1997) in allowing for a positive normative use of the (idealized, de-racialized) theories of Kant, Locke, and so forth, is false. Nowhere in the book do I deny that such an employment is possible, indeed desirable. Rather, I say explicitly at the start (Mills 1997, 7) that I am seeking to engage constructively with contractarianism, that the point of understanding "the original and continuing 'contract' [i.e., the Racial Contract]" is "so that we can correct for it in constructing the ideal 'contract'" and that "I believe contract theory can be put to positive use once this hidden [racial] history is acknowledged" (136–37). So there is no retreat from an originally more "startling" position. From the outset, I am quite clear that the aim is to salvage contract theory by putting it on a more realistic historical basis. But the reason it is "important and revealing" to distinguish sanitized "Kantianism" and "Lockeanism" from actual Kantianism and Lockeanism is twofold: first, to set the philosophical and historical record straight—that is, that these and other Enlightenment theorists were arguing for a *white* egalitarianism, not a nonracial egalitarianism, and that this distinction affects the "content" of their actual theories; second, to better position ourselves for tackling matters of corrective racial justice, which are currently obfuscated by the mystificatory mainstream orthodoxy that the modern period ushers in egalitarianism as the dominant norm, when in fact *white racial superiority* has been the actual norm.[5]

The Integrated Contractarian Framework Claim

Finally, Garcia (2001, 38) rejects as clearly wrong my claim in Mills (2000) that what I call the "domination contract" provides a superior basis for doing normative contractarian theory:

> [B]ecause [the Racial Contract] is plainly immoral, it is plainly nonbinding. . . . Besides, the Millsian claim that people act as though they were fulfilling an agreement is so different from the Rawlsian claim that people ought to act in accordance with agreed-upon principles that the appearance of 'an integrated framework' for our normative inquiries is, as far as I can tell, superficial, specious.

I think this is just a simple misunderstanding (as against his earlier, more complicated misunderstandings). Following Jean Hampton, I pointed out in the book (again, all in the early endnotes) that the classic contractarians generally used "contract" to model the actual polity (in a suitably abstract sense) and to prescribe a better, more just one. Modern contractarians, however, such as John Rawls (1971) in his famous thought experiment, just use it normatively (though my claim [e.g., Mills 1997, 121–22] is that they generally proceed as if moral egalitarianism *were* the actual norm obtaining, and in this respect they do presuppose the misleading descriptive contract). The advantage of reviving the older use, I argue, is to provide a more realistic sense of the actual history, structure, and functioning of the sociopolitical, which can guide us in our normative inquiries (in Mills 1997 and, in greater detail, in Mills 2000, which is where the phrase "an integrated conceptual framework" [455] comes from). Moral judgments about the world involve both value commitments and factual claims about that world. As any rational ethicist must, Rawls concedes that knowledge of the facts is important, and he does allow that people will take behind the veil "general knowledge" of history, how society works, and so forth. But nowhere behind the veil, as Rawls reconstructs things, is there any awareness of white supremacy as a dominant structure of recent world history. (Nor, similarly, as feminists have long complained, is there any awareness of patriarchy and how the family needs to be rethought.)

The "domination contract," as I call it in Mills (2000), would then be one way of modeling the (nonideal) sociopolitical facts about race, gender, and so forth, about which we need to be aware when articulating ideal policies. (How else will issues of corrective justice get on the table except through having them as part of the factual picture?) And in this respect, the framework would be "integrated" since contractarianism would be used on both sides, the factual and the normative. The nonideal "Racial Contract" (or, more general, the nonideal domination contract) would encapsulate the "agreements" *actually* made; and the ideal normative contract (for example, the Rawlsian apparatus) would then be employed to prescribe what "agreements," on the basis of this history, *should* be made. So we would use the "Racial Contract" as a way of summarizing the important facts about race and white supremacy (factual contract), and then, from behind the veil, we would thus prescribe on this basis (normative contract). (As for example—though without a gender contract—Susan Moller Okin [1989] argues that Rawls' method can be used to go beyond Rawls' own conclusions once knowledge of the workings of the real-life family is taken behind the veil.)

CONCLUSION

As can be seen, I am in disagreement with most of Garcia's critical points, and I think that the majority of them rest either on misunderstandings of my claims or factual–theoretical errors of his own. Nevertheless, I hope that our exchange will stimulate further discussion on the usefulness of a contractarian strategy for de-ghettoizing issues of race in political philosophy. Tacitly in his critique of me, and more explicitly in his other recent writings, Garcia is presupposing a framework in which racism is best understood as a matter of individual ill-will; and institutional racism and white supremacy (though, as seen, he balks at the latter term) are to be conceptualized as founded *on* individual racism. Given my own theoretical perspective, then, he has things upside down.[6] My claim from chapter 5 onward is that white supremacy should be our theoretical starting point, with individual racism theoretically second. In this respect, I am, of course, following the classic model of Marxist theory, which famously rejects the "Robinsonades" of liberalism for social-structural accounts of class domination and which seeks to explain prevailing norms and belief patterns in terms of people's socialization and interactions with this structure.

Historically, social contract theory has been thought to be antithetical to radical approaches in political theory because of its misleading presuppositions of voluntary consent and egalitarian inclusion. But by working with the concept of what I call the "domination contract," one can turn a mainstream conceptual apparatus to radical theoretical ends. The strength of the liberal political tradition has always been its values of freedom, moral–juridical equality, rights protection, and self-realization; and those socialist theorists of the past who sneered at these as "bourgeois" values were, I believe, mistaken. (In the wake of the collapse of official communism, of course, this claim is hardly controversial.) The sensible approach is to argue that there is nothing wrong with the values themselves, but rather their limited realization in a society structured by relations of exclusion. Liberals have usually ignored or downplayed these problems, a theoretical neglect facilitated by an apparatus that, by its initial positing of abstract atomic individuals, obfuscates the relations of domination among them. In the mainstream contract, all humans are regarded as paradigm "contractors," thereby blurring over the history of class, gender, and racial subordination. The domination contract, by contrast, makes explicit the differential power of the rich (Rousseau), and it highlights the fact that women and people of color were *not* seen as full persons in the modern Western and Western-imposed polity (Pateman, Mills). So by making this our theoretical starting point, it precludes the routine glossing over of the distinctive normative challenges posed by the demands of justice for subordinated populations. By replacing orthodox contractarianism's mystified factual picture of the sociopolitical with the more realistic picture of radical contractarianism, we can reclaim what is valuable about liberalism while not accepting its social ontology. Insofar as critical theory seeks the completion of the Enlightenment, or the radicalization of the Enlightenment, such an approach, I would claim, is fully in keeping with its traditional agenda.

So if my title is *From Class to Race*, it is, finally, nonetheless obvious that I have retained many of the crucial claims of traditional left theory, and I have even left open the door for a historical materialist explanation of white supremacy. The challenge for new critical theorists must be to win the normative battle with mainstream theorists by demonstrating that by their own ostensible values, the current social order is unjust and thus requires transformation. Racial emancipation will ultimately free whites as well as nonwhites.

NOTES

1. In Mills (2000), I argue that Rousseau's "class contract" from *A Discourse on Inequality* (1984), Carole Pateman's "sexual contract" (1988), and my "racial contract" (1997) can all be illuminatingly generalized as examples of the "domination" contract. Unlike the mainstream egalitarian contract, the domination contract begins

from an earlier social stage rather than a mythical state of nature, and it takes moral and political exclusion to be the norm. Thus it makes group oppression central rather than marginal; and since this, of course, has been the actual history of humanity, it provides a far more illuminating framework within which to do sociopolitical theory. In her recent book, Naomi Zack criticizes my idea of a racial contract on the basis that "the victims and objects of colonialism did not consent to their enslavement and exploitation" (Zack 2002, 123–24, n. 30), thereby missing the blindingly obvious point that this contract (following Rousseau) is an exclusionary contract made *among the dominant group*. Nor have others had the slightest difficulty in seeing the "irony and sarcasm" manifest throughout the book that she claims not to be able to find.

2. Goldberg writes:

> Mills takes at face value the realist interpretation of social contract theory, the claim that individuals become modern political subjects of the state as a result of some general agreement among them. Mills accordingly assumes that social contract theory accounts for an actual contractual arrangement, implicit and indirect though it often was, as the basis for modern state establishment and legitimacy. People on this account are considered actually to have agreed to the structures of state formation. (Goldberg 2002, 37)

Many of my criticisms of Garcia's misinterpretation of what I am trying to do with the contract idea would therefore be equally applicable to Goldberg. The carelessness of Goldberg's reading is all the more striking when one considers that the follow-up expository paper I mentioned at the start, "Race and the Social Contract Tradition" (Mills 2000), which makes clear that I am *not* using the "contract" literally, appeared in Goldberg's own journal, *Social Identities*, for a special issue on race and democracy; and it was commissioned and read by him as the editor!

3. The qualification is necessary because of a point of disanalogy between race and gender: that while there is only one female sex, there are several nonwhite races; and their statuses in Western racist thought have traditionally differed. Asians (Chinese, Indians) were usually ranked higher than blacks and Native Americans, the latter two generally seen as "savages," the former two grudgingly conceded to have civilizations, albeit inferior ones.

4. For another of Goldberg's misunderstandings, see Goldberg (2002, 54, n. 1). Here he cites this sentence, and my earlier claim that "The Racial Contract . . . underwrites the social contract" (Mills 1997, 72), as putative evidence of my vacillation between conceptions of the contract as necessarily racist and as contingently racist. But there is no such vacillation: I say from the start (Mills 1997, 7, 137), and maintain consistently throughout the book, that the racial exclusions in the contract are historically contingent, a result of European imperialism. The "underwriting" and the "real meaning" referred to are *within* this specific historical context, not transhistorical truths.

5. Apparently because he too sees me as arguing for the rejection of (sanitized) liberal Enlightenment values, Glenn Loury says he finds the book "provocative but in my view ultimately unpersuasive" (Loury 2002, 211, n. 1):

> But here is the problem, and the source of my dissatisfaction with Mills's argument. . . . What are we to do? Overthrow Kantian ethics? And put what, exactly, in its place? . . . To

recognize the flaws of the liberal tradition is one thing; to replace it with something workable is quite another. . . . Thus a historically oriented effort to expose the particularity at the core of universalistic arguments may be interesting, but it is not a refutation of the universalistic claims. (120–21)

As my argument above should have made clear, this response is doubly mistaken: first, it assumes that Enlightenment thinkers like Kant were nonetheless making universalistic, rather than racially bounded, claims; second, it imputes to me a desire to reject universalism, when in fact I am arguing—and did argue in the book—that we *do* need to strive for genuine universalism. However, the best starting point for such an enterprise, I would contend, is an honest recognition of the racial particularisms in Enlightenment theory, so that we can self-consciously correct for them (for starters, by *not* pretending that the "contract" included everybody). The challenging work of my colleague Tony Laden exemplifies an alternative approach to this common project, that of making liberalism "radical" (see Laden [2001]).

6. See my recent critique of Garcia's "ill-will" analysis of racism: Mills (2003).

References

Acton, H. B. 1955. *The Illusion of the Epoch: Marxism-Leninism as a Philosophical Creed*. London: Cohen and West.

Alcoff, Linda Martín. 1999. "Towards a Phenomenology of Racial Embodiment." *Radical Philosophy*, no. 95 (May–June): 15–26.

Allen, Anita. 1992. "Legal Rights for Poor Blacks." In *The Underclass Question*, ed. Bill E. Lawson. Philadelphia: Temple University Press, 117–39.

Allen, James, Hilton Als, Congressman John Lewis, and Leon F. Litwack. 2000. *Without Sanctuary: Lynching Photography in America*. Santa Fe, N.Mex.: Twin Palms Publishers.

Allen, Theodore W. 1994–1997. *The Invention of the White Race*. 2 vols. New York: Verso.

Almaguer, Tomás. 1994. *Racial Fault Lines: The Historical Origins of White Supremacy in California*. Berkeley: University of California Press.

America, Richard F., ed. 1990. *The Wealth of Races: The Present Value of Benefits from Past Injustices*. New York: Greenwood Press.

Amin, Samir. 1988. *Eurocentrism*. Trans. Russell Moore. New York: Monthly Review Press.

Anderson, Claud. 1994. *Black Labor, White Wealth: The Search for Power and Economic Justice*. Englewood, Md.: Duncan & Duncan.

Anderson, Perry. 1985 [1976]. *Considerations on Western Marxism*. New York: Verso.

Ansley, Frances Lee. 1989. "Stirring the Ashes: Race, Class and the Future of Civil Rights Scholarship." *Cornell Law Review* 74, no. 6 (Sept.): 993–1077.

Appiah, K. Anthony, and Amy Gutmann. 1996. *Color Conscious: The Political Morality of Race*. Princeton, N.J.: Princeton University Press.

Arnold, N. Scott. 1987. "Recent Work on Marx: A Critical Survey." *American Philosophical Quarterly* 24, no. 4 (Oct.): 277–93.

Ashcraft, Richard. 1972. "Leviathan Triumphant: Thomas Hobbes and the Politics of Wild Men." In *The Wild Man Within: An Image in Western Thought from*

the Renaissance to Romanticism, ed. Edward Dudley and Maximillian E. Novak. Pittsburgh, Pa.: University of Pittsburgh Press, 141–81.

Auletta, Ken. 2000. *The Underclass*. Rev. and updated ed. Orig. ed. 1982. New York:
Penguin USA.

Ball, Terence, and James Farr, eds. 1984. *After Marx*. Cambridge: Cambridge University Press.

Barker, Sir Ernest, ed. 1960. *Social Contract: Essays by Locke, Hume, and Rousseau.*
New York: Oxford University Press.

Barnet, Richard J. 1993. "The End of Jobs." *Harper's Magazine* 287, no. 1720 (Sept.):
47–52.

Bell, Derrick. 1987. *And We Are Not Saved: The Elusive Quest for Racial Justice*. New
York: Basic Books.

———. 1992. *Faces at the Bottom of the Well: The Permanence of Racism*. New York: Basic Books.

Berman, Marshall. 1988 [1982]. *All That Is Solid Melts into Air: The Experience of
Modernity*. New York: Viking Penguin.

Bernal, Martin. 1987. *Black Athena: The Afroasiatic Roots of Classical Civilization*, vol.
1, *The Fabrication of Ancient Greece, 1785–1985*. New Brunswick, N.J.: Rutgers
University Press.

Bernasconi, Robert. 2001. "Who Invented the Concept of Race? Kant's Role in the
Enlightenment Construction of Race." In *Race*, ed. Robert Bernasconi. Malden,
Mass.: Blackwell, 11–36.

———. 2002. "Kant as an Unfamiliar Source of Racism." In *Philosophers on Race: Critical Essays*, ed. Julie K. Ward and Tommy L. Lott. Malden, Mass.: Blackwell, 145–66.

Berry, Mary Frances. 1994 [1971]. *Black Resistance, White Law: A History of Constitu-
tional Racism in America*. New York: Allen Lane.

Bittker, Boris I. 2003. *The Case for Black Reparations*. 2d ed. Orig. ed. 1973. Boston:
Beacon Press.

Blauner, Robert. 2001. *Still the Big News: Racial Oppression in America*. Rev. and exp.
ed. Orig. ed. 1972. Philadelphia: Temple University Press.

Blaut, J. M. 1993. *The Colonizer's Model of the World: Geographical Diffusionism and
Eurocentric History*. New York: The Guilford Press.

———. 2000. *Eight Eurocentric Historians*. New York: The Guilford Press.

Bonilla-Silva, Eduardo. 2001. *White Supremacy and Racism in the Post-Civil Rights
Era*. Boulder, Colo.: Lynne Rienner Publishers.

Boucher, David, and Paul Kelly, eds. 1994. *The Social Contract from Hobbes to Rawls.*
New York: Routledge.

Boxill, Bernard. 1991. "Wilson on the Truly Disadvantaged." *Ethics* 101, no. 3
(Apr.): 579–92.

———. 1992a. *Blacks and Social Justice*. Rev. ed. Orig. ed. 1984. Lanham, Md.: Rowman & Littlefield.

———. 1992b. "The Underclass and the Race/Class Issue." In *The Underclass Question*, ed. Bill E. Lawson. Philadelphia: Temple University Press, 19–32.

———, ed. 2001. *Race and Racism*. New York: Oxford University Press.

———. 2003. "The Morality of Reparations II." In *A Companion to African-American
Philosophy*, ed. Tommy L. Lott and John P. Pittman. Malden, Mass.: Blackwell,
134–47.

Brenkert, George G. 1980. "Freedom and Private Property in Marx." In *Marx, Justice, and History*, ed. Marshall Cohen, Thomas Nagel, and Thomas Scanlon. Princeton, N.J.: Princeton University Press, 80–105.

———. 1983. *Marx's Ethics of Freedom*. London: Routledge & Kegan Paul.

Brink, David O. 1989. *Moral Realism and the Foundations of Ethics*. Cambridge: Cambridge University Press.

Brodkin, Karen. 1998. *How Jews Became White Folks and What That Says about Race in America*. New Brunswick, N.J.: Rutgers University Press.

Brown, Michael K. 1999. *Race, Money, and the American Welfare State*. Ithaca, N.Y.: Cornell University Press.

Buchanan, Allen E. 1982. *Marx and Justice: The Radical Critique of Liberalism*. Totowa, N.J.: Rowman & Littlefield.

———. 1986. "The Marxist Conceptual Framework and the Origins of Totalitarian Socialism." In *Marxism and Liberalism*, ed. Ellen Frankel Paul, Fred D. Miller Jr., Jeffrey Paul, and John Ahrens. Oxford: Basil Blackwell, 127–44.

———. 1987. "Marx, Morality and History: An Assessment of Recent Analytical Work on Marx." *Ethics* 98, no. 1 (Oct.): 104–36.

Button, James W. 1978. *Black Violence: Political Impact of the 1960s Riots*. Princeton, N.J.: Princeton University Press.

Callinicos, Alex, ed. 1989. *Marxist Theory*. Oxford: Oxford University Press.

Carver, Terrell, and Paul Thomas, eds. 1995. *Rational Choice Marxism*. University Park: Pennsylvania State University Press.

Cell, John W. 1982. *The Highest Stage of White Supremacy: The Origins of Segregation in South Africa and the American South*. Cambridge: Cambridge University Press.

Chase, Allan. 1980. *The Legacy of Malthus: The Social Costs of the New Scientific Racism*. Urbana, Ill.: University of Illinois Press.

Churchill, Ward. 1992. *Fantasies of the Master Race: Literature, Cinema and the Colonization of American Indians*. Monroe, Maine: Common Courage Press.

Clark, Lorenne M. G., and Lynda Lange, eds. 1979. *The Sexism of Social and Political Theory: Women and Reproduction from Plato to Nietzsche*. Toronto: University of Toronto Press.

Cocker, Mark. 1998. *Rivers of Blood, Rivers of Gold: Europe's Conflict with Tribal Peoples*. London: Jonathan Cape.

Cohen, G. A. 1988. *History, Labor, and Freedom: Themes from Marx*. New York: Oxford University Press.

———. 1989. "Reconsidering Historical Materialism." In *Marxist Theory*, ed. Alex Callinicos. Oxford: Oxford University Press, 148–74.

———. 2001. *Karl Marx's Theory of History: A Defence*. Exp. ed. Original edition 1978. Princeton, N.J.: Princeton University Press.

Cohen, G. A., and Will Kymlicka. 1988. "Human Nature and Social Change in the Marxist Conception of History." *The Journal of Philosophy* 85, no. 4 (Apr.): 171–91.

Cohen, Joshua. 1982. Review of *Karl Marx's Theory of History*, by G. A. Cohen. *The Journal of Philosophy* 79, no. 5 (May): 253–73.

Cohen, Marshall, Thomas Nagel, and Thomas Scanlon, eds. 1980. *Marx, Justice, and History*. Princeton, N.J.: Princeton University Press.

Cole, David. 1999. *No Equal Justice: Race and Class in the American Criminal Justice System*. New York: The New Press.

Collier, Andrew. 1979. "Materialism and Explanation in the Human Sciences." In *Issues in Marxist Philosophy*, vol. 2, *Materialism*, ed. John Mepham and David-Hillel Ruben. Atlantic Highlands, N.J.: Humanities Press, 35–60.

Conley, Dalton. 1999. *Being Black, Living in the Red: Race, Wealth, and Social Policy in America*. Berkeley: University of California Press.

Cook, J. Thomas. 1987. "Deciding to Believe without Self-Deception." *The Journal of Philosophy* 84, no. 8 (Aug.): 441–46.

Cose, Ellis. 1993. *The Rage of a Privileged Class*. New York: HarperCollins.

Costello, Dan. 1990. "Mills and McCarney on 'Ideology' in Marx and Engels." *The Philosophical Forum* 21, no. 4 (Summer): 463–70.

Cox, Oliver Cromwell. 2000 [1948]. 50th anniversary ed. *Race: A Study in Social Dynamics*. New York: Monthly Review Press.

Crenshaw, Kimberlé Williams. 1988. "Race, Reform, and Retrenchment: Transformation and Legitimation in Antidiscrimination Law." *Harvard Law Review* 101, no. 7 (May): 1331–87.

Crenshaw, Kimberlé, Neil Gotanda, Gary Peller, and Kendall Thomas, eds. 1995. *Critical Race Theory: The Key Writings That Formed the Movement*. New York: The New Press.

Crossman, Richard H., ed. 2001 [1949]. *The God That Failed*. New York: Columbia University Press.

Currie, Elliott. 1985. *Confronting Crime: An American Challenge*. New York: Pantheon Books.

Dahm, Helmut, Thomas J. Blakeley, and George L. Kline, eds. 1988. *Philosophical Sovietology: The Pursuit of a Science*. Dordrecht, Holland: D. Reidel.

Delany, Martin Robison. 1970 [1859–1862]. *Blake; or, the Huts of America*. Boston: Beacon Press.

Delgado, Richard, ed. 1995. *Critical Race Theory: The Cutting Edge*. Philadelphia: Temple University Press.

di Leonardo, Micaela. 1999. "'Why Can't They Be like Our Grandparents?' and Other Racial Fairy Tales." In *Without Justice for All: The New Liberalism and Our Retreat from Racial Equality*, ed. Adolph Reed Jr. Boulder, Colo.: Westview Press, 29–64.

Djilas, Milovan. 1973. *Memoir of a Revolutionary*. Trans. Drenka Willen. New York: Harcourt Brace Jovanovich.

Dray, Philip. 2002. *At the Hands of Persons Unknown: The Lynching of Black America*. New York: Random House.

Du Bois, W. E. B. 1996 [1903]. *The Souls of Black Folk*. New York: Penguin USA.

———. 1995 [1928]. *Dark Princess: A Romance*. Jackson: University Press of Mississippi.

———. 1998 [1935]. *Black Reconstruction in America, 1860–1880*. New York: The Free Press.

Dudley, Edward, and Maximillian E. Novak, eds. 1972. *The Wild Man Within: An Image in Western Thought from the Renaissance to Romanticism*. Pittsburgh, Pa.: University of Pittsburgh Press.

Dudziak, Mary L. 2000. *Cold War Civil Rights: Race and the Image of American Democracy*. Princeton, N.J.: Princeton University Press.

Dupuy, J., ed. 1998. *Self-Deception and Paradoxes of Rationality*. Cambridge: Cambridge University Press.

Dussel, Enrique. 1995 [1992]. *The Invention of the Americas: Eclipse of "the Other" and the Myth of Modernity*. Trans. Michael D. Barber. New York: Continuum.

Dyer, Richard. 1997. *White*. New York: Routledge.

Dymski, Gary A. 1997. "Racial Inequality and Capitalist Exploitation." In *Exploitation*, ed. Kai Nielsen and Robert Ware. Atlantic Highlands, N.J.: Humanities Press, 335–47.

Edgley, Roy. 1990. "Marxism, Morality and Mr. Lukes." In *Socialism and Morality*, ed. David McLellan and Sean Sayers. London: Macmillan, 21–41.

Edsall, Thomas Byrne, and Mary D. Edsall. 1991. *Chain Reaction: The Impact of Race, Rights, and Taxes on American Politics*. New York: W. W. Norton.

Eisenstein, Zillah R., ed. 1979. *Capitalist Patriarchy and the Case for Socialist Feminism*. New York: Monthly Review Press.

Ellison, Ralph. 1995 [1952]. *Invisible Man*. New York: Vintage Books.

Elster, Jon. 1983. *Sour Grapes: Studies in the Subversion of Rationality*. Cambridge: Cambridge University Press.

———. 1985. *Making Sense of Marx*. Cambridge: Cambridge University Press.

Eze, Emmanuel Chukwudi. 1995. "The Color of Reason: The Idea of 'Race' in Kant's Anthropology." In *Anthropology and the German Enlightenment: Perspectives on Humanity*, ed. Katherine M. Faull. Lewisburg, Pa.: Bucknell University Press, 196–237.

———, ed. 1997. *Race and the Enlightenment: A Reader*. Cambridge, Mass.: Blackwell.

Fainstein, Norman. 1986–1987. "The Underclass/Mismatch Hypothesis as an Explanation for Black Economic Deprivation." *Politics and Society* 15, no. 4: 403–51.

Fanon, Frantz. 1991 [1952]. *Black Skin, White Masks*. Trans. Charles Lam Markmann. New York: Grove Press.

Faull, Katherine M., ed. 1995. *Anthropology and the German Enlightenment: Perspectives on Humanity*. Lewisburg, Pa.: Bucknell University Press.

Feinberg, Joel, ed. 1996. *Reason and Responsibility: Readings in Some Basic Problems of Philosophy*. 9th ed. Belmont, Calif.: Wadsworth.

Fields, Barbara Jeanne. 1990. "Slavery, Race and Ideology in the United States of America." *New Left Review*, no. 181 (May–June): 95–118.

Fisk, Milton. 1980. *Ethics and Society: A Marxist Interpretation of Value*. New York: New York University Press.

Foley, Neil. 1997. *White Scourge: Mexicans, Blacks, and Poor Whites in Texas Cotton Culture*. Berkeley: University of California Press.

Forsyth, Murray. 1994. "Hobbes's Contractarianism: A Comparative Analysis." In *The Social Contract from Hobbes to Rawls*, ed. David Boucher and Paul Kelly. New York: Routledge, 35–50.

Foulkes, Imogen. 2003. "World Jobless Hits Record High." BBC News World Edition, Business, http://news.bbc.co.uk/2/hi/business/2690901.stm (accessed March 30, 2003).

Frank, Andre Gunder. 1966. "The Development of Underdevelopment." *Monthly Review* 18, no. 4 (Sept.): 17–31.

Frankfurt, Harry. 1971. "Freedom of the Will and the Concept of a Person." *The Journal of Philosophy* 68, no. 1 (Jan. 14): 5–20.

Fraser, Nancy. 1998a. "From Redistribution to Recognition? Dilemmas of Justice in a 'Post-Socialist' Age." In *Theorizing Multiculturalism: A Guide to the Current Debate*, ed. Cynthia Willett. Malden, Mass.: Blackwell, 19–49.

———. 1998b. "A Rejoinder to Iris Young." In *Theorizing Multiculturalism: A Guide to the Current Debate*, ed. Cynthia Willett. Malden, Mass.: Blackwell, 68–72.

Fredrickson, George. 1987 [1971]. *The Black Image in the White Mind: The Debate on Afro-American Character and Destiny, 1817–1914*. Hanover, N.H.: Wesleyan University Press.

———. 1981. *White Supremacy: A Comparative Study in American and South African History*. New York: Oxford University Press.

———. 2002. *Racism: A Short History*. Princeton, N.J.: Princeton University Press.

Freeman, Alan David. 1995. "Legitimizing Racial Discrimination through Antidiscrimination Law: A Critical Review of Supreme Court Doctrine." In *Critical Race Theory: The Key Writings That Formed the Movement*, ed. Kimberlé Crenshaw, Neil Gotanda, Gary Peller, and Kendall Thomas. New York: The New Press, 29–46.

Füredi, Frank. 1998. *The Silent War: Imperialism and the Changing Perception of Race*. New Brunswick, N.J.: Rutgers University Press.

Gans, Herbert J. 1990. "Deconstructing the Underclass: The Term's Dangers as a Planning Concept." *Journal of the American Planning Association* 56, no. 3 (Summer): 271–77.

Garcia, Jorge. 1996. "The Heart of Racism." *Journal of Social Philosophy* 27, no. 1 (Spring): 5–45.

———. 2001. "The Racial Contract Hypothesis." *Philosophia Africana* 4, no. 1 (Mar.): 27–42.

Garrow, David J. 2003 [1981]. *The FBI and Martin Luther King, Jr.: From "Solo" to Memphis*. New Haven, Conn.: Yale University Press.

Geras, Norman. 1989. "The Controversy About Marx and Justice." In *Marxist Theory*, ed. Alex Callinicos. Oxford: Oxford University Press, 211–67.

———. 1997 [1990]. "Marxism and Moral Advocacy." In *Discourses of Extremity: Radical Ethics and Post-Marxist Extravagances*. New York: Verso, 3–19.

Gilman, Sander L. 1998. *Creating Beauty to Cure the Soul: Race and Psychology in the Shaping of Aesthetic Surgery*. Durham, N.C.: Duke University Press.

Gilroy, Paul. 1993. *The Black Atlantic: Modernity and Double Consciousness*. Cambridge, Mass.: Harvard University Press.

Glasgow, Douglas C. 1980. *The Black Underclass: Poverty, Unemployment, and the Entrapment of Ghetto Youth*. New York: Random House.

Glausser, Wayne. 1990. "Three Approaches to Locke and the Slave Trade." *Journal of the History of Ideas* 51, no. 2 (Apr.–June): 199–216.

Goldberg, David Theo, ed. 1990. *Anatomy of Racism*. Minneapolis: University of Minnesota Press.

———. 1992. "Critical Notes on the Underclass." *APA Newsletter on Philosophy and the Black Experience* 91, no. 1 (Spring): 15–19.

———. 1993. *Racist Culture: Philosophy and the Politics of Meaning*. Cambridge, Mass.: Blackwell.

———. 2002. *The Racial State*. Malden, Mass.: Blackwell.

Goodin, Robert E., and Philip Pettit, eds. 1993. *A Companion to Contemporary Political Philosophy*. Cambridge, Mass.: Blackwell.

Gordon, Lewis R. 1995. *Bad Faith and Antiblack Racism*. Atlantic Highlands, N.J.: Humanities Press.

Gornick, Vivian. 1983 [1977]. *The Romance of American Communism*. New York: Basic Books.

Gossett, Thomas F. 1997 [1963]. *Race: The History of an Idea in America*. New York: Oxford University Press.

Gottlieb, Roger. 1985. "Forces of Production and Social Primacy." *Social Theory and Practice* 11, no. 1 (Spring): 1–23.

———. 1987. *History and Subjectivity: The Transformation of Marxist Theory*. Philadelphia: Temple University Press.

Gould, Carol C. 1978. *Marx's Social Ontology: Individuality and Community in Marx's Theory of Social Reality*. Cambridge, Mass.: MIT Press.

Gould, Stephen Jay. 1996. *The Mismeasure of Man*. Rev. and exp. ed. Orig. ed. 1981. New York: W. W. Norton.

Gramsci, Antonio. 1971. *Selections from the Prison Notebooks*. Ed. and trans. Quintin Hoare and Geoffrey Nowell Smith. New York: International Publishers.

Gray, John. 1986. "Marxian Freedom, Individual Liberty, and the End of Alienation." In *Marxism and Liberalism*, ed. Ellen Frankel Paul, Fred D. Miller Jr., Jeffrey Paul, and John Ahrens. Oxford: Basil Blackwell, 160–87.

Greenberg, Edward S. 1990. "Reaganism as Corporate Liberalism: Implications for the American Future." *Policy Studies Review* 10, no. 1 (Fall): 103–25.

Griffin, John Howard. 1996 [1961]. *Black like Me*. New York: Signet.

Guinier, Lani. 1994. *The Tyranny of the Majority: Fundamental Fairness in Representative Democracy*. New York: The Free Press.

Gutmann, Amy. 1996. "Responding to Racial Injustice." In *Color Conscious: The Political Morality of Race* by K. Anthony Appiah and Amy Gutmann. Princeton, N.J.: Princeton University Press, 106–78.

Hamill, Pete. 1988. "Breaking the Silence." *Esquire* (March 1988): 91–102.

Hampton, Jean. 1993. "Contract and Consent." In *A Companion to Contemporary Political Philosophy*, ed. Robert E. Goodin and Philip Pettit. Cambridge, Mass.: Blackwell, 379–93.

———. 1997. *Political Philosophy*. Boulder, Colo.: Westview Press.

Hannaford, Ivan. 1996. *Race: The History of an Idea in the West*. Baltimore: Johns Hopkins University Press.

Harding, Sandra, ed. 1993. *The "Racial" Economy of Science: Toward a Democratic Future*. Bloomington: Indiana University Press.

Harris, Cheryl I. 1993. "Whiteness as Property." *Harvard Law Review* 106, no. 8 (June): 1709–91.

Harris, Leonard. 1992. "Agency and the Concept of the Underclass." In *The Underclass Question*, ed. Bill E. Lawson. Philadelphia: Temple University Press, 33–54.

Hayter, Teresa. 1987 [1981]. *The Creation of World Poverty: An Alternative View to the Brandt Report*. London: Pluto Press.

Healey, Dorothy Ray, and Maurice Isserman. 1993 [1990]. *California Red: A Life in the American Communist Party*. Chicago: University of Illinois Press.

Hegel, Georg Wilhelm Friedrich. 1956. *The Philosophy of History*. Trans. J. Sibree. New York: Dover Publications.

Herrnstein, Richard J., and Charles Murray. 1994. *The Bell Curve: Intelligence and Class Structure in American Life.* New York: The Free Press.

Higginbotham, A. Leon, Jr. 1978. *In the Matter of Color: Race and the American Legal Process—The Colonial Period.* New York: Oxford University Press.

———. 1996. *Shades of Freedom: Racial Politics and Presumptions of the American Legal Process.* New York: Oxford University Press.

Hill, Thomas E., Jr., and Bernard Boxill. 2001. "Kant and Race." In *Race and Racism,* ed. Bernard Boxill. New York: Oxford University Press, 448–71.

Hirsch, James S. 2002. *Riot and Remembrance: The Tulsa Race War and Its Legacy.* New York: Houghton Mifflin.

Hobbes, Thomas. 1996. *Leviathan.* Edited by Richard Tuck. Rev. student ed. Orig. ed. 1991. New York: Cambridge University Press.

Hochschild, Jennifer L. 1984. *The New American Dilemma: Liberal Democracy and School Desegregation.* New Haven, Conn.: Yale University Press.

———. 1991. "The Politics of the Estranged Poor." *Ethics* 101, no. 3 (Apr.): 560–78.

Hodges, Donald Clark. 1962. "Historical Materialism in Ethics." *Philosophy and Phenomenological Research* 23, no. 1 (Sept.): 1–22.

Hoetink, Harmannus. 1962. *Caribbean Race Relations: A Study of Two Variants.* London: Oxford University Press.

Honderich, Ted. 1989. *Violence for Equality: Inquiries in Political Philosophy.* Rev. and exp. 3d ed. Orig. ed. 1976. New York: Routledge.

———, ed. 1995. *The Oxford Companion to Philosophy.* New York: Oxford University Press.

Horsman, Reginald. 1986 [1981]. *Race and Manifest Destiny: Origins of American Racial Anglo-Saxonism.* Cambridge, Mass.: Harvard University Press.

Hughes, Mark Alan. 1989. "Concentrated Deviance and the 'Underclass' Hypothesis." *Journal of Policy Analysis and Management* 8, no. 2 (Spring): 274–82.

Hume, David. 1960. "Of the Original Contract." In *Social Contract: Essays by Locke, Hume, and Rousseau,* ed. Sir Ernest Barker. New York: Oxford University Press, 147–66.

———. 1997. "Of National Characters." In *Race and the Enlightenment: A Reader,* ed. Emmanuel Chukwudi Eze. Cambridge, Mass.: Blackwell, 30–33.

Husami, Ziyad I. 1980. "Marx on Distributive Justice." In *Marx, Justice, and History,* ed. Marshall Cohen, Thomas Nagel, and Thomas Scanlon. Princeton, N.J.: Princeton University Press, 42–79.

Hutchinson, Allan C., ed. 1989. *Critical Legal Studies.* Totowa, N.J.: Rowman & Littlefield.

Ignatiev, Noel. 1995. *How the Irish Became White.* New York: Routledge.

Inniss, Leslie, and Joe R. Feagin. 1989. "The Black 'Underclass' Ideology in Race Relations Analysis." *Social Justice* 16, no. 4 (Winter): 13–34.

Isserman, Maurice. 1993 [1982]. *Which Side Were You On? The American Communist Party during the Second World War.* Urbana: University of Illinois Press

Jacobson, Matthew Frye. 1998. *Whiteness of a Different Color: European Immigrants and the Alchemy of Race.* Cambridge, Mass.: Harvard University Press.

Jacoby, Russell, and Naomi Glauberman, eds. 1995. *The Bell Curve Debate: History, Documents, Opinions.* New York: Random House.

Jaggar, Alison M. 1988 [1983]. *Feminist Politics and Human Nature.* Lanham, Md.: Rowman & Littlefield.

James, C. L. R. 1989. *The Black Jacobins: Toussaint L'Ouverture and the San Domingo Revolution*. 2d ed. Orig. ed. 1938. New York: Vintage.

Jencks, Christopher. 1992. *Rethinking Social Policy: Race, Poverty, and the Underclass*. Cambridge, Mass.: Harvard University Press.

Jennings, Francis. 1975. *The Invasion of America: Indians, Colonialism, and the Cant of Conquest*. New York: W. W. Norton.

Jones, David H. 1989. "Pervasive Self-Deception." *Southern Journal of Philosophy* 27, no. 2 (Summer): 217–37.

Jordan, Winthrop. 1995 [1968]. *White over Black: American Attitudes toward the Negro, 1550–1812*. Williamsburg, Va.: Omohundro Institute of Early American History and Culture.

Kagan, Shelly. 2002 [1989]. *The Limits of Morality*. New York: Oxford University Press.

Kairys, David, ed. 1998. *The Politics of Law: A Progressive Critique*. 3d ed. Orig. ed. 1982. New York: Basic Books.

Kamenka, Eugene. 1969. *Marxism and Ethics*. London: Macmillan.

Kelley, Robin. 1990. *Hammer and Hoe: Alabama Communists during the Great Depression*. Chapel Hill: University of North Carolina Press.

Kellner, Douglas. 1981. "Marxism, Morality and Ideology." In *Marx and Morality, Canadian Journal of Philosophy*, supp. vol. 7, ed. Kai Nielsen and Steven C. Patten. Guelph, On.: Canadian Association for Publishing in Philosophy, 93–120.

Kiernan, Victor. 1996 [1969]. *The Lords of Human Kind: European Attitudes to Other Cultures in the Imperial Age*. Seattle, Wash.: Serif and Pixel Press.

Kinder, Donald R., and Lynn M. Sanders. 1996. *Divided by Color: Racial Politics and Democratic Ideals*. Chicago: University of Chicago Press.

King, Desmond. 1995. *Separate and Unequal: Black Americans and the U.S. Federal Government*. Oxford: Clarendon Press.

Kirkland, Frank M. 1992. "Social Policy, Ethical Life, and the Urban Underclass." In *The Underclass Question*, ed. Bill E. Lawson. Philadelphia: Temple University Press, 152–87.

Kline, George L. 1988. "The Myth of Marx's Materialism." In *Philosophical Sovietology: The Pursuit of a Science*, ed. Helmut Dahm, Thomas J. Blakeley, and George L. Kline. Dordrecht, Holland: D. Reidel, 158–82.

Klinkner, Philip A., and Rogers M. Smith. 1999. *The Unsteady March: The Rise and Decline of Racial Equality in America*. Chicago: University of Chicago Press.

Koestler, Arthur. 1954. *Arrow in the Blue*, vol. 2, *The Invisible Writing*. New York: Macmillan.

Kolakowski, Leszek. 1977. "Marxist Roots of Stalinism." In *Stalinism: Essays in Historical Interpretation*, ed. Robert C. Tucker. New York: W. W. Norton, 283–98.

Kosman, L. A. 1980. "Being Properly Affected: Virtues and Feelings in Aristotle's Ethics." In *Essays on Aristotle's Ethics*, ed. Amelie Oksenberg Rorty. Berkeley: University of California Press, 103–16.

Kovel, Joel. 1984 [1970]. *White Racism: A Psychohistory*. New York: Columbia University Press.

Kozol, Jonathan. 1991. *Savage Inequalities: Children in America's Schools*. New York: Crown.

Kymlicka, Will. 1990. *Contemporary Political Philosophy: An Introduction*. Oxford: Clarendon Press.

Laden, Anthony Simon. 2001. *Reasonably Radical: Deliberative Liberalism and the Politics of Identity*. Ithaca, N.Y.: Cornell University Press.

———. 2003. "The House that Jack Built: Thirty Years of Reading Rawls." *Ethics* 113, no. 2 (Jan.): 367–90.

Lawrence, Charles R., III. 1995. "The Id, the Ego, and Equal Protection: Reckoning With Unconscious Racism." In *Critical Race Theory: The Key Writings That Formed the Movement*, ed. Kimberlé Crenshaw, Neil Gotanda, Gary Peller, and Kendall Thomas. New York: The New Press, 235–57.

Lawson, Bill E., ed. 1992a. *The Underclass Question*. Philadelphia: Temple University Press.

———. 1992b. "Uplifting the Race: Middle-Class Blacks and the Truly Disadvantaged." In *The Underclass Question*, ed. Bill E. Lawson. Philadelphia: Temple University Press, 90–113.

Laycock, Henry. 1980. "Critical Notice," review of *Karl Marx's Theory of History*, by G. A. Cohen, and *Marx's Theory of History*, by William H. Shaw. *Canadian Journal of Philosophy* 10, no. 2 (June): 335–56.

Leacock, Eleanor Burke, ed. 1971. *The Culture of Poverty: A Critique*. New York: Simon & Schuster.

Lee, Robert G. 1999. *Orientals: Asian Americans in Popular Culture*. Philadelphia: Temple University Press.

Lemann, Nicholas. 1986. "The Origins of the Underclass." *Atlantic* (June–July): 31–55; 54–68.

Lenin, Vladimir I. 1963. *Collected Works*, vol. 1. Moscow: Progress Publishers.

———. 1969 [1902]. *What Is to Be Done?* New York: International Publishers.

———. 1996 [1916]. *Imperialism: The Highest Stage of Capitalism*. Chicago: Pluto Press.

Levine, Andrew. 1989. "What Is a Marxist Today?" In *Analyzing Marxism*, ed. Robert Ware and Kai Nielsen. *Canadian Journal of Philosophy*, supp. vol. 15. Calgary, Alta.: University of Calgary Press, 29–58.

Levine, Andrew, and Erik Olin Wright. 1980. "Rationality and Class Struggle." *New Left Review* 123 (Sept.–Oct.): 47–68.

Lewis, Oscar. 1975 [1959]. *Five Families: Mexican Case Studies in the Culture of Poverty*. New York: Basic Books.

———. 1966. *La Vida: A Puerto Rican Family in the Culture of Poverty—San Juan and New York*. New York: Random House.

Lipset, Seymour Martin, and Gary Marks. 2000. *It Didn't Happen Here: Why Socialism Failed in the United States*. New York: W. W. Norton.

Lipsitz, George. 1998. *The Possessive Investment in Whiteness: How White People Profit from Identity Politics*. Philadelphia: Temple University Press.

Litwack, Leon F. 1998. *Trouble in Mind: Black Southerners in the Age of Jim Crow*. New York: Alfred A. Knopf.

———. 2000. "Hellhounds." In *Without Sanctuary: Lynching Photography in America*, James Allen, Hilton Als, Congressman John Lewis, and Leon F. Litwack. Santa Fe, N.Mex.: Twin Palms Publishers, 8–37.

López, Ian F. Haney. 1995. "The Social Construction of Race." In *Critical Race Theory: The Cutting Edge*, ed. Richard Delgado. Philadelphia: Temple University Press, 191–203.

————. 1996. *White by Law: The Legal Construction of Race*. New York: New York University Press.

Lott, Tommy L. 1992. "Marooned in America: Black Urban Youth Culture and Social Pathology." In *The Underclass Question*, ed. Bill E. Lawson. Philadelphia: Temple University Press, 71–89.

————, ed. 1998. *Subjugation and Bondage: Critical Essays on Slavery and Social Philosophy*. Lanham, Md.: Rowman & Littlefield.

Lott, Tommy L., and John P. Pittman, eds. 2003. *A Companion to African-American Philosophy*. Malden, Mass.: Blackwell.

Louden, Robert B. 2000. *Kant's Impure Ethics: From Rational Beings to Human Beings*. New York: Oxford University Press.

Loury, Glenn C. 2002. *The Anatomy of Racial Inequality*. Cambridge, Mass.: Harvard University Press.

Lukes, Steven. 1985. *Marxism and Morality*. Oxford: Oxford University Press.

Lustig, Jeff. 1977. "On Organization: The Question of the Leninist Party." *Politics & Society* 7, no. 1: 27–67.

Lycan, William G., and George N. Schlesinger. 1996. "You Bet Your Life: Pascal's Wager Defended." In *Reason and Responsibility: Readings in Some Basic Problems of Philosophy*, 9th ed., ed. Joel Feinberg. Belmont, Calif.: Wadsworth, 119–27.

Lyons, Paul. 1982. *Philadelphia Communists, 1936–1956*. Philadelphia: Temple University Press.

Lyotard, Jean-François. 1984. *The Postmodern Condition: A Report on Knowledge*. Trans. Geoff Bennington and Brian Massumi. Minneapolis: University of Minnesota Press.

Manley, John F. 1990. "American Liberalism and the Democratic Dream: Transcending the American Dream." *Policy Studies Review* 10, no. 1 (Fall): 89–102.

Mann, Coramae Richey. 1993. *Unequal Justice: A Question of Color*. Bloomington: Indiana University Press.

Marcuse, Herbert. 1985 [1961]. *Soviet Marxism: A Critical Analysis*. New York: Columbia University Press.

Marx, Anthony W. 1998. *Making Race and Nation: A Comparison of the United States, South Africa, and Brazil*. New York: Cambridge University Press.

Marx, Karl, and Frederick Engels. 1975 [1942]. *Selected Correspondence, 1846–1895*. Westport, Conn.: Greenwood Press.

————. 1975. *Collected Works*, vol. 1. New York: International Publishers.

————. 1975. *Collected Works*, vol. 2. New York: International Publishers.

————. 1975. *Collected Works*, vol. 3. New York: International Publishers.

————. 1975. *Collected Works*, vol. 4. New York: International Publishers.

————. 1976. *Collected Works*, vol. 5. New York: International Publishers.

————. 1976. *Collected Works*, vol. 6. New York: International Publishers.

————. 1977. *Collected Works*, vol. 7. New York: International Publishers.

————. 1977. *Collected Works*, vol. 8. New York: International Publishers.

————. 1977. *Collected Works*, vol. 9. New York: International Publishers.

————. 1978. *Collected Works*, vol. 10. New York: International Publishers.

————. 1979. *Collected Works*, vol. 11. New York: International Publishers.

————. 1979. *Collected Works*, vol. 12. New York: International Publishers.

————. 1980. *Collected Works*, vol. 14. New York: International Publishers.

————. 1980. *Collected Works*, vol. 16. New York: International Publishers.

———. 1981. *Collected Works*, vol. 17. New York: International Publishers.
———. 1988. *Collected Works*, vol. 23. New York: International Publishers.
———. 1989. *Collected Works*, vol. 24. New York: International Publishers.
———. 1987. *Collected Works*, vol. 25. New York: International Publishers.
———. 1990. *Collected Works*, vol. 26. New York: International Publishers.
———. 1986. *Collected Works*, vol. 28. New York: International Publishers.
———. 1987. *Collected Works*, vol. 29. New York: International Publishers.
———. 1988. *Collected Works*, vol. 30. New York: International Publishers.
———. 1989. *Collected Works*, vol. 31. New York: International Publishers.
———. 1989. *Collected Works*, vol. 32. New York: International Publishers.
———. 1991. *Collected Works*, vol. 33. New York: International Publishers.
———. 1994. *Collected Works*, vol. 34. New York: International Publishers.
———. 1996. *Collected Works*, vol. 35. New York: International Publishers.
———. 1997. *Collected Works*, vol. 36. New York: International Publishers.
———. 1998. *Collected Works*, vol. 37. New York: International Publishers.
———. 1982. *Collected Works*, vol. 38. New York: International Publishers.
———. 1983. *Collected Works*, vol. 40. New York: International Publishers.
———. 1985. *Collected Works*, vol. 41. New York: International Publishers.
———. 1988. *Collected Works*, vol. 43. New York: International Publishers.
———. 1991. *Collected Works*, vol. 45. New York: International Publishers.
———. 1992. *Collected Works*, vol. 46. New York: International Publishers.
———. 1995. *Collected Works*, vol. 47. New York: International Publishers.
———. 2001. *Collected Works*, vol. 48. New York: International Publishers.
———. 2001. *Collected Works*, vol. 49. New York: International Publishers.
Massey, Douglas S., and Nancy A. Denton. 1993. *American Apartheid: Segregation and the Making of the Underclass*. Cambridge, Mass.: Harvard University Press.
Mayer, Tom. 1994. *Analytical Marxism*. Thousand Oaks, Calif.: Sage Publications.
McBride, William L. 1999. *Philosophical Reflections on the Changes in Eastern Europe*. Lanham, Md.: Rowman & Littlefield.
———. 2001. *From Yugoslav Praxis to Global Pathos: Anti-Hegemonic Post-Post-Marxist Essays*. Lanham, Md.: Rowman & Littlefield.
McCarney, Joe. 1980. *The Real World of Ideology*. Atlantic Highlands, N.J.: Humanities Press.
———. 1990. "'"Ideology" in Marx and Engels': A Reply." *The Philosophical Forum* 21, no. 4 (Summer): 451–62.
McCumber, John. 2001. *Time in the Ditch: American Philosophy and the McCarthy Era*. Evanston, Ill.: Northwestern University Press.
McGary, Howard. 1992. "The Black Underclass and the Question of Values." In *The Underclass Question*, ed. Bill E. Lawson. Philadelphia: Temple University Press, 57–70.
———. 1999. *Race and Social Justice*. Malden, Mass.: Blackwell.
McLaughlin, Brian P., and Amelie Oksenberg Rorty, eds. 1988. *Perspectives on Self-Deception*. Berkeley: University of California Press.
McLellan, David. 1995. *Ideology*. 2d ed. Orig. ed. 1986. Minneapolis: University of Minnesota Press.
McLellan, David, and Sean Sayers, eds. 1990. *Socialism and Morality*. London: Macmillan.

McMurtry, John. 1978. *The Structure of Marx's World-View*. Princeton, N.J.: Princeton University Press.

Mele, Alfred. 1987. "Recent Work on Self-Deception." *American Philosophical Quarterly* 24, no. 1 (Jan.): 1–17.

———. 2001. *Self-Deception Unmasked*. Princeton, N.J.: Princeton University Press.

Mepham, John, and David-Hillel Ruben, eds. 1979. *Issues in Marxist Philosophy*, vol. 2, *Materialism*. Atlantic Highlands, N.J.: Humanities Press.

Merleau-Ponty, Maurice. 1969 [1947]. *Humanism and Terror: An Essay on the Communist Problem*. Trans. John O'Neill. Boston: Beacon Press.

Mill, John Stuart. 1989. *On Liberty; with the Subjection of Women; and Chapters on Socialism*. Ed. Stefan Collini. Cambridge: Cambridge University Press.

Miller, Richard W. 1984. *Analyzing Marx: Morality, Power, and History*. Princeton, N.J.: Princeton University Press.

Mills, Charles W. 1985. "'Ideology' in Marx and Engels." *The Philosophical Forum* 16, no. 4 (Summer): 327–46.

———. 1988. "Alternative Epistemologies." *Social Theory and Practice* 14, no. 3 (Fall): 237–63.

———. 1989. "Determination and Consciousness in Marx." *Canadian Journal of Philosophy* 19, no. 3 (Sept.): 421–46.

———. 1997. *The Racial Contract*. Ithaca, N.Y.: Cornell University Press.

———. 1998. *Blackness Visible: Essays on Philosophy and Race*. Ithaca, N.Y.: Cornell University Press.

———. 2000. "Race and the Social Contract Tradition." *Social Identities* 6, no. 4 (Dec.): 441–62.

———. 2003. "'Heart' Attack: A Critique of Jorge Garcia's Volitional Conception of Racism." *The Journal of Ethics* 7, no. 1: 29–62.

Mills, Charles W., and Danny Goldstick. 1989. "A New Old Meaning of 'Ideology.'" *Dialogue* 28, no. 3: 417–32.

Minority Rights Group, ed. 1995. *No Longer Invisible: Afro-Latin Americans Today*. London: Minority Rights Publications.

Mishler, Paul C. 1999. *Raising Reds: The Young Pioneers, Radical Summer Camps, and Communist Political Culture in the United States*. New York: Columbia University Press.

Morris, Christopher. 1999. "Introduction." In *The Social Contract Theorists: Critical Essays on Hobbes, Locke, and Rousseau*, ed. Christopher Morris. Lanham, Md.: Rowman & Littlefield, ix–xi.

Morrison, Toni. 2000 [1970]. *The Bluest Eye*. New York: Penguin USA.

Moses, Wilson Jeremiah, ed. 1996. *Classical Black Nationalism: From the American Revolution to Marcus Garvey*. New York: New York University Press.

Mosse, George L. 1997 [1978]. *Toward the Final Solution: A History of European Racism*. New York: Howard Fertig.

Mudimbe, V. Y. 1988. *The Invention of Africa: Gnosis, Philosophy, and the Order of Knowledge*. Bloomington: Indiana University Press.

———. 1994. *The Idea of Africa*. Bloomington: Indiana University Press.

Munck, Ronaldo. 1986. *The Difficult Dialogue: Marxism and Nationalism*. Atlantic Highlands, N.J.: Humanities Press.

Murray, Albert. 1990 [1970]. _The Omni-Americans: Some Alternatives to the Folklore of White Supremacy._ Cambridge, Mass.: Da Capo Press.

Murray, Charles A. 1995. _Losing Ground: American Social Policy, 1950–1980._ 2d ed. Orig. ed. 1984. New York: Basic Books.

Myrdal, Gunnar. 1962. _The Challenge to Affluence._ New York: Pantheon Books.

———. 1996 [1944]. _An American Dilemma: The Negro Problem and Modern Democracy._ 2 vols. New Brunswick, N.J.: Transaction Publishers.

Naison, Mark. 1983. _Communists in Harlem during the Depression._ Urbana: University of Illinois Press.

Nielsen, Kai. 1989. _Marxism and the Moral Point of View: Morality, Ideology, and Historical Materialism._ Boulder, Colo.: Westview Press.

Nielsen, Kai, and Robert Ware, eds. 1997. _Exploitation._ Atlantic Highlands, N.J.: Humanities Press.

Nielsen, Kai, and Steven C. Patten, eds. 1981. _Marx and Morality, Canadian Journal of Philosophy,_ supp. vol. 7. Guelph, On.: Canadian Association for Publishing in Philosophy.

Nisbett, Richard, and Lee Ross. 1980. _Human Inference: Strategies and Shortcomings of Social Judgement._ Englewood Cliffs, N.J.: Prentice Hall.

Nussbaum, Martha C. 1999. _Sex and Social Justice._ New York: Oxford University Press.

Nussbaum, Martha C., and Amartya Sen, eds. 1993. _The Quality of Life._ Oxford: Clarendon Press.

Okihiro, Gary Y. 1994. _Margins and Mainstreams: Asians in American History and Culture._ Seattle: University of Washington Press.

Okin, Susan Moller. 1989. _Justice, Gender, and the Family._ New York: Basic Books.

Oliver, Melvin L., and Thomas M. Shapiro. 1995. _Black Wealth/White Wealth: A New Perspective on Racial Inequality._ New York: Routledge.

Omi, Michael, and Howard Winant. 1994. _Racial Formation in the United States: From the 1960s to the 1990s._ 2d ed. Orig. ed. 1986. New York: Routledge & Kegan Paul.

O'Neill, Onora. 1993. "Justice, Gender, and International Boundaries." In _The Quality of Life,_ ed. Martha C. Nussbaum and Amartya Sen. Oxford: Clarendon Press, 303–23.

O'Reilly, Kenneth. 1991 [1989]. _Racial Matters: The FBI's Secret File on Black America, 1960–1972._ New York: The Free Press.

Outlaw, Lucius, Jr. 1990. "Toward a Critical Theory of 'Race.'" In _Anatomy of Racism,_ ed. David Theo Goldberg. Minneapolis: University of Minnesota Press, 58–82.

Parekh, Bhikhu. 1982. _Marx's Theory of Ideology._ Baltimore: Johns Hopkins University Press.

Pateman, Carole. 1988. _The Sexual Contract._ Stanford, Calif.: Stanford University Press.

Pateman, Carole, and Elizabeth Gross, eds. 1997 [1987]. _Feminist Challenges: Social and Political Theory._ Boston: Northeastern University Press.

Paul, Ellen Frankel, Fred D. Miller Jr., Jeffrey Paul, and John Ahrens, eds. 1986. _Marxism and Liberalism._ Oxford: Basil Blackwell.

Peffer, R. G. 1990. _Marxism, Morality, and Social Justice._ Princeton, N.J.: Princeton University Press.

Peterson, Paul E. 1991–1992. "The Urban Underclass and the Poverty Paradox." *Political Science Quarterly* 106, no. 4 (Winter): 617–37.

Pieterse, Jan Nederveen. 1995 [1992]. *White on Black: Images of Africa and Blacks in Western Popular Culture.* New Haven, Conn.: Yale University Press.

Pines, Christopher L. 1993. *Ideology and False Consciousness: Marx and His Historical Progenitors.* Albany: State University of New York Press.

Plekhanov, G. V. 1972. *The Development of the Monist View of History.* New York: International Publishers.

Rasmussen, David M. 1996. "Critical Theory and Philosophy." In *The Handbook of Critical Theory,* ed. David M. Rasmussen. Malden, Mass.: Blackwell, 11–38.

Rawls, John. 1971. *A Theory of Justice.* Cambridge, Mass.: Harvard University Press.

Reed, Adolph, Jr. 1990. "The Underclass as Myth and Symbol: The Poverty of Discourse about Poverty." *Radical America* 24 (Jan.–Mar.): 21–40.

———, ed. 1999. *Without Justice for All: The New Liberalism and Our Retreat from Racial Equality.* Boulder, Colo.: Westview Press.

Richardson, Henry, and Paul Weithman, eds. 1999. *The Philosophy of Rawls: A Collection of Essays.* 5 vols. New York: Garland.

Roberts, Marcus. 1996. *Analytical Marxism: A Critique.* New York: Verso.

Robinson, Cedric J. 2000 [1983]. *Black Marxism: The Making of the Black Radical Tradition.* Chapel Hill: University of North Carolina Press.

Robinson, Randall. 2000. *The Debt: What America Owes to Blacks.* New York: Dutton.

Rodinson, Maxime. 1983. *Cult, Ghetto, and State: The Persistence of the Jewish Question.* Trans. Jon Rothschild. London: Al Saqi Books.

Rodney, Walter. 1981 [1972]. *How Europe Underdeveloped Africa.* Washington, D.C.: Howard University Press.

Roediger, David R. 1999. *The Wages of Whiteness: Race and the Making of the American Working Class.* Rev. ed. Orig. ed. 1991. New York: Verso.

———. 1994. *Towards the Abolition of Whiteness: Essays on Race, Politics, and Working Class History.* New York: Verso.

Roemer, John E. 1982. *A General Theory of Exploitation and Class.* Cambridge, Mass.: Harvard University Press.

———, ed. 1986. *Analytical Marxism.* Cambridge: Cambridge University Press.

Rogers, G. A. J., ed. 1994. *Locke's Philosophy: Content and Context.* Oxford: Clarendon Press.

Rorty, Amelie Oksenberg, ed. 1980. *Essays on Aristotle's Ethics.* Berkeley: University of California Press.

Rose, Steven, Leon J. Kamin, and R. C. Lewontin. 1984. *Not in Our Genes: Biology, Ideology, and Human Nature.* New York: Pantheon Books.

Rose, Tricia. 1994. *Black Noise: Rap Music and Black Culture in Contemporary America.* Hanover, N.H.: University Press of New England.

Rosen, Michael. 1996. *On Voluntary Servitude: False Consciousness and the Theory of Ideology.* Cambridge, Mass.: Harvard University Press.

Rousseau, Jean-Jacques. 1984. *A Discourse on Inequality.* Trans. Maurice Cranston. New York: Viking Penguin.

Russell, Kathy, Midge Wilson, and Ronald Hall. 1992. *The Color Complex: The Politics of Skin Color Among African Americans.* New York: Harcourt Brace Jovanovich.

Said, Edward. 1993. *Culture and Imperialism.* New York: Alfred A. Knopf.

San Juan, E., Jr. 1992. *Racial Formations/Critical Transformations: Articulations of Power in Ethnic and Racial Studies in the United States.* Atlantic Highlands, N.J.: Humanities Press.

Sartre, Jean-Paul. 1949. *Three Plays.* Trans. Lionel Abel. New York: Alfred A. Knopf.

Sawhill, Isabel V. 1989. "Comment on 'Concentrated Deviance and the "Underclass" Hypothesis.'" *Journal of Policy Analysis and Management* 8, no. 2 (Spring): 282–83.

Saxton, Alexander. 2003. *The Rise and Fall of the White Republic: Class Politics and Mass Culture in Nineteenth-Century America.* New ed. Orig. ed. 1990. New York: Verso.

Sayre-McCord, Geoffrey, ed. 1988. *Essays on Moral Realism.* Ithaca, N.Y.: Cornell University Press.

Scheffler, Samuel. 1992. *Human Morality.* New York: Oxford University Press.

Schrecker, Ellen W. 1999 [1986]. *No Ivory Tower.* New York: Oxford University Press.

Schuman, Howard, Charlotte Steeh, Lawrence Bobo, and Maria Krysan. 1997. *Racial Attitudes in America: Trends and Interpretations.* Rev. ed. Orig. ed. 1985. Cambridge, Mass.: Harvard University Press.

Schuyler, George S. (writing as Samuel I. Brooks). 1991 [1936–1938]. *Black Empire.* Boston: Northeastern University Press.

Schweickart, David. 2002. *After Capitalism.* Lanham, Md.: Rowman & Littlefield.

Shapiro, Herbert. 1988. *White Violence and Black Response: From Reconstruction to Montgomery.* Amherst: University of Massachusetts Press.

Siegel, Achim, ed. 1998. *The Totalitarian Paradigm after the End of Communism: Towards a Theoretical Reassessment.* Atlanta, Ga.: Rodopi.

Skillen, Anthony. 1978. *Ruling Illusions: Philosophy and the Social Order.* Atlantic Highlands, N.J.: Humanities Press.

Sleeper, Jim. 1990. *The Closest of Strangers: Liberalism and the Politics of Race in New York.* New York: W. W. Norton.

Smart, J. J. C., and Bernard Williams. 1973. *Utilitarianism: For and Against.* Cambridge: Cambridge University Press.

Smith, Rogers M. 1993. "Beyond Tocqueville, Myrdal, and Hartz: The Multiple Traditions in America." *American Political Science Review* 87, no. 3 (Sept.): 549–66.

———. 1997. *Civic Ideals: Conflicting Visions of Citizenship in U.S. History.* New Haven, Conn.: Yale University Press.

Sombart, Werner. 1976 [1906]. *Why Is There No Socialism in the United States?* White Plains, N.Y.: International Arts & Sciences Press.

Souffrant, Eddy M. 2000. *Formal Transgression: John Stuart Mill's Philosophy of International Affairs.* Lanham, Md.: Rowman & Littlefield.

Sowell, Thomas. 1981a. *Ethnic America: A History.* New York: Basic Books.

———. 1981b. *Markets and Minorities.* New York: Basic Books.

Spann, Girardeau A. 1995. "Pure Politics." In *Critical Race Theory: The Cutting Edge,* ed. Richard Delgado. Philadelphia: Temple University Press, 21–34.

Steger, Manfred B., and Terrell Carver, eds. 1999. *Engels After Marx.* University Park: Pennsylvania State University Press.

Steinberg, Stephen. 2001a. *The Ethnic Myth: Race, Ethnicity, and Class in America.* 3d ed. Orig. ed. 1981. Boston: Beacon Press.

————. 2001b. *Turning Back: The Retreat from Racial Justice in America*. 3d ed. Orig. ed. 1995. Boston: Beacon Press.

————. 1999. "Occupational Apartheid in America: Race, Labor Market Segmentation, and Affirmative Action." In *Without Justice for All: The New Liberalism and Our Retreat from Racial Equality*, ed. Adolph Reed Jr. Boulder, Colo.: Westview Press, 215–33.

Sterba, James P. 1998. *Justice for Here and Now*. New York: Cambridge University Press.

Stocker, Michael. 1990. *Plural and Conflicting Values*. Oxford: Clarendon Press.

Sushinsky, Mary Ann. 1990. "Ideology and Epistemology: A Discussion of McCarney and Mills." *The Philosophical Forum* 21, no. 4 (Summer): 471–76.

Takaki, Ronald. 2000. *Iron Cages: Race and Culture in 19th-Century America*. Rev. ed. Orig. ed. 1979. New York: Oxford University Press.

Teresi, Dick. 2002. *Lost Discoveries: The Ancient Roots of Modern Science—From the Babylonians to the Maya*. New York: Simon & Schuster.

Thurow, Lester C. 1969. *Poverty and Discrimination*. Washington, D.C.: Brookings Institution.

Timpanaro, Sebastiano. 1996 [1975]. *On Materialism*. Trans. Lawrence Garner. New York: Routledge.

Tucker, Robert C., ed. 1977. *Stalinism: Essays in Historical Interpretation*. New York: W. W. Norton.

————, ed. 1978. *The Marx-Engels Reader*. 2d ed. Orig. ed. 1972. New York: W. W. Norton.

Tucker, William H. 1994. *The Science and Politics of Racial Research*. Urbana: University of Illinois Press.

Tully, James. 1994. "Rediscovering America: The *Two Treatises* and Aboriginal Rights." In *Locke's Philosophy: Content and Context*, ed. G. A. J. Rogers. London: Clarendon Press, 165–96.

Ture, Kwame (formerly Stokely Carmichael), and Charles V. Hamilton. 1992 [1967]. *Black Power: The Politics of Liberation in America*. New York: Vintage Books.

Turner, Patricia A. 2002 [1994]. *Ceramic Uncles and Celluloid Mammies: Black Images and Their Influence on Culture*. Charlottesville: University of Virginia Press.

Twine, France Winddance. 1998. *Racism in a Racial Democracy: The Maintenance of White Supremacy in Brazil*. New Brunswick, N.J.: Rutgers University Press.

Unger, Peter. 1996. *Living High and Letting Die: Our Illusion of Innocence*. New York: Oxford University Press.

Uzgalis, William. 1998. "'. . . The Same Tyrannical Principle': Locke's Legacy on Slavery." In *Subjugation and Bondage: Critical Essays on Slavery and Social Philosophy*, ed. Tommy L. Lott. Lanham, Md.: Rowman & Littlefield, 49–77.

————. 2002. "'An Inconsistency Not to be Excused': On Locke and Racism." In *Philosophers on Race: Critical Essays*, ed. Julie K. Ward and Tommy L. Lott. Malden, Mass.: Blackwell, 81–100.

Valentine, Charles A. 1968. *Culture and Poverty: Critique and Counter-Proposals*. Chicago: University of Chicago Press.

Van Deburg, William L., ed. 1997. *Modern Black Nationalism: From Marcus Garvey to Louis Farrakhan*. New York: New York University Press.

van den Berghe, Pierre L. 1978. *Race and Racism: A Comparative Perspective.* 2d ed. Orig. ed. 1967. New York: John Wiley & Sons.

Von Eschen, Penny M. 1997. *Race Against Empire: Black Americans and Anticolonialism, 1937–1957.* Ithaca, N.Y.: Cornell University Press.

Waldron, Jeremy. 1994. "John Locke: Social Contract versus Political Anthropology." In *The Social Contract from Hobbes to Rawls,* ed. David Boucher and Paul Kelly. New York: Routledge, 51–72.

Walker, David. 2000. *David Walker's Appeal: To the Colored Citizens of the World,* ed. Peter P. Hinks. University Park: Pennsylvania State University Press.

Walzer, Michael. 1995. "Contract, Social." In *The Oxford Companion to Philosophy,* ed. Ted Honderich. New York: Oxford University Press, 163–64.

Ward, Julie K., and Tommy L. Lott, eds. 2002. *Philosophers on Race: Critical Essays.* Malden, Mass.: Blackwell.

Ware, Robert, and Kai Nielsen, eds. 1989. *Analyzing Marxism. Canadian Journal of Philosophy,* supp. vol. 15. Calgary, Alta.: University of Calgary Press.

Welchman, Jennifer. 1995. "Locke on Slavery and Inalienable Rights." *Canadian Journal of Philosophy* 25, no. 1 (Mar.): 67–81.

Welton, Donn, ed. 1998. *Body and Flesh: A Philosophical Reader.* Malden, Mass.: Blackwell.

Wertheimer, Alan. 1999 [1996]. *Exploitation.* Princeton, N.J.: Princeton University Press.

White, Shane, and Graham White. 1998. *Stylin': African American Expressive Culture from its Beginnings to the Zoot Suit.* Ithaca, N.Y.: Cornell University Press.

Willett, Cynthia, ed. 1998. *Theorizing Multiculturalism: A Guide to the Current Debate.* Malden, Mass. Blackwell.

Williams, Eric. 1994 [1944]. *Capitalism and Slavery.* Chapel Hill: University of North Carolina Press.

Williams, Robert A., Jr. 1990. *The American Indian in Western Legal Thought: The Discourses of Conquest.* New York: Oxford University Press.

Willie, Charles V. 1988. "Review of *The Truly Disadvantaged.*" *Policy Studies Review* 7: 865–74.

Wilson, James Q., and Richard J. Herrnstein. 1998 [1985]. *Crime and Human Nature.* New York: Simon & Schuster.

Wilson, William Julius. 1978. *The Declining Significance of Race: Blacks and Changing American Institutions.* Chicago: University of Chicago Press.

———. 1987. *The Truly Disadvantaged: The Inner City, the Underclass, and Public Policy.* Chicago: University of Chicago Press.

———. 1991. "*The Truly Disadvantaged* Revisited: A Response to Hochschild and Boxill." *Ethics* 101, no. 3 (Apr.): 593–609.

Winant, Howard. 1994. *Racial Conditions: Politics, Theory, Comparisons.* Minneapolis: University of Minnesota Press.

———. 2001. *The World Is a Ghetto: Race and Democracy since World War II.* New York: Basic Books.

Wood, Allen. 1980a. "The Marxian Critique of Justice." In *Marx, Justice, and History,* ed. Marshall Cohen, Thomas Nagel, and Thomas Scanlon. Princeton, N.J.: Princeton University Press, 3–41.

———. 1980b. "Marx on Right and Justice: A Reply to Husami." In *Marx, Justice, and History*, ed. Marshall Cohen, Thomas Nagel, and Thomas Scanlon. Princeton, N.J.: Princeton University Press, 106–34.

———. 1985 [1981]. *Karl Marx*. Boston: Routledge & Kegan Paul.

———. 1986. "Marx and Equality." In *Analytical Marxism*, ed. John E. Roemer. Cambridge: Cambridge University Press, 283–303.

Wright, Richard. 1993 [1940]. "The Ethics of Living Jim Crow: An Autobiographical Sketch." In *Uncle Tom's Children*. New York: HarperPerennial, 1–15.

X, Malcolm. 1989 [1971]. *The End of White World Supremacy: 4 Speeches by Malcolm X*, ed. Imam Benjamin Karim. New York: Arcade Books.

Young, Iris Marion. 1990. *Justice and the Politics of Difference*. Princeton, N.J.: Princeton University Press.

———. 1998. "Unruly Categories: A Critique of Nancy Fraser's Dual Systems Theory." In *Theorizing Multiculturalism: A Guide to the Current Debate*, ed. Cynthia Willett. Malden, Mass.: Blackwell, 50–67.

Zack, Naomi. 2002. *Philosophy of Science and Race*. New York: Routledge.

Index

ACORN. *See* Association of Community Organizations for Reform Now
Acosta, Joseph de, 236
Acton, H. B., 67–68
affirmative action, 201, 204, 212. *See also* racial justice
Africa/Africans: and colonialism, xviii, 118n14, 152, 185, 188, 214, 228, 240; as historyless, xix, 189, 231; as rulers in alternative universe, 243; and slavery (*see* slavery, New World African). *See also* Afrocentrism; South Africa
African-American philosophers, 123, 129–30, 145n8
Afrocentrism, 134, 196, 214
Alcoff, Linda Martín, 168, 192
alienation from the body, 191–92. *See also* class, alienation
Allen, Anita, 130
Allen, James, Hilton Als, Congressman John Lewis, and Leon F. Litwack, 239
Althusser, Louis, 5, 158
America, Richard F., 206
American Communist Party (CPUSA), 90, 91, 93, 94, 106, 111–12, 113

American Revolution, 149, 201
analytic philosophy, 2–3, 192, 198; as apolitical, xix–xx, 177–78
Analytical Marxism, xiv–xv, 5–6, 37, 41, 55–56, 89; and race, 155, 172n3
Anderson, Claud, 206
Anderson, Perry, 90
Annenkov, P. V., 46
Ansley, Frances Lee, 179
anti-objectivism, moral, 3, 6, 30–31, 59–65, 67–76
apartheid, 99, 134, 136–37, 146n12, 179, 201
Appiah, Anthony, 137–38
Aristotelianism, 94, 124, 236
Arnold, N. Scott, 31n1, 41
Ashcraft, Richard, 235–38
Asia/Asians, 118n14, 149, 188, 215, 242–43, 248n3
Association of Black Sociologists, 135
Association of Community Organizations for Reform Now (ACORN), 211
Australia and Native Australians, 152, 239, 240

Baldwin, James, 193
Barker, Sir Ernest, 221

271

About the Author

Charles W. Mills is professor of philosophy at the University of Illinois, Chicago. He did his Ph.D. at the University of Toronto, and previously taught at the University of Oklahoma. He is the author of two other books, *The Racial Contract* (1997) and *Blackness Visible: Essays on Philosophy and Race* (1998), as well as numerous articles on Marxism, Africana philosophy, and critical race theory. For academic years 1999–2002, he was a University Scholar at the University of Illinois at Chicago.

Made in the USA
Coppell, TX
27 December 2021